2

Politics in Russia

FIFTH EDITION

Politics in Russia

Thomas F. Remington
Emory University

PEARSON
Longman

New York   San Francisco   Boston
London   Toronto Sydney   Tokyo   Singapore   Madrid
Mexico City   Munich   Paris   Cape Town   Hong Kong   Montreal

Editor in Chief: Eric Stano
Acquisitions Editor: Vikram Mukhija
Executive Marketing Manager: Ann Stypuloski
Production Coordinator: Scarlett Lindsay
Project Coordination, Text Design, and Electronic Page Makeup: TexTech, Inc.
Cover Design Manager: Nancy Danahy
Cover Image: © Digital Vision/Veer
Senior Manufacturing Buyer: Roy L. Pickering, Jr.
Printer and Binder: R. R. Donnelley, Harrisonburg
Cover Printer: R. R. Donnelley, Harrisonburg

Library of Congress Cataloging-in-Publication Data

Remington, Thomas F.,
    Politics in Russia / Thomas F. Remington. —5th ed.
        p.   cm.
    Includes bibliographical references and index.
    ISBN-13: 978-0-205-58602-8
    ISBN-10:   0-205-58602-3
    1.   Russia (Federation)—Politics and government—1991–
    2.   Constitutional history—Russia (Federation) 3.   Soviet Union—
    Politics and government.   I. Title.
    JN6695.R46 2008
    320.947—dc22   2007025870

Please visit our website at www.ablongman.com

Between the time website information is gathered and published, some sites
may have closed. Also, the transcrip[...] [...]hical
errors. The publisher would apprecia[...] notification where these occur so that
they may be corrected in subsequent [...]

ISBN-13: 978-0-205-58602-8
ISBN-10:   0-205-58602-3

Printed in the United States of Amer[...]

    2 3 4 5 6 7 8 9 10—DOH—10 09 0[...]

Brief Contents

Contents

5 Ideology and Political Culture   119

6 Interest Groups and Political Parties   146

7 State and Market in Russia's Economic Transition   189

Preface

The fifth edition of *Politics in Russia* has been substantially revised to take account of the many developments that have occurred in Russian political life since the fourth edition was published. It discusses the authoritarian trends that have grown increasingly pronounced since Vladimir Putin ascended to the presidency. It argues that while President Putin has made the strengthening of state power his central priority, there is a fundamental incompatibility between his demand to accelerate economic growth through far-reaching structural reforms and his drive to centralize and concentrate political power by suppressing political opposition and civil society. This edition examines these efforts in detail, focusing in particular on Putin's attempts to reshape the party system in order to give his United Russia party a commanding position in advance of the 2007–2008 electoral cycle; the dramatic growth in state control over the major energy industries; and the taming and cooptation of civil society. The book explores the implications of Russia's reliance on oil and gas exports for its political and economic development, and argues that although the state has benefited from the higher living standards that economic growth has brought, the longer-term sustainability of Russia's development is far from assured.

The book focuses on the effect that changes in the political regime since the end of the Soviet system have had on the capacity of the state to accomplish its goals. Much of President Putin's strategy can be seen as a reaction against the loss of cohesion and discipline in the state that occurred in the 1990s. In order to centralize power, Putin has reverted to some authoritarian methods of rule once used by the Soviet regime. Because we can only understand Russia's post-Communist era in relation to the Soviet regime that was in power from 1917 to 1991, Chapter 2 covers the Soviet system, in particular the period of Gorbachev's reforms, which ended in the disintegration of the Soviet state, while Chapter 3 traces the establishment of Russia's present-day political arrangements out of the turmoil of the late 1980s and early 1990s.

Russia's political life remains subject to rapid change. This edition of *Politics in Russia* covers events roughly through the end of 2006. I believe that although the turbulence of the immediate post-Communist transition period is over, Russia's political system continues to evolve. I have tried to identify some of the forces influencing the development of this system, particularly those stemming from the transformation of its economy from a centrally planned state-socialist system to one with private property and market relations. The severe economic depression that Russia only began to escape at the end of the 1990s has provoked fierce disputes in Russia and around the world about how reform might have been conducted differently. Likewise, the sustained recovery since 1999 poses the question of whether Russia is merely reaping the benefit of high international oil prices, or whether it has turned the corner in economic structure and performance. This edition discusses some of these issues and invites readers to work through the evidence and arguments themselves, in order to come to their own conclusions about why things have turned out as they have.

The final chapter examines Russia's relations with its immediate neighbors, the states that formerly were republics of the Soviet Union. Russia dominates this region, but its position is challenged by several forces, among them the aspiration of some of its neighbors to join Western economic and security alliances, the instability of other neighboring states, and the uneasy mutual dependence between Russia and several of its neighbors for the supply and transit of oil and gas. These factors affect Russia's ability to become a superpower in the post-Soviet region.

I remain deeply indebted to friends and colleagues in Russia for generously sharing with me their knowledge and understanding of developments in their country. I would also like to express my appreciation to colleagues in this country whose studies of Russian politics have advanced our knowledge of present-day Russia and enriched the field of political science. Finally, I would like to thank those reviewers who provided feedback on the fourth edition and helped give shape to this fifth edition: Rossen Vassilev, Ohio State University; Andrei Muntean, Drexel University; B. David Benedict, Houghton College; Donald Pienkos, University of Wisconsin-Milwaukee; and Kent Moors, Duquesne University.

Like the previous editions, the fifth edition of this book is dedicated to my son, Alexander Frederick Remington.

Thomas F. Remington
Emory University

Regions of the Russian Federation, 1993

69 Kaliningrad Oblast

Northern region
1 Karelia Republic
  Komi Republic
2 Nenets AOkr
  Other Arkhangel'sk Oblast
3 Nenets AOkr
  Arkhangel'sk Oblast
4 Vologda Oblast
  Murmansk Oblast

Northwestern region
5 Leningrad
  St. Petersburg city
  Leningrad Oblast
6 Novgorod Oblast
7 Pskov Oblast

Central region
8 Bryansk Oblast
9 Vladimir Oblast
10 Ivanovo Oblast
11 Kaluga Oblast
12 Kostroma Oblast
13 Moscow
  Moscow city
  Moscow Oblast
14 Orel Oblast
15 Ryazan' Oblast
16 Smolensk Oblast
17 Tver' Oblast
18 Tula Oblast
19 Yaroslavl' Oblast

Volgo-Vyatsk region
20 Mariy El Republic
21 Mordova Republic
22 Chuvash Republic
23 Kirov Oblast
24 Nizhnii Novgorod Oblast

Central Black Earth region
25 Belgorod Oblast
26 Voronezh Oblast
27 Kursk Oblast
28 Lipetsk Oblast
29 Tambov Oblast

Volga region
30 Kalmykia Republic
31 Tatarstan Republic
32 Astrakhan Oblast
33 Volgograd Oblast
34 Penza Oblast
35 Samara Oblast
36 Saratov Oblast
37 Ulyanovsk Oblast

Volga region
38 Adygei Republic
39 Dagestan Republic
40 Kabardino-Balkar Republic
41 Karachay-Cherkess Republic
42 North Osetian Republic
43 Chechen and Ingush Republics
44 Krasnodar Krai
45 Stavropol' Krai
46 Rostov Oblast

Urals region
47 Bashkortostan Republic
48 Udmurt Republic
49 Kurgan Oblast
50 Orenburg Oblast
51 Perm' Oblast
52 Komi-Permyat AOkr
  Other Perm' Oblast
53 Sverdlovsk Oblast
54 Chelyabinsk Oblast

West Siberian region
55 Altai Republic
  Altai Krai
56 Kemerovo Oblast
57 Novosibirsk Oblast
58 Omsk Oblast
  Tomsk Oblast
59 Tiumen' Oblast
  Khanty-Mansiisk AOkr
60 Yamalo-Nenetsk AOkr
  Other Tiumen' Oblast

East Siberian region
61 Buryatia Republic
62 Tuva Republic
63 Khakassia Republic
  Krasnoyarsk Krai
  Taymyr AOkr
  Evenki AOkr
  Other Krasnoyarsk Krai
64 Ust'-Ordyn Buryat AOkr
  Other Irkutsk Oblast
  Chita Oblast
65 Agin AOkr
  Other Chita Oblast

Far Eastern region
  Sakha Republic
  Primorsk Krai
  Khabarovsk Krai
66 Jewish AO
  Other Khabarovsk
  Amur Oblast
67 Kamchatka Oblast
68 Koryak AOkr
  Other Kamchatka Oblast
  Magadan Oblast
  Chukotka AOkr
  Other Magadan Oblast
  Sakhalin Oblast

AO—Autonomous Oblast
AOkr—Autonomous Okrug

Note: There are 85 territorial units of the Russian Federation. The 69 numbered regions in this listing correspond to the numbered units on the following map. The remaining 20 regions are indicated by name. Four small autonomous districts have lost their status as constituent territorial units (subjects) of the federation and have been absorbed into their surrounding regions. Therefore, although the maps depicts 89 territorial units, only 85 currently have the status of a federal subject.

The 89 Territorial Units of the Russian Federation

Source: Center for International Research, U.S. Bureau of the Census

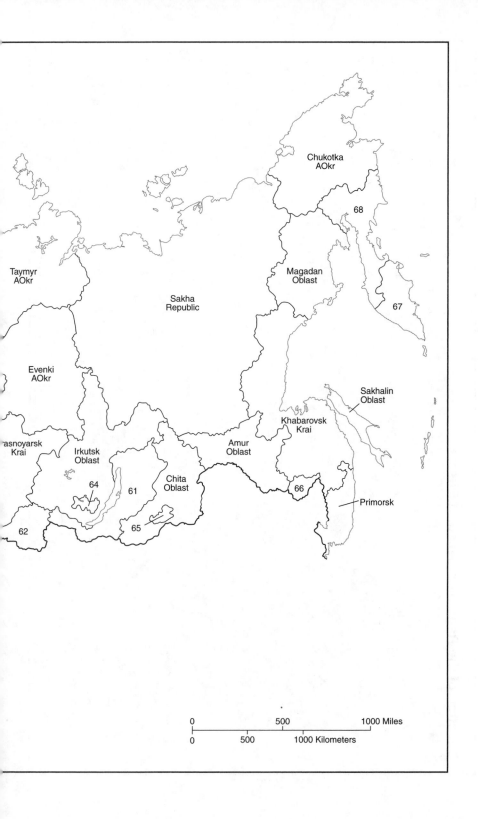

Location of the Regions of Western Russia

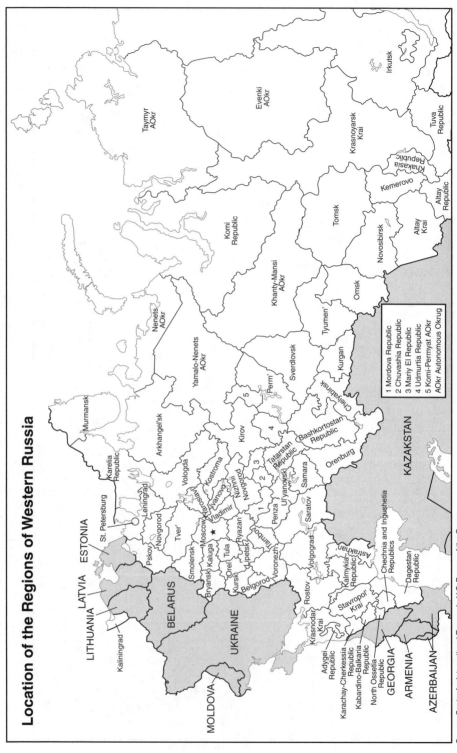

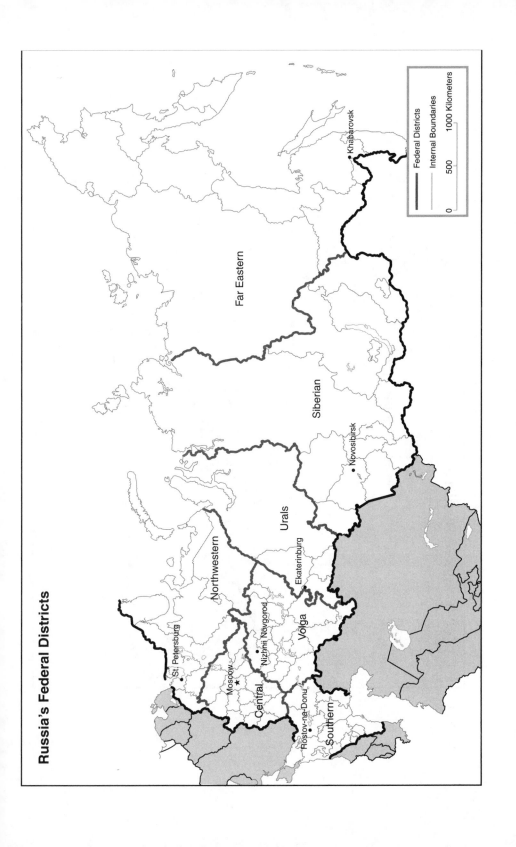

Russia's Federal Districts

Far Eastern

• Khabarovsk

Siberian

• Novosibirsk

Urals

Ekaterinburg

Northwestern

St. Petersburg

• Nizhnii Novgorod

Volga

Moscow ★

Central

• Rostov-na-Donu

Southern

Federal Districts
Internal Boundaries

0   500   1000 Kilometers

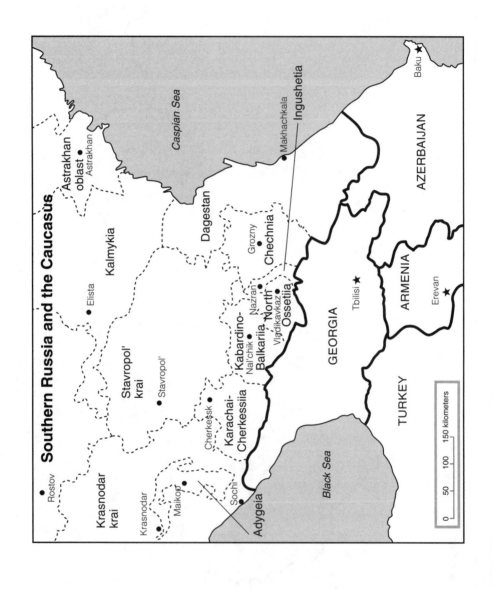

Southern Russia and the Caucasus

Chapter 1

State and Regime in Russia

In July 2006, President Vladimir Putin hosted the annual summit meeting of the leaders of the world's major industrial democracies, the Group of Eight (G-8), in his native city of St. Petersburg. Inclusion of Russia in this group, bringing it from the Group of Seven to the G-8, had been controversial. Allowing Putin to host the group—thus giving him the opportunity to present Russia to the world as a leading industrial democracy—provoked still more criticism. But the American and other Western governments hoped that by making Russia a full partner in this body they would strengthen Russia's integration into the international community. The G-8 summit represented a symbolic victory for Putin's steady effort to rebuild Russian power at home and abroad following nearly two decades of political upheaval—two decades in which Russia's regime had undergone a fundamental transformation, and the power of its state had declined drastically before slowly regaining its integrity under Putin.

Putin's Russia is the successor to the Soviet state, formally called the Union of Soviet Socialist Republics (USSR) or Soviet Union. This was a nominally federal union of 15 national republics ruled by a centralized Communist Party. But in 1991 it fell apart into its constituent national republics and Russia, the largest of the 15 republics, emerged as a newly independent country, and heir to the Soviet Union under international law (for instance, Russia inherited the Soviet Union's seat in the Security Council of the United Nations). The transition was painful in many ways. Bloody ethnic conflicts erupted in several regions on Russia's periphery. And within Russia, people's high expectations for a smooth transition to Western-style living standards, featuring democracy and capitalism, were dashed. Putin took understandable satisfaction from the fact that during his presidency, political order in Russia had been restored, economic growth was running at 6–7 percent per year, and Russia's role as a major oil and gas exporter gave it significant international leverage. The other members of the G-8, recognizing that too much was at stake to allow a new Cold War division of Europe to develop, implicitly endorsed Russia's claim to membership in the club of major powers at the St. Petersburg summit, and agreed to a set of bland resolutions containing statements of agreement on general principles that papered over deep disagreements over energy security and the drift toward authoritarian rule under Putin.

Despite the high economic growth rates in Russia since 1999 and the recovery of living standards, the longer-term sustainability of Russia's great power status is tenuous. Indeed, in several respects, under Putin Russia's transformation from a Communist state into a stable capitalist democracy has gone into reverse. Putin's policies are far from reestablishing a Communist state, but they harken back to an older Russian political pattern in which Russia's rulers seek to restore the power of a weakened state by diminishing the realm of free association outside the state. Moreover, Russia's heavy dependence on oil and gas revenues for its budget leaves it vulnerable to the so-called resource curse, characteristic of states whose budgets are dominated by revenues from the export of state-owned natural resources. Such states typically exhibit high levels of corruption, low accountability, and low investment in human capital. Finally, Russia continues to experience a severe demographic crisis. Mortality rates, particularly among adult males, shot up in the early 1990s and have fallen little since then. High mortality combined with low birthrates is resulting in a net loss of close to a million people per year, posing a grave threat to Russia's national security and economic viability. In view of these deeper structural dilemmas, the longer-term sustainability of Russia's political and economic recovery will require far-reaching institutional reform.

The weakening of Russia's state—the loss of capacity to administer the country, enforce laws, collect taxes, and maintain order—resulted from the breakdown of the old regime and the slow, incomplete establishment of the new regime. This pattern of radical regime change, when the ruling power's breakdown brings about a disintegration of the state, is a recurrent one in Russia's thousand-year history. The previous time the old regime fell apart and brought the state down with it was the Russian Revolution of 1917 and the civil war that followed it. But the revolutionary changes of regime that took place in the late 1980s and 1990s in Russia occurred in an era of mass communications, universal literacy, high educational attainments, and widespread faith in democratic values. Many of the initial changes in political institutions in the 1980s and 1990s, therefore, were aimed at replacing the authoritarian, overbureaucratized, and stagnant Communist regime with one that was democratic and dynamic. But the leadership made a number of fatal compromises along the way, trading off great pieces of state authority for the sake of holding on to power.

For the most part, the project to establish a truly democratic system in place of the Communist regime has failed. Instead, particularly under Putin, the leadership's top priority has been to rebuild the capacity of the state to meet its fundamental objectives. But Putin's methods have been those typically employed by Russian rulers in the past when they were challenged by weak administrative capacity: he has tried to centralize political power by reducing the spheres of autonomy for civil society, regional governments, and market institutions. In doing this he has been greatly helped by the high price of oil and gas on world markets, allowing him to reestablish fiscal solvency in the state and to increase state ownership and control over Russia's major industries. In the longer run, however, only significant institutional reform in the political and economic spheres will ensure that the recovery of state capacity is sustainable.[1]

CURRENT POLICY CHALLENGES

Vladimir Putin took office as president in dramatic fashion. At the time he became president he was little known in Russia or abroad. (See Close-Up 1.1: Who Is

---

Close-Up 1.1   Who Is Mister Putin?

Vladimir Putin's rise to power was so rapid that at the point he succeeded to the presidency, he was virtually unknown. A frequent question asked by Russians and foreigners alike was "Who is Mr. Putin?"

Vladimir Vladimirovich Putin was born on October 7, 1952, in Leningrad (called St. Petersburg since 1991), and grew up in an ordinary communal apartment. From early on, he took an interest in martial arts and became expert at judo. Inspired by heroic tales of the secret world of espionage, at the age of 16 he paid a visit to the local headquarters of the KGB, hoping to become an agent. There he was told, however, that he needed to go to university first. In 1970 he entered the law faculty at Leningrad State University and specialized in civil law. Upon graduation in 1975, Putin went to work for the KGB and was assigned to work first in counterintelligence, and then in its foreign intelligence division. Proficient in German, he was sent to East Germany in 1985. In 1990, after the Wall fell, Putin went back to Leningrad, working at the university there but in the employ of the KGB. When a former law professor of his, Anatolii Sobchak, became mayor of Leningrad in 1991, he went to work for Sobchak. In the mayor's office he handled external relations, dealing extensively with foreign companies interested in investing in the city, and rose to become deputy mayor.

In 1996, Putin was called to Moscow to take a position in Yeltsin's presidential administration. Here he made a rapid career. In July 1998, Yeltsin named Putin head of the FSB (Russia's federal security service), and in March 1999, secretary of the Security Council as well. In August 1999, President Yeltsin appointed him prime minister. Thanks in part to his decisive handling of the federal military operation in Chechnia, following a

(Continued)

wave of bombings of apartment houses in several cities in Russia that were attributed to Chechen terrorists, Putin's popularity ratings quickly rose. On December 31, 1999, Yeltsin resigned, making Putin acting president. Putin went on to run for the presidency and, on March 26, 2000, won with an outright majority of the votes in the first round.

As time passed, Putin's political persona became somewhat clearer. Uncomfortable with the give-and-take of public politics, he prefers the hierarchical style of organization used in the military and police. He has no particular affection for the old Communist regime, and appears to be a pragmatist who strongly desires to strengthen state power in Russia, restoring the country's economic vigor and status as a great power in the world. He has built his political strategy on a foundation of continuity with the past rather than a radical rupture with it. Skilled at projecting an affable, relaxed demeanor, he is also self-possessed and disciplined, and reveals little of himself in dealing with others. Like previous Russian rulers, he has made his first priority the consolidation of his own political power.

Mister Putin?) His predecessor, Boris Yeltsin, had served as president of Russia since 1991. On December 31, 1999, Yeltsin appeared on national television to announce that he was resigning as president as of midnight. Although his term was not due to expire until June 2000, he had decided to resign early so as to allow his chosen successor, Vladimir Putin, to take over at the beginning of the new millenium. Putin was Yeltsin's prime minister and enjoyed Yeltsin's confidence, as well as strong public support. As acting president, Putin had a substantial advantage in the presidential elections, which under the constitution had to be held within three months of the president's departure. Putin's first move was to issue a decree guaranteeing Yeltsin and his family lifetime immunity from criminal prosecution. Although the manner in which the succession occurred was not illegal, it appeared to reflect an unseemly bargain: Yeltsin gave the presidency to Putin in return for security for himself.

Putin went on to win election as president in his own right in March 2000 and to exercise the powers of the presidential office forcefully. Enjoying a strong base of popular confidence, Putin undertook a steady effort to rebuild state power. He attacked the power of the so-called oligarchs—the small group of extremely wealthy figures who held controlling shares of Russia's major natural resource, manufacturing, financial, and media companies and exercised disproportionate influence over government—through prosecutions of two particularly prominent ones. He systematically weakened the independence of the chief executives of the country's regions—the governors—by establishing new federal districts overseen by presidentially appointed representatives, securing the power to dismiss governors for violations of the law, and removing them as ex officio members of the upper chamber of parliament. He placed people whom he had worked with closely in the past into positions of responsibility in the government and his presidential administration.

Putin has continued to enjoy exceptionally high levels of public approval. This has given him considerable latitude in choosing policies to achieve his goals. With time, these goals have become clearer. In foreign policy, he seeks to restore Russia to its place as a major world power, a status it lost with the collapse of the Soviet Union. In the economy, he wants to achieve high, sustainable growth under a model in which there is substantial private, including foreign, ownership and investment coupled with state ownership and control of sectors deemed to be strategically important to the state, notably oil and gas. In politics, he seeks to preserve a framework of democratic institutions but to control the exercise of power through them. Elections are held, but their outcomes are predetermined; civil society is allowed to exist within certain highly restricted limits; individual rights are honored to the extent they do not conflict with the prerogatives of the state.

Many have termed Putin's model of political order "managed democracy," but more recently, Putin's associates have taken to using the term "sovereign democracy." Putin seeks to integrate Russia into the international economic system but at the same time to maintain a wide sphere of control for the state in the polity and economy. A strong state, for Putin, is one with an unbroken chain of executive authority stretching from the president down to the head of each region and district, with accountability running upward to the center rather than downward to the citizenry or society. He sees the president as the central figure directing the flow of power within the state. Putin accepts that Russia forms part of Europe and European civilization, but regards the value of democracy as secondary to that of state sovereignty. Possibly he believes that in a generation or two, Russia will be ready for a system featuring democratic accountability and separation of powers. For now, however, he appears to believe that the capacity and sovereignty of the state require the centralization of executive authority, with the president as the linchpin of the entire political system.

Putin has only been partially successful in realizing his goals. Much of the credit for the economic recovery goes to the high world market prices for oil and gas. Most of the ambitious fiscal and administrative reforms he has introduced have been blunted in implementation. Some of Putin's actions, such as the suppression of independent media and the campaign against the oil giant Yukos, have discouraged business investment and fueled capital flight, leading to slower economic growth. Putin's heavy reliance on the country's "power structures" (the interior ministry with its police and security troops, the regular armed forces, the law enforcement system, and the secret services) to remove or intimidate his rivals has chilled open public discourse. This makes it harder for the center to monitor bureaucratic performance. Actual improvements in the quality of governance under Putin have been modest. Putin has been much more successful in undercutting democratic checks and balances on central power than in making the new authoritarian system work effectively.

Under the constitution, a president is limited to two consecutive four-year terms. Putin's second term will end in March 2008. Many Russians are convinced that Putin will indeed leave power as the constitution requires, and most believe that he will work behind the scenes to ensure that a figure sympathetic to him (or even subject to Putin's quiet manipulation) will succeed him. There have been many calls by public figures for amending the constitution so that Putin can continue as president, but Putin has so far steadfastly refused to consider such an option. For example, in the course of an October 2006 "open line" session at which Putin responded to questions from listeners around the country submitted by phone, text message, and e-mail, one man worried: "What will be with us and the country after 2008?" Putin assured him that everything would work out well.

> As to me, I have said that the constitution—even though I enjoy my work—the constitution does not give me the right to run for a third term in a row. But, even once I lose the levers and powers of the presidency, I think that, without subordinating the Fundamental Law to my personal interests, I will be able to preserve the most important thing that a person who is involved in politics should cherish, your trust. And, making use of that, you and I will be able to influence life in our country and to guarantee its consistent development in order to exercise influence on what happens in Russia.[2]

Putin has consistently made similar comments on a number of occasions, making it increasingly likely that he will indeed step down from the presidency in 2008. How readily his associates would be able to control the succession to ensure that the basic contours of the regime would continue remained an open question—as did the question of what Putin's own role would be.

The popularity of Putin's drive to rebuild the power of the state owes much to the widespread view that the late President Yeltsin had brought the country misfortune and disgrace. In his nationally televised farewell speech on New Year's Eve, 1999, announcing that he was resigning the presidency, Boris Yeltsin gave voice to the sense of loss and disillusionment that many Russians felt. He struck an uncharacteristically contrite tone:

> Today, on this incredibly important day for me, I want to say more personal words than I usually do. I want to ask you for forgiveness, because many of our hopes have not come true, because what we thought would be easy turned out to be painfully difficult. I ask [you] to forgive me for not fulfilling some hopes of those people who believed that we would be able to jump from the grey, stagnating, totalitarian past into a bright, rich and civilized future in one go.
> I myself believed in this. But it could not be done in one fell swoop. In some respects I was too naive. Some of the problems were too complex. We struggled on through mistakes and failures. At this complex time many people experienced upheavals in their lives. But I want you to know that I never said this would be easy. Today it is important for me to tell you the

following. I also experienced the pain which each of you experienced. I experienced it in my heart, with sleepless nights, agonizing over what needed to be done to ensure that people lived more easily and better, if only a little. I did not have any objective more important than that.[3]

Yeltsin's words of regret about how the transition had turned out were a belated acknowledgment of the disappointment and bitterness felt by many Russians about the regime change's effect on their lives. For most people, the passage from the Soviet, Communist regime to a system with the superficial trappings of democracy and a free market had worsened living standards and increased insecurity. Social inequality exploded: a handful of people grew fabulously wealthy from the privatization of state assets while over 40 percent of the population sank into poverty as unemployment rose and high inflation destroyed incomes and savings. The social safety net wore thin. Crime and corruption proliferated. Discipline and accountability in the state bureaucracy—which had deteriorated in the late Communist period—broke down still further. The government attempted to carry out a far-reaching program of fiscal and monetary reform, but with only limited success, as entrenched bureaucratic interests fought at every turn to subvert the government's plans. Many people bitterly reflected that the expansion of democratic freedoms had brought more misery than progress.

Meantime, Russians had to adjust to the fact that their country was no longer a great empire consisting of 15 ethnically diverse, nominally sovereign republics forming a single union; now it was an independent state and its neighbors were likewise free and independent under international law. The political controls that the Communist Party had exercised over the economy, property, culture, and political decision making were gone, but new institutions for coordinating the behavior of the country's citizens and territories had not yet taken hold. The state was extremely weak, a problem made all the more serious by the fact that Russia, even after the dissolution of the Soviet Union, was still by far the largest country in the world in physical expanse. Maintaining the unity of the country under those conditions was a severe challenge.

Little wonder, therefore, that Putin should be so popular or that many would prefer him to remain in power than to face the uncertainties of another political transition. For a majority of Russians, Putin's leadership is associated with the restoration of political order and economic progress, and the return of Russia's international influence. Putin's successes stand out the more starkly because the decade of the 1990s brought insecurity, poverty, and institutional breakdown for the majority of the population. By contrast with Yeltsin, Putin created the impression of a young, energetic, disciplined, and goal-oriented figure, intent on restoring order at home and prestige abroad. Understandably, then, many Russians were willing to support his centralization of power as the cost of rebuilding state capacity.

Russia's transformation over the past two decades gives us a unique opportunity to analyze the factors that influence political change. How do long-term, slow-acting social changes combine with short-term conjunctures of circumstance to produce new patterns of political life? As we shall see, the Soviet regime pursued a program of social modernization that had cumulative effects over the decades of Soviet rule, creating pressures for adaptation that the regime could not accommodate. Changes such as urbanization, mass education, and industrialization resulted in a more demanding and articulate society in the Soviet Union. When the reformist Gorbachev[4] leadership in the late 1980s opened up greater freedom of speech and association, Soviet citizens responded with explosive energy to voice demands and to organize for collective action. Politics became freer, more open, and more contested. Leaders such as Gorbachev and Yeltsin strove to create new political institutions that would enable them to realize their designs for policy and power. Not surprisingly, though, in view of the huge uncertainty and rapid change surrounding them in the late 1980s and early 1990s, they often miscalculated the consequences of their actions. For instance, it is clear now that the central party leadership in the late 1980s seriously underestimated the strength of ethnic-national attachments in the union republics, so that when they granted greater political liberty to Soviet citizens, much of the new ferment that followed swelled into nationalist movements demanding independence for the union republics.

Another critical issue in understanding regime change is the relationship between economic and political liberalization. The monopoly on productive property—that is, wealth such as factories, banks, and land that produces wealth—held by the state meant that the state's rulers could dispose of the country's resources as they saw fit with no effective check on their power. Karl Marx and Lenin (Vladimir Ilyich Ulyanov) had taught that the institution of private property is inimical to Communism because it is associated with a class of independent property-owners who will defend their rights against a government that tries to confiscate their wealth. The reformers fighting for freedom and democracy in Russia therefore regarded the demand to institute private property rights, the rule of law, and a market economy as being inseparable from the demand for democratic rights in the political sphere. Communists fought intensely to prevent the restoration of private property and a market economy. They argued—quite accurately—that privatizing state assets would lead to the concentration of huge wealth and power in the hands of a small number of owners. They downplayed the point that privatization would also deprive them of their lock on political power.

The Communist regime's monopoly on power and property also meant that there were few autonomous social groups that could lend support to newly rising political movements. One of the most distinctive features of Communist systems is their effort to transform all social associations into instruments furthering the reach of the state into people's lives. Trade unions, youth leagues, hobby groups, professional associations, communications media, religious bodies, educational institutions, and the arts were all forced to become instruments of mass mobilization on behalf of the regime. Among the impediments to the establishment of a fully democratic system in Russia, the weakness of civil society—the sphere of organized social associations that link people by their common interests outside family and friends—has proved to be one of the most powerful.[5] This weakness has continued to hold back Russia's post-Communist political development.

The study of Russia's transformation is not only of academic interest. Policymakers throughout the world have drawn lessons from it for their own development strategies. For some observers, Russia's poor performance in the 1990s stands as a devastating indictment of the strategies pursued by the International Monetary Fund (IMF) and Western governments in their aid and advice to transitional economies; instead of preaching open markets and fiscal austerity, critics argue, the world should have been promoting efforts to increase the state's ability to steer the economy.[6] Russia and China are often contrasted as alternative models of reform. Some critics argue that Gorbachev erred in democratizing the political system before opening up the economy, on the grounds that loosening political controls invited a surge of nationalism, corruption, civil war, and administrative decomposition that ultimately brought about the collapse of the state—all without improving the economy.[7] Others argue that under Yeltsin the Russian leadership abandoned its controls over the economy before new market-oriented institutions were in place. The result was a catastrophic decline in production; the loss of much of the country's economic capacity; the flourishing of barter, corruption, and underground economic activity; and the takeover of most of Russia's most profitable resources by a few unscrupulous tycoons. In contrast, say the critics, China has preserved its Communist political controls but encouraged entrepreneurship, foreign investment, and profit making in agriculture, with the result that it has enjoyed a long period of extremely high economic growth without experiencing the loss of political order.[8]

As we shall see in Chapter 7, it is not clear that the model of reform that Russia attempted to pursue was intrinsically flawed, but certainly the implementation of the program was fatally compromised by political factors from the start.[9] For example, other newly post-Communist states pursued similar programs of radical economic reform with far better results. Some reasons for Russia's problems lie in the starting conditions under which Russia launched its reforms, and the particular path it took to post-Communism. We should be wary of assuming that Russian leaders had the same options that Chinese leaders had. Similarly, the unexpectedly rapid recovery of Russia's economy since 1999 raises the question of whether Putin's "strong state" strategy is responsible, or whether Russia is merely benefiting from high world oil prices.

Russia's political evolution also affects international security. Legally, Russia is the successor of the Soviet Union in international law, and, as a practical matter, it inherited an enormous military arsenal and vital geopolitical location. Russia's military might has declined considerably since the 1980s, but, with around 7,200 nuclear weapons still in its active inventory (and another 8,800 or so in reserve or scheduled for dismantlement), it remains one of the two world nuclear superpowers.[10] Of far greater concern for international security than its active nuclear stockpiles, however, is the legacy of its history as a producer of nuclear, chemical, and biological weapons. Many of its factories and laboratories still have the capability of supplying nuclear fuel and other raw materials that could be used to produce weapons of mass destruction. Loose control over nuclear, biological, and chemical materials in the former Soviet Union, in fact, is considered to be the weakest link in international efforts to prevent the proliferation of weapons of mass destruction.[11] The Soviet Union built up a large pool of scientific and technical experts in the production of biological, chemical, and nuclear weapons, and there is widespread concern about their willingness to sell their services to radical states or terrorist groups.

The stockpiles of weapons of mass destruction and their associated labs, factories, raw materials, and technical expertise that exist in the United States and Russia are the legacy of decades of competition between the two superpowers during the Cold War. From the late 1940s until the late 1980s, the United States and other Western democracies fought with the Soviet Union for influence over Europe, Asia, the Middle East, and other regions of the world. The United States committed itself by treaty to defending the security of Europe and other regions, with the threat of nuclear war backing up its commitment. The Soviet Union, in turn, countered by building up its arsenal of nuclear, biological, and chemical weapons to levels that would allow it to deter any military threat to its national interests.[12] In the end, of course, the huge military power at the disposal of the regime proved incapable of preventing its collapse. Indeed, the Soviet Union's insatiable appetite for military spending was one reason its economy lagged far behind the West in most other areas.

The origins of the Cold War conflict between the superpowers lie in the revolutionary aims of the Communist movement in the first half of the century, when Russia sponsored an international Communist movement aimed at overthrowing international capitalism and "bourgeois" (liberal democratic) governments around the world. From the time that the Communists took power in Russia in 1917, their regime adopted a posture of fundamental hostility to the West. For most of the period of Communist rule (1917–1991), Soviet rulers alternated between an aggressive, expansionist policy toward the Western world and an accommodative and pragmatic one. They pursued "peaceful coexistence" but competed for influence by supporting radical socialist movements and fought the spread of the basic democratic and capitalist values of the West. Observers long noted that, in its external relations, the Soviet Union proceeded along two tracks simultaneously.[13] On one track, the regime sought stable economic and diplomatic relations with the powerful countries of the capitalist world. On the other, it constructed a network of political and military alliances with socialist and revolutionary regimes and groups with the goal of increasing its global influence at the expense of that of the West. In turn, the United States constructed a network of alliances and treaty relationships around the world to try to contain the expansion of Soviet influence, provided economic assistance to developing countries, and exerted its power to prevent Communism from spreading. The antagonism between the democratic and market-oriented states of the West and the socialist bloc led by the Soviet Union created a bipolar structure of power in world politics that lasted from shortly after World War II until the momentous reforms of Mikhail Gorbachev.[14]

The strategic rivalry between the two superpowers, the United States and Soviet Union, shaped both political and military relations. Both countries devoted enormous efforts to preparing for possible war. Each side came to accept that a general nuclear war between them would be so devastating to each side, no matter which began it, that it could never be fought; but each accepted that the terrible threat of such a war served to deter the other from taking excessive or provocative risks. Both, moreover, continually upgraded their nuclear arsenals during this period, emphasizing qualities such as destructive power, accuracy, invulnerability, and mobility.

Russia and the United States have agreed on the desirability of deep reductions in their nuclear arsenals. In Helsinki in 1997, Presidents Yeltsin and Clinton committed themselves to the goal of reducing the number of long-range warheads that each side possessed to the level of 2,000–2,500 by the end of 2007. The two sides have also discussed making still deeper reductions. In May 2002, Presidents Bush and Putin signed a treaty in Moscow committing each side to removing around two-thirds of their remaining nuclear weapons from deployment over the next ten years, leaving between 1,700 and 2,200 for each country.[15]

During the Cold War, the United States and the Soviet Union embodied the opposite poles of a great ideological contest between capitalist democracy and Marxist-Leninist socialism. Soviet doctrine claimed that the socialist system was intrinsically superior to capitalism both because it did away with the exploitation of labor by capitalists, and because it concentrated control over productive resources in the hands of leaders who could build up the country's productive potential. The doctrine held that, unlike capitalism, socialism had a clear goal and would one day bring society to the "communist" stage of development, when all property and power would be held in common and all people would be equal. In earlier periods, many Soviet citizens as well as sympathetic foreign observers believed that the Soviet system did indeed offer an alternative model of economic development and social justice to that represented by capitalism. Over time, however, the socialist model showed that it was unable to generate self-sustaining economic growth, technological progress, or political liberty. The Soviet populace lost faith that the bright future of Communism would ever arrive. When the Communist system collapsed, it collapsed quickly, indicating how little popular support Communist rule in fact possessed.

Nevertheless, although the deep ideological confrontation between the Soviet bloc and the American bloc has vanished, there remains a distinct possibility of a new cold war as Russia seeks to "balance" against the West rather than to integrate itself into the fabric of political and economic institutions of the West.[16] Emergence of a democratic, open political system in Russia would make it more likely that Russia and the West would be able to cooperate in countering the global proliferation of weapons of mass destruction and terrorism rather than engaging in an arms race or political competition. An economically healthy and democratic Russia would be a stabilizing factor in the multiple regions on which Russia borders: Eastern Europe, the Middle East, Northeast and Northwest Asia. On the other hand, the renewal of authoritarianism in Russia would very likely herald a return to a climate of international tension, a new division of Europe, and a new arms race.

FOUR DOMAINS OF CHANGE

Let us look more closely at the changes that have occurred in the last two decades in four basic domains of state and regime: state structure, political regime, economic system, and national identity.

State Structure: From Soviet Union to Russian Federation

As of January 1, 1992, the Union of Soviet Socialist Republics (USSR, also often called Soviet Union) ceased to exist. The Soviet Union's red flag with its hammer and sickle no longer flew over Moscow's Kremlin, which has been the seat of Russian state power for four hundred years. In its place was Russia's white-blue-red tricolor flag. Soviet Communism had come to an end, and a newly sovereign Russia took control of that portion of the USSR's territory—comprising some three-quarters of the physical area and half the population—that had formed the Russian Soviet Federative Socialist Republic (RSFSR). Today the RSFSR has been renamed "the Russian Federation" or simply Russia.

The relationship between the Soviet Union and post-Communist Russia can be confusing, both for outside observers and for the people who suddenly found themselves citizens of a new state. Many people thought of Russia and the Soviet Union as interchangeable names for the same country. This was an understandable mental shortcut given Russia's dominance of the union politically and culturally. Formally, however, Russia was only one of fifteen nominally equal federal republics making up the union. Each republic had an ethnic-national identity but the union itself had no ethnic or national affiliation—only an ideological one.

The union collapsed when the governments of Russia and other member republics refused to accept the authority of the central government any longer. Mikhail Gorbachev, the reform-minded leader of the Soviet Union, struggled to find some new framework to preserve the unity of the union, but he was outmaneuvered by Boris Yeltsin, head of the Russian Republic, and frustrated by the powerful aspirations for self-rule on the part of peoples in many of the republics. On June 12, 1990, the Russian Congress of People's Deputies—the newly elected legislative assembly of the RSFSR—approved a sweeping endorsement of Russian sovereignty within the USSR, according to which Russia would only observe those USSR laws that it consented to acknowledge. A year later, on June 12, 1991, Boris Yeltsin was elected president of Russia in the first direct popular presidential elections that Russia had ever had. Probably few Russians foresaw that the union itself would eventually collapse as an outgrowth of these developments. Other events were equally momentous. The Communist Party ceased to rule the country. The familiar contours of the state-owned, state-planned economy were giving way to contradictory tendencies: production in the state enterprises fell, while energetic if frequently corrupt private entrepreneurship spread. Inequality and poverty increased sharply. Everyone agreed that the old Soviet system was breaking down, while a new system had not fully formed.

The final breakup came in 1991. In August 1991, a group of leaders of the main bureaucratic structures of the union government (army, KGB, state economic ministries, etc.) arrested Gorbachev and made a desperate attempt to restore the old Soviet order. Their coup attempt failed, however, when on the third day key elements of the army and security police refused to follow their orders. Thereafter, through the fall of 1991, the breakdown of Soviet state authority accelerated. One by one the union republics issued declarations of independence. The power structures of the union soon were unable to exercise authority. The Finance Ministry could not collect taxes, the military could not conscript soldiers. Trade ties were breaking down across regions and republics. As revenues fell, the Central Bank pumped more and more money into circulation that was not backed up by real values. The economy was sinking into chaos. Union bureaucracies operating on Russian territory were taken over by the Russian government; those in other republics were similarly nationalized by those republics.

In October 1991, Yeltsin announced that Russia would proceed with radical market-oriented reform designed to move the economy from Communism to a free market irreversibly. On December 1, 1991, a referendum was held in the Ukrainian republic on national independence. When the proposal to declare Ukrainian independence passed with 90 percent of the vote, politicians throughout the Soviet Union recognized that the breakup of the union was inevitable, and they looked for ways to preserve at least some of the formal ties among the republics. The leaders of the three Slavic core states—Russia, Ukraine, and Belorussia—met near Minsk, capital of Belorussia, on December 8, and on their own authority declared the USSR dissolved. In its place they agreed to form a new entity, a framework for coordinating their economic and strategic relations, called the Commonwealth of Independent States (CIS). Thirteen days later the CIS was expanded to include all the former republics except for Georgia and the three Baltic states of Lithuania, Latvia, and Estonia. In 1993, Georgia also joined. As we will see in Chapter 9, however, the CIS has never evolved into an effective mechanism for coordinating political and economic decisions in its member states, and has largely been replaced by more specific functional groupings of subsets of its members.

The breakup of the Soviet state enjoyed widespread initial support in Russia, and more still in most of the other former Soviet republics. Very soon, however, opinion polls in Russia were registering a wave of public regret at the loss of the Soviet state. Already by late 1993, a large majority of Russian citizens condemned the breakup of the Soviet Union as harmful.[17] Two-thirds of Russians blamed the breakup of the Soviet Union for their current economic woes. The proportion of Russians who have a favorable opinion of the old, pre-Gorbachev regime rose to about 70 percent by 2000 and has remained at that level.[18] But at the same time, support for the current regime has risen substantially, to almost two-thirds in 2004.[19]

Each year since 1990, Russia has commemorated its independence of the Soviet Union on June 12. June 12, 1990, was the day when the newly elected Russian legislature adopted its "Declaration of Sovereignty" and exactly one year later, Boris Yeltsin was elected president for the first time. Since then, each year on June 12 the government seeks to recapture the optimistic mood of 1990 and 1991 by commemorating Russia's hopes for a bright future as a sovereign nation. Yet the attitude of many Russians toward the holiday is one of irritation and indifference: independence has brought few perceptible benefits. A survey taken in June 2000 revealed that 28 percent of the Russian population did not know what the June 12 holiday was supposed to celebrate. Another 51 percent of the respondents did know that the day was "Independence Day," but few were in a mood to celebrate: 57 percent of the respondents said that independence had brought Russia nothing but harm.[20] Putin renamed the holiday "Russia Day" but there has been little more sense of national unity under the new name; in 2006, fewer than a quarter of respondents were familiar with the new name.[21]

Regime Change

Concurrent with the breakup of the Soviet Union, Russia undertook the revolutionary task of remaking its political institutions. The first steps in democratizing the Communist system were taken by Mikhail Gorbachev, who came to power as General Secretary of the Communist Party of the Soviet Union (CPSU) in 1985. Although Gorbachev did not intend for his reform policies to bring about the dissolution of the Soviet Union, he did push for a far-reaching and radical set of changes in the economic and political institutions of the regime. These changes, in turn, stimulated demands for still more autonomy by regional leaders and to the mobilization of protest against the existing regime by large segments of the population in many republics. In Russia, Boris Yeltsin and other political leaders successfully challenged Gorbachev and the union government for power by championing the cause of liberal democracy, the market economy, and national sovereignty for Russia. After the breakup of the Soviet Union, President Yeltsin and his government continued to press for market-oriented economic reform. In doing so Yeltsin sometimes resorted to undemocratic methods, most spectacularly in 1993, when he dissolved parliament.

Under Putin there has been a significant retrenchment in political freedom. Independent media outlets have been taken over by new management, and the arrests of several media magnates have had a chilling effect on the entire political establishment. Yet even though the scope of free political activity under Putin is narrower than it was in the 1990s, Russia remains freer than it was in the Soviet era before Gorbachev. In comparison with the Communist regime, the current system is much freer.

Individual Rights

The barriers to individual political liberties imposed by the Communist regime are largely removed: the intrusive Communist Party mechanisms for indoctrinating the population and enforcing ideological discipline in public discourse is gone and with them, the network of political informers who reported to the secret police on "anti-Soviet" speech. Citizens may now organize new political parties and associations, albeit under increasingly burdensome registration requirements. And citizens are free to practice their religion.[22] A large body of research suggests that commitment to democratic principles of individual rights is widely shared although not uniformly practiced. Around two-thirds of the public support the idea of democracy, but about 80 percent are dissatisfied with the way democracy is developing in Russia.[23] On the other hand, Russians value the political freedoms that democratization has brought them. Over 85 percent consider freedom of expression, freedom of conscience, and freedom to elect their leaders to be important to them.[24] Citizens' ability to defend their rights against encroachment by central or local authorities remains tenuous, however. The courts are often reluctant to uphold citizens' rights in disputes with powerful central and regional authorities.

Another significant difference between the current regime and the Communist regime is the emergence of autonomous social and civic organizations. In the Soviet era, public organizations were monitored and controlled by the Communist Party. In the Stalin era (1928–1953), the major public organizations, such as trade unions and youth leagues, were considered to be "transmission belts" linking society to the political authorities. "Transmission belt" organizations provided regime-sponsored outlets for organized collective action and ensured that they would serve the regime's political goals. In the Gorbachev period, a huge number of new, autonomous social organizations sprang up under the influence of the regime's political reforms, some with avowedly political purposes, others for cultural or philosophical pursuits.[25] After the demise of the Communist regime, many of these vanished. With time, however, a more stable set of interest groups began to develop. Among these are organizations defending the interests of regions, of collective and state farms, state industrial firms, new entrepreneurs, private farmers, bankers, and industrial workers, not to mention a shifting array of political parties and movements competing for attention. Chapter 6 will discuss the activity of these associational groups.

A third difference between the present regime and the Communist regime is that elections have become competitive and regular. Between the first contested elections of USSR deputies in 1989 and the presidential election of March 2004, Russian voters went to the polls twelve times in nationwide elections:

March 1989: election of USSR deputies
March 1990: election of RSFSR and local deputies
March 1991: referenda on preserving union and creating Russian presidency
June 1991: election of RSFSR president
April 1993: referendum on approval of Yeltsin and government
December 1993: election of deputies to new parliament and referendum
    on draft constitution
December 1995: election of deputies to parliament

June 1996: election of president
December 1999: election of deputies to parliament
March 2000: election of president
December 2003: election of deputies to parliament
March 2004: election of president

In addition to these nationwide elections, there have also been numerous regional and local elections of executive and legislative officials.

However, elections are increasingly subject to extensive efforts at manipulation by state officials through unequal access to media publicity, rigged court decisions about the eligibility of candidates, fraudulent vote counting, and other abuses.[26] Yet voters and leaders take elections seriously as a means of conferring legitimacy on political leaders. Certainly, as many political scientists have pointed out, merely holding elections is no guarantee that a political system is democratic: in many countries, elections are no more than a means of giving the aura of democratic legitimacy to rulers who otherwise trample on democratic principles; they do not give voters an effective instrument for holding leaders responsible for their actions. Some systems are no more than "electoral democracies," in which elections do not in fact decide who has power or what policies they will follow. However, though elections alone are not a *sufficient* condition of democracy, certainly they are a *necessary* condition for it.[27]

Authoritarian Trends

Under Putin, the authoritarian elements of the political system have grown stronger, while the democratic elements have weakened. One result of the democratic movement of 1989–1991 was the creation of a powerful state presidency invested with enormous power to overcome resistance to reform. The new constitution ratified in the nationwide referendum in December 1993 embodied President Yeltsin's conception of the presidency. Under it, the president has wide powers to issue decrees with the force of law and faces few constraints on the exercise of his powers. In practice the president directly oversees foreign policy and national security. Presidents Yeltsin and Putin have interpreted this power broadly. Citing the constitutional provision that the president is the supreme commander in chief of the armed forces, both have claimed the right to mobilize armed forces to preserve order without parliamentary authorization.

In December 1994 and again in September 1999, President Yeltsin ordered the army and security troops to defeat the armed forces fighting for the independence of the separatist Chechen Republic, an ethnic enclave within the Russian Federation. In neither case did the president seek parliamentary approval for the action. The military campaign by the federal forces in 1994–1996 and again in 1999–2000 resulted in massive destruction of Grozny, Chechnia's capital city, and of many other cities and towns in the republic. Tens of thousands of people have been killed, hundreds of thousands of people have fled the republic, and hundreds of thousands more have been left homeless by the fighting. A group of legislators challenged Yeltsin's use of his decree power to wage war in Chechnia by appealing to the Constitutional Court, but the court found that Yeltsin had acted constitutionally in dealing with a threat to national security.

Yeltsin sometimes did use the powers of the presidency to take unconstitutional action. In September 1993, Yeltsin issued a decree summarily dissolving parliament and ordering the holding of elections for a new parliament to be held in December of that year. When a group of hard-line parliamentarians resisted and barricaded themselves in the parliament building, Yeltsin ordered the army to shell the building. Under Yeltsin, television broadcasters also came under pressure to support the Kremlin's candidates in elections. For example, state media coverage of the 1999 parliamentary elections was severely biased in favor of the pro-Kremlin parties.[28] Under President Putin, media freedom has been eroded further, as independent news organizations have been shut down or reorganized.

The concentration of political power in the president and the executive agencies he oversees is reinforced by the weakness of checks on its use. The institutions that could monitor and expose malfeasance by the president and government, such as parliament, the mass media, and interest groups, are hampered by the cloak of secrecy that surrounds the executive and by the fact that the executive controls many of the material and informational resources that they depend on for their activity. For instance, the government can deny licenses to opposition-minded broadcast companies and newspapers. On several occasions Putin has professed to be completely unaware of actions taken by law enforcement officials against individuals whose opposition to his policies went too far—claims that are hard to take at face value. The presidential administration controls a wide array of material resources and administrative levers with which to check the independence of both the legislative and judicial branches.

Russia's regime under Putin resembles the pattern of what political scientist Guillermo O'Donnell has called "delegative democracy."[29] In such a system, common in Latin America, a president may win an election and then proceed to govern as though he were the sole source of authority in the country. The president exercises so much actual power over other political structures, thanks to his control of the police and military and his access to patronage, that he can negate the nominal separation of powers written into the constitution. In such a system, parliamentarians may use their positions not to represent constituents or craft legislation but to trade favors and enrich their friends and family. Judges may deem it safer to tailor their decisions to the wishes of powerful state officials. The editors of major newspapers bury stories unfavorable to the authorities. Interest groups curry favor with officials rather than mobilizing their supporters around particular policy positions. The leaders of opposition parties learn to accept their role on the sidelines.

Under Putin this pattern of "hollowed-out democracy" has become evident: without explicitly violating any constitutional limits on his power, and without abolishing elections or other democratic institutions, Putin has effectively negated the constitutional limits on his power built into the constitution. Using the president's extensive powers over the executive branch, he has neutralized and marginalized all independent sources of political authority, meantime observing formal constitutional procedures. For example, he has enacted his policy program by passing legislation through parliament rather than by relying on his decree power. But having used his control over electoral processes to secure overwhelming majority support in both chambers, parliamentary approval of his proposed agenda is assured. As observers have pointed out, Putin appears to dislike the open give-and-take of democratic politics, preferring more familiar methods of behind-the-scenes bureaucratic maneuvering.[30]

Putin's use of presidential power differs from Yeltsin's. Yeltsin used his presidential powers erratically and impulsively, but respected certain limits: he did not suppress media criticism, and he tolerated political opposition. Faced with an opposition-led parliament, Yeltsin was willing to compromise with his opponents to enact legislation. However, Yeltsin grew dependent on a coterie of powerful financial-media-industrial tycoons for support and let them acquire substantial influence. Likewise, Yeltsin allowed regional bosses to flout federal authority with impunity because he found it much less costly to accommodate them than to fight them. Putin has focused on regaining much of the central power lost in the 1990s. In doing so, he has reduced some of the political freedoms that Russians gained with the collapse of Communism. It would not be an oversimplification to say that Putin has gone about strengthening the state by concentrating ever more power in a hierarchy of executive power (what the Russians call "the vertical of power"— something akin to the principle of the chain of command in a military organization), while placing the entire executive branch under his direct control. This recentralization of power has been accomplished by reducing the autonomy of other centers of political power in the country, among them the parliament, parties, regional governments, mass media, and civil society.

The loss of state capacity under Yeltsin illustrates one danger of an over-centralized political system: when the president does not effectively command the powers of the office, power drifts to other centers of power. Putin's presidency illustrates the opposite danger. When Putin took over, he was faced with the task of reversing the breakdown of political control and responsibility that had accelerated under Yeltsin. Although he has repeatedly called for a system based on respect for the rule of law, he has also steadily restored authoritarian rule. He himself captured the contradictory quality of this vision in his 2004 message to parliament, when he said that creating "a free society of free people is the very most important of our tasks" but at the same time warned that any attempts to effect a significant change in his policy "could lead to irreversible consequences. And they must be absolutely excluded."[31]

Economic Transformation

In addition to the wrenching change in state structure and the transformation of the political regime, a third and equally momentous change has been underway in Russia. This is the transformation from the state-owned, centrally administered economy to one approximating a market system. In a market economy, the right of private ownership of productive resources enjoys legal guarantees; decisions on production and consumption are made by producers and consumers; and coordination of the myriad activities of individuals and organizations is accomplished primarily through their interaction in a competitive environment. Russia is far from reaching this point—in fact, no economy in the real world completely matches this description. But in Russia the state has gone far to dismantle the former socialist system in favor of a rudimentary market framework. Russia's 1992 economic reform program—rapid, radical price liberalization, combined with sharp decreases in state spending and increases in taxation—was called "shock therapy." Russia's version of shock therapy was a very crude policy instrument, but it was never fully implemented and it was often quietly sabotaged in practice. It may have been the only means available to policymakers for making rapid and irreversible changes in the behavior of economic actors, but it created many unwanted side effects and did not succeed in setting Russia onto a path where market incentives would stimulate economic growth.[32]

Among several painful side effects of the reforms, which included the decontrol of most prices, was a huge jump in prices in 1992 and high but slowly declining inflation thereafter. Another consequence was a deep and protracted depression. A mounting dependence by the government on borrowed money to finance current expenditures led to a major financial crisis in August 1998, when the government defaulted on its domestic and international obligations and let the ruble's value against the dollar plummet. By the end of the 1990s, Russia's gross domestic product had fallen to roughly half of its 1989 level. Only in 1999 did the economy begin to recover. But the recovery has been sustained: output has grown at an average annual rate of 6.7 percent from 1999 through 2006, and living standards have improved substantially.[33] The poverty rate fell significantly, from around 40 percent in the late 1990s to around 20 percent by the mid-2000s.

Painful as they were, the economic reforms of the early 1990s did effect some significant changes. One was to create a rudimentary system of market institutions, such as banks, stock exchanges, and property rights. Another was to end most shortages of goods and services in major cities. The public's demand for basic consumer goods could be satisfied, and both domestic and imported food and other goods became widely available throughout the country. The attempt to stabilize state finances was one prong of economic reform in Russia. The other was a shift to private ownership of productive resources through the privatization of state enterprises and through the growth of independent businesses.[34] By 1999, the private sector had grown to the point where it exceeded the state sector in share of employed workers.[35] The results of these policies have been mixed. Market forces now play a far greater role than in the past. But control over real economic assets of factories and farms often remains in the hands of the same managers and officials who held them in the past, the only difference being that now they have acquired legal ownership.[36] A legacy of Communist rule, many of those who held power under the old system wound up in positions of wealth and power in the new system.

Nevertheless, privatization generally improved the economic performance of privatized firms, although only modestly in most industries.

Chapter 7 will examine these economic reforms and their social consequences in more detail.

The Question of Identity: Imperial Russia—USSR—Russian Federation

The breakdown and reconstruction of Russia's state structure, political institutions, and economic system created enormous uncertainty for Russians. No less unsettling was the loss of national identity. Although today's Russian Federation is the direct successor of a thousand-year-old tradition of statehood, the political forms and boundaries of the state as it exists today differ from any that Russia has known. From the late fifteenth century until the early twentieth century, Russia's state was constituted as an imperial monarchy ruling a contiguous expanse of territories and peoples. As a result, Russia's political evolution differed from the typical path taken by Western countries.[37] In Western Europe, nations formed as social communities in territories defined through contests and treaties among state rulers. In Russia, by contrast, the state created a territorial empire spanning a huge landmass and populated by diverse array of European and Asian peoples, who differed profoundly among themselves in religion, way of life, and relationship to Russian authority. Russian national consciousness was not based on ethnicity, therefore, so much as it was on identification with a powerful imperial state. Russia's history lacks a model of a nation-state to serve as a precedent for the post-Communist period.

In the Soviet era, Russia was the core republic of a Communist-ruled union of national republics and Russians were often treated as the "elder brother" of the other peoples of the multinational country. Russia lent its language and much of its political culture to the Soviet Union but in the process it gave up its own character as a distinct national state. In effect, the Soviet Union was a new kind of empire, one whose culture was partly Russian, but which claimed to be a higher type of political organization. Over time, many Russians came to feel that Russia itself as a national entity was being shortchanged by the terms of its membership in the union.

Following the demise of the Soviet Union, Russians were once again called on to form attachments to a redefined state, now called the Russian Federation. As had been the case for much of Russian history, post-Communist Russia's leaders have generally chosen not to base the identity of the newly independent state on an *ethnic* principle. No doubt this was partly out of the practical consideration that some 20 percent of the population was not ethnically Russian, but it also reflected the historical tradition of defining Russia as a multiethnic state rather than a national state. Generally Russia's leaders have characterized the state as a multinational federation in which the major ethnic communities have territorial units within the federation. To build loyalty to the new Russia, the leaders have emphasized Russian and Soviet historical achievements in war, industry, science, technology, and the arts, but they have also sharply differentiated the new post-Soviet Russia from either its Communist-era or tsarist predecessors. They aim at creating a set of overlapping identities for citizens, including the sense of belonging to a particular ethnic community, while at the same time being a citizen of the multiethnic Russian state.[38]

In retrospect, the breakup of the Soviet Union into its constituent republics may appear to have been the logical culmination of the Soviet state's development, but until 1991, most observers considered breakup to be highly unlikely. The reason? Communist rulers were committed to a long-term goal of eradicating differences among peoples based on ethnic or linguistic characteristics, and instead building a new Soviet national identity based on the Soviet socialist way of life. As a practical matter, though, they recognized that harmony in the Soviet state required preserving some cultural rights for territorially based national groups. Therefore they provided territorial political institutions for larger nationalities through which the traditional languages and cultures could be maintained.

In nearly every case, the national minorities in the Soviet Union were the same groups occupying the same lands that the tsarist Russian empire had conquered in previous centuries. But denying that the multinational, Communist state was in any way a Russian empire—the very name was meant to show that the state was neither Russian by national identity nor an empire politically—the Communist regime imposed a common socialist model of economic ownership and administration on the entire territory of the state. Although Soviet ideology held that in the long run, national differences would be subsumed in a common Soviet national identity, during the late 1980s, leaders in the 15 republics pursued demands for greater autonomy for their republics; in many, mass movements for national independence grew powerful. This was true even in Russia: the structures of the union itself were so firmly associated with a conservative, exploitative political arrangement that both nationalist conservatives and democratic reformers in Russia were firmly convinced that progress for Russia was only possible if Russia escaped the USSR's political straitjacket.

Many Russians believe that the Russian state requires a great national mission as a foundation for its values, goals, and legitimacy. They cite the fact that the tsarist political order had regarded itself as the preserver of the true Christian faith, and that the Soviet regime considered itself to be the base of a worldwide revolutionary struggle for socialism. In 1996, shortly after his reelection as president, Yeltsin called for the formulation of a "new national idea." He observed that previous eras of Russian history had been characterized by overarching political ideologies, such as monarchy, totalitarianism, or perestroika. The new Russian state demanded a new national idea, he declared. However, the team he charged with discovering such an unifying ideology in a year's time reported at year's end that they had been unsuccessful in devising one. Perhaps, as one of Yeltsin's advisors commented at the time, it was impossible to frame a single idea that could encompass the full range of contradictory realities of the new political situation. Rather, perhaps the never-ending *search* for a national idea was itself the idea.

CHOICES AND CHANGES IN RUSSIAN POLITICS

Russia has experienced huge changes—the breakup of the Soviet Union, the dismantling of its Communist political system, a shift toward market capitalism, and a change in the very national identity of the state. How have they affected Russian citizens? How much have they changed the distribution of *real* power in the country?

The political changes in Russia in the 1990s have not brought the country into the "rich, bright, and civilized future" that Yeltsin spoke of in his resignation speech: many of the same political elites remain in place and the breakdown of the old regime has brought less democracy, and more disorder and corruption, than anyone had hoped. Still, the degree of change has been significant. The upheavals of the last decade are equivalent to a revolutionary break with the past, comparable to the formation of the Soviet regime in 1917.[39] True, it is easy enough to detect the persistence of older patterns of political life, such as the dual executive of autocrat and government, the impotence of legal institutions and pervasiveness of corruption, the proliferation of centralized state agencies together with the inability to accomplish stated policy purposes, the power and autonomy of the security police, and the survival of the former regime's ruling elite in positions of power. Looking at these phenomena, we might jump to the conclusion that nothing essential has changed, except that social disorder and distress have grown. People are even more likely to say this when they have personally been caught up in hopes and expectations that were subsequently betrayed. Many Russians today say that the apparent democratic revolution in Russia was a fraud and illusion that simply allowed a new group of greedy, power-hungry elites to win a share of control of the country's property and power.

However, it would be as wrong to exaggerate the degree of continuity with the past as it would to overlook the ways in which the transition from Communist authoritarianism to a democratic system is incomplete. The dismantling of the old Communist party mechanisms for exercising its monopolistic power means that political processes are more open. The pluralistic diversity of political interests has now moved from the arena of behind-the-scenes bureaucratic politics to a more open competition among interest groups and parties for influence over policy. Individual rights are more strongly protected than in the past. Contact between Russia and the outside world has expanded enormously. There is far more freedom for economic activity. Overall, these changes in national identity, political institutions, and economic system amount to a vast transformation. When we consider the level of violence required to carry out the Communist revolution and establish the Soviet system in Russia, the peaceful nature of the transition from the old regime seems astonishing.

Yet the peaceful nature of this transformation came at the expense of a grave weakening in state capacity. This occurred because many of the powerful elite groups that persisted from the Soviet period into the post-Soviet system found ways to take advantage of the new conditions. In doing so, they manipulated the new system to their benefit, creating a political system that is not fully democratic and an economy in which property rights are not always secure and market competitition is often overridden by rent-seeking.[40] For this reason, much of the democratic promise of the transition was fatally compromised. Still, the mutual adaptation of elites and institutions may have been the price paid for averting more serious social conflict during the passage from Communism to democracy. As political scientist Valerie Bunce has argued, the poor quality of Russian democracy may account for its survival.[41] It may also account for the lack of resistance to Putin's use of authoritarian methods of rule to restore the state's internal and external power.

PLAN OF THE BOOK

Russia's transformation allows us to explore the interplay between regime change and state capacity. Certainly there is no assumption here that Russia's political transition will ultimately result in a democratic state. But its political future remains open. History suggests that political systems can remain trapped in intermediate zones in which some democratic institutions coexist with strong elements of authoritarianism for decades or longer. Our task, therefore, is to see whether there is some overall direction to the development of Russia's political system.

The rest of the book explores the institutions and processes of Russia's political system in greater detail. Chapter 2 provides a brief overview of the political history of the last decade, when the old Soviet regime collapsed, and a new political order in Russia took shape. The chapter details the main changes in the structures and processes of rule in the Soviet period, describing the Communist Party-dominated regime and showing how power was organized and used. Then it discusses the Gorbachev reforms, their objectives and the succession of schemes he advanced to reorganize the political system. The chapter shows that the reforms had unanticipated effects that resulted in Gorbachev's loss of control over political developments. When the Soviet regime collapsed in 1991, it was succeeded by newly independent successor regimes in the former republics. Already, however, the Russian Republic had initiated its own major reforms that culminated in a political crisis in 1993 and the adoption of a new constitution that remains in force today. In Chapter 3, we describe the institutions and processes of the contemporary Russian regime, analyze the trends of its development, and assess how well President Putin has achieved his goal of rebuilding Russian state power by centralizing executive authority.

In Chapter 4 we look at how the public participates in the political system. The nature of political participation has greatly changed since the Soviet era. In the old regime participation tended to be ceremonial, regimented, and controlled. Today the prevalent pattern is one of political disengagement and mistrust of government, along with high levels of turnout at elections. Some "informal organizations" that sprang up during the late Soviet period evolved into political parties and interest groups, some of which fell by the wayside and others of which have survived.

The second part of the chapter takes up the subject of elite recruitment. In every political system, popular participation in politics is closely related to the process of elite recruitment: through elections, organizational activism, and the exercise of influence over policymakers, some individuals get involved in politics; of them, some become full-time political professionals. Of considerable interest in this connection is the question of the relation between the old political elite in Russia and the contemporary political elite. Is it true, as some charge, that the same crowd is still running things? Is there new blood, and what has happened to the old Communist elite? We will also inquire into the close, sometimes collusive, relations between the political and business elites.

Chapter 5 assesses the findings of public opinion surveys about the values and beliefs of Russians. It observes that although typical Russian citizens value political rights and freedoms, they also expect the state to provide basic social equality and welfare for its citizens. Although most rate the old regime favorably, not many would actually wish to restore it. Confidence in the institutions of the new order is low, but confidence in Putin is remarkably high. For the most part, Russians have accepted the new post-Soviet political regime as one that delivers basic political stability.

In Chapter 6 we ask how Russians voice their political demands and interests through interest groups and political parties. We review several categories of actors—industrial managers, women's groups, organized labor, and the Orthodox Church—to see how the social changes of the last five years have altered the balance of power and interest among different kinds of social groups.

In the second part of the chapter we ask how political parties are developing. How do they tie different groups of the population to the national political arena? The emergence of a dominant ruling party—United Russia—invites us to ask whether the regime is moving to some version of the old Communist Party-led state and whether United Russia can continue to maintain its power after Putin leaves office.

Chapter 7 examines the remaking of the economy. It discusses the "shock therapy" reforms of the early 1990s and the privatization program, trying to understand why these reforms turned out so poorly, and why the financial system collapsed in August 1998. It examines the effects of economic change on the lives of ordinary Russians and assesses the improvement in economic conditions since 1999. In particular, we will consider the importance of Russia's energy resources for its economic performance and international standing. Is Russia's energy wealth in fact a "resource curse" from the standpoint of the sustainability of its economic and political development?

Chapter 8 surveys the system of judicial and law-enforcement institutions. The chapter discusses the problem of law and legal institutions at two levels: the task of putting the activity of state officials and private citizens securely under the rule of law, and the effectiveness of legal institutions in enforcing constitutional and legal rules. The chapter reviews the major institutions of the judicial system and the reforms that are being made in it. Of particular interest is the emergence of a mechanism for judicial review of the acts of other government institutions in the form of the Constitutional Court. We discuss the obstacles impeding the rule of law, including organized crime, pervasive corruption, and the manipulation of the legal system by Putin and other political officials.

The last chapter offers an overview of Russia's changing relationship with its near neighbors, the states of the former Soviet Union. The chapter asks whether Russia has embarked on a project of rebuilding some sort of Russian empire or new Soviet state. It argues that the neoimperial tendencies in Russia that are fueled above all by the use of energy politics as a tool of statecraft could prompt a new cold war.

NOTES

1. OECD, *Russian Federation* (Paris: OECD, 2006).

2. Taken from the transcript of Putin's remarks, as posted to the presidential Web site: <http://president.kremlin.ru/text/appears/2006/10/112959.shtml>.

3. Quoted from text of speech as posted to CNN Web site, www.cnn.com, December 31, 1999.

4. Mikhail Gorbachev became General Secretary of the Communist Party of the Soviet Union in 1985 and quickly launched a program of economic and political reform. In 1990 he became president of the USSR, the first and last individual to hold this post. On December 25, 1991, he resigned as president and turned the formal powers of his office over to Russian president Boris Yeltsin. Gorbachev continued to play an active role in public life after his resignation.

5. Larry Diamond defines civil society as "the realm of organized social life that is open, voluntary, self-generating, at least partially self-supporting, autonomous from the state, and bound by a legal order or set of shared rules." It "involves citizens acting collectively in a public sphere" for a variety of purposes. Larry Diamond, *Developing Democracy: Toward Consolidation* (Baltimore: John Hopkins Press, 1999), p. 221.

6. Among the critics arguing this way is Joseph Stiglitz, formerly the World Bank's chief economist. Joseph Stiglitz, *Globalization and Its Discontents* (New York: Norton, 2002),

especially the chapter "Who Lost Russia?" Other works in this vein include Stephen F. Cohen, *America's Failed Crusade*; and Peter Reddaway and Dmitri Glinski, *The Tragedy of Russia's Reforms: Market Bolshevism against Democracy* (Washington, DC: United States Institute of Peace, 2001).

7. For example, see Minxin Pei, *From Reform to Revolution: The Demise of Communism in China and the Soviet Union* (Cambridge: Harvard University Press, 1994).

8. Barry Naughton, *Growing out of the Plan: Chinese Economic Reform, 1978–1993* (Cambridge: Cambridge University Press, 1995); Yingyi Qian, "How Reform Worked in China," in Dani Rodrik, ed., *In Search of Prosperity: Analytic Narratives on Economic Growth* (Princeton, NJ: Princeton University Press, 2003), pp. 297–333; Stiglitz, *Globalization and Its Discontents,* pp. 133–65.

9. Rudiger Ahrend and William Tompson, "Fifteen Years of Economic Reform in Russia: What Has Been Achieved? What Remains To Be Done?" Paris, OECD, Economics Department Working Papers No. 430, May 13, 2005, pp. 6–8.

10. Figures taken from the Web site of the Carnegie Endowment for International Peace: "Nuclear Numbers," http://www.carnegieendowment.org/npp/numbers/default.cfm, January 7, 2007. The Carnegie Endowment estimates that Russia has around 3,800 strategic nuclear warheads, and the United States around 5,900, in its stockpiles.

11. Graham Allison, "How to Stop Nuclear Terror," *Foreign Affairs* 83:1 (January/February 2004): 64–75.

12. For example, despite signing the 1972 treaty banning all biological weapons, the Soviet Union pursued a large-scale program for research on and production of a number of biological weapons, including smallpox, anthrax, and plague. It is believed that this program employed some 60,000 people. A former top scientist in the Soviet bioweapons program who now lives in the United States has written a memoir of his experiences. Ken Alibek and Stephen Handelman, *Biohazard* (New York: Delta, 2000).

13. A magisterial study of Soviet foreign policy from the beginnings of the Soviet regime through the early 1970s is Adam Ulam, *Expansion and Coexistence: Soviet Foreign Policy, 1917–1973*, 2nd ed. (New York: Praeger, 1974).

14. World War II ended in 1945, and the postwar era of antagonism between the United States and its allies and the Soviet Union and its allies began in 1947–1948. Mikhail Gorbachev, the last leader of the Soviet Union, assumed power as General Secretary of the Communist Party of the Soviet Union in March 1985. In 1990 he created and assumed the position of President of the Soviet Union. He resigned formally from this position in December 1991. The USSR (Union of Soviet Socialist Republics; also known as the Soviet Union) formally dissolved as a legal entity on December 31, 1991. Since the Bolshevik Revolution in 1917, when the Soviet regime was established, the Soviet leaders and the dates of their rule were as follows:

1. Vladimir Lenin (1917–1924)
2. Joseph Stalin (1924–1953)
3. Nikita Khrushchev (1953–1964)
4. Leonid Brezhnev (1964–1982)
5. Yuri Andropov (1982–1984)
6. Konstantin Chernenko (1984–1985)
7. Mikhail Gorbachev (1985–1991)

15. The treaty did not require the dismantling of all the weapons, however. It left open the possibility that either side might simply put the weapons into storage, where they might be vulnerable to theft or could be placed back into deployment.

16. James M. Goldgeier and Michael McFaul, "Russians as Joiners: Realist and Liberal Conceptions of Postcommunist Europe." in M. McFaul and K. Stoner-Weiss, *After the Collapse of Communism: Comparative Lessons of Transition* (Cambridge: Cambridge University Press, 2004), pp. 232–56.

17. Jerry F. Hough, "The Russian Election of 1993: Public Attitudes Toward Economic Reform and Democratization," *Post-Soviet Affairs* 10:1 (January–March 1994): 13.

18. Richard Rose, William Mishler, and Neil Munro, *Russia Transformed: Developing Popular Support for a New Regime* (Cambridge: Cambridge University Press, 2002), p. 132.

19. Ibid., p. 90. The survey data is from a regular poll of Russian public opinion called "the New Russian Barometer." This series is a regular public opinion survey conducted by the Center for the Study of Public Policy of the University of Strathclyde under the direction of Richard Rose, in cooperation with the Levada Center for Public Opinion Research (formerly VTsIOM), a respected survey organization based in Moscow. The Center for the Study of Public Policy maintains a Web site (www.russiavotes.org) publishing survey data concerning Russian electoral dynamics.

20. Results of a survey of a nationally representative sample of 1600 adult Russians conducted by VTsIOM. Cited on the Web site of www.polit.ru on June 12, 2000. However, a survey in 2002 found that a slight majority of Russians now believed that Russia's independence was a positive development. See RFE/RL Newsline, June 11, 2002.

21. From a Levada-Center poll, June 9, 2006, from the Levada Center Web site: <http://www.levada.ru/press/2006060902.html> accessed January 13, 2007.

22. The state has made it difficult for some religious denominations to operate, however, particularly those that have not had a long-standing presence in Russia.

23. Timothy J. Colton and Michael McFaul, "Are Russians Undemocratic?" Carnegie Endowment for International Peace, Working Papers no. 20 (June 2001), pp. 5, 8.

24. Colton and McFaul, "Are Russians Undemocratic?" p. 11.

25. Jim Butterfield and Marcia Weigle, "Unofficial Social Groups and Regime Response in the Soviet Union," in Judith B. Sedaitis and Jim Butterfield, eds., *Perestroika from Below: Social Movements in the Soviet Union* (Boulder, CO: Westview, 1992), pp. 175–95; Marcia A. Weigle, *Russia's Liberal Project: State–Society Relations in the Transition from Communism* (University Park: Penn State University Press, 2000).

26. In his book, *Virtual Politics,* Andrew Wilson describes a huge array of such techniques used in Russia and Ukraine, and argues that these efforts to manipulate elections are so far-reaching that elections themselves are a sham. See Andrew Wilson, *Virtual Politics: Faking Democracy in the Post-Soviet World* (New Haven, CT: Yale University Press, 2005).

27. See the discussion of the conditions of democracy in Diamond, *Developing Democracy,* chs. 1–2.

28. Sarah Oates, "Television, Voters and the Development of the 'Broadcast Party,'" in Vicki L. Hesli and William M. Reisinger, eds., *The 1999–2000 Elections in Russia: Their Impact and Legacy* (New York: Cambridge University Press, 2003), pp. 29–50; also see the report on media bias in the 1999 elections on the Web site of the European Institute for the Media, www.eim.de.

29. Guillermo O'Donnell, "Delegative Democracy," *Journal of Democracy* 5:1 (1994): 55–69.

30. For an alternative interpretation of Putin and his policies, see Richard Sakwa, *Putin: Russia's Choice* (London: Rutledge, 2004).

31. Quoted from text published on Web site polit.ru, May 26, 2004.

32. Among the studies of the economic transformation of Russia and its consequences are Andrei Shleifer and Daniel Treisman, *Without a Map: Political Tactics and Economic Reform in Russia* (Cambridge, MA: MIT Press, 2000); Thane Gustafson, *Capitalism Russian-Style* (Cambridge: Cambridge University Press, 1999); and Anders Aslund, *Building Capitalism: The Transformation of the Former Soviet Bloc* (Cambridge: Cambridge University Press, 2002).

33. OECD Economic Surveys, *Russian Federation* (Paris: OECD, 2006).

34. A valuable analysis of the economic reform program is Shleifer and Treisman, *Without a Map.* Shleifer, a Harvard economist, helped advise the Russian government on the reforms.

35. The remainder work in joint ventures or for public organizations or in other forms of mixed public-private enterprises. Figures drawn from *Rossiiskii statisticheskii ezhegodnik: 1999* (Moscow: Goskomstat Rossii, 1999), p. 114. This publication is the official statistical annual published by the State Statistics Committee of Russia.

36. A useful study of ownership and control of privatized enterprises is Joseph R. Blasi, Maya Kroumova, and Douglas Kruse, *Kremlin Capitalism: Privatizing the Russian Economy* (Ithaca, NY, and London: ILR Press/Cornell University Press, 1997).

37. Roman Szporluk, "The Imperial Legacy and the Soviet Nationalities," in Lubomyr Hajda and Mark Beissinger, eds., *The Nationalities Factor in Soviet Politics and Society* (Boulder, CO: Westview, 1990), pp. 1–23; and idem, "Dilemmas of Russian Nationalism," in Rachel Denber, ed., *The Soviet Nationality Reader: The Disintegration in Context* (Boulder, CO: Westview, 1992), pp. 509–43.

38. Valery Tishkov and Martha Brill Olcott, "From Ethnos to Demos: The Quest for Russia's Identity," in Anders Aslund and Martha Brill Olcott, eds., *Russia after Communism* (Washington, DC: Carnegie Endowment for International Peace, 1999), pp. 61–90.

39. Political scientist Michael McFaul has argued that we should view Russia's transformation since the end of the Soviet Union as a peaceful revolution. See Michael McFaul, *Russia's Unfinished Revolution: Political Change from Gorbachev to Putin* (Ithaca, NY: Cornell University Press, 2001).

40. Rent-seeking refers to activity by individuals, bureaucrats, firms, or other economic actors to use or obtain control rights to assets that allow them to receive above-normal gains from the exploitation of the assets. This problem will be discussed in more detail in Chapter 6.

41. Valerie Bunce, "Rethinking Recent Democratization: Lessons from the Postcommunist Experience," *World Politics* 55 (2003): 167–92.

Chapter 2

The Soviet System and Its Demise

Russia's present-day political institutions are the product of a series of political struggles that began in the late 1980s when Mikhail Gorbachev first began his attempts to reform the Soviet regime. Gorbachev's reforms ultimately brought down the Soviet regime and ignited a contest within Russia itself over how the country was to be ruled. This intra-Russian struggle subsided once the 1993 constitution came into force. The adoption of the constitution settled the problem of how power should be formally organized in the Russian state, but the constitution bears the strong imprint of Yeltsin's own political objectives. In particular, the powerful presidency embodies Yeltsin's vision of a president holding paramount power to set national policy. Likewise the design of the parliament, the Constitutional Court, and the nature of federalism all were shaped by Yeltsin's strategic imperatives—above all, his determination to rid Russia of the legacies of Communist rule. Although a large number of leaders and experts participated in drafting the constitution, Yeltsin had the final say on most points.[1] Vladimir Putin has reinforced some features of the constitution—particularly the sweeping powers of the presidency—while emptying others of all significance. But he has ruled out altering the constitution as such.

In a longer-term perspective, today's political order has been shaped by a thousand-year history of Russian statehood. Both in the Soviet era and before it, Russia's rulers have sought to create the means for extending central control over a vast, cold, and thinly populated land. Before we review the basic elements of the current constitutional order, therefore, we need to know something of its historical origins. This chapter provides a summary overview of the Russian regime before the Communists came to power, before describing the Soviet system and its breakdown. Chapter 3 then discusses the formation of the current Russian regime.

HISTORICAL LEGACIES

The Tsarist Regime

The Russian state traces its origins to the princely state that arose around Kiev (today the capital of independent Ukraine) in the ninth century. For nearly a thousand years, the Russian state was autocratic, that is, it was ruled by a hereditary monarch whose power was unlimited by any constitution. Only in the first decade of the twentieth century did the Russian tsar agree to grant a constitution calling for an elected legislature—and even then, the tsar soon dissolved the legislature and arbitrarily revised the constitution. In addition to autocracy, the historical legacy of Russian statehood includes absolutism, patrimonialism, and Orthodox Christianity. Absolutism meant that the tsar aspired to wield absolute power over the subjects of the realm. *Patrimonialism* refers to the idea that the ruler treated his realm as property that he owned rather than as a society with its own legitimate rights and interests. This conception of power continues to exert an influence over state rulers today.[2]

The patrimonial character of the tsarist state, and the lingering elements of patrimonialism that have survived into the Soviet and post-Soviet eras, owes much to the impact of the physical environment in which Russia's state arose. As Richard Pipes observed, Russia might have developed as a set of decentralized political communities rather than as a mobilizing, centralizing state had it not been for the low productivity of its economy's agrarian base. The harsh climate and low-quality soil tended to push Russians to seek out new lands to plow under rather than to increase the yield of lands already cultivated.[3] This pattern, coupled with the absence of readily defensible natural boundaries to separate Russia from neighboring peoples, meant that the costs of both economic production and external security were high by comparison with European states, tending to induce a pattern of state-led mobilization of resources for economic development and military power.[4] Moreover, the Russian state's historically recurrent drive to mobilize human and natural resources for war and economic development has been far more brutal than in most Western societies owing to the immense expanse of territory over which Russia's state had to maintain its lines of control and communication, its generally harsh and inhospitable climate, and its location on the borders of several European and Asian civilizations and empires. Over time, these pressures have intensified Russia's rulers' demands for absolute power over their society and pushed their ideological doctrines to take on extreme and dogmatic forms. This historical legacy helps to explain why Russians place a particularly high value on state power and why their efforts to accumulate and manage state power have been so difficult.

Finally, the tsarist state identified itself with the Russian branch of the Orthodox Christian Church. In Russia, as in other countries where it is the dominant religious tradition, the Orthodox Church ties itself closely to the state, considering itself a national church. Traditionally the Russian Orthodox Church has exhorted its adherents to show loyalty and obedience to the state in worldly matters, in return for which the state has treated it as the state church—even in those periods when the state subjected it to control and persecution. This legacy is still manifested in the post-Communist rulers' efforts to associate themselves with the heritage of Russia's church, and in many Russians' impulse to identify their state with a higher spiritual mission.

Absolutism, patrimonialism, and Orthodoxy have been recurring elements of Russian political culture. But alternative motifs have been influential as well. At some points in Russian history, the country's rulers have sought to modernize its economy and society. Russia imported Western practices in technology, law, state organization, and education to make the state competitive with other great powers. Modernizing rulers such as Peter the Great (who ruled from 1682 to 1725) and Catherine the Great (1762–1796) had a powerful impact on Russian society, bringing it closer to Western European models. The imperative of building Russia's military and economic potential was all the more pressing because of Russia's constant expansion through conquest and annexation of neighboring territories, and the ever-present need to defend its borders. The state's role in controlling and mobilizing society rose with the need to govern a vast territory. By the end of the seventeenth century, Russia was territorially the largest state in the world. But for most of its history, Russia's imperial reach exceeded its actual grasp.

By comparison with the other major powers of Europe, Russia's economic institutions remained backward well into the twentieth century. However, the trajectory of its development, especially in the nineteenth century, was toward that of a modern industrial society. By the time the tsarist order fell in 1917, Russia possessed a large industrial sector, although it was concentrated in a few cities. The country had a sizable middle class, although it was greatly outnumbered by the vast and impoverished peasantry and the radicalized industrial working class. As a result, the social basis for a peaceful democratic transition was too weak to prevent the Communists from seizing power in 1917.

The thousand-year tsarist era left a contradictory legacy. The tsars attempted to legitimate their absolute power by appealing to tradition, empire, and divine right. They treated law as an instrument of rule rather than a source of authority. The doctrines that rulers should be accountable to the ruled and that sovereignty resides in the will of the people were alien to Russian state tradition. Throughout Russian history, state and society have been more distant from each other than in Western societies. Rulers and populace regarded one another with mistrust and suspicion. This gap has been overcome at times of great national trials such as the war against Napoleon and, later, World War II. Russia celebrated victory in those wars as a triumphant demonstration of the unity of state and people. But Russia's political traditions also include a yearning for equality, solidarity, and community, as well as for moral purity and sympathy for the downtrodden. And throughout the Russian heritage runs a deep strain of pride in the greatness of the country and the endurance of its people.

THE SOVIET REGIME BEFORE GORBACHEV

In October 1917, Vladimir Lenin, leader of the Russian Communists, overthrew a weak parliamentary government, which itself had overthrown the tsarist regime several months before.[5] From 1917 until 1991, Russia was ruled by the Communist Party, which held a monopoly on political power (see Close-Up 2.1: Socialism,

---

Close-Up 2.1   Socialism, Communism, Marxism, Leninism

Terms such as socialism and Communism can be confusing because they have been used in a number of different ways and often by people with strongly held ideological visions of what they *want* these concepts to mean. But there is a coherent core of meaning to each of these terms, and it is helpful to recognize the distinctions.

Socialism has a very broad range of meaning. Generally, it refers to the elimination of private property in some or all of the means of production of a society—that is, those forms of wealth that can be used to produce more wealth (including land, factories, natural resources, banks, etc.). Instead, society or some agent of society such as the state would be the owner of the wealth and would use its control of resources to eliminate poverty, exploitation, and inequality in society as well as to build up the productive potential of the society to a higher level. Socialists disagree over how comprehensive state ownership of productive property should be: some advocate that the state own only certain basic industries and natural resources; others want to end private property altogether. Some link socialism with political freedom and popular democracy; others would allow the state to suppress some freedoms for the sake of a larger collective goal. Some advocate immediate action; others prefer to allow society to evolve gradually from capitalism to socialism. In recent decades, socialism in advanced industrial democracies has turned into "social democracy," a system in which the state uses its power not to eliminate private property but rather to use its taxing and spending power to promote equality of opportunity and provide for basic social well-being, all the while seeking to encourage the incentives of a market economy to promote economic growth, productivity, and national competitiveness.

Communism has a more specific meaning. It can be used to refer either to an economic system or to a type of political regime. As an economic system, Communism refers to a society in which there is no private property in the means of production. Most Communists would subscribe to the view that the ultimate goal of Communism is the elimination not only of private property but also of the state itself. They would argue that the state should take ownership and control of society's wealth from the capitalists,

(Continued)

but should gradually give way to a system of self-organized, self-managed communal life—the kind of society that is to be found in a commune, where all share and share alike both in producing and in consuming. However, no large-scale society has ever been able to operate in the way that small communal societies operate. And even small communal societies have generally been short-lived. Communists are therefore always socialists, in that they want to do away with capitalism (the system comprising a market economy and private-property rights). But not all socialists are Communists, since not all socialists would want to eliminate all private property and dismantle the institutions of political democracy.

In the political sense, Communism refers to the type of regime in which a Communist party—meaning a party devoted to the Communist doctrine—holds power. In fact, no Communist regime has ever taken any serious steps to dismantle the machinery of state power. To the contrary, Communist regimes always expand the power of the state over individuals, not merely taking control of all or some of the means of production, but also intervening to different degrees in social and private life, suppressing political opposition, and sometimes putting society on a quasi-military footing. In the twentieth century, some Communist regimes turned into extraordinarily violent and bloody dictatorships. Communist regimes continued to promote the vision that one day everyone would live as in a commune and that the state would at some very distant point "wither away"; but in practice they placed heavy emphasis on building up the power of the state to control society, so they demanded absolute loyalty to the state, its principles, and its goals. As a regime type, nearly all Communist regimes have collapsed. As of this writing, North Korea remains Communist, as does Cuba; Vietnam and China combine capitalism with political monopolies by their Communist parties: but no serious observer now believes that Communism as a regime type has a future.

Marxism is a form of Communist doctrine, developed by Karl Marx and Friedrich Engels, which holds that the end of capitalism will come about when the working class seizes control of the means of production from the capitalists and uses it to establish socialism, and eventually Communism. Marxists are therefore Communists. *Leninism* refers to the brand of Marxism developed by Lenin: Lenin emphasized the need for political revolution even before all the economic conditions for socialism were met, and he was especially insistent about the need for an iron dictatorship over society to be exercised by the Communist Party "in the name of" the working class. Through most of the Soviet period, the official doctrine taught to all citizens was called "Marxism-Leninism," because it was officially regarded as a system of thought originated by Marx and Engels and subsequently developed by Lenin and his successors. Over time, the doctrine became rigid, hollow, formulaic, and dogmatic—no longer of any relevance to Soviet leaders faced with the realities of the world in the twentieth century, where capitalism proved itself considerably more dynamic than the Soviet system.

Communism, Marxism, Leninism). Originally, the Communist Party was a revolutionary movement aimed at overthrowing the tsarist state. Indeed, its ambitions went much further than that. The Communists' long-range goal was the overthrow of capitalism throughout the world and the establishment of a worldwide socialist system. In the end, the Communist movement succeeded in establishing Communist regimes in Russia, Eastern Europe, much of Asia, and a few isolated countries in other regions (among them Cuba). But the worldwide Communist revolution never arrived, and Russia's Communists devoted most of their energies to building up the power of the Soviet state. They constantly invoked the language of class war as they sought to portray their drive for economic and military power, and for moral unity and loyalty, as a struggle against the capitalist world.

To the Russian Communists, socialism meant a society without private ownership of the means of production, in which the state owned and controlled all important economic assets, and in which political power was exercised in the interests of the working people. *Vladimir Ilyich Lenin* (1870–1924; in power 1917–1924) formed the Russian Communist Party and headed the Soviet Russian government after the revolution.[6] In keeping with Lenin's model of the Communist Party as a "vanguard party," the Soviet regime divided power between the *soviets,* which were elective councils through which workers and peasants could voice their desires, and the Communist Party, which would lead the soviets. The Communists regarded the soviets as useful channels for participation in the state by the masses, but ensured that they would be dominated by the more tightly organized and disciplined Communist Party. The party, as the bearer of the guiding vision, would direct the soviets and their executive organs, but it would remain organizationally separate from them.[7]

Lenin's successor, *Joseph Stalin* (1879–1953; in power 1924–1953), consolidated the institutional underpinnings of Lenin's model of rule, but also took its despotic impulses to extremes: Stalin's regime employed mass terror against large categories of the population, killing millions of Soviet citizens through executions, induced famine, forced labor under inhuman conditions, and deportations.[8] Stalin's regime expanded Soviet state power and defended it in World War II; it carried out a crash program of forced industrialization and agricultural collectivization. Stalin was a state-builder, in the sense that under his rule the Soviet state extended its capacity to rule over all regions of the country and in all aspects of social life. Under Stalin the vast state hierarchies of military and police power were built up, together with factories, mines, power stations, highways, canals, and railroad lines; vast numbers of schools, clinics, and cultural and scientific institutions were built; whole cities were constructed, and Moscow itself was remade. Soviet society was penetrated with networks of informers, and millions of people were arrested on charges of "anti-Soviet" activity. Yet there was also a profound strain of hope and pride running through Soviet culture, as many people believed that they were building the bright socialist future.

Stalin was a state-builder, but he also left a legacy of very weakly institutionalized power because political authority was heavily dependent on fear, suspicion, reverence for Stalin, and a tendency by all officials to leave all decisions to Stalin himself. Stalin's power was as close to being absolute as any leader in history has ever come: he set the country's priorities in every sphere; intervened in any issue he cared to take up (whether deciding whether a particular movie or play should be released or forbidden, or editing the words to the new Soviet national anthem). He fostered a quasi-religious devotion to himself personally that his successor, Nikita Khrushchev, labeled "the cult of personality." Stalin personally approved lists of "enemies of the people" who were to be arrested and shot. His own tendency toward paranoia only intensified the climate of fear and mistrust that permeated official life. Moreover, the pattern of personal despotism was repeated in many subordinate organizations, where smaller-scale "little Stalins" ruled with an iron fist in their own organizations. Within the state were no checks on the power of the ruler, and the secret police were outside the control of any law or institution save the will of the supreme ruler. Little wonder that on Stalin's death in 1953, there were no agreed rules and procedures for transferring power to another leader nor was there a clear division of authority between the leader at the top, the party, and the state.

Therefore Stalin's successors, beginning with *Nikita Khrushchev* (1894–1971; in power from 1953–1964), grappled with the challenge of defining a new and more institutionalized framework for ruling the state. Lacking Stalin's unchallengeable power, they agreed on the need to make the regime less dependent on fear and more on popular consent without relinquishing their power.[9] They made the system less personalistic and more rule-governed, agreeing that the system should return to the Leninist tradition that the Communist Party was the seat of power in the country. And within the party, they agreed, power was to be exercised collectively. They ended the use of mass terror and raised living standards somewhat, but they retained the basic Leninist tenets of state ownership of the means of production and the Communist Party's role as the source of political direction for state and society. Under Khrushchev and his successor, Leonid Brezhnev, the rules and structures of the Communist Party–governed state became more firmly defined and less subject to the caprices of a single leader.

A key to understanding the structure of the Soviet regime is the theory of the "leading role" of the Communist Party. The idea was that the Communist Party should control government without itself replacing government. The party was to set goals, resolve conflicts, and monitor all basic political processes, including political socialization, elite recruitment, and policy implementation. It would coordinate the many agencies of the state and ensure that they worked together to maintain the system and achieve its goals. But the party was not supposed to usurp the actual functions of government, such as managing the economy; policing the society; or running schools, factories, and television stations. The Soviet model was a strategy for building state power in a society at a low level of development: it created opportunities for mass participation and the recruitment of leaders, and gave experience in government to ordinary working people. It presented a democratic facade to the Soviet population and the outside world, while concealing the enormous brutality and wastefulness of its methods. With time, the model also demonstrated its incapacity to respond to new kinds of political imperatives that arose from the immobilism and self-interest of its powerful bureaucratic components.

The model incorporated a federal element. Formally, the state comprised 15 sovereign national republics, but centralized political control over them was guaranteed by the Communist Party's hierarchical chain of command that stretched across all governmental and societal organizations. Soviet citizens learned to switch back and forth between a world of fictions proclaimed in Soviet doctrine, taught in schools, and repeated endlessly in the mass media, and a world of everyday realities: the fictions concerned the shining ideals of Soviet Communism, the nominally democratic political institutions in which citizens were said to be the masters of the state, and the progress the society was making toward a life of abundance and justice. The realities reflected the stagnation in living standards, the acceptance of endless venality and cant in public life, the gap between the modest living standards of a majority of the population and those of the elite whose political status entitled them to lives of privilege.

The word "soviet" means council, and the Soviet model of government revolved around a system of soviets. These were elected bodies symbolizing the principle of democratic self-government. There were soviets in every territorial unit of the country—village, town, county, province, and so on, all the way up to the Supreme Soviet of the USSR itself. In theory, the soviets exercised all state power in the Soviet Union, but in reality it was understood that the soviets had no real policy-making power. The USSR Supreme Soviet, for instance, met only twice a year, and then for a few days each time, to hear official reports and approve motions proposed by the leadership. Generally, everyone accepted that the soviets served the function of creating a formal appearance of representative democracy, when in fact the party and the executive organs of government made all the major decisions. The only sense in which the soviets "represented" the public was descriptive, in that the candidates were selected by the party to ensure the presence of fixed quotas from each major demographic category: occupation, sex, age, ethnic group, and party status. This allowed the regime to boast that large proportions of particular groups of the population were serving as elected representatives (called deputies). Usually only one candidate ran for a given seat, so that the elections offered voters only the opportunity to vote for or against the candidate offered. Elections were not an institution for making officials accountable to voters for their actions, but they were treated as grand national ceremonies in which the nearly universal voter turnout demonstrated the unity of the people and their state.

Formally, the deputies of a soviet elected a set of executive officials to manage government in its territory, making the executive arm of each soviet accountable to the soviet for its actions. In reality, the soviet simply ratified a choice that had been made by Communist Party authorities. Nonetheless, executive officials had real bureaucratic power, and together they formed an executive branch chain of command that stretched all the way from the lowest level of government up to

Moscow. Meantime, the Communist Party supervised and directed—but was not supposed to usurp—the work of government executives. At the highest levels—union republics and the all-union central government—there was a Supreme Soviet, which had the power to enact laws. Executive power was invested in the Council of Ministers. The USSR Council of Ministers was thus formally equivalent to the cabinet of a parliamentary government in a Western democracy and its chairman was the functional equivalent of a prime minister. As the person in charge of the executive branch for the entire Soviet Union, the chairman of the Council of Ministers was in fact a very powerful figure—but never as powerful as the head of the Communist Party of the Soviet Union.

Federalism in the Soviet state was used to give symbolic rights to ethnic minorities, especially those located on the outer perimeter of Russia's territory that had traditions of national autonomy or statehood. So, unlike federalism in the United States or Germany, the constitutional form that federalism took in the Soviet Union was linked to the goal of giving ethnic-national populations a means to maintain their national cultures but to do so without challenging the center's power. In Soviet federalism, 15 nominally sovereign republics were considered to be the constituent units of the federal union. Each republic gave a particular ethnic nationality a certain formal opportunity for representation. Most structures of power at the central level were replicated in the 15 union republics; of course, the army and the money supply were exclusively central functions.

Power was so highly centralized in the Soviet regime that the federal structure of the state was largely a formality. Yet the effect of organizing the state around ethnic territories, each with its own trappings of statehood, proved to have powerful cumulative effects on Soviet political development. The development of "national" educational systems, cultural institutions, and mass media reinforced ethnic-national identities in all 15 republics, even in those where there was only a weak sense of national consciousness before Soviet rule. At the same time, the centralization of political and economic power in Moscow prevented the national leaders of the federal republics from making any serious claims on the union government for greater autonomy. As time passed, members of the indigenous nationalities in the republics came to take certain rights for granted, including the right to maintain their national cultures so long as these did not directly contradict Soviet ideological doctrine. The stability of these informal rules and understandings about how far each nationality could go in preserving its national identity fostered a tendency for its leaders and peoples to think of the territory and institutions of the republic as "theirs," a kind of collective national property. Coupled with the steady rise in the population's educational levels over the decades of Soviet rule, this tacit but powerful assumption contributed to the growth of ethnic self-consciousness in each republic among the indigenous nationality.[10]

The Soviet state was federal in form, unitary in fact. Political scientists say that under federalism, the constituent regions of a particular state possess one or more constitutionally protected domains of power in which they are autonomous and can make policy so long as they do not violate constitutional rules, while the federal authorities also are autonomous in one or more other realms (typically national security and monetary policy).[11] In the Soviet Union, the central government (the Communist Party leadership and central executive authorities) had ultimate control over the political, economic, and cultural life of the republics, choosing how much autonomy each could exercise at any given time. Each jurisdictional unit was treated as subordinate to the higher-level unit within which it was located, in keeping with the chain of command principle: the union center controlled major productive resources throughout the country, including land, natural resources, industry, and human capital; the constituent republics were given the right to manage lesser assets on their territories. Strategic decisions about economic development in the republics were determined by the center. The pattern resembled colonial imperialism in that a dominant metropolitan state developed the economies of peripheral territorial possessions for its benefit. However, the Soviet state made all it ruled into citizens and brought them under a common set of political and economic institutions. Establishing and maintaining control over so large and diverse a state was in fact a great achievement by comparison with the many failed states of the contemporary period. Yet the political regime preserved control over the state by denying its citizens many elementary political and economic rights.

The place of the Russian Republic within the union state was anomalous. The fact that the Soviet regime was dominated by Russians did not mean that the Russian Republic benefited from the arrangement. The Russian Republic (RSFSR) was by far the largest of the 15 union republics in territory and population, and its language and culture dominated the entire union. Yet the republic itself lacked even the weak instruments of statehood that the other republics possessed, such as its own republic-level Communist Party branch, KGB (Committee for State Security—the secret police), trade union council, Academy of Sciences, and the like. The reason, of course, is that if these organizations had had branches at the level of the Russian Republic, they would have threatened the power of the union-level structures. Union-level party and state organs thus doubled as Russian ones. One could say that Russia used the Soviet state to rule a quasi-imperial state.

Empires are costly to rule. In the USSR, the balance of trade among republics was not favorable to the Russian Republic, even though Russia dominated the union politically. Because of the deliberately low prices set for energy and other industrial inputs supplied by Russia, Russia ended up subsidizing the development of other republics. By 1991, Russia was providing the equivalent of one-tenth of its gross domestic product to other republics in the form of implicit trade subsidies.[12] Yet the economies of the other republics were also forced to develop along the lines dictated by the central plan. Central planning and controlled prices made it impossible to judge who was exploiting whom, and within each republic people became convinced that the union was exploiting their republic.[13] Meantime, ethnic federalism enabled republican party and state leaders to build up political machines and expand their own political control. Many leaders in the union republics were keen to win greater control over state resources, not necessarily to put them to better or more productive use, but rather to build up their own political power by distributing the stream of benefits these resources yielded to their favored constituents. Thus when the political leaders in the union republics demanded the *decentralization* of economic administration, often what they wanted was to capture control over state resources for their own political benefit rather than to make more productive use of them—to transfer the *union*'s bureaucratic control over the economy to control by the *republic-level* bureaucracy. Decentralization in this sense was neither democratic nor market-oriented. Republic-level leaders often played the ethnic card in behind-the-scenes bureaucratic bargaining, demanding greater economic autonomy for their territories on the grounds that the ethnic nationalities residing in those territories needed more opportunities for development.[14]

This point is a clue to the struggle for power between the union and Russian republican levels of the Soviet system. The demand for decentralization was one on which both democratic forces and bureaucratic officials in the republics could agree: the democrats wanted to break the hold of the Communist Party and the central government over citizens' political rights, whereas the republic-level officials were eager to claim a share of control over Soviet state assets located in their republics. They found common cause in the desire to weaken the central government. Thus to a large extent, the struggles over sovereignty in 1989–1991 resulting in the breakup of the union were a contest for control over state resources between elites whose institutional position was at the union level, and the political forces at the next level down who sought to gain autonomy within their territorial jurisdictions. As far as the Russian Republic was concerned, this strategy meant that when the Russian leaders won sovereign power over the Russian territory, they had to give up their power over other republics.

The fight for national sovereignty had a strong economic component because the state owned and controlled the means of production: land, natural resources, factories and farms, and wealth in all its forms. The struggle for power in the old regime was a struggle for the right to control the immense wealth of the country. Political and economic power were closely intertwined in the Soviet system. The relationship between these two domains is a key to understanding the difference of the Soviet system from liberal democracies, even those in which the state has a large ownership stake in the economy. Even the most strongly social democratic polity in Europe differs sharply from the state socialism of the Soviet-type system. In contrast to societies in which there is private ownership of productive property, in the Soviet system an individual's power, prestige, and wealth depended on his or her position in the political hierarchy. Productive wealth could not be passed on through inheritance to others.[15] State ownership of productive resources meant that political and social status derived from the same source; even the most powerful leaders depended on the favor of party officials because all lines of advancement and opportunity converged in the Communist Party. The "new class"—those who rose to power and privilege in the system—sought to use the Communist Party to protect their interests, but the absence of firm political rights or popular legitimacy created insecurity, which they compensated for by the use of propaganda and repression that fended off political challenges to their positions.[16]

In the planned economy, output growth was the standing imperative. The heads of enterprises were under intense pressure to fulfill their plan targets, and generally the authorities gave them substantial autonomy in choosing how to meet their output goals. Managers could generally get by with cutting corners, for instance reducing quality, so long as they met the basic target for raw output set by the planners. Managers had little incentive to innovate or modernize because the risk that a new technology might fail outweighed the potential benefits of increased productivity. In short, the incentives faced by enterprise managers tended to militate against flexibility, adaptiveness, entrepreneurship, and innovation. With time, as a result, the economy tended to grow stagnant and unable to compete in the global market. Its abundant natural resources (minerals, oil, timber, and many other goods) gave it the capacity to export and earn foreign exchange, but by the 1960s it was experiencing chronic shortfalls in agricultural production and the quality of its manufactured goods (apart from the defense industry) was appallingly low.

Stalin's strategy of rapidly industrializing Russia brought about another important feature of the state socialist model—the reliance on the enterprise as a source of noneconomic benefits to the populace. Goods such as housing, child care, subsidized meals, groceries, scarce durable goods such as cars, and subsidized vacations have long been allocated through enterprises alongside the ordinary retail distribution system. In the late 1970s, when the economy's performance began slipping seriously and food rationing had to be introduced in many cities, enterprise "social funds" assumed a greater political importance. As the supply of housing, food, and ordinary services fell ever further behind demand, enterprise managers exercised still more leverage over the state. Workers and managers were tightly bound to one another in mutual need. Managers needed a large and cheap labor force to enable them to fulfill their plan targets, and workers needed a secure position in a state enterprise to obtain a range of social benefits that were unavailable except through the enterprise. This created a bond of reciprocal dependence between workers and managers, which some have termed an implicit "social contract." Under the social contract, the regime committed itself to providing job security, social benefits, and relative income equality, in exchange for quiescence and compliance from workers.[17]

The social contract tended to weaken trade unions. In the Soviet model, trade unions were organized around entire economic branches, so that the managers of a firm were members of the same trade union as the engineers, the bench workers, and the cafeteria staff. Their common dependence on the state for the well-being of their workplace gave both managers and workers an incentive to pressure the state to maintain a steady stream of orders and financing regardless of whether the enterprise was profitable and productive or a wasteful drain on society's resources. Just as the economy created little incentive for entrepreneurship or innovation, it also discouraged the restructuring or closing of loss-making firms. Indeed, because the price system was set according to political criteria rather being set by the play of demand and supply, it was next to impossible to know whether a given enterprise was operating profitably or not. Some, in fact, were subtracting value from the economy by producing goods that were worth less than the materials that went into making them. The deadweight cost of inefficiency grew from year to year, as the economy stifled innovation that would have raised productivity.

Moreover, the weakness of financial constraints on enterprises' appetites for resources created a chronic syndrome of excess demand, shortages, and repressed inflation.[18] Low efficiency and failure to innovate on the part of enterprises did not incur economic penalties. To some extent enterprises were able to conceal the facts of their performance by falsifying reports or concealing damaging information. Administrative demands from the center for improved productivity were never sufficient because managers themselves lacked incentives to take risks. The center itself was constantly pressured to satisfy the needs of powerful industrial and regional officials to protect their interests. As a result, the system settled into inertia and decay: each year the plan represented a modest incremental change over the previous year. Any serious attempts at reform were defeated by the combination of weak central power and inertial resistance by those who were called on to carry out the reform. A very powerful coalition of interests—ministries, regional officials, enterprise directors, and workers—shared a latent interest in the preservation of the status quo because any serious change threatened them. (It was a latent interest because they did not organize collectively, but rather acted in concert by working to preserve the status quo.) By the beginning of the 1980s, the economy had all but stopped growing. But zero growth meant that competing with the United States on military spending placed an ever heavier burden on the economy. By the time Gorbachev came to power, defense expenditures were running at about a quarter of gross domestic product, and the share was still increasing.[19] The deadweight economic loss caused by high military expenditures was a major reason Gorbachev undertook his program of radical reform.

The deteriorating performance of the economy in the 1960s, 1970s, and 1980s placed a greater burden on the regime's ability to meet social expectations. It meant that fewer jobs were opening up in managerial and professional positions. Yet the stream of graduates with specialist degrees kept growing. More and more people occupied jobs below their educational qualifications. This affected both manual and specialist social strata. Many groups considered themselves underpaid and undervalued. Many of the grievances voiced in the early years of glasnost centered around the low professional autonomy and esteem of managerial and professional groups, including the administrative staff of the Communist Party itself. These strains were in part the consequence of the Brezhnev leadership's policy of levelling by raising the wage levels and educational qualifications at the lower end of the social hierarchy without achieving a corresponding transformation of the structure of labor. As a result, a sizable part of the workforce occupied jobs for which they were significantly overqualified.

Economic stagnation exacerbated popular resentment of the privileges of the political elite. Crucial to understanding the explosive quality of social protest in the late 1980s is the accumulation of popular alienation, which often took nationalist forms, but which also arose from other issues, such as environmental degradation, the perception that the ruling "nomenklatura" was indifferent and parasitic, anger over shortages in the economy, and the conviction on the part of nearly every region and republic that it was being economically exploited by a distant, bureaucratized center.

In addition to the soviets' role as the building block of the state, the principle of ethnic federalism, and the centralization of economic power, the political dominance of the Communist Party was the fourth defining characteristic of the old regime. Lenin's model of rule ensured that the organizational structure of the Communist Party maximized central control over all levels of government. The party itself was kept rather small, emphasizing that membership was a privilege and an obligation, and taking pains to admit only individuals whose political loyalties and social backgrounds passed stringent review. At its peak, the Communist Party had around 20 million members, around 9 percent of the adult population.[20] In many professions the membership rate was higher, and generally membership was higher among the more educated strata of society. Among individuals in positions of high political and administrative responsibility, party membership was nearly obligatory. Indeed, for most individuals with high career ambitions, Communist Party membership was not just useful, it was a requirement.

The party's own organization paralleled that of the government, which it supervised and directed. In every territorial jurisdiction—district, town, province and so on—the party maintained its own full-time organization. For instance, each city had its own CPSU organization with a governing committee; a more powerful inner body called the "bureau"; and a set of functional departments overseeing industry, agriculture, ideology, and personnel with their own full-time staff, who were overseen by managers called secretaries. The first secretary of the municipal party organization was always the city's most powerful official. The top party official was not the chief executive of the city: that was the chairman of the local executive committee of the city soviet. The first secretary of the party organization worked closely with the chairman of the executive committee, but the party official was superior in status. Directives and advice from the party secretary were binding on executive branch officials, but, by the same token, if the city government needed special help from Moscow, the party represented a direct channel of access to the highest levels of power in the country.

At the top, final power to decide policy rested in the CPSU Politburo. The Politburo was a small committee made up of the country's most powerful leaders that made decisions in all important areas of policy at its weekly meetings. Supporting the Politburo was the powerful Secretariat of the Central Committee of the Communist Party. The Secretariat ran the party's central headquarters, which was linked to all lower party organizations. Here the party monitored the political and economic situation throughout the country and around the world, and determined which problems needed to be addressed, developing policy options for the Politburo. Here the party managed the political careers of thousands of top political officials. Here it determined the ideological line that was to be reinforced and echoed throughout the country through the channels of party propaganda and the mass media. And here it supervised the vast government bureaucracy, the army, the police, the law-enforcement system, the KGB, and the governments of the republics and regions. The description of the Communist Party's political role given in the 1977 Soviet Constitution, to the effect that the party was "the leading and guiding force of Soviet society, the nucleus of its political system of [all] state and public organizations," was reasonably accurate.[21] Three of the party's most important powers were deciding policy, recruiting officials, and policing the ideological doctrine of the country. All major policy decisions were made by the party, at every level of the political system. All responsible officials were chosen with the approval of the party. And the ideas discussed in the media, the arts, education, or any public setting had to meet with the approval of the party's ideological watchdogs.

Sweeping as the party's powers were, they were undermined by bureaucratic immobilism. This problem grew more severe in the 1970s and 1980s as a result of the growing complexity of the political system, the loss of social cohesion, and the declining capacity of the aging leaders to manage the system coherently. The role that fear of arrest had played in reinforcing central power in the Stalin era gradually diminished, and gave way to the certainty on the part of many officials that they could behave incompetently or even criminally with impunity. Certainly it is true of hierarchical organizations everywhere that overcentralization brings its own pathologies of control, through distortions of information flow, tacit resistance to the center's orders by officials at lower levels who have their own agenda, and the force of inertia.[22] By the time Mikhail Gorbachev was elected General Secretary of the CPSU in 1985, the political system of the USSR had grown top-heavy, unresponsive, and muscle-bound.[23]

The old regime appeared stable, but in fact its institutions were weak. More than in political systems in which legal rules and traditions govern the way power is exercised by those holding political office, Soviet politicians had to struggle for power constantly, even when they occupied an important position. Behind the surface unity and consensus of Soviet politics, Soviet political leaders were engaged in a continuous competition for power. Naturally, Soviet leaders did not advertise their moves in this game. Nonetheless, by close examination of the public record, it is possible to identify the political alliances and commitments formed by top political leaders of the CPSU. Contenders for power consolidated power by showing that they could solve policy problems: successes here tended to strengthen their hand in attracting supporters and eliminate opponents, whereas failures weakened the incentives that other officials had for supporting them.[24] The contest was not carried out in the electoral realm as there was no electoral link between the desires of the public and the policy choices considered by the regime. Nonetheless the contest was real, and played for high stakes. It resembled games of bureaucratic politics played out in other complex hierarchical organizations but with lower agreement over the rules and with a high risk factor: failure in the political arena could lead, at best, to forced retirement and disgrace, and at worst to arrest and imprisonment—in Stalin's time, to the concentration camps.

Because there was no agreed mechanism for deciding when and how power would be transferred from one leader to another, political succession often set off an intense struggle for power. Once a leader climbed to the top, and won the office of General Secretary of the CPSU, he sought to use the powers of the office to stay there for the rest of his life. Nikita Khrushchev was removed from power by a successful conspiracy in 1964; he spent the rest of his life as a pensioner out of the public eye.[25] The ringleader of the conspiracy, *Leonid Brezhnev* (1906–1982; in power 1964–1982), quickly consolidated his own power. He built a base of support that allowed him to remain in that office, despite obviously worsening health, until his death in November 1982. Brezhnev learned the lessons of Khrushchev's fall only too well. He owed his success at holding power for 18 years to avoiding any serious attempts at political reform that might have upset the balance of ministerial and regional power centers that dominated the regime. There was relatively little turnover of political officeholders and even less policy innovation. The result was drift in policy, worsening government performance, and a gradual aging of the entire ruling elite of the USSR, as the political system grew increasingly unresponsive to the imperative of economic and political reform.

Brezhnev was succeeded by *Yuri Andropov* (1914–1984), who had served as chairman of the KGB and as a secretary of the CPSU Central Committee. Although Andropov initially launched a policy program to reverse the decline in national economic performance, it soon turned out that he was gravely ill and could only rule from his hospital bed. When he, in turn, died in February 1984, he was succeeded by another aging, ailing member of the Brezhnev generation, *Konstantin Chernenko* (1911–1985). Chernenko had been a loyal member of Brezhnev's personal clientele and tried to hold on to power by allying himself with the remnants of the old Brezhnev political machine. This meant halting the limited reform programs launched under Andropov and returning to the conservatism and drift of the Brezhnev era. But Chernenko, too, was fatally ill, and died in March 1985. At this point, the senior leadership was evidently concerned at the impression of debility and weakness created by this rapid succession of deaths, and agreed to turn to a much younger, more dynamic, and open-minded figure as the new General Secretary. The youngest member of the Politburo at the time he was named its leader (born in 1931, he was only 54 when he took over) *Mikhail Gorbachev* quickly grasped the levers of power that the system granted the General Secretary, and moved both to strengthen his own political base, and to carry out a program of economic reform.

Gorbachev Comes to Power

One of the enduring mysteries about Gorbachev is how so radical a reformer could ever have reached the pinnacle of power under the old regime. One explanation lies in the fact that he could appeal not only to groups who wanted to liberalize the regime, but also to conservatives alarmed at the deterioration of discipline and morals in state and society. These conservatives could accept a certain amount of administrative reform in the interests of strengthening socialism. They, and pro-reform elements in the party apparatus and intelligentsia, were therefore a natural base of support for an ambitious and ingenious political leader such as Mikhail Sergeevich Gorbachev. At the same time, probably few within the party leadership realized how radical Gorbachev was until it was too late for them to remove him: his youth, self-confidence, intelligence, exposure to the West, and personal instincts all helped fuel his drive to carry out far-reaching changes in the Soviet system, aimed at transforming it into some version of a socialist democracy. Shortly before he was made General Secretary of the Communist Party of the Soviet Union, Gorbachev and his future foreign minister Eduard Shevardnadze (who later became president of post-Soviet Georgia) chatted while walking along a beach at a resort on the Crimean Sea. They agreed, according to their recollections of the conversation, that "everything was rotten" and "we cannot go on living this way."[26] At that point, although he knew that the system was deeply dysfunctional, neither the model of the change he intended to bring about nor the means of achieving it was clear to Gorbachev. He possessed enormous confidence, energy, ambition, and zeal for reform, but would he have launched his reforms had he known how they would turn out?

Gorbachev's remarkable rise began in the late 1970s. In 1978 he was named Secretary of the Central Committee; in 1979 he became candidate member, and in 1980 full member of the Politburo. In March 1985, upon Chernenko's death, Gorbachev was named General Secretary of the party. He needed to build a broader base of support in the Politburo for a policy of reform. To help persuade his colleagues to embark on real reform, Gorbachev needed to generate an elite perception of impending crisis in order to overcome his colleagues' reluctance to accept the risks of major reform.

Emphasizing the need for greater openness—glasnost—in relations between political leaders and the populace, Gorbachev stressed that the ultimate test of the party's effectiveness lay in improving the economic well-being of the country and its people. By highlighting such themes as the need for market relations, pragmatism in economic policy, and less secretiveness in government, he identified himself as a champion of reform.[27] The party amplified his modestly unorthodox message through its propaganda machine, disseminating to officials and citizens everywhere the new leader's appeals for glasnost, modernization, and intensification of economic development. Gorbachev called his program for reforming the Soviet system perestroika, which means a restructuring. He meant by this that he wanted to overhaul the entire structure of the Soviet economy and state system, but to leave its foundations intact.

Gorbachev moved rapidly to consolidate his own power using the General Secretary's power over the appointment of ranking elites. Acting cautiously at first, and then with increasing decisiveness, Gorbachev removed opponents and promoted supporters. Gorbachev not only stripped power away from the Brezhnev-era old guard, but he began transferring power away from the Communist Party altogether. Gorbachev also made use of the party's control of national policy to set new directions in domestic and foreign policy. In the economic sphere, he demanded "acceleration" of technological progress and economic growth through an infusion of capital, including stepped-up foreign investment. He also promised to loosen the suffocating bureaucratic controls that discouraged innovation on the part of enterprise managers. He called for breathing new life into the desiccated democratic forms of Soviet political life by making elections and public debate real and meaningful. In the sphere of foreign policy he pursued a new, active diplomacy in Europe and Asia, served up a series of disarmament proposals, and promised greater flexibility in relations with the West.

Gorbachev not only called for policy reform, he also made far-reaching institutional changes in the economy and political system. He pushed through a reform bringing about the first contested elections for local soviets in many decades.[28] He sponsored a Law on State Enterprise that was intended to break the stranglehold of industrial ministries over enterprises through their powers of plan-setting and resource allocation. He legalized private, market-oriented enterprise for individual and cooperative businesses and encouraged them to fill the many gaps in the economy left by the inefficiency of the state sector. He called for a "law-governed state" (*pravovoe gosudarstvo*) in which state power—including that of the Communist Party—would be subordinate to law. He welcomed the explosion of informal social and political associations that formed. He made major concessions to the United States in the sphere of arms control, resulting in a treaty that, for the first time in history, stipulated the destruction of entire classes of nuclear missiles.

In 1988, he proposed still more far-reaching changes at an extraordinary gathering of party members from around the country, where in a nationally tele-vised address he outlined a vision of a democratic, but still socialist, political sys-tem. In it, legislative bodies made up of deputies elected in open, contested races, would exercise the main policy-making power in the country. The Supreme Soviet would become a genuine parliament, debating policy, overseeing government officials, and adopting or defeating bills. Moreover, the judiciary would be sepa-rated from party control, and at the top of the system there would be a body called on to adjudicate the constitutionality of legislative acts. The party conference itself was televised, and treated the Soviet public to an unprecedented display of open debate among the country's top leaders. Using to the full the General Secretary's authoritarian powers, Gorbachev quickly railroaded his proposals for democrati-zation through the Supreme Soviet, and in 1989 and 1990 the vision Gorbachev laid out before that party conference was realized as elections were held, deputies elected, and new soviets formed at the center and in every region and locality. When nearly half a million coal miners went out on strike in the summer of 1989, Gorbachev declared himself sympathetic to their demands.

Gorbachev's radicalism received its most dramatic confirmation through the astonishing developments of 1989 in Eastern Europe. All the regimes mak-ing up the socialist bloc collapsed and gave way to multiparty parliamentary regimes in virtually bloodless popular revolutions (Romania was the only country where the ouster of the ruling Communist elite was accompanied by widespread bloodshed)—and the Soviet Union stood by and supported the revolutions![29] The overnight dismantling of Communism in Eastern Europe meant that the elaborate structure of party ties, police cooperation, economic trade, and military alliance that had developed since Stalin imposed Communism on Eastern Europe after World War II vanished. Divided Germany was allowed to reunite, and, after initial reluctance, the Soviet leaders even gave their sanction to the admission of the reunified Germany to NATO. In the Soviet Union itself, meantime, the Communist Party was facing massive popular hostility and a critical loss of authority. Gorbachev forced it to renounce the principle of the "party's leading role" and to accept the legitimacy of private property and free markets. Real power in the state was being transferred to the elective and executive bodies of government— marked, above all, by the new office of state president that Gorbachev created for himself in March 1990. One by one, the newly elected governments of the national republics making up the Soviet state declared their sovereignty within the union; and the three Baltic Republics had declared their intention to secede altogether from the union. Everywhere, inside and outside the Soviet Union, Communist Party rule was breaking down.

POLITICAL INSTITUTIONS OF THE TRANSITION PERIOD: DEMISE OF THE USSR

Gorbachev's inability to overcome resistance to his economic programs by the party and state bureaucracy prompted him to push for still more radical reform by opening up channels for democratic elections and representation. He was careful not to go too far, however. His design for the democratization of the soviets had clear roots in the Leninist past, and, not incidentally, also served to reinforce his own power at the top. In introducing his political reforms in 1988, Gorbachev made it amply clear that he was not endorsing a move to a multiparty system as well. Gorbachev saw a limited role for parliamentarism as a further extension of glasnost, but wanted to make sure that the power to make major decisions on domestic and national policy would still remain with the Communist Party leadership. Gorbachev sought to play the new parliamentary structures off against the party bureaucracy, bringing pressure to bear on party officials to carry out his reform policies, while ensuring that the newly elected deputies would not overstep the boundaries of their power. Gorbachev's political reforms had both direct and strategic purposes. Gorbachev did want to open up the system to more democratic participation. But he intended for the new channels of mobilization to expand his base of support for the reforms he wanted to make: he calculated that if he created new political arenas in which supporters of liberal reform could gain influence, they would pressure the bureaucracy for more perestroika. But by creating these new arenas of participation, including media glasnost, elections, and democratized soviets, Gorbachev made it possible for a wide variety of political tendencies—radical democrats, hard-line Communist conservatives, and nationalist movements—to seize the initiative. Many of these groups had entirely different aims from his own.

In retrospect it is clear that Gorbachev underestimated the centrifugal force of demands for national sovereignty and independence in a number of the union republics. As the liberalization of political life enabled new autonomous political movements to press for changes going far beyond what he was then prepared to tolerate, he concluded that the two posts he held—General Secretary of the CPSU and Chairman of the Supreme Soviet of the USSR—did not give him enough power. Although he had initially opposed the idea of creating a state presidency, he changed his mind and declared early in 1990 that a presidency was needed in order to control the executive branch. Accordingly, in March 1990, he rammed constitutional amendments creating a presidency through the Congress of People's Deputies. He coupled this with a change in the constitution that had the effect of legalizing multiparty competition. Both of these reforms, needless to say, seriously threatened the Communist Party's power. Now Gorbachev would set policy and oversee the bureaucracy in his capacity as president, not as General Secretary; even worse from the Communist Party's standpoint was the fact that the party would be forced to compete for popular support in competitive elections against legal rivals.

Once again, Gorbachev's reforms had consequences he clearly did not intend. Although he was readily elected president of the Soviet Union, he was elected by the Congress of People's Deputies, not in a direct popular election (which he might have lost). Elimination of the long-standing provision that assigned the Communist Party the "leading role" in government and society authorized opposition movements to contest the party's mandate to rule. Therefore the 1990 elections of deputies to the Supreme Soviets in all 15 republics, and for soviets in regions and towns all across the country, stimulated competition among political movements and parties. In Russia, a coalition of democratic reformers ran under the banner of a movement called "Democratic Russia," which sought to form caucuses in each soviet to which its candidates were elected. In the March 1990 elections the Democratic Russia movement succeeded in winning a majority of seats in both the Moscow and Leningrad (a year later the city took back its old name of "St. Petersburg") soviets. And in the races for the Russian Congress of People's Deputies, the Democratic Russia contingent claimed as many as 40 percent of the newly elected deputies as adherents. (Of course, as events later showed, many of these deputies had only a very weak, opportunistic commitment to the radical democratic tenets of its program.) A roughly equal number of the new Russian deputies identified themselves with the conservative, antireform, prosocialist ideology of the Communists of Russia. Under the influence of the democratic aspirations and national self-awareness that the electoral campaign awakened, the Congress narrowly elected Boris Yeltsin chairman of the Russian Supreme Soviet in June 1990. As chief of state in the Russian Republic, Yeltsin was now well positioned to challenge Gorbachev for preeminence.[30]

A course of developments then followed in the Russian Republic that paralleled those occurring at the level of the USSR federation during the previous year. Like Gorbachev a year earlier, Yeltsin, too, decided in early 1991 to create a state presidency in Russia. Unlike Gorbachev, Yeltsin put the matter to a national referendum. But he did so in such a way as to challenge Gorbachev. When Gorbachev held a USSR-wide referendum in March 1991 on whether the populace desired to preserve the Soviet Union in some new, vaguely defined form, Yeltsin added a question to the ballot distributed in the Russian Republic. This asked whether voters approved the idea of instituting a national presidency for the Russian Republic. Both measures—the preservation of the union and the introduction of a Russian presidency—passed by wide margins (71 percent of Russian voters supported preservation of the union, 70 percent a Russian presidency), but the popularity of the principle of a Russian presidency effectively undercut Gorbachev's desire to win a national mandate for his efforts to defend central power.

Moreover, Yeltsin linked his power and the cause of Russian national freedom with a program of radical market-oriented economic reform. In the spring of 1990, Yeltsin had endorsed a program of rapid, uncompromising economic transformation intended to dismantle the old system of state ownership and planning, and set loose the forces of private enterprise. The strategy discussed by Yeltsin's economic advisors had much in common with the programs of stabilization being adopted in Poland and Czechoslovakia. First, the central government would relinquish many of its administrative controls over the economy, allowing prices to rise to meet demand and freeing producers to determine their own production goals. Second, the government would launch a massive effort to privatize state assets and create a broad base of property owners who would help ensure that Communism would never return. In Russia, the "500 Days" program that was developed embodying these ideas had the added feature of allowing the republics to claim sovereign control over the assets on their territories. This provision helped make the program palatable to republic leaders and publics, but would have eliminated most remaining controls that the union center still had to regulate the economy. Little wonder that Gorbachev, pressured by conservative elements in the Politburo, military, government, and KGB, rejected the plan after having initially considered it; and little wonder that Yeltsin embraced it in his struggle with Gorbachev.

The winter of 1990–1991 saw an intense political struggle between Gorbachev and Yeltsin. Gorbachev fought to hold on to his power in the central leadership while maneuvering to defeat Yeltsin. By April 1991, Yeltsin had defeated the conservative forces in the Russian parliament and Gorbachev had failed to bring Yeltsin down. Gorbachev was forced to accept Yeltsin's power, and that of Russia's sovereign status within the federal union. Gorbachev then sought to find terms for a new federal or confederal union that would be acceptable to Yeltsin and the Russian leadership, as well as to the leaders of the other republics. He initiated negotiations with the republic leaders aimed at drafting a new constitutional framework for the Soviet Union. In pursuing these talks, though, he was negotiating from a position of weakness: he lacked the support of the conservative, bureaucratic elements of the union government, and democratic forces were shifting their support to Yeltsin and the cause of a sovereign Russia.

Nonetheless, in April 1991, Gorbachev succeeded in reaching agreement on the outlines of a new treaty of union with nine of the fifteen republics, including Russia. The agreement would have established a new balance of power between the federal union government and the constituent republics. The union government would have preserved its responsibility for defense and security, energy and transportation, money and finance, and other coordinating functions. The member republics would have gained the power to make economic policy and control productive assets within their territories. Most of the union bureaucracy's power would have been transferred to the republics. Gorbachev once again underestimated the strength of his opposition, based in the great bureaucracies of the union government. On August 19, 1991, his own vice president, prime minister, defense minister, KGB chief, and other senior officials moved to prevent the signing ceremony of the treaty by forming the "State Committee on the State Emergency" and seizing power in what became known as the August "putsch." They put Gorbachev (then vacationing in the Crimea) under house arrest and attempted to restore the shaken power of the Soviet regime. The coup organizers made some critical errors, however. Evidently they counted on widespread public support for their actions, but instead, the tide of public sympathy in Moscow and Leningrad was against them. Thousands of people came out to defend the "White House," the building where Russia's parliament met. The organizers failed to arrest Boris Yeltsin, who rallied mass opposition to the coup. After three days, the coup collapsed, the organizers were arrested, and Gorbachev returned again as president of the Soviet Union. But Gorbachev's power was now fatally compromised. Neither union nor Russian power structures heeded his commands. Through the fall of 1991, the Russian government took over the union government, ministry by ministry. In November 1991, Yeltsin issued a decree formally outlawing the Communist Party of the Soviet Union. In rapid succession, the union republics declared their independence and on December 9, 1991, the leaders of the Russian, Ukrainian, and Belorussian Republics met to issue a declaration that the Soviet Union was dissolved and replaced by the Commonwealth of Independent States (CIS). Gorbachev became a president without a country. On December 25, 1991, he resigned as president of the USSR and turned the powers of his office over to Boris Yeltsin.

As his nemesis Yeltsin would do eight years later, Gorbachev appeared on national television to announce his resignation. Bitterness alternated with self-justification in his speech. He explained the necessity of his attempt to reform the system, even though his efforts had led to the country's dissolution, by arguing that it would have been wrong for him simply to win office and then cling to power as long as possible (as Brezhnev, he was implying, had done). He had no alternative but to initiate major reforms:

> All the attempts at partial reform—and there were any number of them—suffered failure one after the other. The country lost its vision of the future.

It was impossible to live like that any longer. What was needed was a radical change. That is why I have never, ever regretted not taking advantage of the post of general secretary merely to reign for a number of years. I would have viewed that as irresponsible and amoral. I realized that it was an extremely difficult and even risky business to begin reforms on that sort of scale and in our sort of society. Even today I am convinced of the historical correctness of the democratic reforms begun in the spring of 1985.[31]

Mikhail Gorbachev's reputation stands considerably higher in the West than it does in his own country. He attempted to overcome the paralysis of the Soviet political system by introducing partial measures toward a market-oriented economy and a democratic political system while retaining the essential features of Communist Party domination, state ownership of productive property, and a centralized union state. The wave of demands that his reform awakened stimulated political leaders to make still more far-reaching demands for democratization, decentralization, and market capitalism. These demands provoked a backlash in the form of the August 1991 coup attempt, which in turn fueled a wave of independence movements in all the union republics—even Russia. With the collapse of the union itself each former republic became a nominally independent, sovereign state. Their leaders were each faced with the challenge of finding a new basis for legitimate rule and adapting the Soviet institutional legacy to new tasks. In Russia, the struggle between the defenders of the old Communist order and the advocates of a Western-oriented democratic and capitalist system now grew intense.

NOTES

1. Michael McFaul, *Russia's Unfinished Constitution: Political Change from Gorbachev to Putin* (Ithaca, NY: Cornell University Press, 2001).

2. Ibid., pp. 128–65.

3. Richard Pipes, *Russia under the Old Regime* (New York: Scribner's, 1974), p. 19.

4. Allen C. Lynch, *How Russia Is Not Ruled: Reflections on Russian Political Development* (Cambridge: Cambridge University Press, 2006), pp. 42–43.

5. Note that Communist revolution's date was October 25 under the Julian calendar then in force, but was commemorated on November 7 each year thereafter once the regime switched over to the Gregorian calendar then in use in the West. Similarly, the fall of the tsarist regime occurred in February under the old calendar, March under the new one.

6. Vladimir Ilyich Lenin (1870–1924) was the leader of the wing of the Russian Marxist movement that insisted that socialism in Russia would only be possible if the revolutionaries seized state power and used it to construct a modern, industrial, and socialist economic base in Russia, as well as to launch similar revolutions elsewhere. This wing, which later became a separate party, was called the Bolsheviks. Still later it was renamed the Russian Communist Party, and finally the Communist Party of the Soviet Union. Lenin and his fellow Bolsheviks carried out their plan after seizing power in October 1917 in the name of the workers and peasants, and establishing a government formed around state socialist principles. As de facto leader of the Bolshevik (later Communist) party, and chairman of the new Soviet Russian government, Lenin established the basic governing institutions of the new Soviet regime. Throughout Soviet history, Soviet citizens were taught to revere Lenin as the

infallible source of guidance about ideological doctrine and his teachings were codified, systematized, and joined to official versions of Marxist theory. Together, these bodies of official teachings were given the name "Marxism-Leninism." In the Soviet Union and throughout the Communist world, Marxism-Leninism had the status of dogma.

7. Two useful historical surveys of the Soviet regime are Sheila Fitzpatrick, *The Russian Revolution: 1917–1932* (New York: Oxford University Press, 1984); and Mary McAuley, *Soviet Politics: 1917–1991* (New York: Oxford University Press, 1992).

8. For an authoritative biography of Stalin that explains much of his behavior in psychological terms, see Robert C. Tucker, *Stalin as Revolutionary, 1879–1928: A Study in History and Personality* (New York: Norton, 1973); and Robert C. Tucker, *Stalin in Power: The Revolution from Above, 1928–1941* (New York: Norton, 1990).

9. On Khrushchev, see William Taubman, *Khrushchev: The Man and His Era* (New York: Norton, 2003); and William J. Tompson, *Khrushchev: A Political Life* (New York: St. Martin's Press, 1995).

10. Ronald Grigor Suny, *The Revenge of the Past: Nationalism, Revolution, and the Collapse of the Soviet Union* (Stanford, CA: Stanford University Press, 1993). On early Soviet policies toward ethnic nationalities aimed at building ethnic-national identities within a common multinational Soviet state, see Terry Martin, *The Affirmative Action Empire: Nations and Nationalism in the Soviet Union, 1923–1939* (Ithaca, NY: Cornell University Press, 2001).

11. Mikhail Filippov, Peter C. Ordeshook, and Olga Shvetsova, *Designing Federalism: A Theory of Self-Sustainable Federal Institutions* (Cambridge: Cambridge University Press, 2004).

12. Anders Åslund, *How Russia Became a Market Economy* (Washington, DC: Brookings Institution, 1995), p. 108.

13. Stephen White, Graeme Gill, and Darrell Slider, *The Politics of Transition: Shaping a Post-Soviet Future* (Cambridge: Cambridge University Press, 1993), p. 85.

14. On national mobilization in the republics, see Mark R. Beissinger, *Nationalist*

Mobilization and the Collapse of the Soviet State (Cambridge: Cambridge University Press, 2002).

15. A person could leave "personal" property to his heirs, including money, but not property that was used to create other forms of wealth or income.

16. The famous theory of the "new class" was devised by Yugoslav dissident Milovan Djilas to explain how there could be a ruling class in a supposedly classless society.

17. Linda Cook, *The Soviet Social Contract and Why It Failed: Welfare Policy and Workers' Politics from Brezhnev to Yeltsin* (Cambridge, MA: Harvard University Press, 1993).

18. Janos Kornai, *The Socialist System: The Political Economy of Communism* (Princeton, NJ: Princeton University Press, 1992).

19. Ibid.

20. On the Communist Party, see Ronald J. Hill and Peter Frank, *The Soviet Communist Party,* 3rd ed. (Boston: Allen & Unwin, 1986); and Graeme J. Gill, *The Collapse of a Single-Party System: The Disintegration of the CPSU* (Cambridge: Cambridge University Press, 1994).

21. From Article Six of the USSR constitution as given in Robert Sharlet, *The New Soviet Constitution of 1977: Analysis and Text* (Brunswick, OH: King's Court Communications, 1978), p. 78.

22. Anthony Downs, *Inside Bureaucracy* (Boston: Little, Brown, 1967).

23. Philip G. Roeder, *Red Sunset: The Failure of Soviet Politics* (Princeton, NJ: Princeton University Press, 1993).

24. George W. Breslauer, *Khrushchev and Brezhnev as Leaders: Building Authority in Soviet Politics* (Boston: Allen & Unwin, 1982).

25. He did dictate his memoirs into a tape recorder. The tapes were smuggled out and published under the title *Khrushchev Remembers* (Boston: Little, Brown, 1970) and *Khrushchev Remembers: The Last Testament* (Boston: Little, Brown, 1974). Both volumes were translated and edited by Strobe Talbott.

26. Archie Brown, *The Gorbachev Factor* (New York: Oxford University Press, 1996), p. 81.

27. Brown, *The Gorbachev Factor.*

28. Stephen White, "Reforming the Electoral System," *Journal of Communist Studies* 4:4 (1988): 1–17.

29. The eyewitness reports by Timothy Garton Ash, *The Magic Lantern* (New York: Random House, 1990), are exceptionally valuable firsthand accounts as well as brilliant political analysis of the revolutions of 1989 in Eastern Europe. A thorough history of this period is Gale Stokes, *The Walls Came Tumbling Down: The Collapse of Communism in Eastern Europe* (New York: Oxford University Press, 1993).

30. On the 1989 and 1990 elections and the new representative bodies they formed, see Yitzhak M. Brudny, "The Dynamics of 'Democratic Russia,' 1990–1993," *Post-Soviet Affairs* 9:2 (1993): 141–70; Giulietto Chiesa, with Douglas Taylor Northrop, *Transition to Democracy: Political Change in the Soviet Union, 1987–1991* (Hanover and London: Dartmouth College; University Press of New England, 1993); Robert T. Huber and Donald R. Kelley, eds., *Perestroika-Era Politics: The New Soviet Legislature and Gorbachev's Political Reforms* (Armonk: M.E. Sharpe, 1991); Brendan Kiernan, *The End of Soviet Politics: Elections, Legislatures and the Demise of the Communist Party* (Boulder, CO: Westview, 1993); Michael E. Urban, *More Power to the Soviets: The Democratic Revolution in the USSR* (Aldershot, England, and Brookfield, Vermont: Edward Elgar, 1990); and Thomas F. Remington, ed., *Parliaments in Transition: New Legislative Politics in Eastern Europe and the Former USSR* (Boulder, CO: Westview, 1994).

31. "Gorbachev Resigns as USSR President," FBIS-SOV-91-248 (December 26, 1991), 20–21.

Chapter 3

Russia's Constitutional Order

THE RUSSIAN REPUBLIC IN THE TRANSITION PERIOD

The last chapter showed that the Soviet regime established a highly centralized political order in which power flowed from the center and political institutions formed a hierarchy of repeating structures. Each of the 15 union republics was a smaller-scale replica of the whole union in its political organization. Each had its own Supreme Soviet, its own government with its own ministries (even a foreign ministry!), its own republic-level branch of the KGB and of the Communist Party. A uniform, centrally planned economic system and political ideology kept the system closely knit. In each national republic, the language of the dominant ethnic nationality could be taught in schools and used in the cultural sphere, but Russian served as a lingua franca across the union, and was the language of politics, science, diplomacy, and security.

As the core republic of the union, the Russian Republic comprised half the population and three-quarters of the territory of the whole union. Although Russia had no republic-level Communist Party, it did have a Supreme Soviet and executive branch at the republican level. When Gorbachev introduced the new two-tiered parliamentary structure consisting of a Congress of People's Deputies and Supreme Soviet for the USSR, the Russian Republic dutifully followed suit one year later and created its own congress and supreme soviet. These became the political base for the radical democratic movement and gave Boris Yeltsin a platform. Over the period from 1990–1993, Yeltsin mounted his challenge to Gorbachev for preeminence in Russia by building support in the Russian legislative branch for a directly elected presidency, running for and winning the office of president, and then defying

Gorbachev by demanding a program of radical economic reform. When the Soviet Union broke up at the end of 1991, these executive and legislative bodies of the Russian Republic became the supreme organs of power in a sovereign state.

Boris Yeltsin clearly understood that if he won the mantle of legitimacy that comes from being a directly elected president, he would have a political advantage over Gorbachev that he could use in dealing with the executive bureaucracy of the Russian Republic. Once he succeeded in being elected president of Russia in June 1991, he was able to outflank Gorbachev every time Gorbachev attempted to assert the power of the union government over the republics.

But Yeltsin's political strategy also had a weakness. When he ran for president in June 1991, he held the office of chairman of the Supreme Soviet. As chairman, he was effectively both the chief officer of the legislature and, because state power was constitutionally seated in the legislature rather than divided between legislative and executive branches, he was also the highest official in the state. But as soon as he was elected president of the Russian Federation, he left his position as chairman of the Supreme Soviet to assume the new office of president. The legislature's deputy chairman, Ruslan Khasbulatov, replaced him as chairman. At that point Yeltsin no longer could directly control the Supreme Soviet. Over the next two years, Khasbulatov and the legislature moved from a posture of support for Yeltsin and his policies to one of sharp opposition. The conflict reached a bloody climax in September and October 1993 when Yeltsin dissolved parliament by decree, and the opposition forces launched an armed uprising against him, which he suppressed. Yeltsin demanded that the legislature adopt a new constitution giving him sweeping authority as president; the legislature refused. The growing confrontation between Yeltsin's allies and his opponents in the period between August 1991 and October 1993 very nearly resulted in civil war.

1990–1993: Deepening Constitutional Conflict

In the fall of 1991, with the union government losing power, economic shortages were spreading and prices rising; some regional authorities even erected roadblocks to prevent the sale of foodstuffs from their territories. Tax collections were plummeting. Invoking the very real danger of a breakdown of state authority, Yeltsin demanded that the Russian legislature grant him extraordinary powers to cope with the country's economic crisis. Yeltsin made it clear that he believed that only a decisive program of dismantling state controls on production and prices would restore economic activity again. In October 1991, he was given the power to carry out his radical economic program by decree. The Congress also consented to his demand that he be authorized to appoint the heads of government in each region of the country, rather than holding local elections for heads of the executive branch. Yeltsin then named himself acting prime minister and proceeded to form a government led by a group of young, Western-oriented leaders determined to carry out a decisive economic transformation. Charged with planning and carrying out the program was his deputy prime minister, Egor Gaidar.

Under the program—widely called "shock therapy"—the government undertook several radical measures simultaneously that were intended to stabilize the economy by bringing government spending and revenues into balance, and by letting market demand determine the prices and supply of goods. Under the reforms, the government let most prices float, raised taxes, and cut back sharply on spending in industry and construction. These policies caused widespread hardship as many state enterprises found themselves without orders or financing. The rationale of the program was to squeeze the built-in inflationary pressure out of the economy so that producers would begin making sensible decisions instead of chronically wasting resources. By letting the market rather than central planners determine prices, output levels, and the like, the reformers intended to create an incentive structure in the economy in which efficiency would be rewarded, and waste would be punished. Removing the causes of chronic inflation, the reform's architects argued, was a precondition for all other reforms: hyperinflation would wreck both democracy and economic progress; only by stabilizing the state budget could the government proceed to restructure the economy. A similar reform program had been adopted in Poland in January 1990, with generally favorable results.

Radical economic stabilization affects many interests and causes acute hardship for society, at least in the short run. Groups that are particularly hard-hit, including those dependent on state subsidies that are being cut, make their voice heard through the political process. In Russia's case, the program caused particularly deep distress and led to bitter collision between the president and the parliament, each representing a powerful coalition of organized political interests. Each claimed to represent Russia's true interests, the president backing the cause of liberal reform, the parliament demanding a return to state socialism.

The reform program took effect on January 2, 1992. The first results were immediately felt as prices skyrocketed, government spending was slashed, and heavy new taxes went into effect. A deep credit crunch shut down many industries and brought about a protracted depression. Quickly a number of politicians began to distance themselves from the program: even Yeltsin's vice president, Alexander Rutskoi, denounced the program as "economic genocide."[1] Through 1992, opposition to the reform policies of Yeltsin and Gaidar grew stronger and more intransigent. Increasingly, the political confrontation between Yeltsin and the reformers on one side, and the opposition to radical economic reform on the other, became centered in the two branches of government. Yeltsin expanded the powers of the presidency beyond constitutional limits in carrying out the reform program. In the Russian Congress of People's Deputies and the Supreme Soviet, the deputies refused to adopt a new constitution that would enshrine presidential power into law. They refused to allow Yeltsin to continue to serve as his own prime minister, and rejected his attempt to nominate Gaidar. They demanded modifications of the economic program and directed the Central Bank, which was under parliament's control, to continue issuing credits to enterprises to keep them from shutting down. The Central Bank's liberality wrecked the regime of fiscal discipline that the government was attempting to pursue: the money supply tripled in the third quarter of 1992 and for the year, prices rose over 2300 percent.[2] Through 1992, Yeltsin wrestled with the parliament for control over government and government policy.

In March 1993, Yeltsin threatened to declare a regime of special emergency rule in the country, and to suspend parliament, but then backed down. The Congress of People's Deputies immediately met and voted on a motion to impeach Yeltsin. The motion failed by a narrow margin. Yeltsin countered by convening a large conference to hammer out a constitution that would give him the presidential powers he demanded. On September 21, shortly before the deputies were to meet to adopt a law that would have lowered the threshold for decisions in the Congress and thus would have made it easier for them to impeach the president, Yeltsin declared the parliament dissolved, and called for elections to a new parliament to be held in December. Yeltsin's enemies, who included Yeltsin's vice president, Alexander Rutskoi, and the chairman of parliament, Ruslan Khasbulatov, then barricaded themselves inside the White House, as the building where the parliament was situated was popularly known. Refusing to submit to Yeltsin's decrees, they held a rump congress that declared Rutskoi president. After ten days, during which Yeltsin shut off electric power to the building, they joined with some loosely organized paramilitary units outside the building and assaulted the building next to the White House where the Moscow mayor's offices were located. Then they tried to take over the television tower where Russia's main national television broadcast facilities are housed, driving trucks through the entrance, smashing offices, and exchanging gunfire with police. They evidently hoped their action would set off a national revolt against Yeltsin or win the army over to their side. Finally, the army decided to back Yeltsin and suppress the uprising. Khasbulatov, Rutskoi, and the other leaders of the rebellion were arrested. The army even lobbed artillery shells against the White House, killing an unknown number of people inside.

In subsequent decrees soon afterward, Yeltsin dissolved all local soviets and called for the formation of new local representative bodies. He also called on regional soviets to disband and hold new elections to new assemblies under guidelines that he also issued. Yeltsin was in fact ending the system of soviet power. He had made his views on this issue amply clear the previous June when, at the constitutional assembly that he convened, he declared that the system of soviet power was intrinsically undemocratic because it failed to separate legislative from executive power. In place of soviets he decreed that there be small, deliberative bodies at the local and regional levels, and a national parliament called the Federal Assembly representing Russia as a whole.

Yeltsin's plan for the parliament was embodied in the draft constitution that he put before the country in December 1993. According to it, the Federal Assembly would have two chambers. The upper house, the Federation Council, would give equal representation to each of Russia's 89 regions and republics (called "subjects of the federation"). As in many other parliaments, it would be weaker than the lower, or popular, chamber. The latter, called the State Duma, would be formed in a manner entirely new to Russia. It was to have 450 seats. Half were to be filled in proportion to the share of votes that parties received for their party lists.[3] The other 225 seats were to be filled in traditional single-member district races. Each voter in December 1993 therefore cast four votes for the Federal Assembly: two for the seats from his or her region in the Federation Council, and two for the deputies of the State Duma. One of these was for a candidate running for the local district seat, and one was for a party list.[4]

In the national referendum on December 12, 1993, Yeltsin's constitution was approved. According to the official figures, turnout was 54.8 percent, and of those who voted, 58.4 percent voted in favor of the constitution.[5] The constitution therefore came into force. Figure 3.1 presents a schematic overview of the main structures of the current constitutional order.

The 1993 Constitution and the Presidency

The new constitution was designed to establish a dominant presidency: Yeltsin referred to the model as a "presidential republic." We can call the Russian system "presidential-parliamentary." In such a system there is both a president and a prime minister. The president appoints the prime minister and other cabinet ministers, but the cabinet must also have the confidence of parliament to govern.[6] In Russia, the president does have the power to make law by decree, and to dissolve parliament, although he is subject to several specific constitutional constraints. His decrees may not violate existing law and can be superseded by laws passed by parliament. The president appoints the prime minister (who is formally termed the Chairman of the government), subject to the approval of parliament. The Duma can refuse to confirm the president's choice, but if after three attempts, the president still fails to win the Duma's approval of his choice, he dissolves the Duma and calls for new elections. Likewise, the Duma may hold a vote of no confidence in the government. The first time a motion of no confidence carries, the president and government may ignore it, but if it passes a second time, the president must either dissolve parliament or dismiss the government. The president's power to dissolve parliament and call for new elections is also limited by the constitution. He may not dissolve parliament within one year of its election, or once it has filed impeachment charges against the president, or once the president has declared a state of emergency throughout Russia, or within six months of the expiration of the president's term.[7] The president can veto legislation passed by parliament, but parliament can override the veto by a two-thirds vote in each chamber. Thus although the constitution gives the president the upper hand in relations with parliament, it is not an entirely free hand.

Moreover, the president cannot bypass parliament and put an issue to a popular referendum on his own authority, nor may he block one. Only once a citizens' initiative has gathered two million signatures can a ballot proposition be put before the country as a national referendum.

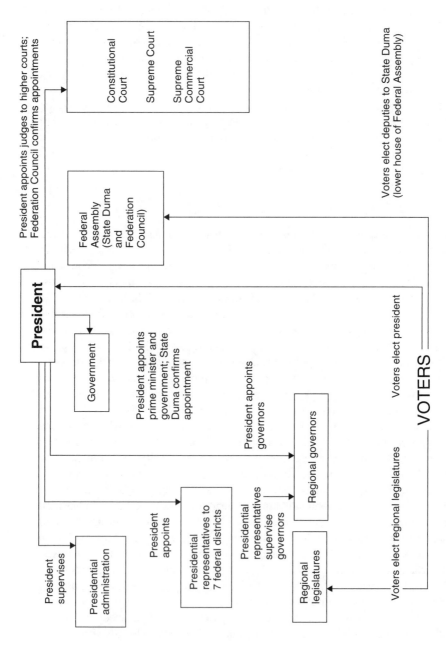

Figure 3.1 ■ Structure of Russian Government.

President appoints judges to higher courts;
Federation Council confirms appointments

Constitutional
Court

Supreme Court

Supreme
Commercial
Court

Federal
Assembly
(State Duma
and
Federation
Council)

Voters elect deputies to State Duma
(lower house of Federal Assembly)

President

Government

President appoints
prime minister and
government; State
Duma confirms
appointment

President appoints
governors

Voters elect president

VOTERS

Regional governors

President
supervises

Presidential
administration

President
appoints

Presidential
representatives to
7 federal districts

Presidential
representatives
supervise
governors

Voters elect regional legislatures

Regional
legislatures

Voters elect regional legislatures

The constitution calls the president "head of state" and "guarantor of the constitution." He "ensures the coordinated functioning and collaboration of bodies of state power" (Article 80, paragraphs 1 and 2). He is not made chief executive. Although the president's nominee for prime minister must be confirmed by parliament, the president can appoint and remove deputy prime ministers and other ministers without parliamentary consent. These decisions are, nonetheless, to be made "on the proposal" of the prime minister.

Formally, at least, the president's power to name the government is the same as that of the French president, and the language of the relevant provisions of the two constitutions is the same.[8] However, both Yeltsin and Putin have taken liberties with their power to name the government, and have directly controlled the appointment and dismissal of both the prime minister and the other members of the government. On the other hand, the constitution could also accommodate a very different relationship between president and parliament. Although a powerful and popular president is likely to dominate policy making in all spheres, with his prime minister serving as an executive in charge of formulating specific policy options and administering the machinery of government, a weaker president might find it necessary to appoint a prime minister whose base of power lay in a parliamentary majority—as happened in France during periods of "cohabitation."

The major difference between Russia's semipresidential system and that of France is that Russia's government is not formed from a party majority in parliament. The president appoints the government based on calculations about the relative power of different bureaucratic and personal factions, taking care to balance competing interests. The weakness of institutional authority is offset by the strength of the president in relation to other centers of power. Putin, for example, has used his presidential administration, his near-total control over the mass media, the security organs, and a number of appointed consultative bodies, to rule with little regard to the formal structures of the constitution.

The Russian president has far-reaching formal and informal powers.[9] The president exercises his power through a staff structure called the "administration of the president." This is an immense organization. The French president, for example, gets by with a staff of 40 to 50 people; the American president has a White House staff of over 400 people and another 1,300 in the Executive Office of the President. In Russia, the presidential administration comprises around 2,000 people, and as often as the president may try to trim it, the number keeps creeping upward. It is made up of many units, such as the press office; divisions for liaison with other bodies of power and with the regional governments; a division overseeing law-making and judicial institutions; even a unit that owns and manages the properties belonging to the presidency, among which are apartment buildings, office buildings, hotels, health resorts, and other facilities—even the buildings of parliament itself.

To some extent, the presidential administration duplicates the ministries of government. Some units of it work to ensure that governments in the regions carry out federal policy. The "power ministries," that is, the state agencies directly concerned with national security, report directly to the president. These include the Foreign Ministry, Federal Security Service (formerly the Committee for State Security, or KGB), Defense Ministry, and Interior Ministry. There are, in addition, a large range of official and quasi-official commissions and administrations that are funded and directed by the president that carry out a variety of supervisory and advisory functions.

The president also directly oversees the Security Council, which consists of a full-time secretary, the heads of the power ministries and other security-related agencies, the prime minister, and, more recently, the president's representatives to the seven federal "superdistricts" through which he keeps tabs on the 89 federal regions of the country. The president can appoint other officials to the Security Council as well. Its powers are broad but shadowy. President Putin has relied on it to develop policy initiatives, and he has appointed senior generals from the FSB (security police) and military as its top staff.[10] There is still no legislation establishing the rights and obligations of the Security Council, and so its structure, role, and power at any given time depend on the president's discretion.[11]

Both Yeltsin and Putin have regularly created and dissolved new institutions answering directly to the president. For example, in 2000, Putin created the State Council, which comprises the heads of regional governments and thus parallels the Federation Council. Five years later, he created the Public Chamber, which will be discussed in Chapter 6. Both the State Council and the Public Chamber duplicate some of the deliberative and representative functions of parliament, and therefore weaken parliament's role. They illustrate the tendency, under both Yeltsin and Putin, for the president to create and dissolve new structures answering directly to the president. These improvised structures can be politically useful to the president by acting as counterweights to constitutionally mandated bodies such as parliament, as well as providing policy advice and feedback. They help ensure that the president is always the dominant institution in the political system, but they undermine the authority of other formal institutions.

Under Putin, the presidential administration has expanded its role in shaping and guiding political processes far beyond the federal executive branch. The president's staff manages relations with the parliament, the courts, big business, the media, political parties, and major interest groups. A good indication of the degree to which Putin has revived Russia's traditional authoritarian style of rule is the informal rule that no significant political undertaking (such as a new political party) in Russia is possible without prior clearance with the presidential administration.

In addition to the formal powers of the president are the symbolic resources at his disposal. The president's offices are in the Kremlin. The Kremlin—a term that means fortress or citadel—was the symbolic seat of the Russian state under Ivan the Terrible in the sixteenth century. It remained the center of Russian state power until Peter the Great moved the capital of the country to the new city of St. Petersburg, which he founded on the Baltic Sea at the beginning of the eighteenth century; the Bolsheviks moved the capital back to Moscow in 1918 and again made the Kremlin the physical and symbolic center of the Soviet state. Today's Russian presidents deliberately identify themselves with Russian rulers of the tsarist and Soviet eras in order to underline the continuity of state power.

Far more than Yeltsin did, Vladimir Putin has quietly fostered a cult of personality through such methods as the use of official portraits that officials are encouraged to hang in their offices, and signals to the mass media to portray him in a flattering light. In keeping with the old tradition by which notable officials from the tsar down to local dignitaries are expected to listen to the complaints of ordinary people, Putin's staff annually receives over half a million letters from Russian citizens. He holds periodic call-in sessions with the public during which he responds to questions submitted by telephone, e-mail, text message, or live from broadcast sites around the country. (His detailed, information-filled answers are possible because the questions have been vetted and selected beforehand.) Putin's staff have promoted a media image of Putin as a straight-talking, firm, and authoritative president, who shares the thoughts and feelings of his fellow citizens and even allows himself to use profane language on occasion. Occasional televised clips of Putin arm wrestling or engaged in a martial arts contest reinforce the official message that he is youthful, energetic, and in charge. The presidential Web site (the English-language version is at: <http://president.kremlin.ru/eng/>) identifies Putin both with the symbols of Russian statehood and the direction of Russian policy.

The personalization of state power is not confined to Putin and the presidency. Many structures in Russia's post-Communist state, such as regional governments and political parties, are closely identified with the personalities of their heads: the leader's personal priorities often define the rights and responsibilities of the office. Rules remain undeveloped and fluid. Despite efforts under Putin to reform the system of state administration, the bureaucracy remains inefficient, frequently corrupt, and susceptible to political manipulation.

Increasingly, under Putin, the Russian political system has adopted the practices and forms of rule used by the Soviet regime. These include the concentration of decision-making power at the top, the accepted gap between democratic appearances and the reality of monopolistic power, and the reliance on police methods to keep political opposition in check. The president's role is similar to that of the old party General Secretary, his administration something like the machinery of the Central Committee.[12] The administration's far-reaching influence and coordinating role in the political system is equivalent to that of the old Secretariat of the Communist Party. Indeed, the presidential administration is located in the same offices on Old Square, adjacent to the Kremlin, that the secretariat once occupied. In the absence of other mechanisms for control, such as effective parliamentary oversight, vigorous media scrutiny, a politically independent judiciary, or a rational legal foundation for bureaucratic authority, direct political supervision from above seems to be the only means Russian rulers know for controlling the sprawling state bureaucracy.[13] Although political centralization is an ineffective means of managing the state bureaucracy, no president wants to relinquish the enormous formal and extraconstitutional powers he can exercise over the state.

Many observers have called the Russian system "superpresidential" because the president's powers are so broad.[14] Indeed, Timothy Colton and Cindy Skach have counted the specific powers granted to the Russian president and find that he has twice as many formal, constitutionally granted powers as does the French president.[15] There are a number of dangers in superpresidentialism: the regime depends heavily on the person of the president, who may be (or become) unfit for the job; president and parliament have competing electoral mandates and so may well come into conflict; and the government is in an ambiguous position because it must serve both president and parliament.[16] Overly powerful presidencies also tend to weaken the development of robust party competition, because strong presidents often avoid lending their political authority to institutions outside their direct control; in comparative perspective, the stronger the president, the weaker the party system.[17] And of course, as both Yeltsin and Putin have shown, the Russian president may expand the use of his informal, "metaconstitutional" powers at the expense of the formal checks and balances built into the system.

One other weakness of a superpresidential system should be noted. In a system that relies so heavily on the president's power for making and carrying out policy, the president's power inevitably turns out to be inadequate to achieve large-scale policy goals that require extensive coordination, persuasion, and public support. Even a strong president soon discovers how limited are the resources at his disposal for changing the behavior of large state bureaucracies across a wide range of policy issues simultaneously. The real problem with presidentialism is not that presidential power is too strong—it is that it is too *weak*.

The Government

The "government" refers to the senior echelon of leadership in the executive branch. It is charged with formulating the main lines of national policy, especially in the economic and social realms, and overseeing its implementation. (The president oversees the formulation and execution of foreign and national security policy.) It corresponds to the Cabinet in Western parliamentary systems. In the Russian system, the government answers primarily to the president, and only nominally to the parliament.

Successful performance under a system featuring both a president and a prime minister requires a constructive working relationship between the two. Either this comes about through the prime minister's clear subordination to the president, or they work out a mutually acceptable division of labor between them. Russia has shown examples of several different types of relationship beween president and prime minister. For example, Prime Minister Chernomyrdin and President Yeltsin achieved a surprisingly harmonious working relationship that lasted over five years. First appointed by Yeltsin as head of government in December 1992 and finally dismissed in March 1998, Viktor Chernomyrdin had a comparatively long tenure as head of government. His successors as prime minister under Yeltsin did not hold on to power so long.[18] The relationship between president and prime minister is variable. When Yeltsin was ill and removed from much day-to-day policy making, his prime minister could exercise a considerable degree of autonomy in running the government. Under Putin, however, it is clear that the president has the major say in setting policy direction, and sees the government as the executive machinery for achieving his goals. And as in other dual executive systems, the president finds it very convenient to be able to use the government as whipping boy for failures of policy, and to claim credit for its successes.[19]

An indication of the strongly presidential tilt of the system is the fact that the makeup of the government is not directly determined by the party composition of the parliament. Indeed, there is scarcely any relationship between the distribution of party forces in the Duma and the political balance of the government. Nearly all members of the government are career managers and administrators rather than party politicians. Instead, the government's composition reflects the president's calculations about how to balance considerations such as personal loyalty, professional competence, and the relative strength of major bureaucratic factions. When Putin chose Mikhail Fradkov to be prime minister on March 1, 2004—two weeks *ahead* of presidential elections—the political establishment was taken by surprise; Fradkov was a relatively obscure figure who had headed the Federal Tax Police for two years. His very lack of independent political clout underscored the fact that Putin would be the main source of policy direction for the country.

A goal of Putin was to streamline the system of state administration to make it a more effective and accountable instrument. From 2002 to 2004 a commission under Putin's direction labored to develop a new scheme for organizing the federal executive. In March 2004 the restructuring was implemented. In principle, the new organization chart matched the structure of the government more closely with its functions. There were now to be three types of government bodies, ministries, services, and agencies. Ministries, of which there were to be only 15, were to be broadly responsible for developing policy within their domains. Services were to be organized around supervision and regulation, and agencies were to be in charge of service delivery and management of state property.[20] Ten of the new ministries were to be under the direction of the prime minister (chair of the government), and five under the president's direction supervision (these are the "power ministries"). The cabinet was to be considerably slimmed down, and to comprise fifteen ministries and three state committees that in turn would oversee dozens of other state committees and agencies responsible for managing the federal executive branch. The guiding principle of the reform was to replace the old "branch" style of government, under which each branch of the economy was supervised by a corresponding state structure, with a "functional" basis of organization. But observers were very skeptical that the new system would improve bureaucratic performance. They noted that although the aim was to streamline the structure of government, the total number of federal-level executive bodies rose from 57 to 72.[21]

Moreover, the actual lines of control and accountability remained confused. How much actual control ministers would have over agencies and services under their jurisdiction was unclear, and few people expected the new scheme to do away with the chronic problems of redundancy, overlap, and competition among arms of the bureaucracy that have impeded effective management and coordination for decades.

The Parliament

The parliament—Federal Assembly—is distinctly inferior to the president in power but, under Yeltsin, sometimes succeeded in blocking the president. Under Putin its independence has steadily diminished to the point that it serves in effect as a rubber stamp for the president's initiatives. Nonetheless it remains a central element in the political system for several reasons. One is the fact that political parties and politicians compete hard to win seats in the State Duma, which gives them opportunities to lobby the bureaucracy for their own interests and those of their constituents. Another is the role parliament plays as a forum for public debate. Pro-government and opposition parties are able to voice their positions on issues of the day even if their actual influence on legislation is limited. Finally, the president values the legal legitimacy that passage of legislation by parliament generates, which helps explain why Putin goes to the trouble of submitting bills to parliament and shepherding them through the legislative process rather than simply promulgating his policy decisions by decree.

State Duma

The State Duma has the constitutional right to originate legislation except in certain categories of policy that are under the jurisdiction of the upper house, the Federation Council. Upon passage in the State Duma, a bill goes to the Federation Council. If the upper house rejects it, the bill goes back to the Duma, where a commission comprising members of both houses may seek to iron out differences. If the Duma rejects the upper house's changes, it may override the Federation Council by a two-thirds vote (see Figure 3.2).

When the bill has cleared parliament, it goes to the president for signature. If the president refuses to sign the bill, he returns it to the Duma, outlining his objections. The Duma may pass it with the president's proposed changes by a simple absolute majority, or override the president's veto, for which a two-thirds vote is required. The Federation Council must then also approve the bill, by a simple majority if the president's amendments are accepted, or a two-thirds vote if it chooses to override the president. Under Yeltsin, the Duma occasionally overrode the president's veto and, on several occasions, overrode Federation Council rejections. In other cases under Yeltsin, the Duma passed bills rejected by the president after accepting the president's amendments. Even when parliament and president were at odds over policy—as happened frequently during Yeltsin's presidency—the two sides avoided provoking a conflict that could trigger a major constitutional

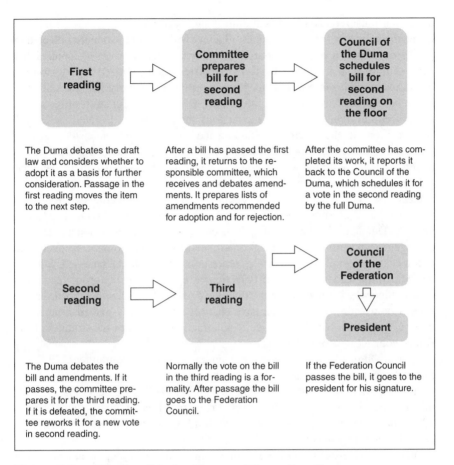

First reading

The Duma debates the draft law and considers whether to adopt it as a basis for further consideration. Passage in the first reading moves the item to the next step.

Committee prepares bill for second reading

After a bill has passed the first reading, it returns to the responsible committee, which receives and debates amendments. It prepares lists of amendments recommended for adoption and for rejection.

Council of the Duma schedules bill for second reading on the floor

After the committee has completed its work, it reports it back to the Council of the Duma, which schedules it for a vote in the second reading by the full Duma.

Second reading

The Duma debates the bill and amendments. If it passes, the committee prepares it for the third reading. If it is defeated, the committee reworks it for a new vote in second reading.

Third reading

Normally the vote on the bill in the third reading is a formality. After passage the bill goes to the Federation Council.

Council of the Federation

President

If the Federation Council passes the bill, it goes to the president for his signature.

Figure 3.2 ■ The Legislative Process: Three Readings.

crisis. In the 1990s, around three-quarters of the laws passed by parliament were eventually signed into law by Yeltsin.

Under Putin the relationship between parliament and president is far closer. Both chambers of parliament firmly support virtually every initiative submitted to them by the president or government (sometimes extracting minor concessions as the price for their support). Following the sweeping success of the pro-presidential party, United Russia, in the December 2003 election, the president's followers enjoy a huge majority in the Duma and have marginalized all opposition. The number of presidential vetoes has dropped almost to zero; the Duma and Federation Council pass virtually everything submitted by the president and almost nothing the president does not support.

A distinctive feature of the State Duma is that it is organized around its party factions. Every party that has won at least 5 percent of the party list voting in the proportional representation half of the ballot is entitled to form a faction in the Duma made up of its elected deputies, together with any of the deputies elected in single-member districts who care to join.[22] Moreover, any group of deputies that can assemble 55 members has the right to register as a recognized deputy group to obtain exactly the same rights and benefits as those the party factions obtain.[23] These benefits are valuable to deputies: they include funds for staff, office space, and procedural rights. Moreover, the factions and groups divide up all the leadership positions in the chamber, including the committee chairmanships, among themselves.[24] The factions and groups see the Duma as a means for showcasing their pet legislative projects, giving their leaders a national forum, obtaining crucial organizational support for their party work, and providing service to their constituents. Not surprisingly, nearly all deputies join one of the factions or groups.

The steering committee of the Duma is the Council of the Duma. The Council of the Duma makes the principal decisions in the Duma with respect to legislative agenda and proceedings, and sometimes forges compromises to overcome deadlocks among the political groups represented in the Duma. Until 2004, it was made up of the leaders of each party faction or registered deputy group regardless of size. Since the United Russia faction took control of the chamber, however, the rules and structure of the Duma have changed considerably and made it much more majoritarian. Now the United Russia faction dominates the Council of the Duma, controlling 8 of its 11 seats.

The Duma also has a system of standing legislative committees, 29 in the Duma that convened in January 2004. Each deputy is a member of one committee. Committees help draft legislation and sift through the amendments that are submitted once a bill has been passed in first reading. In the Duma that convened in 2004, commmittees have less work to do drafting legislation, because nearly all major legislation is developed by the government.

Bills are considered in three readings. In the first reading, the Duma simply decides whether to approve the basic conception of a piece of legislation. If so, the bill goes back to the committee, which then collects and evaluates the amendments that are offered to the bill by deputies (sometimes thousands of amendments are offered to a single bill). When the committee has agreed on its recommended version of the bill, it reports it out again to the floor for a second reading, and the whole chamber decides on which amendments to approve and which to reject. At that point the floor votes on the bill in its entirety, and sends it back to the committee for a final editing and polishing. The third reading then gives the Duma's final approval to the bill and it goes to the Federation Council.

The December 2003 elections gave the pro-Putin party, United Russia, a commanding position in the Duma with two-thirds of the seats. Around 80 percent of all single-member district deputies joined the United Russia faction—a good indication of its drawing power. Because United Russia votes with a high degree of discipline, the Duma is consistently able to deliver the president legislative majorities. Other factions have very little opportunity to influence the agenda, let alone the outcomes of legislative deliberations. This has given Putin even more opportunity to reshape political institutions and processes, centralizing power even further at the expense of rival institutions. After the Beslan tragedy in 2004, Putin pushed through parliament a series of reforms that reinforce centralization both vertically and horizontally. First, in place of directly elected governors, the president now nominates governors for confirmation by regional parliaments. Second, Putin eliminated all single-member district seats from the Duma; instead, all 450 seats will be filled by national party-list proportional representation elections. Third, he called for the creation of a new "public chamber" to filter and review all legislative proposals before they were submitted formally to the Duma. Taken together, these changes severely reduce the ability of members of parliament to develop any independent local base of political support: lacking local constituencies, they will have to rely on ties to the leaders of national parties; governors will have little opportunity or ability to influence deputies from their regions; and the Duma will find it more difficult to engage in legislative entrepreneurship in order to influence public policy.

These reforms reinforce the trend under Putin toward the suppression of independent sources of political initiative that could oppose Putin's power and policies. They make both the regional governments and the federal parliament instruments for carrying out the president's will. The reforms illustrate the authoritarian tendencies that have strengthened since Putin took office. They do not eliminate all elements of political pluralism in the society, however. Although political parties face increasing obstacles, they continue to compete at the regional and federal level for representation. In the longer term, the viability of political pluralism in Russia will depend on the slow accumulation of material and organizational resources in society, the growth of political self-awareness and organizational capacity on the part of social groups and interests, and the formation of linkages between political parties and social associations.

Federation Council

The upper chamber of parliament is called the Federation Council. Constitutionally, it has some important rights. It approves presidential nominees for high courts such as the Supreme Court and the Constitutional Court. It approves presidential decrees declaring martial law or a state of emergency, and any actions altering the boundaries of territorial units in Russia. It must consider any legislation dealing with taxes, budget, financial policy, treaties, customs, and declarations of war. Under Yeltsin the Federation Council defied the president's will on a number of issues, rejecting some of his nominees for the Constitutional Court, as well as his candidates for Procurator General.[25] Putin, however, has made the chamber firmly subordinate to his will.

On matters of ordinary legislation, where the Federation Council does not have exclusive jurisdiction, the State Duma can override a veto by the Federation Council with a two-thirds vote. The president can then choose whether to support the Duma's position and sign the law, or to uphold the Federation Council and veto it.

The Federation Council is designed as an instrument of federalism in that (like the U.S. Senate) every constituent unit of the federation is represented in it by two members. Under the constitution, they must come from the executive and legislative branches of the regional governments. As in the United States, equal representation from territories of unequal population means that the populations of small territories (which in Russia are often ethnic-national units) are greatly overrepresented compared with more populous regions. The first members of the Federation Council were elected by direct popular vote in December 1993 but, under a law passed in 1995, the heads of the executive and legislative branches of each constituent unit of the federation were automatically given seats in the Federation Council as of 1996.

In 2000, Putin changed this procedure as part of a package of reforms intended to strengthen the power of the federal government vis-à-vis the regions. Under Putin's new procedure, each region's chief executive names a full-time representative to serve as a member of the Federation Council, and each regional legislature names another. Despite initial resistance by the Federation Council, the new law was passed with only minor modifications. It soon became clear that although the Federation Council's members were delegated by the regions, politically they were controlled by the Kremlin.[26]

In its new composition, the Federation Council has consistently supported President Putin and his program, and has passed nearly every law he has proposed even when the legislation directly countered the interests of the regions. The members have found the credentials (and immunity from all criminal prosecution) that go with parliamentary membership to be useful to them in lobbying for the interests of the regions that delegated them. But both among members and the political elite generally there continues to be a great deal of dissatisfaction over the chamber's current role and most observers believe that the current law on the composition of the chamber should be replaced by one providing that the members of the upper house are popularly elected. This must be reconciled in some way, however, with the constitutional requirement that the two members of the chamber from each of Russia's territorial subjects represent the executive and legislative branches.[27]

Executive–Legislative Relations

Relations between president and parliament during the Yeltsin period were often stormy. The first two Dumas, elected in 1993 and in 1995, were dominated by the Communist and other leftist factions hostile to President Yeltsin and the policies of his government. This was particularly true in economic policy. On other issues, however, such as matters concerning federal relations, the Duma and president often reached agreement—sometimes over the objections of the Federation Council, whose members fought to protect regional prerogatives. Yeltsin sometimes replaced members of the government in response to political pressure from the Duma.[28]

The election of 1999 produced a Duma with a pro-government majority. Putin and his government worked to build a reliable base of support in the Duma for their legislative initiatives comprising a coalition of four centrist political factions. The 2003 election produced a still wider margin of support for the president in the Duma and an overwhelming majority for the United Russia party. This has meant that Putin does not need to expend much effort in bargaining with the Duma to win its support for his policies. Generally speaking, the pro-presidential deputies in the Duma need the Kremlin much more than the Kremlin needs them. For example, deputies rely on support from the presidential administration for their reelection campaigns. The recent electoral reforms will only reinforce this dependency. Because, starting with the 2007 parliamentary elections, all seats will be filled through proportional representation from nationwide party list ballots, deputies will need the backing of their party leaders to gain a good place on the party list. The parties, in turn, will need the favor of the Kremlin to clear the new 7 percent electoral threshold (e.g., the Kremlin will influence media coverage for the parties' electoral campaigns). As a result, for the foreseeable future, the balance of power in the political system will continue to leave the parliament in a marginalized position.

Superpresidentialism and the Separation of Powers

Article 10 of the constitution declares that: "State power in the Russian Federation is exercised on the basis of the separation of legislative, executive and judicial powers. Bodies of legislative, executive and judicial power are independent." Under President Yeltsin, there was some real separation of executive, legislative, and judicial power, both because there was effective, well-organized opposition to Yeltsin, and because at crucial moments Yeltsin himself chose to respect the provisions of the constitution he had instituted.[29] But under President Putin, little remains of the separation of powers. Putin has rendered parliament an ineffectual and largely ceremonial body, and has increased executive control over the judiciary. The encroachment of presidential power extends to the Constitutional Court, which under the constitution exercises the power of judicial review. That is, the Constitutional Court has the authority to review the legality and constitutionality of actions of the president and parliament. (We will discuss the Constitutional Court in more detail in Chapter 8.) Occasionally the court defied Yeltsin. It has never defied Putin. Nevertheless, even the possibility that it might exert a measure of independent political influence has led Putin to propose moving the seat of the court to St. Petersburg. This is widely considered to be a tactic to distance the court from the tight web of governing bodies located in Moscow and thus to marginalize it still further politically.

The formal concentration of power in the presidency under the constitution allows the president to use informal, extraconstitutional instruments of power to strip other institutions of the ability to resist presidential authority. Once elected, a president can dominate the government and put pressure on the courts, the governors, the mass media, and business leaders to support his policies.

In this respect Russia somewhat resembles the pattern that political scientist Guillermo O'Donnell has called "delegative democracy."[30] In such a system, common in Latin America, a president may win an election and then proceed to govern as if he were the sole source of authority in the country. The president exercises so much actual power over other political structures, thanks to his control of the police and military and his access to patronage, that he can negate the nominal separation of powers written into the constitution. In such a system, parliamentarians may use their positions not to represent constituents or craft legislation but to trade favors and enrich their friends and family. Judges may deem it safer to tailor their decisions to the wishes of powerful state officials. The editors of major newspapers bury stories unfavorable to the authorities. Interest groups curry favor with officials rather than mobilizing their supporters around particular policy positions. The leaders of opposition parties learn to accept their role on the sidelines.

Under Putin this pattern of "hollowed-out democracy" has become evident: without explicitly violating any constitutional limits on his power, and without abolishing elections or other democratic institutions, Putin has effectively negated the constitutional limits on his power built into the constitution. Using the president's extensive powers over the executive branch, he has neutralized and marginalized most independent sources of political authority, meantime observing formal constitutional procedures. But having used his control over electoral processes to secure overwhelming majority support in both chambers, parliamentary approval of his proposed agenda is assured. As observers have pointed out, Putin appears to dislike the open give-and-take of democratic politics, preferring more familiar methods of behind-the-scenes bureaucratic manoevering.[31]

Putin's use of presidential power presents a sharp contrast to the Yeltsin period. Yeltsin used his presidential authority erratically and impulsively, but respected certain limits on his power: he did not suppress media criticism, and he tolerated political opposition. Faced with an opposition-led parliament, Yeltsin was willing to compromise with his opponents to enact legislation. However, Yeltsin grew dependent on a coterie of powerful financial-media-industrial tycoons (the so-called oligarchs) for support, allowing them to acquire substantial influence over policy. Likewise, Yeltsin allowed regional bosses to flout federal authority with impunity because he found it much less costly to accommodate them than to fight them.

The loss of state capacity under Yeltsin illustrates one danger of an overcentralized political system: when the president does not effectively command the powers of the office, power drifts to other centers of power. Putin's presidency illustrates the opposite danger. When Putin took over, he was faced with the task of reversing the breakdown of political control and responsibility that had accelerated under Yeltsin. Although he has repeatedly called for a system based on respect for the rule of law, he has also steadily restored authoritarian rule. Many call his model of rule "managed democracy," that is, a system in which the formal trappings of democracy are preserved, but all political processes are thoroughly controlled by the president.[32] Putin's chief political ideologist, Vladislav Surkov, prefers a different term for Putin's regime: "sovereign democracy." He has described this concept in a number of speeches as a model in which Russia develops its own distinctive national form of democracy, one that reconciles the twin values of individual rights and state sovereignty. He envisions a vigorous role for the state in building up the social prerequisites for Russia to be a great power into the foreseeable future.[33] Russia must benefit from participation in the global economy, he argues, but it must not adopt foreign models for its political system. It is telling that while Putin and his team do not reject democracy as an ideal, they have redefined it in such a way as to rule out any limitations on presidential power.

THE FEDERAL DIMENSION

Many Russians feared that the breakup of the Soviet Union would lead to the breakup of the Russian Federation, and many still harbor this fear.[34] Yet apart from the two wars fought in Chechnia since 1991, Russia's path of development during the transition period has not culminated in the state's dissolution along national-territorial lines like those that ended the Soviet Union's existence. As was true of the USSR under Gorbachev, Yeltsin's government confronted the twin crises of relations between the central government and the constituent members of the federation, and of carrying out deep economic reform in the face of powerful opposition. The breakdown of the Soviet order eroded both the central government's power to enforce its power in the regions and limited the inducements it could offer regional governments to comply with federal law. Because both Gorbachev and Yeltsin had made liberal offers of autonomy to the subnational governments of Russia as part of their rivalry in 1990–1991, Russia found it particularly difficult to reestablish the primacy of its own central authority. Through the Yeltsin period, subnational governments fought with the Russian federal authorities over their respective spheres of power. This was particularly true for several of the ethnic-national territories that enjoy a privileged constitutional status in Russia. In several cases, the federal government even conceded to ethnic republics the right not to forward taxes collected in the republic to the central government. Under Putin, however, there has been a strong reassertion of the center's power over the regions.[35]

By far the most intractable case is that of the Chechen Republic (Chechnia), whose leaders declared independence in 1991 and where the federal government intervened with massive force in 1994 and again in 1999 (see Close-Up 3.1: Chechnia and the Terrorist Threat). Nevertheless, Chechnia has proved to be the sole case in which the federal government had to resort to force to preserve the unity of the state. Unlike the union government, the Russian state preserved itself despite centrifugal pressures from the regions. Several factors distinguishing Russia's situation from that of the USSR help to explain the different outcomes.

One is the demographic factor. The Soviet population was more ethnically fragmented that was that of the Russian Republic. Whereas half of the Soviet population was ethnically Russian, and the other half consisted of a diverse array of

Close-Up 3.1   Chechnia and the Terrorist Threat

Chechnia, or the Chechen Republic, is located in the mountainous region of the North Caucasus, between the Black and Caspian Seas, amid a belt of ethnic republics that includes several other predominantly Muslim republics. (Note that Dagestan is a kind of "dormitory" republic providing a common homeland to several small mountain peoples.) (See map of Southern Russia and the Caucasus in frontmatter.) The Chechen people were subjugated by the Russian imperial army in the nineteenth century but continued to resist Russian, and later Soviet, rule. In 1944, the entire Chechen people were deported by Stalin to Kazakhstan on suspicion that the entire nation was disloyal and would collaborate with the Germans. The Chechens were allowed to return to their homeland after the war, after suffering terrible hardships, but harbored deep grievances against Moscow. In 1991, with the USSR breaking up, the leader of the republic declared independence from Russia. Yeltsin rejected the declaration as invalid but did not initially attempt to coerce the republic into rescinding it. However, in December 1994, following unsuccessful efforts to restore federal authority in Chechnia through back-channel negotiations and covert armed intervention, Russia launched a large-scale military assault, employing heavy and often indiscriminate force. Fighting between Russian federal troops and the forces fighting for Chechen independence continued for nearly two years, punctuated by mass hostage-taking raids by Chechens on Russia soil and unsuccessful cease-fire declarations. Tens of thousands of civilians fled their homes. Finally, in October 1996, when both sides had had enough, the Chechen authorities and the federal government signed a treaty permitting the withdrawal of federal troops and granting Chechnia wide de facto autonomy.*

   The agreement only led to a pause in the fighting, however. The government in Chechnia was unwilling or unable to impose basic civil and political order. Quasi-independent paramilitary forces continued to operate with impunity from Chechen soil. Kidnappings for ransom and drug trafficking flourished. In the summer of 1999, armed guerrilla forces (said to have been supported by radical international Islamist groups) crossed the

---

* On the Chechen war, see John B. Dunlop, *Russia Confronts Chechnya: Roots of a Separatist Conflict* (Cambridge: Cambridge University Press, 1998); Carlotta Gall and Thomas de Waal, *Chechnya: Calamity in the Caucasus* (New York: New York University Press, 1998); Anatol Lieven, *Chechnya: Tombstone of Russian Power* (New Haven, CT: Yale University Press, 1998); and Matthew Evangelista, *The Chechen Wars: Will Russia Go the Way of the Soviet Union?* (Washington, DC: Brookings Institution, 2002). For a thoughtful Russian perspective, see Dmitri V. Trenin and Aleksei V. Malashenko with Anatol Lieven, *Russia's Restless Frontier: The Chechnya Factor in Post-Soviet Russia* (Washington, DC: Carnegie Endowment for International Peace, 2004).

border from Chechnia into the neighboring republic of Dagestan and attempted to seize power in several villages, the beginning of what they called a crusade to liberate the entire North Caucasus region. Federal forces pushed them back into Chechnia. Soon afterward, bombs exploded in apartment buildings in several Russian cities. The federal authorities immediately claimed that Chechen terrorists were responsible and began a new ground operation in Chechnia intended to destroy all the rebel units. However, neither the massive aerial bombardment of cities and suspected rebel bases nor the massive federal intervention succeeded in wiping out all of the resistance, and hostilities continued with hit-and-run raids and suicide car bomb attacks on federal troops. Federal forces used brutal tactics to pacify the population, including massive roundups of civilians accompanied by interrogations and torture to identify supporters of the rebels. The harshness of federal military tactics aroused worldwide condemnation. Although the federal government appropriated funds for rebuilding the republic, nearly all the funds were pilfered. Chechens continued to live in misery, many in squalid refugee camps outside the republic. Russian news coverage of the Chechen war was subject to drastic censorship, so that most Russians received a distorted picture of the war.

At the same time, international sympathy for the Chechen cause was weakened by the rebels' use of terrorism to achieve their goals. Chechen terrorists have conducted a number of highly visible operations. For example, they seized a maternity hospital in the town of Budennovsk in June 1995, taking about 1,000 people hostage; in January 1996 they seized another hospital in the town of Kizlyar with at least 1,000 hostages; in September 1999 a series of bombings of apartment buildings in several Russian cities killed some 300 people and were believed to have been carried out by Chechen terrorists; in October 2002, a band of terrorists took over a theater in Moscow (all 41 of the terrorists and some 129 of their hostages were killed in the assault on the theater, which the special forces carried out after infiltrating a powerful sleeping agent into the theater); in July 2003, two female suicide bombers killed 15 people at a rock concert in Moscow; the next month, suicide bombers killed at least 50 at a military hospital; in December 2003, suicide bombers killed 46 people on a commuter train; in February 2004, a suicide bomb on the Moscow metro killed 39 people; in June 2004, an attack on a police headquarters in the capital of Ingushetia, which neighbors Chechnia, killed at least 92 people; in May 2004, the pro-Moscow president of Chechnia was assassinated by a bomb planted in the sports stadium of Groznyi, capital of Chechnia; in August 2004, two passenger airplanes taking off from a Moscow airport were brought down by explosions detonated by female suicide bombers; and in August 2004, another suicide bomber set off an explosion outside a major market in Moscow, killing ten people.

(Continued)

Probably the most shocking attack of all was the seizure of a school in the North Osetian town of Beslan by a group of terrorists on September 1, 2004. As the map on page xvi indicates, North Ossetia is an ethnic republic located between Ingushetia and Kabardino-Balkaria in the North Caucasus. September 1 is a date of particular significance because it is the first day of school each year throughout Russia. Children, accompanied by their parents, often come to school bringing flowers to their teachers. A group of around 32 heavily armed militants organized by the Chechen warlord Shamil Basaev chose September 1 to storm a school and take hostage the parents, teachers, and children who were there. The terrorists crowded the captives into the school gymnasium, which they proceeded to fill with explosives to prevent any attempt at a rescue attempt. Attempts at negotiations over the release of the hostages failed; the terrorists even refused to allow water and food to be brought into the school. Reports on the terrorists' demands varied. Some suggested that the terrorists were demanding the release of some of their comrades who had been captured earlier that summer; other reports said that the terrorists called for the withdrawal of federal troops from Chechnia.

On the third day of the seige, something triggered the detonation of one of the bombs inside the school. In the chaos that followed, many of the children and adults rushed to escape. The terrorists fired at them. Federal forces stormed the school, trying to rescue the escaping hostages and to kill the terrorists. Many of the bombs planted by the terrorists exploded. Ultimately around 350 of the hostages died, along with nearly all the terrorists and an unknown number of security troops.

The media covered the events closely. The Beslan tragedy had an impact on Russian national consciousness comparable to that of September 11 in the United States because, although there had been a number of previous attacks tied to Chechen terrorists, none had cost so many innocent lives. Although many Russians blamed corruption and poor organization among the police for allowing the terrorists to take over the school in the first place and for failing to prevent the destruction at the end, they also recognized that the terrorists had made it impossible for the security forces to attempt a rescue for fear of provoking a massacre of the children inside.

President Putin and other senior government officials claimed that the terrorists who had carried out the Beslan massacre and other recent episodes were part of an international terrorist movement aimed ultimately at the dismemberment of Russia itself. Putin studiously avoided linking the incident to Russian policy in Chechnia. In response to the crisis, Putin called for a series of measures to reinforce national security, particularly in the North Caucasus, and to improve the effectiveness of federal police, security, and military agencies. By the same token, however, Putin has placed his own political reputation on the line by tying his strategy of centralizing power to the goal of strengthening state security.

smaller national groups, Russia's population is 80 percent Russian. Its ethnic minorities thus form a very small proportion of the total. The Soviet population, moreover, was never an ethnic nationality, whereas Russia's national culture provided a historic identity that encouraged (and sometimes required) other national groups to assimilate to it. Finally, the national republics of the Soviet Union were all located on the perimeter of the country, and thus bordered other countries. The national territories of Russia are mainly internal to the Russian Republic, and therefore have had less direct interaction with the outside world.[36]

A second factor has to do with Russia's internal administrative structure. In Russia, only around 17 percent of the population lives in territories designated as ethnic homelands.[37] In the Soviet state, by contrast, all territory was included in one or another of the ethnic-national republics. The republic of Russia took up three-quarters of Soviet territory and half its population. In the Soviet state, most national groups giving their names to the republics had lived in the territory of their republics for centuries, and had some reason to consider them "national homelands." In most cases, these peoples had a national history and had been subjugated by the Soviet Russian state. Like the USSR, the Russian Republic was also formally considered a federation and had internal ethnic-national subdivisions. But in contrast to the larger union, only some of its constituent members are ethnic-national territories. Most are pure administrative subdivisions, populated mainly by Russians. In the past, Russia's internal ethnic-national territories were classified by size and status into autonomous republics, autonomous provinces, and national districts; today all the former autonomous republics are simply termed republics. In many, the indigenous ethnic group comprises a minority of the population. Since 1991, the names and status of some constituent units in Russia have changed, sometimes in order to restore an older, pre-Soviet name, and in other cases as a result of a change in their legal status in the federation.

As of 2007, Russia comprises 85 constituent territorial units; in Russian constitutional terminology, these are called the "subjects of the federation." Of these, 21 are republics, 8 are "krai's" (territories), 6 are autonomous districts (all but one of them located within other units), 1 is an autonomous oblast, 2 are cities, and 47 are oblasts. (See Map 1.) Republics, autonomous okrugs (districts), and the one autonomous oblast are units created specifically to give some political recognition to populations living in territories with significant ethnic minorities. Autonomous okrugs are located within larger territorial entities, although they are treated as constituent members of the federation. Along with republics, the single autonomous oblast, oblasts, krais, and the two great cities of Moscow and St. Petersburg. Republics, on the other hand, have inherited certain special rights. They may adopt their own constitution so long as it does not contradict the federal constitution. They may maintain state symbols, such as a flag. In contrast, oblasts and krais are simply administrative subdivisions with no special constitutional status. Not surprisingly, therefore, between the oblasts and krais, on the one hand, and the republics on the other, there is constant rivalry. Leaders of oblasts and krais complain of the special privileges that republics are given that enable them to circumvent federal law but receive benefits such as federal subsidies.

Republics, in turn, jealously guard their special status. Over 1990–1992, all the republics adopted declarations of sovereignty and two made attempts to declare full or partial independence of Russia: Chechnia and Tatarstan. Tatarstan, situated on the Volga, is an oil-rich and heavily industrialized region. Eventually Russia and Tatarstan worked out a special treaty arrangement satisfactory to both sides, and the separatist movement in Tatarstan gradually subsided. This treaty then served as a precedent for subsequent bilateral agreements signed by the federal executive branch with the executives of 45 other subjects over the period from 1994 to 1998. These treaties delineated the rights and obligations of the federal and regional government, and in some cases granted special privileges and exemptions to the region, for example, an exemption from certain taxes, or permission to retain a higher share of earnings from the exploitation of regional resources, or even relief from having to contribute soldiers to the army.

One centralizing measure Putin has pursued is the absorption of smaller ethnic districts into larger neighboring units. Four such mergers have already been implemented since 2005, reducing the total number of federal subjects from 89 to the current 85.* More still are in the planning stages. Most observers believe that the Putin administration seeks to eliminate most or all of the smaller ethnic units by absorbing them into their surrounding regions, thus reducing the patronage rights and political voice that come with their status as constituent members of the federation.

Under the old regime, federalism was largely nominal; it served symbolic purposes but did not provide any actual autonomy on the part of the constituent regions of the country. In recent years, Russia's constitutional order has evolved toward a more meaningful form of federalism, in which constituent units of the federation possess a defined sphere of autonomy. Even so, the 1993 constitution failed to specify a particular set of rights and powers where the subjects of the federation possessed exclusive jurisdiction. Instead, after defining those powers where the federal level has exclusive jurisdiction (such as providing for the national defense and a money system), the constitution defines a set of rights in which the federal and regional governments *share* responsibility, among them regulation of the use of natural resources. The constitution thus leaves it to laws and agreements to work out how they are to share power. Still, the new constitution went some way to make federalism real by ensuring that each of the federal subjects had an equal number of representatives in the Federation Council. The Federation Council has strongly defended the prerogatives of the regions, which has helped to mitigate some of the problem's intensity. With time, some of the nationalist passions that helped to drive the movements for separatism in the republics have subsided as populations have concluded that their economies are not likely to benefit from independence.

---

* The Taimyr and Evenki autonomous districts were absorbed into Krasnoyarsk krai; the Koryak autonomous district was absorbed into Kamchatka oblast; and the Komi-Permyak autonomous district was merged with Perm' oblast to form Perm' krai.

The relations between the central government and the governments of regions and republics continue to evolve. Putin made it clear that the reform of federal relations was a top priority for him. Among his first steps as president were several measures intended to impose greater uniformity in the relations of regions with the central government and to ensure that regional governments adhered to federal law. In this he had to reverse Yeltsin's strategy of appeasing regional leaders with grants of power and bilateral treaties as a way of obtaining their support for his battles with his Communist opposition. For example, there was an especially intense phase of treaty making when President Yeltsin was out on the hustings during his 1996 presidential election campaign. Typically, as part of a visit to a region, he would ceremoniously sign a treaty on power-sharing with the governor or head of state, clearly using the occasion of a treaty between the federal government and a region as a means of appealing to the regional authorities for their electoral support.[38] After the election the pace of treaty making slowed down considerably.

Putin made clear his intention to reassert the authority of the federal government. His proposed law reforming the makeup of the Federation Council was one step toward this end: by stripping the regional governors[39] and parliamentary speakers of their seats in the upper house, he was explicitly demoting them in political status. Another law that Putin pushed through parliament gave him the ability to remove a sitting governor if a court found that the governor had refused to bring his actions into line with the federal constitution and law. Needless to say, the governors strongly opposed these changes. But the Duma overrode the upper house's veto and, with some modifications, the law was passed and signed by the president.

One of the most dramatic actions taken by Putin to recentralize control over the regions was his decree on May 13, 2000, creating seven new "federal districts," each with a special presidential representative whose task was to monitor the laws and actions of the governments of a set of regions. The purpose of the new districts was to strengthen central control over the activity of federal bodies in the regions; often, in the past, local branches of federal agencies had fallen under the de facto influence of powerful governors. The new structure was intended to ensure that federal revenues were not diverted into local coffers, and to supervise and coordinate federal law enforcement bodies that had sometimes developed cozy relations with local interests. That the new presidential representatives were to rely more on military-style than political methods was underscored by the fact that five of the seven individuals whom Putin appointed had made their careers in the army, the security police, or the Interior Ministry. Critics of Putin's reform complained that it was a step in the direction of creating a hypercentralized, authoritarian system of rule. Defenders argued that many regions had effectively become dictatorial fiefdoms and that decisive steps were needed to bring them back under central control. In practice, presidential representatives' impact has been modest. They have succeeded in bringing many regional laws into conformity with federal law, and have increased federal supervision of regional government.

On the other hand, they have not made the performance of regional government appreciably more efficient or transparent, and they have frequently clashed with the federal ministries whose branch offices they try to coordinate.

At present, executive power in Russia's regions is a good deal more powerful than the legislative bodies.[40] Regional assemblies are generally very weak and in most cases are dominated by regional chief executives. For the most part, deputies work in regional assemblies on a part-time basis; only a few are full-time employees of the assembly. Often, in fact, officials of the executive branch form the largest body of representatives to the local assemblies. There is little separation of powers at the regional and local level, and few checks on the power of governors from regional legislatures, interest groups, or mass media. In most regions, governors dominate their regional legislatures and control most of the regional media. In most regions, the only constraints on governors' powers are the presidential representatives to the federal districts, who coordinate the work of the federal agencies in their areas, and major business firms that control substantial shares of the region's employment and revenues. In some regions, the governors and the mayors of the capital cities are rivals for power, but usually the governors have a stronger position because of their control over most taxes.[41]

Until new legislation in 2004, regional chief executives were elected in direct popular elections in their regions. Following the Beslan terrorist incident, however, Putin enacted legislation eliminating direct elections for governors. Under the new system, the president nominates a candidate for governor to the regional legislature, which then approves the nomination (no legislature has dared to oppose one of Putin's appointments). Many Russians supported this change, believing that the institution of local elections had been discredited by corruption and fraud and that elections were more often determined by the influence of wealthy insiders than by public opinion. The presidential administration had routinely intervened in gubernatorial contests to help bring about a favorable outcome for its preferred candidate. Voters had little real choice over alternative policy programs: party leanings or affiliations had little to do with how governors acted.[42] More important than party leanings were the connections between particular governors or challengers and powerful industrial and financial interests. For this reason, Putin hopes that appointed governors will be more accountable to the Kremlin than were the elected ones, but past experience suggests that centralizing power by itself is unlikely to improve governance in the regions in the absence of other mechanisms for monitoring government performance and enforcing the law.

The 21 ethnic republics have the constitutional authority to determine their own form of state power so long as their decisions do not contradict federal law. All 21 have established presidencies.[43] In many cases, the republic presidents have constructed personal power bases around appeals to ethnic solidarity and demands to preserve the cultural autonomy of the indigenous nationality. Often they have used this power to resist the expansion of political and economic rights. In the 1990s, the central government's power to enforce federal law in the republics tended to be weaker than in ordinary regions, and hence relied more on a combination of fiscal sticks and carrots. Putin has moved cautiously in his drive to reduce the autonomy of the ethnic republics, allowing a number of the long-serving presidents to remain in power while gradually whittling away at their prerogatives. They, in turn, have generally supported Putin's policies in public but sometimes have quietly encouraged local ethnic-nationalist movements.[44]

Relations between the federal government and the governments of regions and republics reveal a considerable degree of conflict. In the 1990s many regions passed laws that violate the Russian constitution. For instance, several republics declared that they had sovereign control—in effect, ownership—over the natural resources located within their borders. Putin has reined in these separatist tendencies, however, using political and legal methods. The federal procuracy has demanded that regional governments revise thousands of laws that it believes violate federal legislation. The Constitutional Court has heard several cases involving republics' claims of sovereignty. In June 2000, the court took advantage of Putin's tough stance against regional separatism to strike down the claims to sovereignty that were asserted in the constitutions of several ethnic republics. Now no region may claim that it has "sovereignty" in any area of law, even areas that are not under federal jurisdiction.

Below the tier of regional government are units that are supposed to enjoy the right of self-government—municipalities and other local government units. Under recent legislation, the right of local self-government has been expanded to a much larger set of units, such as urban and rural districts and small settlements. This has raised the total number of locally self-governing units to 24,000. In principle, local self-government is supposed to permit substantial policy-making autonomy in the spheres of housing, utilities, and social services (and to reduce the federal government's burden in providing such services). However, the new legislation, which is being phased in gradually, provides no fixed independent sources of revenue for these local entities. They thus depend on the regional governments for most of their revenues, although they have growing responsibility for the delivery of education, health, and social services to the population. For their part, regional governments resist allowing local governments to exercise any significant powers of their own. In many cases, the mayors of the capital cities of regions are political rivals of the governors of the regions. Moscow and St. Petersburg are exceptional cases because they have the status of federal territorial subjects like republics and regions. The mayor of Moscow, Yuri Luzhkov, in fact wields a great deal of political power at the level of the federal government. Other cities lack the power and autonomy of Moscow and St. Petersburg, and must bargain with their superior regional governments for shares of power.[45]

The fears that Russia would split apart much as the Soviet Union did proved to be exaggerated despite the tragic case of Chechnia. Although Russia also underwent a wave of ethnic national mobilization within its national republics, separatism never brought Russia itself to the brink of dissolution. The different demographic makeup of Russia, and Moscow's willingness to negotiate special arrangements with some national republics, have preserved Russia's integrity. On the other hand, despite President Putin's concerted effort to reverse the decentralization of power that occurred in the 1990s, the central government's power over regional governments remains limited. In many areas, regional authorities wield arbitrary power much as they did before Communism fell. Successful federalism requires a balancing of the demands by regional units for greater autonomy of the center and the federal government's power to enforce common legal standards throughout the country. In Russia, as in other federations, the pendulum has swung between periods of decentralization and centralization. Russia remains deficient, however, in the supply of mediating organizations, such as parties and interest groups, that help to integrate the diverse territorial units and diffuse conflict to other arenas.[46]

NOTES

1. Celestine Bohlen, "Yeltsin Deputy Calls Reforms 'Economic Genocide,'" *New York Times,* February 9, 1992.

2. See Table 6.3 in Chapter 6.

3. To receive any seats, however, a party or electoral association had to have been legally registered and to have won at least 5 percent of the party list votes. For the 225 proportional representation seats, the entire Russian federation was considered a single district. Votes for each party's list were added, and the sum was divided by the total number of votes cast to determine the share of PR seats that each party would receive. Certain parties further divided their lists into regional sublists to determine which of their candidates would win parliamentary mandates.

4. On the new parliament and the manner of its formation, see Thomas F. Remington, *The Russian Parliament: Institutional Evolution in a Transitional Regime, 1989–1999* (New Haven, CT: Yale University Press, 2001).

5. Serious charges of fraud in the vote counting were made by a team of Russian analysts. Combining individual reports of irregularities from a number of regions with statistical modeling techniques, they estimate that actual turnout may have been as low as 46 percent and that, as a result, the constitution did not pass. They also claimed that the election results for parliamentary candidates were extensively falsified as well. Although these accusations created a stir, all sections of the political elite tacitly agreed not to challenge the validity of the referendum or the elections.

6. Matthew S. Shugart and John M. Carey, *Presidents and Assemblies: Constitutional Design and Electoral Dynamics* (New York: Cambridge University Press, 1992), ch. 2, "Defining Regimes with Elected Presidents," pp. 18–27. An alternative type of system is "premier-presidential" in which the president lacks the power to appoint and dismiss cabinet ministers unilaterally.

7. The restriction on dissolving the Duma within one year of its election applies to the no-confidence procedure but not to the requirement of parliament confirmation of the president's nominee for prime minister. Thus whereas the president may not dissolve the Duma twice within one year of its last election when (1) it votes no confidence in the government twice within three months or (2) defeats a motion of confidence in the government, he is not so limited if the Duma rejects the candidates he nominates for prime minister three times in a row.

8. The French Constitution, Article 8, says that "On the proposal of the Prime Minister, he [the president] shall appoint and dismiss the other members of the Government."

9. Vladimir Gel'man, "The Unrule of Law in the Making: The Politics of Informal Institution Building in Russia," *Europe-Asia Studies* 56:7 (2004): 1021–40.

10. Ilia Bulavinov and Elena Tregubova, "Druz'ia, prekrasen nash Sovbez!" *Kommersant Vlast',* 13 June 2000, 14–17.

11. Article 83 of the Constitution provides that the president forms and heads the Security Council but stipulates that its

powers and duties are to be prescribed by law. To date, however, no such law has been passed.

12. Eugene Huskey called attention to this pattern in the 1990s, when Yeltsin was president. The restoration of Soviet methods of rule has gone considerably further under Putin. See Eugene Huskey, *Presidential Power in Russia* (Armonk, NY: M. E. Sharpe, 1999), p. 59.

13. The size of the Russian state bureaucracy is now estimated at around one million employees, which represents a doubling since the end of the Soviet era (Polit.ru, November 21, 2002). Only about a third of these work at the federal level, however. The rest are employed at the regional or local level. By the standards of Western capitalist democracies, the size of the Russian public administration is relatively small. See William Tompson, "The Political Implications of Russia's Resource-Based Economy," *Post-Soviet Affairs* 21:4 (2005): 335–59.

14. Steven M. Fish, *Democracy Derailed in Russia: The Failure of Open Politics* (Cambridge: Cambridge University Press, 2005). In his review of the powers of presidents in 24 postcommunist countries, Timothy Frye observes that Russia's president has the largest number of formal and residual powers of all of them. Timothy Frye, "A Politics of Institutional Choice: Post-Communist Presidencies," *Comparative Political Studies,* 30:5 (October 1997): 523–52. By formal powers he means powers exercised under a grant of authority where the exercise of power is specified by law or constitution. By residual powers he means the right to exercise power under circumstances that the law does not specify.

15. Timothy J. Colton and Cindy Skach, "The Russian Predicament," *Journal of Democracy* 16:3 (July 2005): 119.

16. Stephen White, "Russia: Presidential Leadership under Yeltsin," in Ray Taras, ed., *Postcommunist Presidents* (Cambridge: Cambridge University Press, 1997), pp. 57–61.

17. Matthew Soberg Shugart, "The Inverse Relationship Between Party Strength and Executive Strength: A Theory of Politicians' Constitutional Choices," *British Journal of Political Science* 28 (1998): 1–29.

18. President Yeltsin appointed Victor Chernomyrdin, an experienced state official who had run Russia's natural gas monopoly, as prime minister in December 1992. However, as economic difficulties mounted, Yeltsin suddenly dismissed Chernomyrdin in March 1998 and appointed a young reformer named Sergei Kirienko to take his place. Under heavy pressure from Yeltsin, the Duma confirmed the nomination on the third vote. Kirienko's government proved unable to prevent a financial collapse in August 1998. Yeltsin then dismissed Kirienko and tried to bring back Chernomyrdin again as prime minister. This time the Duma, incensed at the president's actions, balked. Twice the president submitted Chernomyrdin's candidacy, and twice the Duma rejected it. Another constitutional crisis loomed. But this time Yeltsin yielded. Instead of nominating Chernomyrdin a third time, he proposed Foreign Minister Evgenii Primakov to head the government. Primakov, a pragmatist with long diplomatic and foreign intelligence service experience, enjoyed good relations with both the pro-government and the opposition factions in the Duma. He was quickly confirmed, and the political crisis was, for the moment, resolved.

Primakov did not remain in his post long, however. Yeltsin grew suspicious that Primakov was gaining in strength and popularity and dismissed him in May 1999, after only eight months in office. Yeltsin named Sergei Stepashin, who had formerly been head of the FSB and later been Interior Minister, to replace him. The Duma confirmed the appointment on the first ballot by a wide margin.

However, Stepashin's tenure was even shorter than Primakov's. In August 1999, Yeltsin once again abruptly dismissed the government, and named Vladimir Putin as his candidate to head the new government (see Close-Up 1.1: Who Is Mister Putin?). The Duma narrowly voted to confirm Putin and Putin quickly established himself both in public opinion and in Yeltsin's estimation as a competent and trusted head of government. After the success of the political forces close to Putin in the December 1999 parliamentary elections, Yeltsin decided to resign from the presidency in order to make Putin the acting president and thus give Putin the advantages of incumbency in running for president in his own right. Putin handily won the election in March 2000 and named Mikhail Kas'ianov as his prime minister. Shortly before the 2004 presidential election, Putin dismissed Kas'ianov and the rest of the government, naming Mikhail Fradkov as his new prime minister. Fradkov, a figure with little independent political stature, has held the office since then.

19. The same game applies in the United States as well, of course. President Kennedy once commented of a particular foreign policy initiative that if it failed, it would be another State Department failure, whereas if it worked, it would be another White House success.

20. World Bank, *Russian Economic Report,* June 2004, no. 8. From Web site: www.worldbank.org.ru.

21. Konstantin Smirnov, "Vse pravitel'-stvo: ekonomicheskii blok," *Vlast',* June 28, 2004, 63–78.

22. The electoral legislation was changed to provide that, as of the 2007 elections, a party must receive at least 7 percent of the vote to be entitled to parliamentary seats.

23. Until the rules changes of 2004, the Duma allowed any group that had 35 members to form a registered group. In the previous Dumas, there were always a few groups that gathered at least 35 members and registered in order to obtain the benefits of faction status. By raising the threshold, the president's allies ensured that it would be next to impossible for any opposition groups to form.

24. In 2004, United Russia claimed the chairmanships of all the committees. In previous Dumas, committee chairmanships were distributed to factions and groups in rough proportion to the number of seats they held.

25. The Procurator General oversees the Procuracy, a branch of the legal system somewhat similar to government prosecutors in the American system, but with far broader powers. For more details, see Chapter 8.

26. Thomas F. Remington, "Majorities without Mandates: The Federation Council since 2000," *Europe-Asia Studies* 55:5 (July 2003): 667–91.

27. The stipulation that the two members from each region had to represent the executive and legislative branches—which creates a good deal of confusion and rigidity—was added at the last minute by President Yeltsin and sent out for publication before his aides could stop him.

28. Edward Morgan-Jones and Petra Schleiter, "Governmental Change in a President-Parliamentary Regime: The Case of Russia 1994–2003," *Post-Soviet Affairs* 20:2 (April–June 2004): 132–63.

29. Herbert J. Ellison, *Boris Yeltsin and Russia's Democratic Transformation* (Seattle: University of Washington Press, 2006).

30. Guillermo O'Donnell, "Delegative Democracy," *Journal of Democracy* 5:1 (1994): 55–69.

31. For an alternative interpretation of Putin and his policies, see Richard Sakwa, *Putin: Russia's Choice* (London: Rutledge, 2004).

32. Harley Balzer has argued that the term "managed pluralism" better describes Putin's regime. Putin, he believes, is willing to tolerate a range of political and social interests so long as they do not directly oppose him. Rather than imposing a single ideological doctrine on society or closing off the economy to the outside world, he wants to establish a cooperative relation between state and economic, civic, religious, and other social associations. As Putin sees it, their role is to assist the state in managing society rather than to support a political opposition. See Harley Balzer, "Managed Pluralism: Vladimir Putin's Emerging Regime," *Post-Soviet Affairs* 19:3 (2003): 189–227.

33. For example, see Vladislav Surkov, "Natsionalizatsiia budushchego [Nationalization of the Future]," *Ekspert* no. 43 (20), November 2006, on Web site <ekspert.ru>.

34. See Daniel S. Treisman, *After the Deluge: Regional Crises and Political Consolidation in Russia* (Ann Arbor: University of Michigan Press, 1999) argues that Yeltsin used a deliberate strategy combining carrots and sticks in preventing the dissolution of the Russian Federation, averting the fate that befell the Soviet Union, Yugoslavia, and Czechoslovakia, which collapsed as states when their Communist regimes fell.

35. There are a number of studies of regional government and relations between the central government and the regions,

including Kathryn Stoner-Weiss, *Local Heroes: The Political Economy of Russian Regional Governance* (Princeton, NJ: Princeton University Press, 1997); Cameron Ross, *Federalism and Democratisation in Russia* (Manchester and New York: Manchester University Press, 2002); Peter Kirkow, *Russia's Provinces: Authoritarian Transformation versus Local Autonomy?* (New York: St. Martin's Press, 1998); Blair A. Ruble, Jodi Koehn, and Nancy E. Popson, eds., *Fragmented Space in the Russian Federation* (Washington, DC: Woodrow Wilson Center Press, 2001); Jeffrey W. Hahn, ed., *Regional Russia in Transition: Studies from Yaroslavl* (Washington, DC: Woodrow Wilson Center Press, 2001); and Robert W. Orttung, *From Leningrad to St. Petersburg: Democratization in a Russian City* (New York: St. Martin's Press, 1995).

36. Ian Bremmer and Ray Taras, eds., *New States, New Politics: Building the Post-Soviet Nations* (Cambridge: Cambridge University Press, 1997).

37. Note that some of these territorial units are huge in physical terms: Sakha (formerly Yakutia) alone constitutes 17 percent of the territory of Russia. Altogether, a little over half of Russian territory is located in ethnic republics and regions.

38. OMRI Russian Regional Report, vol. 2, no. 9, March 6, 1997.

39. All the chief executives of the subjects of the federation are commonly referred to as governors, whether they are the head of a regular oblast or krai, or the president of one of the ethnic republics. All are conventionally referred to as "the governors."

40. Ross, *Federalism and Democratisation;* Vladimir Gel'man, Sergei Ryzhenkov, and Michael Brie, eds., *Making and Breaking Democratic Transitions: The Comparative Politics of Russia's Regions* (Lanham, MD: Rowman & Littlefield, 2003); and Mary McAuley, *Russia's Politics of Uncertainty* (Cambridge: Cambridge University Press, 1997).

41. Darrell Slider, "Governors versus Mayors: The Regional Dimension of Russian Local Government," in Evans and Gel'man, eds., *Politics of Local Government,* pp. 145–68.

42. Kathryn Stoner-Weiss, "The Limited Reach of Russia's Party System: Underinstitutionalization of Dual Transitions," *Politics and Society* 29:3 (September 2001): 385–414; Debra Javeline, "Does It Matter Who Governs? The Effects of Partisanship on Leadership Behavior in Russia's Regions," paper presented to 1998 Annual Meeting of the American Political Science Association, Boston, MA, 3–6 September 1998.

43. In Mordovia, this office is formally called "head of the republic."

44. Emil Pain, "Reforms in the Administration of the Regions and Their Influence on Ethnopolitical Processes in Russia, 1999–2003," *Dynamics of Russian Politics: Putin's Reform of Federal-Regional Relations, vol. I,* eds. Peter Reddaway and Robert W. Orttung (Lanham, MD: Rowman & Littlefield, 2005), p. 349.

45. Alfred B. Evans, Jr., and Vladimir Gel'man, eds., *The Politics of Local Government in Russia* (Lanham, MD: Rowman & Littlefield, 2004).

46. Mikhail Filippov, Peter C. Ordeshook, and Olga Shvetsova, *Designing Federalism: A Theory of Self-Sustainable Federal Institutions* (Cambridge: Cambridge University Press, 2004), esp. pp. 301–15.

Political Participation and Recruitment

POLITICAL PARTICIPATION AND SOCIAL CAPITAL

In Communist systems, leaders make strenuous efforts to involve citizens in mass ceremonies of civic participation, such as voting in noncompetitive elections and joining in youth groups, trade unions, and other associations. But such participation has a ritualistic quality and does not in fact aggregate demands from citizens or allow citizens to remove their leaders from power. In some authoritarian systems, regimes maintain democratic forms such as parties, elections, and legislatures to create the illusion that the rulers have been granted their power by the choice of the voters. In such systems (sometimes called "elective democracies" or "competitive authoritarian regimes"), elections do not actually confer power on the rulers or hold them accountable to the public.[1] Some authors see a tendency spreading throughout much of the modern world for apparently democratic forms of participation to expand without a similar expansion of constraints on government power or mechanisms for making government responsible to the will of its citizens.[2]

Public participation in a liberal democracy enables citizens to influence government policy and to hold government to account for its consequences. The forms of democratic participation include both directly political activity, such as voting, party work, organizing for a cause, demonstrating, lobbying and the like; and indirect forms, such as membership in civic groups and voluntary associations. Both kinds of participation influence the quality of government. Through their participation in civic groups people learn about public affairs, share and shape their views, and communicate their preferences. Collectively they influence policy. Moreover, through associations, activists rise to positions of leadership, sometimes entering politics. Of course, despite the legal equality of citizens in democracies, individuals' political engagement in any society varies with differences in resources, opportunities, and motivations. The better-off and better-educated tend to be disproportionately involved in public life everywhere, but in some societies the disparity is much greater than in others.[3]

Political scientists have shown that the pattern of political participation in a society is structured by two factors. One is the way resources such as time, money, and civic skills are distributed among citizens. The other is how the political system provides institutional channels for active involvement in politics.[4] In democratic societies, the tendency for policymakers to be more responsive to powerful, wealthy, and well-organized private interests than to weaker or more diffuse interests is offset, to some extent, by the ability of parties and elections to mobilize large masses of citizens into participating at the voting booth.

Parties and elections also offer channels to bring politically motivated individuals into politics, including individuals from outside the established circles of wealth and privilege.[5] Parties and other civic associations such as community organizations, trade unions, and religious groups give opportunities to individuals to gain civic skills, such as the ability to stand up in front of a group of people and persuade them to take action on an issue and to manage a collective undertaking. In the United States, churches and other religious institutions have been an especially important setting where individuals, regardless of their incomes or education, have been able to acquire civic skills.[6] So have large, national associations made up of numerous local branches, such as the Rotary Club, League of Women's Voters, and the Grange.[7] Politically relevant civic participation does not only mean involvement in directly political activities such as campaigning and voting. A growing body of scholarship confirms that the character of civic life more generally affects the quality of democracy.[8]

The Importance of Social Capital

A strong fabric of voluntary associations has been recognized since de Tocqueville's time as an important component of democracy. Recently, political scientist Robert D. Putnam has offered an influential theory explaining why this should be so. Fair, honest, responsive government, Putnam argues, is a public good.[9] Everyone is interested in obtaining its benefits but few are willing to invest much time and effort to provide it. In this dilemma, individuals are strongly tempted to let others bear the costs of informing themselves about issues, getting involved in politics, running for office, monitoring the actions of officeholders to make sure that they do not misuse their power, and so on. If everyone cooperated in getting involved, no one person would bear a disproportionate share of the costs of keeping government responsive. And no one would have a disproportionate amount of influence in government. As with other public goods, therefore, providing good government is a collective action problem: if everyone cooperates, everyone is better off—and yet each individual is better off individually by free riding on others' efforts.

The stock of cooperation in a community or a society varies, Putnam shows. In some societies, people are convinced that even if they themselves are willing to act in accordance with the public interest, others will look out for their own interest at the expense of others, for instance, by cheating on their taxes, avoiding civic responsibilities, and even bribing officials to get something done. As no one wants to play a sucker's game, everyone is tempted to cheat first. What can induce members of a community to be willing to trust one another enough to engage in collective activity for the common good? Putnam calls this quality of a society its "social capital." Social capital refers to the network of ties that keep people engaged in various kinds of cooperative endeavors. These do not need to be political. Putnam finds that one can predict the quality of government by counting how many people in the society belong to all sorts of voluntary associations—whether chuch choirs or birdwatching clubs or softball leagues or parent–teacher associations.[10] A key to the importance of social capital is that when there is a strong likelihood that people who have a relationship in a community also know some of the same people, they know that they have a reputation that depends on their behavior. The fact that each person's circle of acquaintance is part of a larger network of social ties reinforces the propensity for trust and cooperation in social relations.

Social capital therefore rests on a set of mutual understandings about the kinds of behavior that people can expect from one another, and is reinforced by an actual fabric of social relations in which people encounter one another frequently— and their friends and family encounter one another as well. The denser the accumulated social capital, the likelier it is that members of society will be able to cooperate for the collective good in the public realm. This applies equally to politics and economics. Remarkably, in societies in which social capital is thick, both the quality of government and the spread of economic opportunity are greater than in societies in which the absence of trust, cooperativeness, and social capital impede people's ability to hold government accountable and to take advantage of opportunities for economic development.[11]

A society with a low level of social capital and correspondingly poor quality of government can persist over long periods of time, as a result of the stability of mutually reinforcing expectations. In a society in which social capital is weak, people come to expect that nothing will change, at least for the better, and fall into what Richard Rose calls a "low-level equilibrium trap" as people adjust their *demand* for better conditions downward as they grow discouraged and frustrated with the quality of government. As a result, the *supply* of good government and economic development stays low:

> The lowering of popular demands to the actual behaviour of government can create a low-level equilibrium trap. Citizens can adopt what the French describe as *incivisme,* a preference for government leaving people alone and a refusal to cooperate to make it better. This can be stable, in so far as reform is off the political agenda and both the people and political elites tolerate a very imperfect democracy as a lesser evil by comparison with undemocratic alternatives.[12]

In such a case, people may prefer a "strong hand" in the form of a harsh, unresponsive central government to supply public order, as they cannot rely on society to provide it. They may be convinced that only an authoritarian state can prevent anarchy and that democratization will only make government vulnerable to the pressures of powerful and wealthy interests. Where there is low trust and low social capital, people are likelier to seek *private* favors through *vertical* relations with bosses and patrons rather than to work for good *public* policy through *horizontal* institutions of self-government.

The Problem of "Dual Russia"

Putnam developed his theory of the importance of social capital for effective democracy in the context of Italy, but it offers a powerful insight into many other societies, including Russia. In Russia, indeed, an enduring pattern of political life has been the social distance and political alienation between state and society: state authorities have rarely been integrated into the fabric of social relations, but rather have stood above society, extracting what resources they needed from society but not cultivating ties of reciprocity or obligation to it. In a famous essay, Robert C. Tucker characterized this problem as the "image of dual Russia." He quotes the Russian liberal statesman and historian, Pavel Miliukov, who wrote that, in Russia, the state had traditionally been:

> an outsider to whom allegiance was won only in the measure of [its] utility. The people were not willing to assimilate themselves to the state, to feel a part of it, responsible for the whole. The country continued to feel and to live independently of the state authorities.[13]

To a large extent, the gap between state and society still remains today, both in Russians' attitudes and behavior. Mass participation in voting is at a high level, but participation in other forms of political activity is very low. Public opinion polls show that most people believe that their involvement in political activity is futile, and few believe that government serves their interests.[14]

In the late 1980s, political participation in Russia saw a brief, intense surge followed by a protracted ebb. But tens of thousands of voluntary associations do exist, reflecting a wide range of interests and causes. Although participation in public life is low compared with European or North American societies, it is higher than in most periods of Russian history. Certainly there is more participation in voluntary associations today than there was in the Soviet period despite what appeared to be extremely high levels of mass participation in state-sponsored political organizations.

In the Soviet period, the authorities devoted tremendous efforts to urging people to take part in the regime-sponsored forms of mass participation. For instance, they placed huge emphasis on achieving extremely high turnout levels in the uncontested, single-candidate elections of deputies to the soviets. The façade of mass participation served the needs of Soviet propaganda, which promoted the idea that the state was the instrument of the people's collective will. But most mass participation in Soviet times was purely nominal. People joined mass organizations because it took an active effort *not* to be a member. Today, few Russians are members of civic organizations, partly out of an aversion to having been pressured into joining state-sponsored associations during the Soviet period, and partly out of disillusionment with how the democratization wave turned out.[15]

Yet even though Russians are skeptical about their ability to influence government through political participation, all the evidence suggests that Russians today *do* take elections seriously, highly value their new political freedoms including the freedom *not* to participate in public life, and are involved in a dense set of social networks with family and friends. But unfortunately for democracy's prospects, these networks are largely outside the sphere of state power; often, in fact, they reinforce antidemocratic patterns of behavior. The persistence of close networks of family and friendship seems to come at the expense of a wider web of civic life.[16]

Participation in voluntary associations in contemporary Russia is extremely low: according to 2005 survey data, 95 percent of the population do not belong to any sports or recreational club, literary or other cultural group, political party, local housing association, or charitable organization. Only 15 percent claimed to belong to a trade union and no more than 6 percent reported attending church services at least one time per month.[17] Attending religious services and trade union membership are very passive forms of participation in public life, which in Russia overall, is thus far lower than in the West.

Compare these figures with the United States: in the 1990s, even after several decades of steadily declining civic involvement, around 70 percent of Americans belonged to one or more voluntary associations and half consider themselves *active* members.[18] To be sure, the United States is still distinctive in the world for the high degree to which citizens actively take part in voluntary associations. But Russia stands out for the pronounced disengagement of its citizens.

This is not to say that Russian citizens are *psychologically* disengaged from public life. Half of the Russian adult population reports reading national newspapers "regularly" or "sometimes" and almost everyone watches national television "regularly" (81 percent) or "sometimes" (14 percent). Sixty-nine percent read local newspapers regularly or sometimes. Sixty-four percent discuss the problems of the country with friends regularly or sometimes and 48 percent say that people ask them their opinions about what is happening in the country. A similar percentage of people discuss the problems of their city with friends.[19] Seventy-nine percent of Russians in a survey conducted just after the 1999 elections responded that they do favor an election system that has a wide choice of candidates and parties for parliament and president.[20] Moreover, Russians accept that voting is a civic duty. Asked whether it is important to vote in national elections, 46 percent responded that they should make every effort to vote (31 percent responded that there is no need to vote if it is not convenient to do so, and only 23 percent responded that there is no point in voting because it doesn't do any good).[21] Indeed, Russians do vote in high proportions in national elections—higher, in fact, than their American counterparts.[22]

Moreover, Russians prize their right to participate in politics as they choose, including the right *not* to participate. Asked to compare the present regime to the old regime before Gorbachev, large majorities of Russians regard the present system as better in providing political freedoms: with respect to the right to say what one thinks, 76 percent think the present situation is "better" or "much better" than previously; concerning the right to join any organization one pleases, 78 percent consider the present regime "better" or "much better" than the old regime. On freedom of religion, 83 percent rate the present regime as better or much better, and 72 percent regard the present as better or much better in allowing individuals to choose whether to participate in politics or not.[23]

But Russian citizens rate government's performance itself very negatively: concerning whether "people like me" have any ability to influence government, only 9 percent rate the situation as better than before perestroika; 45 percent say that it is unchanged; and 46 percent say that the present situation is "worse" or "much worse" than before. And concerning whether government treats everyone equally and fairly, only 8 percent think the situation has improved, 42 percent think it is much the same, and half respond that things have gotten worse.[24] Evidently Russian value their political rights, including the right not to take part in politics, but are convinced that these rights do not afford them any influence over government. In one late 2000 survey, 85 percent of the respondents expressed the opinion that they have no influence to affect the decisions of the authorities.[25] In another survey, 60 percent said that their vote would not change anything; only 14 percent of the respondents thought that Russia was a democracy; 54 percent said that "overall" it is not a democracy.[26] The political authorities are viewed very negatively (except for Putin). Fifty-five percent of the respondents in a survey in late 2000 said that the authorities are concerned only with their own material well-being and career. Another 13 percent regarded them as honest but weak, whereas another 11 percent considered them honest but incompetent.[27]

The evidence suggests that Russians regard their regime with deep mistrust although valuing their political rights. One reason for this may be that the reforms of the Gorbachev period and the revolutionary breakdown of the old regime raised people's hopes to unrealistically high levels about how quickly conditions would improve. In the late 1980s there was a great surge of popular mobilization in Soviet society. It took multiple forms, including mass protest actions such as strikes and demonstrations, as well as the creation of tens of thousands of new informal organizations. But following the end of the Soviet regime, this wave subsided. The disengagement and skepticism voiced in public opinion today certainly reflects deep disillusionment with how conditions have turned out after the wave of public enthusiasm and mobilization in the late 1980s.

Another reason for citizens' alienation from the regime, however, has to do with the fact that the old mechanisms of participation and recruitment have not been replaced with an effective system of democratic institutions that would allow voters to exercise influence over public policy and make officeholders accountable to the public for their actions. The old regime did have a system for holding officials to account, but it worked hierarchically, as in a military organization. Government officials answered up the chain of command to their administrative superiors and to the party for their actions, not to the voters. Officials, by the same token, often had the discretion and the ability to get around the rules, for instance to grant a favor, to speed up the processing of a bureaucratic transaction, to ignore a rule, or to forgive an offense. Social capital in the sense of thick "horizontal" ties among people may have been lacking, but "vertical" ties compensated for this to some extent. Today, even these have broken down. Most people think that the new system is run for the benefit of a few wealthy and powerful interests, leaving most ordinary citizens without much opportunity to exert any influence through the political process.

In the old system, citizens who had a problem often sought the intercession of an influential individual, someone placed high in the hierarchy of power. They turned to party and government officials, newspaper editors, soviet deputies, managers at their place of work, or other influential individuals. Or they could trade favors with people. In a centrally planned economy, when many items were in short supply, it required using connections to obtain scarce goods and services.[28] Now, however, Russians believe that it takes money—to buy things that are available but expensive, or to bribe an official for a routine service. Russians believe that the level of corruption in the country's institutions is very high: 82 percent say that the police are "somewhat" or "totally" corrupt; 77 percent think local government is corrupt; the same percentage say the Duma is corrupt; 64 percent consider the army corrupt; and 56 percent consider the presidential administration to be corrupt. Interestingly, the institution with the least corrupt reputation is the FSB (successor to the KGB, or secret police): only 46 percent think it corrupt.[29]

In short, connections, political influence, and informal networks used to be critical to coping with daily life in the old system. Now it appears that money is replacing personal connections as the way to get around bureaucratic difficulties and greedy officials. Richard Rose's New Russia Barometer survey in 1998 asked respondents whether they agreed with the following pair of propositions: "Some people say that in Soviet times to get anything done by a public agency you had to know people in the Party" and "Some people say that nowadays to get anything done by a public agency you have to pay money on the side." Sixty-eight percent agreed with the first statement and 90 percent agreed with the second. The problem is that in the old system, more people had access to influential connections than have access to money today. As a result, the sense of powerlessness and alienation from the state is pervasive.

Participation and recruitment are closely related processes, so it is not surprising that the breakdown of the old system of participation has been accompanied by the breakdown of the old system's mechanism for elite recruitment. Elite recruitment refers to the set of institutions in a society by which individuals enter careers that give them access to influence and responsibility. Educational institutions, voluntary associations, civil service examinations, political party work, and elections are all means by which societies' need for officials and leaders are met. In the Soviet system, the formal channels of mass participation were closely linked to its method for grooming officials and placing them in positions of responsibility. Given that the old system has not been replaced by an open, transparent, democratic system of participation and recruitment, a closer look at how the old system operated will help explain why its breakdown has produced so pronounced a sense of disengagement from the political system by the public today. It will also shed light on why Russians today report that money, rather than democratic politics or bureaucratic connections, is the new medium of exchange in public life.

PARTICIPATION AND RECRUITMENT UNDER THE SOVIET REGIME

Channels of Mass Participation

For most rank-and-file citizens of the old Soviet regime, participation in membership organizations was mainly formal—a matter of attending required meetings, paying monthly dues, and obtaining the benefits these organizations distributed. Virtually everyone who was employed belonged to a trade union, if only because trade unions administered social insurance funds and subsidized vacations. Youth groups provided recreational opportunities as well as political indoctrination, and nearly all youth belonged to the organization appropriate for their age group. Millions of people were members of voluntary public associations. For most people, membership in such organizations was largely nominal. For some individuals, however, and especially those who were keen on making political careers, mass organizations were an essential rung on a career ladder through which energetic activism, coupled with political reliability, could bring ambitious individuals to the attention of the party's personnel managers, who in turn could ensure that the individual received the right combination of political education, volunteer assignments, and job opportunities to allow him or her to rise through the ladder of promotions.

A good example of mass participation was the soviets, the elected councils that served as representative and law-making bodies. Elected deputies were expected to help their constituents with various individual problems, but they were not able to make policy decisions in their jurisdictions without the guidance of the Communist Party. In every territorial subdivision of the state—every town, village, rural district, city, province, ethno-territory, and republic—there was a corresponding soviet. (In the case of the union and autonomous republics, and at the level of the union government itself, it was called the Supreme Soviet.) Soviets tended to be quite large: in 1987, 2.3 million deputies were elected to 52,000 soviets across the country. A deputy's calling was not full-time; soviets usually met on a quarterly or biannual basis, for a day or two at a time, hearing reports and approving the proposed budget and plan. Soviets were not deliberative, policy-making bodies, but were means of acquainting deputies and citizens with the policies and priorities of the regime at each level of the state, for giving deputies a feeling of personal responsibility for the well-being of the system, and for showcasing the democratic character of the state. This last function was particularly evident in the care taken to ensure a high level of participation by women, blue-collar workers, youth, nonparty members, and other categories of the populace who were severely underrepresented in more powerful organs. To this end, the party employed a quota system to select candidates to run, controlling the outcome of the nomination process to obtain the desired mix of social characteristics among the elected deputies.[30] Generally speaking, the party tried to select as candidates people who could serve as role models to society, leading citizens from all walks of life who were politically reliable and socially respectable. Virtually all prominent Soviet citizens were deputies to soviets at one level or another.

In addition to service as deputies, Soviet citizens were brought into the work of local government and administration in other ways. Many served as volunteer members of the standing committees of local soviets, monitoring government's performance in housing, education, trade, catering, public amenities, and other sectors of community life. Still others joined residential committees and neighborhood self-help groups. These activities were not entirely ceremonial. Often they gave public-spirited citizens an outlet for community service.[31]

Parochial Contacting

The habit of turning to deputies for help with private problems is characteristic of a pattern called "parochial contacting," which is a form of citizen participation focused on obtaining private benefits rather than influencing public policy. The Soviet authorities encouraged citizens to transmit their grievances, hopes, and petitions to a wide range of official institutions. The volume of letters and personal visits was huge. For 1983 alone, it was estimated that Central Television received about 1.7 million letters; all-union radio over 600,000; Moscow radio, over 170,000; the central newspapers, around half a million each; provincial newspapers, 30–35,000 letters each; the trade unions, two million letters and personal visits; and party organizations, 3.3 million letters and visits.[32] At the local level, ordinary citizens had some opportunity to influence government administration, pushing for improvements in the condition and availability of housing, for example, or for better provision of stores and cultural amenities. But these demands were generally nonpolitical in nature, not aimed at influencing basic policy or challenging the incumbents' right to rule.[33] Often this kind of contact between citizen and state generated a pattern of individualized, clientelistic participation, in which individuals became adept at "working the system" for their own private benefit rather than changing the allocation of resources for whole classes of people.[34] The regime in fact encouraged the *demobilization* of society. That is, they gave people numerous opportunities to pursue particularistic demands but repressed any effort by people to get involved in the political system to satisfy general policy-related demands, whether by organizing independent political movements or by taking to the streets in protest.[35]

Voting

Voting for deputies to soviets was another example of the directed, formal aspect of political participation in the old system. The regime went to great lengths to ensure that everyone cast a ballot, and treated the massive turnout and near unanimous endorsement of the candidate as a sign of the unshakeable unity of regime and people, despite the fact that virtually every race was uncontested.[36] The act of voting was a matter of dropping a ballot with a single, preprinted name into a ballot box at a polling station, where, after the polls closed, officials would count the number of ballots cast for the candidate, and duly announce the candidate's election by an overwhelming majority. The campaign emphasized the ideological solidarity of society—there was no room for an "opposition platform"—but voters were encouraged to see the deputies they elected as go-betweens who could intercede with the bureaucracy for their particular needs. Soviet elections illustrate the ritualistic quality of much participation under the old regime. For the authorities, the *appearance* of mass support was evidently of great importance, whereas for much of the population, participation in such ceremonies was regarded as part of the harmless pageantry of everyday life.

Party Control of Social Organizations

As time went on, the growth of repressed popular grievances far exceeded the slow growth of regularized opportunities for Soviet citizens to voice their demands. As a result the gap between approved gestures of participation and the actual realities of power widened. Those new public organizations that formed with official approval quickly grew into branches of the state rather than autonomous expressions of a public interest.[37] Even the Russian Orthodox Church had a quasi-official status, despite the constitution's declared separation of church and state. The KGB had a large network of informers and agents working within the church for surveillance of believers and to guide the church's social and political activity in directions congruent with the regime's purposes.[38] The party, in short, claimed a "licensing" power over organized social bodies through which it ensured control over their choice of leaders and the direction of their activity.[39] Because the nominally public (*obshchestvennye*—meaning formally nonstate) organizations in fact carried out state-set goals and operated under close political control, the boundary lines between state and society were never distinct. However, precisely because social organizations were so heavily controlled by the party, they did not foster much usable social capital in the form of generalized social trust and autonomous collective action. Until the end of the Soviet regime, people continued to rely much more heavily on personal networks of family and friends to exchange information and favors than in democratic societies, and much less on voluntary participation in public life.[40] At home and at work, in the intimate company of trusted family and friends, Soviet citizens swapped information and opinion. Such networks were necessary for coping with the bureaucratized Soviet system, but at the same time they undermined both its basic ideological premise—that the people and the state were one—and its centralized control over resources.[41]

Informal social networks remain a powerful and important feature of Russian society today as well. Surveys show that around 90 percent of Russians can name at least one person (a family member or a friend) with whom they can discuss serious personal matters, including politics. Most Russians can name at least two such people.[42] Most Russians feel confident that they can ask their family and friends for help, for example, by borrowing money or asking someone to look after them if they are ill. Such relationships are also an important source of political information and opinion. For instance, 11 percent say that talking with family and friends is an important source of guidance to them in deciding how to vote in Duma elections.[43]

But is the continuing strength of such informal social ties a sign that Russia has a civil society supportive of democratic values and institutions? There is some disagreement on this point. Political scientist James Gibson finds that Russian social networks are characterized by a high degree of exchange of political information and opinion, and that there is a high level of trust among such networks, even outside immediate family members. He argues that such networks can therefore help to transmit information and values consistent with democratization. Richard Rose draws exactly the opposite conclusion, for three reasons. First, he points out that in Russia, informal social networks for many years have been means of surviving in an environment where the state was remote, harsh, and corrupt. They therefore reflect the alienation between state and society. Second, the density of social ties is not accompanied by high levels of associational membership. They may reinforce bonds of personal reciprocity, but they do not contribute to the capacity for cooperation in collective action. They are therefore not useful social capital for democracy. Finally, individuals are extremely mistrustful toward state authorities, particularly those who are supposed to represent them and be accountable to them. Therefore, social networks do not serve as vehicles for keeping government responsive or honest. Freedom, argues Rose, is valued because it allows people to keep their distance from a corrupt and exploitative state.[44] In short, although the pattern of close ties of family and friendship continues into the present, often as a buffer against the hardships of the transition, it tends to work *against* the formation of wider networks of civic participation.[45]

Dissent and the Intelligentsia

During the Soviet period, some groups operated outside the state and, as a result, risked being repressed. Overt dissent from the official doctrines was treated by the authorities as a criminal offense. Beginning in the mid-1960s, various small, unofficial groups pressed the regime to respect the civic and political rights that were granted by the Soviet constitution but were denied whenever the authorities found that a particular act violated the limits of permitted expression.[46] Those individuals who stepped outside the limits of permissible public expression—called dissenters or dissidents—were harassed, arrested, or even incarcerated in mental hospitals; a few were forced to emigrate. Many more people, particularly members of the cultural and scientific intelligentsia, chose not to take actions that could provoke their arrest, but shared similar democratic values. Working in institutions such as theaters, labs, research institutes, universities, the mass media, and professional bodies, many of these individuals formed strong ties of mutual trust. Some of them later came to lead the movements for democratic, national, and religious rights that blossomed in the Gorbachev period.

Some prominent dissident and nondissident intellectuals became leaders of new political movements in the late 1980s, such as Andrei Sakharov, the most famous of the democratic dissidents, who became the moral leader of the democratic group of USSR deputies elected in 1989. Another dissident-turned-politician is Sergei Kovalev, a close friend and collaborator of Sakharov's in the democratic movement who became chairman of the human rights committee of the Russian Republic's parliament in 1990 and was a member of the Russian parliament throughout the 1990s. Another intellectual—a nondissident, who remained within the system—who entered politics in 1989 was Anatolii Sobchak. Sobchak was a law professor at Leningrad State University, where Vladimir Putin was a student of his. Sobchak joined the democratic movement and won election to the Leningrad city soviet in 1990 and then went on to become mayor of Leningrad (later St. Petersburg), where Putin worked with him as deputy mayor. In Russia and a number of other republics of the union, scientists, professors, cultural figures, some with dissident backgrounds, others not, comprised the first wave of leaders when the opportunity for democratic politics opened up in 1989–1990. They drew on their networks of friends and acquaintances for support and could articulate coherently the principles on which they based their opposition to the Soviet system—ideals such as liberal democracy and an open, market-oriented economy; in many republics, these were linked to the cause of national sovereignty.

Although the forms of public association that were allowed in the Soviet regime did foster some capacity for collective action among intellectuals, artists, ethnic groups, workers, and other groups, most civic associations operated as extensions of the state's power. Those groups that chose to remain outside the state to avoid political control by the Communist Party were considered suspect and were usually suppressed. Elimination of most forms of private property, the suppression of opposition, and the spread of state control over social organizations left a vacuum of nonstate structures when the political regime fell apart. This vacuum in turn created opportunities for a surge of radical politics, particularly radical ethnonationalism, because of the destruction of class and other cleavages that cut across national divisions.[47] Ties among intellectuals cemented in the post-Stalin era enabled figures from the scientific and cultural elite to assume leading roles in the wave of political activism that crescendoed at the end of the 1980s and beginning of the 1990s. The most widespread type of such political activity was the drive for national independence in the union republics.

Participation and Recruitment in the Old Regime: Interlocking Directorates

The close link between mass participation and elite recruitment in the Soviet regime thus helps explain the explosive quality of political activity in the late 1980s and early 1990s and the sudden emergence of new kinds of elites to lead it.

Without a system of open, competitive parties and interest groups, the state lacked institutional channels for the articulation and aggregation of demands, and the resolution of conflicts. The old leadership was well skilled in coping with a bureaucratic, authoritarian environment, but most officials who had made their careers in the old regime were ill equipped to manage in the new competitive political arena.

One reason the Communist regime placed such emphasis on mass participation was that it contributed directly to the recruitment of leaders.[48] The numerous governing bodies of social organizations created positions for activists and leaders who directed mass participation. Leaders in these organizations, in turn, belonged to the governing bodies of other organizations. The Communist Party likewise formed its own party committees at every level: its members always included the ranking full-time party officials in the given jurisdiction, as well as the heads of government and social organizations. Serving as the hub from which a series of membership ties extended into a locality's organized institutions, the party committee at each level of the hierarchy was a vehicle for the *horizontal integration* of elites by drawing together the key government and societal leaders in any given jurisdiction. At the same time such channels provided for the *vertical integration* of elites through the inclusion of heads of subordinate organizations on nominally elective collective bodies at higher levels. For example, the first secretaries of the most important regional party committees were members of the Central Committee of the Communist Party of the Soviet Union. This helped maintain political unity across the vast and diverse expanse of the country.

Integration of elites through organizational cross-representation helped cement ties among the members of different elite groups in the Soviet system and thus facilitated central control and coordination throughout the political system. Although in practice, the old regime vested actual decision-making authority in administrative bodies, it also preserved elements of the old Bolshevik model of "democratic centralism" and "soviet democracy." These were embedded in the system of soviet elections as well as within the party. Party members cast ballots for representatives to governing bodies that were supposed to oversee the work of its own executive organs. These governing bodies included the Central Committee at the summit of the party hierarchy, as well as party committees at each level of the party organizational ladder. But, as in elections of deputies to soviets, elections within the party were noncompetitive, and the act of voting was purely ceremonial. Likewise, the authority of party committees that were "democratically elected" in this way was understood by everyone to be a formality. The entire system was regarded as lip service to the party's claim to be democratic and representative. It was considered unthinkable to demand that the party actually behave as though it were democratically accountable to its members.[49]

By comparison with many present-day failed states, the Soviet system had a high level of organizational capacity. It had institutions for the recruitment of elites, the coordination of policymakers, and the participation of the population in political routines that acquainted them with the basic institutions of the state. It enabled central policymakers to communicate their goals and priorities down to lower-level elites, and provided political leadership throughout the state. By comparision with more developed political systems, however, the Soviet state demonstrated serious failings. It did a poor job of holding officials accountable either to central authorities or to the citizens at large. Its reliance on self-nominating, closed procedures for appointing and "electing" officials made it vulnerable to pathologies such as corruption, favoritism, and incompetence. Perhaps most fatally, the system became rigid and immobile, so that it could not modernize the economy without upsetting powerful and well-entrenched political interests. Ultimately the system proved incapable of adapting itself to pressures for better performance and greater international competitiveness.

Participation and Recruitment in the Old Regime: Conclusions

Reviewing the patterns of state-sponsored mass political participation and elite recruitment under the old regime, we can draw three conclusions. First, the high volume of formal civic involvement reflected the mobilizing impulses of a political regime that was born in revolution and that sought to impose comprehensive controls on public attitudes and behavior. However ritualized and formalistic these forms of participation became, they demonstrated a massive effort by the regime to control society. Second, they generated little social capital that could form the basis for a democratic regime following the collapse of Communism. For the most part, citizens continued to rely heavily on networks of family, friends, and coworkers for communication and on parochial contacts in their dealings with state authorities; these, as we saw, tended to counteract wider civic involvement. The webs of voluntary, overlapping social association that are the base of support for democratic societies were replaced in the Soviet system by a series of interlocking state hierarchies. As a result, officials were accountable to their superiors rather than to their constituents, and there was a wide gap between the political elite and ordinary citizens.

Finally, there were some important exceptions to this generalization. Some arts organizations, research institutes, universities, and other institutions fostered ties of generalized trust and social cooperation through the long decades after Stalin's death. When Gorbachev finally opened the doors to freer public communication and political action, intellectuals based in these institutions initiated new forms of collective action. In some republics, these movements were aimed at winning national independence for their republics. In several major cities of Russia, these groups spearheaded political movements for democratic reform and became the nucleus of new democratic coalitions and parties that competed in the elections of 1989 and 1991. Intellectuals, in alliance with some radicalized members of the ruling elite, mobilized popular pressure for democratization, linking populist demands for an end to elite power and privilege with the longing for a more prosperous, open, "civilized" way of life. These aspirations were soon succeeded, however, by disillusionment with the outcome of the transition.

SURGE AND EBB IN POLITICAL PARTICIPATION

The Mobilization of Discontent

In a famous comment on the fact that the minor reforms under Louis XVI in France not only failed to relieve the revolutionary pressure of mass discontent, but actually seemed to stimulate it, Alexis de Tocqueville noted that "the most dangerous time for a bad government is when it starts to reform itself." In our time there have been many examples of authoritarian regimes attempting to release the pressure of popular discontent by holding elections or legalizing opposition groups, only to find that the public's desire for radical, fundamental change was more powerful than they calculated. The process of democratization results in a peaceful transition if the leadership is willing to concede power without suppressing its opponents. But its ability to do so depends on the civilian leadership's ability to preserve the support of the military and secret police *and* the ability of the opposition to remain sufficiently united as it pushes the regime to prevent popular demands from spilling out and provoking large-scale repression. Often in such revolutionary settings, mass frustrations and grievances, having accumulated over a long period, sweep away the more moderate elements of the leadership that could mediate between regime and opposition, and instead thrust forward maximalist leaders, with the result that confrontation results in new violence. Both sides need to be willing and able to compromise if the transition is to result in a peaceful and democratic outcome.

In the case of the Soviet Union, new channels of participation and recruitment quickly sprang up in response to the opening that Gorbachev's democratic reforms provided. In 1986 and especially 1987 and 1988, an explosion of associational activity in society occurred.[50] Much of this was not explicitly political in character, and took the form of rock music groups; body-building and martial arts clubs; loose associations of pacifists, hippies, and religious mystics; and cultural and environmental preservation movements. But even many groups without an explicit political agenda were expressions of "identity politics" as they joined in asserting the right to a public voice.[51] They were *implicitly* political, because they challenged party controls over ideology and personnel selection. They could therefore become nuclei of opposition ideas and organization. Moreover, in a rapidly changing environment, the clash between groups seeking to preserve their independence and the party-state bureaucracy tended to politicize and radicalize society. With time, therefore, and particularly as opportunities opened up for forms of political expression, such as mass demonstrations, publication of independent newsletters and leaflets, and electoral campaigning, more and more groups were drawn into politics. This process of politicization of the informal groups reached a peak in the 1988–1989 period, as society was drawn into the debate over democratization.[52] Broadly speaking, two processes occurred simultaneously over the 1987–1989 period: the proliferation of independent social associations (Soviet authorities estimated that 30,000 unofficial groups had formed in 1988, and perhaps as many as 60,000 by 1989) and the aggregation of smaller groups into larger movements and organizations.

One of the most common forms of independent, organized political activity in the 1988–1989 period was the popular front. Typically the popular front was a broad popular movement with a democratic orientation that aggregated several overlapping causes: environmental preservation, the expansion of political freedoms, and, for those operating in national republics, greater autonomy for the national homeland. Another important form of spontaneous collective action was strikes. Strikes by industrial workers usually were motivated by a set of grievances revolving around degrading living and working conditions, demands for meaningful workplace and regional autonomy, and resentment at the privilege and power of the ruling elite. In many regions, however, strikes were vehicles of ethnic-national protest, beginning in 1988 with strikes in Transcaucasia and the Baltic Republics.[53] The largest labor action was the strike by coal miners in July 1989, when, at its peak, the strike was joined by 300–400,000 workers. Generally, nationalism mobilized more strikes than did the labor movement. The evidence from the count of workdays lost to strikes and protest in 1989 indicates that far more downtime was caused by ethnically related movements than from economically inspired protest.[54] The national fronts, strikes, and other political movements that sprang up were not only vehicles for popular participation; they also created opportunities for grassroots leaders to enter politics and for figures from the cultural and scientific intelligentsia to frame demands and plot strategy. Gorbachev's call for open elections in 1989 caused many new activists to enter electoral politics, thus opening a new channel of elite recruitment.

The informal, often anomic, character of much popular political participation in the late Gorbachev period had important effects on the subsequent development of Russian politics. The explosiveness of demands for decent living conditions, ending bureaucratic privilege, autonomy for the national culture, and redress of other broad popular grievances substantially raised the costs to the regime of using force to suppress protest. They therefore helped to bring about radical change, such as the acknowledgment of the right to strike, the legalization of opposition parties, and ultimately the breakup of the union. Because the Soviet regime had suppressed almost all forms of organized participation except those it controlled and directed, there were few independent associations able to channel popular protest in the perestroika period. Many informal organizations sprang up but quickly faded away. The regime attempted to coopt others by drawing them under state sponsorship. Most organizations found it very hard to survive as the economy continued to be overwhelmingly state-owned and state-administered: new informal organizations struggled simply to obtain office space and equipment. In contrast to Central Europe, Soviet society lacked a network of civic associations that could assume responsibility for mobilizing and managing popular pressure for democratic change. In the Soviet case, the mass outpouring of popular protest in 1989–1991 therefore gave way to a rapid demobilization. Still, the surge of popular participation in this period left two lasting institutional changes: regular democratic elections and the nuclei of a number of political parties and interest groups. In the next section we will discuss electoral participation before turning to the relationship between participation and the formation of the political elite. Then in the next chapter we will take a closer look at the dynamics of Russians' attitudes and values.

Electoral Participation

Yeltsin and Electoral Politics

The mobilization of popular political participation had the effect of generating new leadership and new organizations voicing a variety of populist, democratic, and nationalist demands. In many areas it forced former Communist Party and government executives to adapt themselves to a pluralized political environment that they could no longer control. Some were swept away, but most managed to hold on to their power, and a few emerged as champions of reform. A prominent example of the latter was Boris Yeltsin (see Close-Up 4.1: Boris Yeltsin—Russia's First President).

Close-Up 4.1   Boris Yeltsin—Russia's First President

Boris Yeltsin was Russia's first president and the architect of its breakaway from the USSR. As a leader he embodied all the contradictions of the stormy passage from the Communist to the post-Communist era. He alternated between taking radical steps toward democracy and retreating toward opportunistic alliances with wealthy and powerful interests that could keep him in power. Gifted with a brilliant instinct for political strategy, he was also prone to fits of depression, heavy drinking, and passivity. Ill for much of his presidency with serious heart disease, he was also capable of summoning enormous energy when battling against his enemies. Most of the breakthroughs as well as the fatal compromises of Russia's transition are the direct result of decisions he made.

Yeltsin rose through the ranks as a Communist Party leader in the heartland industrial region of the Urals. Born in 1931, he graduated from the Urals Polytechnical Institute in 1955 with a diploma in civil engineering and worked for a long time in construction. From 1976 to 1985, he served as first secretary of the Sverdlovsk oblast (provincial) Communist Party organization. He was known there as a hard-driving, imperious leader, blunt and impatient with subordinates who failed to measure up to his standards, but genuinely devoted to improving the well-being of his region.

Early in 1986 he became first secretary of the Moscow city party organization but was removed in November 1987 for speaking out against

Gorbachev. Positioning himself as a victim of the party establishment, Yeltsin made a remarkable political comeback. In the 1989 elections to the Congress of People's Deputies, he won a Moscow at-large seat with almost 90 percent of the vote. The following year he was elected to the Russian Republic's parliament with more than 80 percent of the vote. He was then elected its chairman in June 1990. In 1991, he was elected president of Russia, receiving 57 percent of the vote. Thus, he had won three major races in three successive years. He was reelected as president in 1996 in a dramatic, come-from-behind race against the leader of the Communist Party.

In foreign policy, Yeltsin generally regarded maintaining good relations with the United States as being of paramount importance, despite a growing set of serious policy differences over issues such as Russia's brutal war in Chechnia, the admission of new members to NATO, American military actions against Serbian aggression in Bosnia and in Kosovo, and Russia's squandering of IMF loans and credits through corruption. It was extremely important to Yeltsin that the West grant Russia the status of an equal partner in great-power deliberations, and he recognized how important Western trade and investment were for the future revival of the economy. Russia's methods for fighting Chechen rebel forces provoked worldwide condemnation because of the massive civilian destruction and refugee flight they brought about, but it was also Yeltsin who, in 1996, accepted the need for a peaceful political resolution of the conflict and signed a truce agreement with the Chechen leadership providing for a withdrawal of federal forces.[*]

Yeltsin's last years in office were notable for his lengthy spells of illness and for the carousel of prime ministerial appointments he made. The entourage of family members and advisers around him, dubbed colloquially "the Family," seemed to exercise undue influence over him on behalf of a clique of powerful state bureaucrats and financial tycoons. He became preoccupied with finding a successor who would protect his security and his political legacy and in 1999 settled on Vladimir Putin as the right candidate. Following the success of the hastily concocted pro-Kremlin party, Unity, in the Duma elections of December 1999, Yeltsin decided to resign six months ahead of the expiration of his term to give Putin an edge in running

---

[*] For a firsthand account of U.S.–Russian relations during the 1990s, see Strobe Talbott, *The Russia Hand* (New York: Random House, 2002). Talbott was President Clinton's senior policy adviser on Russia policy, and offers fascinating firsthand accounts of meetings with Yeltsin. For a detailed biography of Yeltsin, see Leon Aron, *Yeltsin: A Revolutionary Life* (New York: St. Martin's Press, 2000). *George Breslauer, Gorbachev and Yeltsin as Leaders* (Cambridge: Cambridge University Press, 2002), provides a systematic comparison of the leadership styles of Gorbachev and Yeltsin.

(*Continued*)

for president. Upon his retirement, Yeltsin became a private citizen and generally stayed out of the public eye. Yeltsin died of heart failure on April 23, 2007. His funeral at the Cathedral of Christ the Savior in Moscow was attended by dignitaries from Russia and around the world. President Putin eulogized him by saying, "To very few is it given to become free themselves and to lead millions behind them, to arouse the Fatherland to truly historic changes and thus to transform the world. Boris Nikolaevich Yeltsin was able to do that—never turning back, never wavering, never betraying the people's choice and his own conscience. Such personalities do not leave us. They continue to live in the ideas and aspirations of people, in the successes and achievements of the Motherland."

Radical Democratic Populism

The elections to the all-union Congress of People's Deputies in 1989 and the republican and local soviets in 1990 illustrate the turn from the directed political participation characteristic of the old system to the new politics of competitive elections. The 1989 and 1990 elections were conceived by Gorbachev as ways of giving the wave of popular political participation stimulated by glasnost a constructive outlet, one that would help weaken Gorbachev's conservative opposition while at the same time enabling him to continue to set the country's basic policy direction. But the elections had much more far-reaching effects than he anticipated, by activating popular movements and generating new opposition leaders with large popular followings. Although the elections of 1989, 1990, and 1991 were not organized around competing parties for the most part, protopartisan tendencies formed as candidates aligned themselves with competing political causes—some emphasizing liberal democracy, others hard-line Communism, still others ethnic nationalism.

The surge of electoral participation in 1989–1990 had a strongly populist impulse. Campaigns were not organized around political parties as much as they focused on antiestablishment causes and personalities. In many cases they were a referendum on the system rather than a choice between alternative political programs. The 1989 elections to the USSR Congress of People's Deputies enabled the populace to register their opposition to the old party and government elites, resulting in some dramatic upsets. Dozens of leading party and government officials were defeated, and a group of three to four hundred deputies identified with liberal democratic views were elected to the Congress. In some republics, however, particularly in Central Asia, the entrenched political elite was able to maintain its control in much the same way as it had done in the past. The same pattern was apparent in the 1990 elections as well: candidates who were state officials managed for the most part to win their races by avoiding direct confrontation with well-organized opposition movements, but, especially in major cities, new political movements succeeded in electing democratically minded candidates to the republican and local soviets.

Democracy and the End of "Descriptive Representation"

The results of the new, open elections differed considerably from the old system in social makeup of the elected deputies. For one thing, voters generally rejected the social tokenism of the old system. This is reflected most dramatically in the sharp decline in the number of women, workers, and collective farmworkers among the new deputies. Women fared poorly in the 1989 all-union elections, comprising only 17 percent of the candidates and an equal percentage of the winners. They were still more disadvantaged in the 1990 elections to the Russian Republic parliament, when they comprised 7.2 percent of candidates and 5.4 percent of winners. Workers suffered a similar drop in their representation.[55] Table 4.1 illustrates the sharp decline in the rates of representation of two of the social groups affected by the old system of quotas in the soviets, women, and workers.

Second, these early elections were not structured by party. Broad political coalitions with ideological identities did form, but they were informal, loose movements based on shared ideological outlooks rather than organized parties capable of turning out loyal followers. Only in the 1993 and 1995 parliamentary elections did voters have a choice among actual parties. For the first time, parties began to link the preferences of segments of the electorate with the policy-making processes of the state. Yet the process of developing a system of nationally competitive parties remained painfully slow.

As in other countries undergoing a transition from Communism to democracy, members of the "prestige" elite formed a large share of the first generation of

Table 4.1 ■ Workers' and Women's Representation in USSR and Russian Federation Assemblies (as percentage of elected deputies)

	Manual Workers	Women
1. USSR Supreme Soviet (1970) (N = 1,500)	31.7	30.5
2. USSR local soviets (1971) (N = approx. 2 million)	36.5	45.8
3. USSR Supreme Soviet (1984) (N = 1,500)	35.2	32.8
4. Russian Republic Supreme Soviet (1985) (N = 975)	35.8	35.3
5. USSR Congress of People's Deputies (1989) (N = 2,250)	18.6	17.1
6. USSR Supreme Soviet (1989) (N = 542)	24.7	18.4
7. Russian Republic Congress of People's Deputies (1990) (N = 1,026)	5.9	5.4
8. Local Russian Republic soviets (1990) (N = 702,268)	24.9	35.0
9. State Duma of the Federal Assembly (January 1994) (N = 450)	1.3	13.5
10. State Duma of the Federal Assembly (January 1996) (N = 450)	n.a.	10.2
11. State Duma of the Federal Assembly (January 2000) (N = 450)	0.65	7.7
12. State Duma of the Federal Assembly (January 2004) (N = 450)	n.a.	10.0

Note: N refers to the number of seats or mandates in the given assembly.

elected politicians as voters looked to turn out the existing political establishment.[56] Candidates' prior political experience was often a liability in the voters' eyes. Later elections, however, witnessed a backlash against the antiestablishment politics of the 1989–1990 period. This is because of the sharp disappointment that most people felt over the results of the change of regime. The very label of "democrat" became a pejorative name, often coupled with the term, "so-called." The intellectuals who entered politics in 1989–1991 either turned into career politicians, or left the political arena.

Disillusionment with the early wave of democratic populism resulted in a sharp decline in electoral turnout. In 1989 total turnout for elections of deputies to the new all-union Congress of People's Deputies was 90 percent. In 1990, turnout for the elections of deputies to the new Russian Congress of People's Deputies was 76 percent. Seventy-four percent of the electorate took part in the 1991 presidential election in Russia. Sixty-nine percent voted in the Russian referendum of April 1993 on approval of President Yeltsin and his government.

At the end of 1993, after Yeltsin forcibly dissolved the parliament and demanded new elections to a parliament whose structure he instituted by decree, turnout fell further. Anticipating that turnout would be low, Yeltsin decreed that elections of representatives to the parliament would be valid if turnout in a district was at least 25 percent, and that a candidate would be elected if he or she received more votes than any other candidate. For passage of the constitutional referendum, however, Yeltsin decreed that at least half of the registered voters in the country would have to take part in the voting and that at least half of them would have to have approved it. Yeltsin and his administration went to considerable lengths to ensure the constitution's passage. Regional heads of administration were placed under heavy pressure by Yeltsin to achieve a 50 percent turnout and a majority for the constitution. In the end, the government declared that some 54.8 percent of the electorate had voted and that of these, 58.4 percent cast their ballots in favor of the constitution. However, these official figures may overstate the actual level of turnout. According to estimates by a respected team of researchers, actual turnout was probably closer to 46 percent, which implied that the constitution had, in fact, not been adopted.[57] Although these charges were stoutly refuted by election officials,[58] the precipitous decline in electoral participation was a warning to all sides that many citizens no longer considered voting worth the effort. Turnout in many regional and local races was still lower in the 1990s.

However, turnout, at least in national elections, began to rise again in the mid-1990s. Perhaps because of the efforts by parties to mobilize voters for their leaders, voter turnout in the December 1995 parliamentary elections was almost 65 percent and it was even higher for the two rounds of the presidential election in 1996. Table 4.2 shows the figures for electoral participation in parliamentary and presidential elections in the 1990s.[59]

It may be that the vigorous campaigns mounted by the parties in the elections, including heavy—but heavily biased—television news coverage and advertising, had the effect of persuading voters that their interests were at stake in these elections.[60]

Table 4.2 ■ Voter Turnout in Russian Parliamentary and Presidential Elections (official figures)

Election	Turnout (%)
Presidential election 1991	74.7
Duma election 1993	54.8
Duma election 1995	64.8
Presidential election 1996	
First round	69.8
Second round	68.9
Duma election 1999	60.4
Presidential election 2000	68.8
Duma election 2003	55.7
Presidential election 2004	64.4

Evidently no matter how disillusioned voters may feel with democratic politics, they see a link between their participation in the electoral process and the country's future. Political scientists Timothy Colton and Michael McFaul find that 60 percent of the population believe that voting matters and that 86 percent consider voting to be a civic duty.[61] Few Russians feel a strong sense of loyalty to or identification with a party, and fewer still trust parties in general. The issue of how to measure "party identification" (which is a concept commonly used in the study of American elections to refer to the psychological attachment many voters feel to a particular party, whether they agree with its current policy positions or like its leaders or not) is hard to apply in the Russian context, because parties are a relatively new phenomenon and the names and identities of parties have been so fluid. Timothy Colton finds that there is a fair amount of "protopartisanship" or "transitional partisanship" in Russia; over 40 percent of voters say that there is a party they can call "my party" or that "more than others reflects my interests, views and concerns." On the other hand, this level of attachment is loose and voters often switch their loyalties between elections. Moreover, there has been no growth in the degree of partisanship since the mid-1990s.[62]

The low level of attachment between voters and parties helps explain the fact that small but significant shares of the electorate choose the "against all" box on the ballot form, or cast an invalid ballot. (See Table 4.3.) It is a telling indication of the desire by the Putin regime to limit opportunities for the expression of opposition as much as possible that it enacted legislation in the summer of 2006 eliminating the "against all" option from ballots. Dropping it removed the last vestige of the populist, antiestablishment voting of the late 1980s.[63]

Backlash Against Democratic Populism

Besides the ebbing turnout in elections in the early to mid-1990s, another effect of the disillusionment with radical democratic expectations was a backlash against

Table 4.3 ■ "Against all" Votes and Invalid Ballots

As percentage of all valid ballots cast:	Against all (%)	Invalid ballots (%)
1993 Duma election (party list vote)	4.36	3.10
1995 Duma election (party list vote)	2.8	1.9
1996 presidential election		
First round	1.5	1.4
Second round	4.8	0.7
1999 Duma election (party list vote)	3.3	1.29
2000 presidential election	1.99	0.94
2003 Duma election (party list vote)	4.77	1.56
2004 presidential election	3.45	0.83

democratic candidates and parties. This trend strengthened the hand of Yeltsin's political opponents. Yeltsin's political successes had always come about through his ability to appeal to the public at large for support. Yeltsin was able to appeal to the fear that the Communists would come back in his presidential reelection bid in 1996, but by the end of the 1990s, the very term "democrat" had been badly discredited by association with the excesses of the Yeltsin era—the widespread corruption, venality, cynicism of many politicians; the apparent giveaways of state property to manipulative tycoons; and the weakening of the fabric of public order and morality. Disillusionment with the promise of democracy to a large extent fostered a massive retreat from public political participation and a return to the more immediate day-to-day tasks of private life.

Thus from the late 1980s to the late 1990s, political participation in Russia underwent enormous change. Perestroika upset the old model of directed participation—in which the rituals of lip service to Communist ideals were complemented by a modest undercurrent of unlicensed activity and a great deal of parochial contacting between citizens and state. Initially Gorbachev's reforms stimulated a great surge of popular involvement in new forms of participation. This wave of activism brought a generation of democratic political leaders to power, some of them intellectuals from outside the political establishment, others young and ambitious politicians. A few, like Yeltsin, were ranking officials of the old regime who became champions of change. Then this wave passed, leaving many fewer informal organizations behind but still giving citizens numerous opportunities to cast ballots in local and national elections. In its wake was widespread disillusionment with the promise of reform and a broad withdrawal of the populace from political participation except for voting in elections.

Still, although participation in public life is far lower than it was at its peak in the late 1980s and early 1990s, what participation there is today is voluntary. Voting still provides some opportunity for citizens to express their preferences over candidates and parties, and involvement in social associations, though much less widespread than in the West, nonetheless gives many citizens an opportunity to become engaged in the larger public life of their communities. As we shall see in Chapter 6, these forms of involvement more often concern social and cultural interests than directly political ones. But throughout the country, the upheavals of the 1980s and 1990s have left a small but durable residual core of civic life outside the state's direct control.

The very limited scope of participation in civic life, however, compared with Western societies, replicates a much older pattern of political disengagement by the Russian people from the authorities. This pattern may even have been reinforced by the Soviet regime's strenuous efforts to turn the masses out in a variety of forms of state-sponsored channels of activity, which triggered the surge of informal, extrasystemic participation of the late 1980s, followed by the ebbing of such involvement over the course of the 1990s. The low expectations that people had for the government were matched by government's poor performance, forming a "low-level equilibrium trap" in which the low level of actual demand for good government is matched by an equally meager supply of it.[64]

The alienation of the populace from public life is reinforced by the high level of inequality in income and wealth, which widened sharply as a result of the economic changes occurring in Russia since 1991 before falling somewhat. Many feel that the dramatic gap in living standards that has arisen between the newly rich and the rest of society has reduced the sense of community.[65] As in other societies with high disparities in economic resources, the political system may act so as to deepen inequality rather than to offset it.[66] As we saw, in most countries, people with higher levels of education and income tend to be more active in politics.[67] However, in most societies *voting* reflects a somewhat different pattern than other forms of participation, such as joining political associations or taking part in campaigns. Voting requires much less effort than many other forms of political activity and so tends to be more readily accessible to poorer, less mobile, and more marginal strata of a society. Participation in elections for individuals with low education and income levels therefore depends on the success of parties and interest groups in motivating them to take part. A competitive party system thus offsets some of the effects of inequality in social status that are reflected in other forms of political participation. Therefore, even though participation in Russia lacks a sturdy foundation in organizational membership, the relatively high partipation in elections could theoretically help link citizens and rulers. But, in the absence of an effective party system, elections do little to compensate for the great disparities in power and wealth in society.

ELITE ADAPTATION AND REPLACEMENT

Political Recruitment, Old and New

To understand how elite recruitment works today, we have to go back again to the Soviet system because so much of the present-day elite was shaped under it. Like other features of the pre-Gorbachev Soviet political system, the method by which political elites were chosen was carefully regulated by the Communist Party. The filling of any position that carried important administrative responsibility or that was likely to affect the formation of public attitudes was subject to party approval. The system for recruiting, training, and appointing individuals for positions of leadership was called the *nomenklatura* system, and those individuals who were approved for the positions on *nomenklatura* lists were informally called "the *nomenklatura*." Many citizens thought of them as the true ruling class in Soviet society.

Members of the *nomenklatura* did enjoy certain privileges, minor ones in the case of lesser posts, substantial ones for positions carrying greater status and authority. For much of the post-Stalin era, their careers were relatively secure: only in cases of severe incompetence or malfeasance were they likely to be removed entirely from the ranks of the privileged. Some organizations, such as the trade unions, were considered "retirement homes" for older or less able officials, whereas postings to others were considered necessary stepping-stones for political advancement. Many officials, for instance, spent a tour of duty as a full-time functionary for the Communist Party itself before reentering jobs in government or economic management.

The party used the *nomenklatura* system to keep lower officials accountable for their actions, although it was a relatively inefficient mechanism. Among other effects, the *nomenklatura* system fostered the formation of patron–client relationships: a leader was often more interested in subordinates' political loyalty in party power struggles than in their merits as administrators. These networks evidently contributed to elite cohesion and coordination and thus helped stabilize the political regime in much the same way that corruption, to which patronage was often linked, helped to redistribute resources and therefore iron out certain rigidities in the centrally planned economy. But this flexibility came at a very high price, which was ultimately paid by the political regime as a whole. The undermining of party policy and principles by the pursuit of private ends, the ubiquity of mediocrity and incompetence, and the impunity of corruption all corroded the foundations of the regime. Finally, as the entire Brezhnev-era political elite entrenched itself into power, growing older and older through the 1960s, 1970s, and 1980s, upward mobility ground to a near halt, blocking the opportunities for advancement by succeeding cohorts of elites. Not the least of the reasons for the collapse of the Soviet system was the frustration of their aspirations for a larger share of power.[68]

Changing Patterns of Elite Recruitment

The democratizing reforms of the late 1980s and early 1990s made two important changes in the process of elite recruitment. First, the old *nomenklatura* system crumbled along with other Communist Party controls over society. Second, although most members of the old ruling elites adapted themselves to the new circumstances and stayed on in various official capacities, the wave of new informal organizations, popular elections, and business entrepreneurship brought about an infusion of new people into elite positions. Thus the contemporary Russian political elite consists of some people who were recruited under the old *nomenklatura* system together with a smaller share of individuals who have entered politics through new channels such as elections and business. The political elite has not simply reproduced itself from the old regime to the new, nor has it been completely rejuvenated.[69] It would be fairer to say that it has been expanded to accommodate the influx of new, often younger, politicians who have come in to fill positions in representative and executive branches. In numerous cases, the old guard have successfully adapted themselves to the new conditions, and, drawing on their experience and contacts, have found different high-status jobs for themselves. But the new wave of young politicians who have come up through elections to local and national soviets have also found positions in the political elite both in the legislative and executive branches. And a large number of both old-guard officials and new-wave entrepreneurs have become part of a new business elite.

The Russian public opinion research institute, the Levada Center (formerly known as VTsIOM) conducted a survey of Russia's social and political elite.[70] The center compared a sample of over a thousand people who had held senior *nomenklatura* jobs in 1988 with an equivalent group holding leading positions in the state administration, politics, science, culture, and economic management in 1993. The results showed that the great majority of the 1993 elite had either held *nomenklatura* jobs in 1988, or came from positions that were in the "reserve *nomenklatura*"—positions such as deputy director of important institutions rather than director. Only 16 percent had entered elite positions without having had any administrative experience at all. By the same token, 57 percent of the old *nomenklatura* group had been able to stay in administrative positions in the state or economy; another 18 percent found reasonably high but not top-level positions. Most of those who failed to stay in the elite were over 60 years of age. Clearly the old elite managed to survive in positions of power and influence.

One major reason for their success in staying in power was the value of their social connections. Among those of the current elite who were former Communist Party members, former full-time party officials made up three-quarters, suggesting that their personal networks had helped them withstand the collapse of Communist rule. Another factor, however, is education and youth. The new elite, on average, was ten years younger than the old one, reflecting a generational turnover that had probably been overlong in coming. Over 20 percent had never been Communist Party members.

Turnover was lowest among the economic managers and greatest among those in politics. Seventy percent of those in economic elite positions in 1993 had held *nomenklatura* jobs in 1988 as enterprise managers or ministerial officials. But of those holding top government positions, only one-third had been in *nomenklatura* jobs in 1988. Still, even those holding jobs in the state and Communist Party bureaucracy in 1988 were often able to hold on to their elite status: one-third of 1988's state bureaucrats were still in the state bureaucracy in 1993. Of party officials in 1988, 20 percent had taken top-level positions in the state bureaucracy and 40 percent were in high managerial jobs, such as executives in state firms and holding companies.

Continuity through adaptation thus accounts for a larger share of the members of the new Russian political elite than does turnover through democratic renewal. Strikingly few of the old elite were displaced, one reason for the largely peaceful nature of the transition from Communist rule in Russia.[71] Quite clearly, the old *nomenklatura*—which comprised most of the people who possessed leadership and administrative experience at the time that the old system fell apart—had to be the principal pool from which political and bureaucratic officials in the post-1991 period were drawn.

As in other areas of political life, old Soviet institutional mechanisms for recruitment are being restored under Putin, including elements of the old *nomenklatura* system. In the Communist regime, the party maintained schools for training political leaders, where rising officials were given a combination of management education and political indoctrination. Today, most of those schools serve a similar function as academies for training civil servants and are overseen by Putin's presidential administration. Putin has created a system for identifying, training, and promoting "reserve cadres" with a view to ensuring that competent and politically reliable cadres are available for recruitment not only to state bureaucratic positions but even for management positions in major firms.[72]

But while there are major continuities between elite recruitment in the old regime and the present, there are also differences. The *nomenklatura* system of the Soviet regime ensured that in every walk of life, those who held positions of power and responsibility were approved by the party. They thus formed different sections of a single political elite and owed their positions to their political loyalty and usefulness. Today, however, there are multiple elites (political, business, scientific, cultural, etc.), reflecting the greater degree of pluralism in post-Soviet society. Second, there are more channels for recruitment to today's *political* elite. Many of its members come from positions in the federal and regional executive agencies; Putin in particular has recruited officials for his administration heavily from among the police (the regular police and the security services) and from the military.[73] But other prominent political figures climbed the ladder by winning local or national elections, or after making successful business careers. Overall, however, there has been much less turnover of elites under Putin than there was in the 1990s.[74]

Regions also differ in the degree to which the political elite is open to outsiders. Some regions have political regimes that have tended to preserve the old patterns of elite recruitment and the old political elite. In others, democratization and economic reforms have brought an influx of new people into the political elite.[75] In many regions, the business elite and political elite have merged, as prominent businesspeople have entered government and as leading officials run business firms on the side. In a few regions, organized crime and government overlap so closely that leading government officials are closely tied to criminal rackets, or are even themselves heads of organized crime syndicates.[76]

One of the most marked changes since the fall of the Soviet regime has been the formation of a new business class. To be sure, many of its members come out of the old Soviet *nomenklatura,* as old-guard bureaucrats discovered ways to cash in on their political contacts, "turning power into money," as a Chinese expression puts it. Some people estimate that money from the Communist Party found its way into the establishment of as many as a thousand new business ventures, including several of the first commercial banks. (Party officials also diverted money into overseas investments, creating several hundred firms outside the former Soviet Union.)[77] As early as 1987 and 1988, officials of the Communist Youth League (Komsomol) began to see the possibilities of cashing in the assets of the organization and started liquidating its assets to set up lucrative business ventures, such as video salons, banks, discos, tour agencies, and publishing houses.[78] They benefited from their insider contacts, obtaining business licenses, office space, and exclusive contracts with little difficulty. One of these early ventures evolved into the Menatep Bank, which later became the holding company for the Yukos oil company.

But many other members of the new business elite rose through channels outside the state. Many, in fact, entered business in the late 1980s, as new opportunities for legal and quasi-legal commercial activity opened up. A strikingly high proportion of the first generation of the new business elite comprised young scientists and mathematicians working in research institutes and universities.[79] The new commercial sector sprang up very quickly: by the end of 1992 there were nearly one million private businesses registered, with some 16 million people working in them.[80] Since then, though, there has been no net growth in the number of small enterprises.

Much of the business elite maintains close and often collusive relations with ranking state administrators and legislators. The same pattern is evident at the regional and local levels as well, as political leaders and business elites form close relations of mutual dependence. Businesses need licenses, permits, contracts, exemptions, and other benefits from government; political officials in turn need financial contributions to their campaigns, political support, favorable media coverage, and other benefits that business can provide. In the 1990s, the climate of insider relations between many businesses and many political leaders nurtured widespread corruption and the meteoric rise of the oligarchs. Under Putin, the regime has reasserted its dominance in the relationship between the state and big business. Under Yeltsin, state officials often became dependent on business for access to funds, favorable media coverage, and political support. Now the situation is often reversed, as businesses depend on the political favor of state officials for their continued success. In the Yeltsin period, business interests often sought to "capture" state power for their benefit: for instance, to protect themselves from arbitrary treatment or a predatory state. In other cases, state officials and businesses "colluded" to share the benefits from privileged treatment.[81] Certainly there is little concern on either side with avoiding conflict of interest between government and business. Under Putin, however, the top echelons of the business elite no longer have the upper hand in dealing with the state but are increasingly being forced to accept a subordinate role.[82] For example, Putin has appointed a number of his close associates to top positions in Russia's largest firms.[83]

We will come back to the evolution of the private sector in Chapter 7. Our purpose here is to make two points. First, as we have already seen, a major shift occurred in the pattern of recruitment of political elites in the 1990s, although the pace of change has slowed considerably. Today's political elite is relatively diverse in its origins, but members of the old *nomenklatura* elite continue to populate many of the highest-level posts in state and society. Second, although there is no longer a single unified system for controlling the selection of elites to all corners of the state and society, under Putin the regime has attempted to reestablish some control by the executive branch over the recruitment of elites for many state positions and even some in business.

Summing Up

In this chapter we have seen that the pattern of political disengagement that characterizes Russia today followed a surge of popular mobilization in the late 1980s and early 1990s, much of it motivated by radical democratic, populist, and nationalist aims. This wave then ebbed and left widespread disillusionment and mistrust toward government in its wake. At the same time, survey research consistently finds that Russians value their democratic freedoms, including the freedom to vote (or *not* to vote), to practice religion, and to criticize the regime. Turnout in national elections is reasonably high, but involvement in other forms of public life is meager.

We noted that the current alienation of citizens from the state echoes an older model of Russian political life, which some have called the image of "dual Russia," although looking very different—on the surface, at any rate—from the picture of mass participation in public life that the Soviet regime presented. In the Soviet period, everyone belonged to a trade union; participation in youth activities was nearly universal; a massive voter turnout effort got nearly all citizens to the polls to elect deputies to soviets in uncontested elections; two million people served on a part-time basis as deputies to soviets at different levels; and membership figures in huge, state-directed public associations were enormous.

Yet actual participation in the Soviet period was much lower than the reported figures suggested, and public associations did not result in the formation of much usable social capital that could help people cooperate in bearing the burden of providing good government. In today's Russia, political participation is voluntary. However, there is so little active involvement in civic or directly political activity that social capital is low, by comparison with Western societies. Political rights such as the right of association and expression are not coupled with the habits of civic cooperation for collective goods. Moreover, the chilling of the climate for open opposition activity under Putin may have discouraged some from involvement in civic life. And the stark inequalities in income and wealth within society further reinforces the pattern of detachment from and mistrust of public institutions. Still, as we shall see in Chapter 6, there are some forms of autonomous civic participation, often by taking advantage of opportunities for collaboration with regional and local authorities.

The pattern of elite recruitment also shows major differences with the old regime as well as some continuities with it. In the Soviet regime, the selection, grooming, and appointment of officials was tightly regulated by the Communist Party, which used the *nomenklatura* system to ensure that the political elite was loyal to and dependent on the party. No matter what sphere of state or society responsible officials worked in, they owed their positions and future careers to the party's favor. *Nomenklatura* officials came up through the ranks of mass organizations such as the party, youth leagues, trade unions, and so on, so the breakdown of party control over mass participation meant that elites in the 1990s became more diverse in their origins. Some entered politics through elections, others from business. Similarly, some of the old *nomenklatura* elite, having lost their former positions, readily found new jobs in the state administration or in business. Today's elite, therefore, consists of a number of individuals who survived and adapted to the new conditions, as well as many more who have entered through the new channels created by the change of regime.

NOTES

1. Cf. Steven Levitsky and Lucan A. Way, "Elections without Democracy: The Rise of Competitive Authoritarianism," *Journal of Democracy* 13:2 (2002): 52–65.

2. Fareed Zakaria, *The Future of Freedom: Illiberal Democracy at Home and Abroad* (New York: Norton, 2004).

3. Sidney Verba, Norman H. Nie, and Jae-on Kim, *Participation and Political Equality: A Seven-Nation Comparison* (Cambridge: Cambridge University Press, 1978).

4. Sidney Verba, Kay Lehman Schlozman, and Henry E. Brady, *Voice and Equality: Civic Voluntarism in American Politics* (Cambridge, MA: Harvard University Press, 1995). This volume presents a detailed examination of the way time, money, and civic skills affect patterns of political participation in the United States.

5. Joel D. Aberbach, Robert D. Putnam, and Bert A. Rockman, *Bureaucrats and Politicians in Western Democracies* (Cambridge, MA: Harvard University Press, 1981).

6. Verba, Schlozman, and Brady, *Voice and Equality*, pp. 313–33.

7. Theda Skocpol, *Diminished Democracy: From Membership to Management in American Civic Life* (Norman: University of Oklahoma Press, 2003): Theda Skocpol, "Advocates without Members: The Recent Transformation of American Civic Life," in *Civic Engagement in American Democracy,*

ed. Theda Skocpol and Morris P. Fiorina (Washington, DC: Brookings Institution Press, 1999), pp. 461–509; Douglas Rae, *City* (Yale University Press, 2003).

8. Robert D. Putnam, *Bowling Alone: The Collapse and Revival of American Community* (New York: Simon & Schuster, 2000).

9. A public good, as opposed to a private good, is *nonrivalrous,* that is, it cannot be diminished in quantity as individuals consume it; one person's enjoyment of it does not lessen another's person's opportunity to enjoy it. And it is *nonexcludable,* that is, one person cannot keep another from enjoying it. So, public goods typically tempt people to "free ride" on the efforts of others, because those who produce them cannot measure or meter others' use of them.

10. Robert D. Putnam, with Robert Leonardi, et al., *Making Democracy Work: Civic Traditions in Modern Italy* (Princeton, NJ: Princeton University Press, 1993); Robert D. Putnam, *Bowling Alone: The Collapse and Revival of American Community* (New York: Simon and Schuster, 2000).

11. As Putnam and other scholars have pointed out, social capital can divide groups as well as link them. The members of an ethnic minority or religious cult may have dense social ties with one another but these may serve more to isolate them from the rest of society than to integrate them. At their most

extreme, divisive forms of social capital can foster extremism, intolerance, and exclusion.

12. Richard Rose, William Mishler, and Christian Haerpfer, *Democracy and Its Alternatives: Understanding Post-Communist Societies* (Baltimore, Johns Hopkins University Press, 1998), p. 14.

13. Quoted from Robert C. Tucker, "The Image of Dual Russia," in Robert C. Tucker, *The Soviet Political Mind: Stalinism and Post-Stalin Change,* rev. ed. (New York: W. W. Norton & Co., 1971), p. 122. Miliukov was a political leader in the late tsarist period who went into exile after the Bolshevik Revolution.

14. A study by political scientist Marc Morje Howard has shown that not only Russia, but all the postcommunist societies are low in levels of civic participation. Even controlling for other factors associated with involvement in public life, such as age, income, and education, citizens of the entire postcommunist sphere are far more disengaged than are their counterparts in other postauthoritarian societies, let alone established democracies.

Marc Morje Howard, *The Weakness of Civil Society in Post-Communist Europe* (Cambridge: Cambridge University Press, 2003).

15. Marc Howard finds that three factors in particular—distaste for the mobilized participation of the old regime, the continuing strength of family and friendship ties, and disappointment with the results of the regime change—are most closely associated with individuals' decisions about whether to join civic organizations, both in Russia and East Germany. Howard, *Weakness of Civil Society,* pp. 105–45.

16. Howard finds that (although more in East Germany than in Russia), "the vibrant private networks that developed under communism remain an impediment or an alternative to organizational membership today" (*Weakness of Civil Society,* p. 109). In Russia, more than in East Germany, the close ties among friends and family continue to help buffer people from the hardships of the transformation, so there has been less change to observe.

17. Richard Rose, William Mishler, and Neil Munro, *Russia Transformed: Developing Popular Support for a New Regime*

(Cambridge: Cambridge University Press, 2006), pp. 139, 114.

18. Putnam, *Bowling Alone,* p. 59.

19. Richard Rose, *Getting Things Done with Social Capital: New Russia Barometer VII,* paper no. 303, Studies in Public Policy (Glasgow, UK: Centre for the Study of Public Policy, University of Strathclyde, 1998), pp. 32–33.

20. Richard Rose, Neil Munro, and Stephen White, *The 1999 Duma Vote: A Floating Party System,* Studies in Public Policy no. 331 (Glasgow: Centre for the Study of Public Policy, University of Strathclyde, 2000), p. 16.

21. Ibid., p. 39.

22. Turnout levels in American presidential elections in the 1970s, 1980s, and 1990s averaged 52–54 percent. Turnout for congressional elections was much lower.

23. Rose, Mishler, and Munro, *Russia Transformed,* p. 134.

24. Rose and Munro, *Elections without Order,* p. 67.

25. VTsIOM survey findings, as reported on Polit.ru Web site, January 10, 2001.

26. From a survey in *Novoe vremia,* no. 34, 2001, as reported in RFE/RL Newsline, September 4, 2001.

27. VTsIOM survey findings, as reported on Polit.ru Web site, January 10, 2001.

28. A good study of the pervasive use of informal connections and means of exchange in the old Soviet system, see Alena V. Ledeneva, *Russia's Economy of Favours: Blat, Networking and Informal Exchange* (Cambridge: Cambridge University Press, 1998).

29. Rose and Munro, *Elections without Order,* p. 222. Results of NRB X, conducted in 2001.

30. See Stephen White's discussion of this process in *Gorbachev and After* (Cambridge: Cambridge University Press, 1991), pp. 27–29.

31. Friedgut, *Political Participation*; L. G. Churchward, "Public Participation in the USSR," in Everett M. Jacobs, ed., *Soviet Local Politics and Government* (London: Allen & Unwin, 1983), pp. 38–39; Jeffrey W. Hahn, *Soviet Grassroots: Citizen Participation in Local Soviet Government* (Princeton, NJ: Princeton University Press, 1988).

32. Remington, *Truth of Authority,* pp. 123–24.

33. On popular participation in local government, see Theodore H. Friedgut, *Political Participation in the USSR* (Princeton, NJ: Princeton University Press, 1979); and Jeffrey W. Hahn, *Soviet Grassroots.*

34. Wayne Di Franceisco and Zvi Gitelman, "Soviet Political Culture and 'Covert Participation' in Policy Implementation," *American Political Science Review* 78 (1984): 603–21. These forms of "participation," if that is the right term, included many kinds of parochial contacting (e.g., letters and visits to influential officials and organizations) as well as the use of networks of favor-trading and influence-peddling.

However, Donna Bahry and Brian D. Silver take issue with this view of Soviet citizen participation. In their article, "Soviet Citizen Participation on the Eve of Democratization," *American Political Science Review* 84 (1990): 821–48, they argue that there is a higher degree of continuity between Brezhnev-era mass participation and the explosive informal associational activity under Gorbachev than is commonly supposed. Analyzing data about attitudes toward and forms of citizen participation from the Soviet Interview Project (SIP), the large U.S. government-funded study of 3,000 emigres to the United States during the 1970s, they show that some of the same attitudes (higher than average levels of interpersonal trust and a sense of personal political efficacy) characterize both within-system and extrasystemic ("dissent") political activists under the Brezhnev regime, and that citizen participation can be differentiated according to the types of individuals and types of activities in which people were engaged. They therefore refute the proposition that citizen participation was largely "for show" and devoid of all interest or benefit for ordinary citizens.

35. A particularly vivid example of the fate of labor protest in the Soviet period occurred in 1962. Following a government decision to raise prices on meat and butter and to lower wages, workers at a large locomotive plant in the city of Novocherkassk went out on a wildcat strike. The government arrested the leaders of the strike. In protest, large numbers of people from the city demonstrated peacefully. Government troops fired on the demonstrators, killing 70 or 80 people. Some leaders of the protests were sentenced to death. The state media kept silent about the episode, but news of it spread throughout the country by word of mouth.

See Donald W. Treadgold and Herbert J. Ellison, *Twentieth Century Russia,* 9th ed. (Boulder, CO: Westview, 2000), p. 383.

36. On elections, see Victor Zaslavsky and Robert J. Brym, "The Functions of Elections in the USSR," *Soviet Studies* 30:3 (July 1978): 362–71.

37. On the Rodina Society, see John B. Dunlop, *The Faces of Contemporary Russian Nationalism* (Princeton, NJ: Princeton University Press, 1983), p. 38. See also the article, published posthumously, by the great Soviet journalist Anatolii Agranovskii, "Sokrashchenie apparata," *Izvestiia,* May 13, 1984, which discusses the bureaucratization of the Rodina and other nominally public organizations.

38. On the politics of the Church, see John Dunlop, "The Russian Orthodox Church as an 'Empire Saving' Institution," in Michael Bourdeaux, ed., *The Politics of Religion in Russia and the New States of Eurasia* (Armonk, NY: M.E. Sharpe, 1995), pp. 15–40; and Dimitry V. Pospielovsky, "The Russian Orthodox Church in the Postcommunist CIS," in ibid., pp. 41–74.

39. John H. Miller, "The Communist Party: Trends and Problems," in Archie Brown and Michael Kaser, eds., *Soviet Policy for the 1980s* (Bloomington: Indiana University Press, 1982), p. 2.

40. Soviet sociologists worked under severe political constraints, but were able to shed some light on how social communication and the formation of public opinion worked in fact. One major study found that despite the fact that the vast majority of the population watched Soviet television and read Soviet newspapers, half or more of the population still relied heavily on conversations with friends, family members, and coworkers for basic information and opinion. Until Gorbachev introduced glasnost, the relative lack of credibility of the mass media meant that people depended heavily on contacts with individuals whom they trusted for acquiring information and shaping opinion.

See Thomas Remington, "The Mass Media and Public Communication in the USSR," *Journal of Politics* 43:3 (August 1981): 804.

41. This point is extensively documented in Alena V. Ledeneva, *Russia's Economy of Favours,* p. 103 and passim.

42. James L. Gibson, "Social Networks, Civil Society, and the Prospects for Consolidating Russia's Democratic Transition," *American Journal of Political Science* 45:1 (January 2001): 51–68; Richard Rose and Neil Munro, *Elections without Order: Russia's Challenge to Vladimir Putin* (Cambridge: Cambridge University Press, 2002), pp. 223–24.

43. Rose and Munro, *Elections without Order,* p. 125.

44. Rose and Munro, *Elections without Order,* p. 227.

45. Howard, *Weakness of Civil Society,* p. 136.

46. A comprehensive chronicle of such movements is Ludmilla Alexeyeva, *Soviet Dissent: Contemporary Movements for National-Religious, and Human Rights* (Middletown, CT: Wesleyan University Press, 1987). See also Frederick C. Barghoorn, *Detente and the Democratic Movement in the USSR* (New York: Free Press, 1976).

47. Zbigniew Brzezinski, "Post-Communist Nationalism," *Foreign Affairs* (Winter 1989/90): 1–2. A comprehensive study of nationalist mobilization in the last years of the Soviet Union is Mark R. Beissinger, *Nationalist Mobilization and the Collapse of the Soviet State* (Cambridge: Cambridge University Press, 2002).

48. See Bohdan Harasymiw, *Political Elite Recruitment in the Soviet Union* (New York: St. Martin's Press, 1984).

49. In a similar vein, Stalin once supposedly commented that every republic of the Soviet Union had the right to secede from the union under the 1936 constitution. But, he added, no republic had the right to exercise that right.

50. Vladimir Brovkin, "Revolution from Below: Informal Political Associations in Russia, 1988–1989," *Soviet Studies* 42:2 (April 1990): 233–57; Judith B. Sedaitis and James Butterfield, eds., *Perestroika from Below: New Social Movements in the Soviet Union* (Boulder, CO: Westview, 1991).

51. Michael Urban, with Vyacheslav Igrunov and Sergei Mitrokhin, *The Rebirth of Politics in Russia* (Cambridge: Cambridge University Press, 1997), p. 115.

52. Brovkin, "Revolution from Below," 234.

53. Peter Rutland, "Labor Unrest and Movements in 1989 and 1990," in Ed A. Hewett and Victor H. Winston, eds., *Milestones in Glasnost and Perestroika: Politics and People* (Washington, DC: The Brookings Institution, 1991), p. 290.

54. Elizabeth Teague, "Soviet Workers Find a Voice," *Report on the USSR,* Radio Liberty 302/90, 13 July 1990, pp. 13–17.

55. On women's participation in postcommunist parliaments, see Richard E. Matland and Kathleen A. Montgomery, eds., *Women's Access to Political Power in Post-Communist Europe* (New York: Oxford University Press, 2003).

56. Gerhard Loewenberg, "The New Political Leadership of Central Europe: The Example of the New Hungarian National Assembly," in Thomas F. Remington, ed., *Parliaments in Transition: The New Legislative Politics in the Former USSR and Eastern Europe* (Boulder, CO: Westview, 1994), pp. 29–53.

57. V. Vyzhutovich, "Tsentrizbirkom prevrashchaetsiia v politicheskoe vedomstvo," [The Central Electoral Commission is Turning into a Political Agency] *Izvestiia,* May 4, 1994. While it is impossible to assess the validity of the researchers' charges, it is worth noting that the Central Electoral Commission (CEC) reported that the total number of voters on the registration rolls in December 1993 was lower by 1.14 million voters than the number in April 1993. The lower figure, of course, eased the task of declaring that a majority of voters had turned out for the election. How a million voters had vanished between April and December was not indicated. Moreover, the CEC refused to publish a full tally of election results by electoral district, confining itself only to publishing a list of winners. No independent verification of the CEC's own conclusions was thus possible.

See Vera Tolz and Julia Wishnevsky, "Election Queries Make Russians Doubt Democratic Process," *RFE/RL Research Report* 3:13 (1 April, 1994): 3.

58. Iu. Vedeneev and V. I. Lysenko, "Vybory-93: Uroki i al'ternativy," *Nezavisimaia gazeta,* June 28, 1994.

59. Note that the Duma elections in 1993, 1995, and 1999 were held in December—when days are shortest and the weather cold. The 1991 presidential election was held on June 12, and required only one round. The 1996 presidential election required two rounds because no candidate won an outright majority on the first round. These were held June 16 and July 3, respectively. The presidential election in 2000 did not require a second round because Vladimir Putin won an absolute majority of votes on the first round. It was held on March 26 rather than in June, because President Yeltsin's premature resignation forced new elections within three months of his resignation.

60. On the role of the media in the parliamentary elections of 1995 and 1999, see Sarah Oates, "Vying for Votes on a Crowded Campaign Trail," *Transition* (1996) 2: 26–29; and Sarah Oates, "The 1999 Russian Duma Elections," *Problems of Post-Communism* 47:3 (May/June 2000): 3–14.

61. Timothy J. Colton and Michael McFaul, *Popular Choice and Managed Democracy: The Russian Elections of 1999 and 2000* (Washington, DC: Brookings Institution, 2003), pp. 39–40.

62. Colton and McFaul, Popular Choice, pp. 42–43; Timothy J. Colton, *Transitional Citizens: Voters and What Influences Them in the New Russia* (Cambridge, MA: Harvard University Press, 2000).

63. One survey found that a majority of Russian citizens opposed dropping the "against all" option from Russian elections, and that over 30 percent of respondents had availed themselves of it at some point. RFE/RL Newsline, July 3, 10:121 (2006) at <http://www.rferl.org/newsline/>.

64. Rose, Mishler, and Munro, *Russia Transformed.*

65. Howard, *Weakness of Civil Society,* pp. 130–36.

66. Carles Boix, *Democracy and Redistribution* (Cambridge: Cambridge University Press, 2003).

67. Sidney Verba, Norman H. Nie, and Jae-on Kim, *Participation and Political Equality: A Seven-Nation Comparison* (Cambridge: Cambridge University Press, 1978); and Samuel H. Barnes and Max Kaase, eds., *Political Action: Mass Participation in Five Western Democracies* (Beverly Hills, CA: Sage, 1979).

68. Boris Golovachev, Larisa Kosova, and Liudmila Khakhulina, *<<Novaia>> rossiiskaia elita: starye igroki na novom pole? Segodnia,* February 14, 1996.

69. David Lane and Cameron Ross, *The Transition from Communism to Capitalism: Ruling Elites from Gorbachev to Yeltsin* (New York: St. Martin's Press, 1999).

70. Golovachev, Kosova, and Khakhulina, *<<Novaia>>. rossiiskaia elita.*

71. Olga V. Kryshtanovskaia, "Has-Beens: Trends of Downward Mobility of the Russian Elite," *Russian Social Science Review* 46:2 (2005): 4–51.

72. Eugene Huskey, "Nomenklatura Lite? The Cadres Reserve (*Kadrovyi reserv*) in Russian Public Administration," NCEEER Working Paper, October 24, 2003, Washington, DC: National Council for Eurasian and East European Research.

73. Olga Kryshtanovskaya and Stephen White, "Putin's Militocracy," *Post-Soviet Affairs* 19:4 (2003): 289–306.

74. Kryshtanovskaia, "Has-Beens," 47–50.

75. Sharon Werning Rivera, "Elites in Post-Communist Russia: A Changing of the Guard?" *Europe-Asia Studies* 52:3 (2000): 413–32.

76. Kirkow, *Russia's Provinces,* p. 172; Vadim Volkov, *Violent Entrepreneurs: The Use of Force in the Making of Russian Capitalism* (Ithaca, NY: Cornell University Press, 2002).

77. Igor M. Bunin, ed., *Biznesmeny Rossii: 40 istorii uspekha* (Moscow: OKO, 1994), p. 373.

78. Steven L. Solnick, *Stealing the State: Control and Collapse in Soviet Institutions* (Cambridge, MA: Harvard University Press, 1998), pp. 112–24.

79. Bunin, *Biznesmeny Rossii,* p. 386.

80. Bunin, *Biznesmeny Rossii*, p. 366.

81. Joel S. Hellman, Geraint Jones, and Daniel Kaufmann, *"Seize the State, Seize the Day": State Capture, Corruption, and Influence in Transition* (Washington, DC: World Bank Institute, 2000).

82. Balzer, "Managed Pluralism," 212–17.

83. A few examples: Dmitrii Medvedev, the first deputy prime minister, is chairman of the board of Russia natural gas monopoly, Gazprom; Igor Sechin, deputy chief of the presidential administration, is chairman of the state-owned oil firm, Rosneft; Vladislav Surkov, the president's chief political strategist and a deputy chief of the presidential administration, is chairman of the board of the state-owned firm, Transnefteprodukt, which manufactures oil pipeline equipment; Igor Shuvalov, an advisor to the president, is a member of the board of the state railroad monopoly; Viktor Ivanov, another advisor of the president, is on the board of the Russian airline, Aeroflot.

Chapter 5

Ideology and Political Culture

Contemporary Russian political culture has been shaped by the long and turbulent history of Russian statehood. The character of the state, and the values and beliefs of the populace, have been reforged repeatedly under the impact of war and revolution. The very identity of the state—whether Russia was to be a nation-state, an empire, a Communist republic, a crusade, or a democracy—has been bitterly contested and remains unsettled today. Many Russians believe that their country needs a national idea or spiritual calling to define its institutions and goals, which some still find in Communism and others in the country's Russian Orthodox religious heritage. Still others argue that there is no alternative to adopting the universal values of human rights, individual freedom, and the rule of law. Russia's citizens are deeply conscious of being part of a cultural tradition that is neither entirely Western nor Asian, but that has absorbed elements of a number of neighboring civilizations with which it has come into contact.[1]

Under President Putin, the authorities have begun to make a concerted effort to articulate a new post-Communist ideology for the Russian state. They are attempting to combine widely shared values and beliefs inherited from the Soviet and pre-Soviet past in Russian society with the strategic goals of the Putin regime in a new ideological synthesis that they hope will provide a new shared vision of Russia's future. The success of this effort remains uncertain, but the effort to build a new ideology as an instrument of rule clearly represents a point of continuity with the use of ideology by both the Soviet and tsarist rulers for maintaining unity within the state and between state and society. But whereas over time the actual attitudes and values of the Soviet population came to diverge ever farther from the formal doctrines of Marxism-Leninism, the new ideology that the Putin team is forging to define Russia's place in the world corresponds more closely to

119

Russia's contemporary political culture and therefore may find greater public acceptance.

Historically, Russia's political culture has been shaped by four factors: the state's geographic location, climate, and territorial expanse; the tradition of autocratic and patrimonial rule; the country's Orthodox Christian heritage; and, in the last two centuries especially, state-directed modernization. These elements of Russia's development as a political community have influenced the values and beliefs of the population as well as the mutual expectations between rulers and populace.

The Russian state became the largest state in the world in territorial terms by the end of the seventeenth century through the centralization of the rule of the Muscovite princes and the expansion of their dominion southward and eastward. Wars, both of defense and for conquest of new lands, strongly influenced the way the state structured its relations with the people. The challenge of ruling so large a domain with a relatively small population and an extremely meager foundation of productive economic resources always strained the resources of the state. As a result, historically the state was organized around the imperative of creating a capacity for extracting human and material resources from the populace.[2]

A distinctive feature of Russia's development has been that, much more than in other societies, patterns of human settlement have been planned. In their drive to acquire and assimilate new lands through territorial expansion, make the country's borders secure, and exploit its immense natural resource wealth, Russian and Soviet leaders built great cities in remote and inhospitable regions to exploit natural resources such as coal, oil, gas, gold, diamonds, and hydropower and to defend the country's territorial frontiers. But this pattern of planned spatial development has taken a huge toll on Russia's economy because of the necessity of overcoming the obstacles of cold temperatures and long distances. As Allen Lynch puts it, compared with other states in the world, Russia's geography makes both the costs of security and the costs of production high. In the Soviet period, when prices were set administratively and resources were allocated by the planning mechanism, leaders could act as though these costs were irrelevant. Of course, they were not irrelevant: ultimately, the tremendous cost of maintaining the system exceeded its capacity. Today, as Russia struggles to free itself of the legacy of the failed socialist experiment and to integrate itself into the international economy, it cannot ignore the costs geography imposes on social development and national security any longer.[3] But because of the huge investment already spent in the human, military, and economic assets it has inherited, the state is forced to play a much larger role in redistributing economic resources than it would in other economies.[4]

The political legacy of autocratic, patrimonial rule is also critical. By comparison with European states, Russia's state was more absolutist and centralized, and its society weaker in independent resources for self-expression and organization. Russia did not experience the Enlightenment; doctrines of civic and human rights penetrated Russian intellectual culture long after they had been absorbed in

Europe. As of the beginning of the twentieth century, four-fifths of Russia's population was still rural and illiterate. The growth of urban property-holding classes was very limited and late by comparison with Western Europe. The ideology of liberal democracy had a negligible following among Russians in the nineteenth century: much more widespread, particularly among workers and peasants, were radical doctrines of revolutionary socialism. The rise of revolutionary ideologies focusing on the overthrow of the state reflected the long heritage of "dual Russia." For many Russians, the state was an alien and intrusive power that conscripted their young men into the army, enforced the institution of serfdom, rendered arbitrary justice, and sent opponents into exile or hard labor.

For centuries, the tsars embodied the aspirations of state power and glory. Tsarism also provided a focal point for a patrimonial pattern of rule that pervaded Russian political culture. In patrimonialism, the ruler considers his domain to be his private property rather than a community with sovereign rights and interests. A patrimonial ruler is not accountable to his subjects, but treats them as a landowner treats an estate—neglecting it or developing it, as the case might be, but never conceiving it as autonomous of his rule. Some tsars sought to expand the state, others to rationalize their rule, but none until the twentieth century thought it necessary to grant the country a constitution. The bureaucracy was secretive, riddled with corruption, and averse to change. Neither in the tsarist era nor the Soviet period were there institutions providing for the control of the bureaucracy by elected representatives or by courts of law: state officials were accountable to their superiors and ultimately to the tsar, but not to the people.

In turn the tsar was considered to be subordinate only to God; the people—nobles and commoners alike—were expected to submit to the tsar's absolute authority. The tsar sought to maintain an equal distance from all his subjects, because all classes and estates were equally bound in service obligations to the state. There was no conception of a public sphere or nation outside the state until late in the history of the empire. The idea that a strong state required a strong civil society was largely alien to Russian political culture until the late 1980s and the 1990s. Even when the tsar finally granted a constitution, following the 1905 revolution, the state did not evolve into a constitutional monarchy. Soon afterward, the First World War, which imposed insuperable strains on Russia's capacity to mobilize and supply a huge army, overwhelmed tsarism in the revolutions of 1917. First the tsar abdicated and was replaced by a short-lived provisional government. A half year later that government was pushed aside by the Bolsheviks in the October revolution.

Besides patrimonialism, Russia's cultural heritage was also marked by the close identification between state and church. Tradition holds that Grand Prince Vladimir of the Kievan city-state called Rus' (officially regarded by Russian historians as the predecessor of the contemporary Russian state), was baptized into the Eastern Orthodox faith in 988. By choosing the Byzantine or Eastern branch of Christianity for the spiritual ideology of his rule, Vladimir linked Russia with the Byzantine empire for trade and political relations. The impact of Orthodoxy has been felt strongly in Russian political culture, much as Roman Catholicism and Protestant Christianity have shaped West European legal and political traditions. Orthodox Christianity is organized into national churches, which are regarded as the spiritual patrimony of particular national communities, and in worldly matters each national church practices accommodation to the state authorities. In religious doctrine Orthodoxy values faithfulness to changeless forms of worship and resists new practices or ideas. Its doctrine emphasizes the distance separating the kingdom of heaven from the sinful world.

Some scholars see elements of democratic values in the spiritual heritage of Orthodoxy. These include the church's traditional concern with social equality and community, as well as the ideal of an organic harmony—rather than separation or conflict—between civil and religious authorities. They believe that it is possible for Russia today to recover these elements and to incorporate them into a new and distinctive model of Russian democracy.[5] However, other scholars point out that Russia's history lacks a tradition of natural law or right, such as developed early in the Middle Ages in Europe and lent itself to the development of a doctrine of popular sovereignty. Instead, Russia's Orthodox thought reinforced the doctrine of unlimited power in the autocracy and undivided power in the state.[6] Certainly there is little in the Russian Orthodox tradition that could nurture political doctrines of liberal democracy.

Orthodoxy in Russia not only reinforced the values of collectivism and communal harmony and opposed the West's individualism and materialism. It also fostered a sense of a special mission for Russia. In the sixteenth century, some writers went so far as to proclaim Russia the "Third Rome," arguing that with the fall of the two previous seats of Christianity's political power, Rome and Constantinople, Moscow was now destined to become the source of the message that would bring salvation to the world. The great nineteenth-century writer, Fedor Dostoevsky, had a similar conception of Russia's destiny, and echoes of this idea reappeared in the messianic ideology of Russian Communism, which claimed to be a doctrine of universal force.

The fourth element of Russia's legacy that shapes contemporary political development is the recurring pattern of state-led modernization. Over and over in Russian history, technological and organizational changes designed to raise efficiency and productivity have been imposed on society by autocratic rulers, generally with highly uneven effects on society. Tsars such as Peter the Great and Catherine the Great had pressed for adopting some features of European industrial technology to increase Russia's productivity and competitiveness in the competitive international environment. The late nineteenth century saw an intense spurt of industrialization. By the beginning of World War I, Russia was one of the world's leading producers of steel, oil, cotton, and other goods, and its railroad network was second only to that of the United States in total length.[7] But modernization affected different regions and strata differently, exacerbating inequality in living standards and widening the gap in values and beliefs between social elites and the mass of the population.

For their part, the founders of the Soviet regime saw socialism as a form of modernity, and worked to transform society by creating an urbanized industrial economy, a comprehensive educational system, and a powerful scientific-technical infrastructure. They suppressed cultural traditions in many parts of the country that were antithetical to modern values, such as the veiling of women in Central Asia, and imposed the Soviet model of modernity.[8] They regarded modernization as critical to state building: a state that could accomplish its long-term goals, defeat its enemies on the battlefield and its ideological rivals in the Cold War required, Soviet leaders believed, a dynamic industrial economy. However, the Soviet model for industrial development had exhausted its capacity for further growth by the early 1980s. Factor productivity was declining, and the economy lacked the human and material resources needed to keep expanding investment. To a large degree, the economy was locked into a model of modernization that was increasingly obsolete.

This inheritance of stalled development in turn has shaped Putin's agenda. He has identified as his top priority the reinvigoration of Russian economic growth in order to make Russia a powerful and respected state in the world and to raise the living standards of its populace. Yet, like Russian rulers before him, he has looked for ways to adopt modern institutions without allowing them to threaten the state's control over society.

These forces—geography, patrimonialism, Orthodoxy, and modernization—continue to shape Russian political culture. Although contemporary Russians are deeply conscious of their distinctive political heritage, they differ over what this legacy means for the future. We saw in the last chapter that the mistrust and alienation separating ordinary Russians from the state continue to be felt, but that Russians also value the democratic freedoms that have been won since the end of the Communist regime. In this chapter we will explore some attitudes and values that underpin this contradictory pattern of democratic aspirations and deep skepticism among Russians about the quality of government they expect from the state. We will look at some enduring features of Russian political culture as well as ask what long-term and short-term forces are affecting it. And we will ask how political values and beliefs differ across social groups, by age, education, gender, and ethnicity. Before we look at Russia's political culture more closely, however, let us ask what we mean by political culture and why we study it.

THE CONCEPT OF POLITICAL CULTURE

Political scientists define political culture as the distribution of people's values, beliefs, and feelings about politics in a particular society. Values are views about what is right or wrong, good or bad. Beliefs are conceptions of the state of the world. Emotions include pride, shame, desire, anger, or resentment felt toward objects in the political environment. A political culture is the totality of the values, beliefs, and emotions of the members of a society expressed about the political regime and about their own place in it.[9]

The subject of political culture has been the source of lively controversy in political science and in the study of Russia and the Soviet Union.[10] A major point of contention is how political culture is related to the structures and institutions of a political system. Political culture is never static, but culture tends to change gradually and incrementally, whereas political regimes sometimes undergo drastic and discontinuous changes. Therefore, if political culture *directly* determined how a national political system operates, we could not explain some of the startling transformations in regimes that we have observed in our time. Some countries formerly considered to have deeply conservative, authoritarian political cultures have succeeded in sustaining viable and successful democratic polities after a major constitutional transition. Other countries considered to have had democratic political cultures have experienced spells of authoritarian rule. Clearly there can be no simple causal path leading from the distribution of values and beliefs in a society to its form of government at any given point in time. Likewise we should not expect that any particular set of political and social institutions will transform the nature of a country's political culture. If so, we could not explain why so many regimes that have poured resources into shaping their populace's hearts and minds have had so little to show for their effort. Political culture may be malleable, but only up to a point. A country's institutions and its political culture interact and shape one another over time. Where institutions and culture stand in mutually reinforcing equilibrium, we expect change to occur without major ruptures. But in cases in which institutions and culture are not congruent, the chances are stronger that there will be abrupt, discontinuous changes in the political regime.

Differences across countries in the composition of political cultures are stable over time, but certainly not static. "Culture," political scientist Ronald Inglehart writes, "is not a constant. It is a system through which a society adapts to its environment: Given a changing environment, in the long run it is likely to change."[11] He provides evidence that the political culture of a country does influence its political and economic performance. In turn, the country's performance has a feedback effect on its political culture. For instance, where democracy is successful, its operation is likely to reinforce people's belief that democracy works better than the alternatives. A country may remain stuck in an equilibrium between poor-quality government and its population's low expectations of government for long periods of time because people have no faith that a different regime could work any better.

Still, political cultures can evolve, sometimes changing in significant ways. The succession of generations can bring about deep and lasting changes in the values and beliefs of a society. People in their late teens and early twenties are especially susceptible to formative influences in their political and economic environment. At that age, people often come to adhere to orientations that continue to shape their outlook on politics and society for the rest of their lives. We shall see evidence of this phenomenon in Russia.

Political scientists believe that a country's political culture affects the development of its political system through both direct and indirect pathways. The direct path is through the influence of people's values and beliefs on their political behavior, including their voting choices at election time. The second is the indirect influence of people's everyday habits, expectations, and values on their relations with the political environment. As we saw in the last chapter, to the extent that people are able to sustain ties of mutual trust and cooperation in settings outside their immediate circles of family and friends, they are much likelier to be able to solve collective dilemmas, such as how to keep government honest, fair, and responsive. The direct and indirect routes by which political culture affects political life therefore parallel the kinds of political participation discussed in the last chapter: direct participation that takes place in the political sphere, such as voting and campaigning, and people's involvement in public life more generally.

The *direct* influence of political culture on the political system by means of voting can be compared to the relationship between consumers and producers in a market economy. In the abstract, consumer demand is supposed to guide the decisions of producers to offer the desired mixture of goods and services at competitive prices. But in the real world, individual consumers have little actual control over the economy because information about what consumers want and need may be hidden to producers and because consumers' knowledge about the quality and availability of what producers offer is never perfect. In a perfect market economy, consumers in the aggregate are sovereign, but no one consumer has much influence over what is produced or the price at which goods are sold. Matching demand and supply is a complex process that in the long run tends to yield an equilibrium between price and quantity. But at any one moment, there is likely to be a gap between what people want and what the economy provides.

The analogy between economic demand and supply and the relationship between political culture and political institutions is useful up to a point. A democracy usually will do a better job of matching what people demand and what politicians provide them than would a dictatorship, just as a market economy usually matches demand and supply for goods more efficiently than would a centrally planned economy. In a democracy, the distribution of people's preferences will influence the way parties and candidates compete for votes. Over time, as people's values and expectations change, leaders offer new policies that match the shifts in voter demand, moving the demand for and supply of policies toward equilibrium.

But, just as there are many obstacles to the smooth matching of demand and supply in real-world economies, political systems likewise may suffer from a gap between the policies and institutions that people want and those that the political leaders offer them. In some societies, people give up expecting that government will supply them with honest, fair, and efficient administration; effective public order; or simple justice in the courts. The few brave souls who try to fight for an improvement may quit in frustration when they fail to stir up their discouraged fellow citizens to join them in the cause. Observing the low demand for good government, rulers do not supply it, and instead treat the state as a source of private plunder. Such situations can also become stable and last for long periods of time. In extreme cases, central government disappears altogether, and is replaced by warlords or criminal rackets.

Although the influence of political values and beliefs on voting and other kinds of political action is important in guiding political elites about what sorts of promises to make at election time, the indirect path by which political culture influences the political system probably is still more important. Through their daily interactions, members of a society shape one another's values and expectations, including their expectations about government. The patterns of behavior that influence how government operates are established through these channels of association, many of them entirely outside the government sphere. In political cultures in which individuals harbor mistrust for one another, they fear that combining for the common good is a sucker's game: reasoning that others will take advantage of them if they do not look out for themselves, they avoid committing themselves to any collective effort for which the cost is known and immediate, and the payoff distant and uncertain—and dependent on the collective effort. Because good government requires collective effort on the part of citizens to keep officials honest, responsive, and effective, societies pervaded by norms of mistrust for those outside the immediate circles of family and friends are likely to be poorly governed. When people discount the common interest in favor of private benefit, government is likelier to be both more oppressive and more corrupt. Therefore, in studying political culture, we need to look both at people's values and beliefs about government and their expectations about social life more generally.

RUSSIAN POLITICAL CULTURE IN THE POST-SOVIET PERIOD

A good deal of public opinion research has been devoted to analyzing the dynamics of Russian political culture. On some points, the findings of a large number of recent opinion studies converge. Surveyers have found that there is a high level of support for principles associated with liberal democracy, including support for the values of political liberty and individual rights, rights of opposition and dissent, independence of the communications media, and competitive elections.[12] In a 2005 survey, 66 percent of Russians agreed that "Russia needs democracy," but 45 percent said that the kind of democracy Russia needs is "a completely special kind corresponding to Russian specifics."[13] At the same time, 50 percent of the public regard Stalin as a positive figure in Russian history; only 36 percent assess him negatively.[14] Russians rate the Soviet regime before perestroika positively as a time of relative security and prosperity, but reject the notion of bringing back Communism. Nearly half of the population (48 percent) agrees with the statement that it would have been better if perestroika had never been attempted, but 40 percent disagree.[15] Over 70 percent of Russians regret the breakup of the Soviet Union, but 72 percent say that restoring it is neither possible nor necessary.[16] Over 85 percent regarded freedom of speech, the media, and conscience to be important to them.[17] A majority believe that Russia can have both democracy and a strong state.[18]

Political scientist James Gibson sums up the findings of a number of studies by drawing three conclusions: there is rather extensive support in Russia for democratic institutions and processes so long as people see these as rights for themselves; there is much less support for extending rights to unpopular minorities; and the segments of the population who are the most exposed to the influences of modern civilization (younger people, better-educated people, and residents of big cities) are also those most likely to support democratic values. This would suggest that as Russia becomes more open to the outside world, support for democratic values will grow.[19]

The rather high levels of support found for basic democratic principles such as religious liberty, freedom of speech, competitive elections, and other rights challenge an impression that was widely held in the West, that Russian political culture was authoritarian after decades of Soviet indoctrination and hundreds of years of tsarist autocracy.[20] Certainly Soviet propaganda reinforced some older values, such as the enormous emphasis placed on state power, the expectation that the state would provide for the material well-being of its citizens, the patrimonial conception of power, and the priority of collective over individual needs. Consequently, it is not surprising to find a rather high degree of continuity in the level of support for values concerning the state's responsibility for ensuring society's prosperity and for providing individuals with material security.[21] More than in Western Europe or the United States, Russians continue to believe that the state is responsible for providing a just moral and social order, with justice being understood as social equality more than as equality before the law.[22] This pattern reflects the impact of traditional conceptions of state and society in Russian political culture. Older patterns of collectivism and statism in Russian political culture remain prevalent. A number of surveys find that there is broad support for the idea that the state has a responsibility for maintaining basic equality, cohesion, and security for members of society, while guaranteeing economic and political freedom to individuals to the extent consistent with society's well-being. For example, faced with a hypothetical choice between democratic freedoms and a guaranteed income, Russians are closely divided[23] (see Table 5.1).

Surveys consistently find that the patterns of values differ significantly across generations and between social groups. Elites and the mass public differ; younger differ from older generations; men differ from women in their political outlooks; urban from rural residents; and the more educated differ from the less educated. People in elite positions and those who participate more in the culture of the modern world are significantly more likely to resemble people in Europe, North America, and other advanced industrial democracies in their values and beliefs.[24]

The strength of support for democratic values among the general public raises some obvious questions. For one, if most Russians express a belief in democratic values, why do they support President Putin and his authoritarian policies? For another, where did support for democracy come from if the old regime suppressed all ideologies except Marxism-Leninism? We will take up the second question in the

Table 5.1 ■ **Democratic Freedoms vs. Guaranteed Income**

Question: "Are you agreed with the following opinion: If state guarantees to me a normal wage and decent pension, I am prepared to give up freedom of speech and the right to travel freely abroad."

Agree	26%
More agree than disagree	17%
More disagree than agree	23%
Disagree	25%

Source: Yuri Levada, "Svoboda ot vybora? Postclektoralnye razmyshleniia," www.polit.ru, May 18, 2004.

next section. For now, let us consider why Russians might support both Putin and democracy.

Putin has adroitly identified himself with Russians' democratic aspirations by consistently voicing his own faith in its principles while emphasizing the idea that Russia must create its own form of democracy rather than mechanically adopting Western models. This is the implication of the phrase that he and his aides often use to describe their vision for Russia: "sovereign democracy." Putin's aide Vladislav Surkov is in charge of formulating and popularizing this concept. Surkov claims that Russian society was not ready for democracy when the Soviet regime fell. As a result, a handful of corrupt oligarchs were able to enrich themselves at the expense of the state. The state must restore its sovereignty at home (where it has to reclaim power from the oligarchs) and abroad (where it has to fight against the dominance of the United States), he argues. Then Russia can build its own form of democracy—part of the community of nations in the world but not dependent on any of them. Thus the state must take the lead in reconstructing a strong and self-aware middle class, a competent and honest bureaucracy, an effective military, and a productive, flourishing economy. And for that to happen, Surkov argues, the United Russia Party should rule the country for 15 or 20 years, much as the PRI ruled Mexico for decades and the LDP ruled Japan.[25]

Surkov's belief that the state needs to create the social foundation for its own future echoes an older historical pattern of state-led modernization in Russia. A widespread tacit acceptance of this idea also may help explain why many Russians associate Putin with democracy. Over half of the population (55 percent) thought that following Putin's reelection as president in 2004 the country would develop as a democracy; the comparable figure in 2000 was only 35 percent. A majority of Russians in 2004 thought that of all the candidates running for president, Putin was best suited to handling issues such as foreign policy, the Chechen war, crime, and corruption—and democracy.[26] The faith in Putin's competence, in short, helps drive the view that Putin is creating a state that is both democratic and sovereign.

SOVIET POLITICAL SOCIALIZATION

To understand how contemporary Russian values and beliefs are shaped, let us briefly review the old regime's system of political socialization. The Soviet regime was remarkable for the effort it made to inculcate knowledge of and commitment to regime doctrine among the population. The system of formal political socialization embraced virtually every setting of education and communication in society—from schools and youth activity, to the mass media, the arts and popular culture, and to collective activity in the workplace, place of residence, and avocational groups. As much as possible, influences that contradicted Marxist-Leninist doctrine were suppressed, while the rhetoric of public life constantly reaffirmed the doctrine of the leading role of the Communist Party, the superiority of socialism, devotion to the Soviet fatherland, and the correctness of the party's general policies at home and abroad. Because of the importance the regime assigned to the means of mass communications as agencies of political socialization and of mass mobilization, it saturated Soviet society with multiple channels of print and broadcast communications.[27]

The doctrine that guided political socialization—Marxism-Leninism—was based on the ideas of Karl Marx and Friedrich Engels as interpreted and applied by Vladimir Lenin and by the Soviet Communist Party's leaders. Each new leadership that came to power reinterpreted Marxist-Leninist ideas to serve its policy interests, often discarding concepts promulgated by the preceding leaders. The doctrine was flexible (although not on core issues, such as the idea that capitalism was incompatible with socialism) and was regularly revised to justify the current preferences and decisions of the party leadership. Ideological doctrine and political authority were always closely linked, because power and ideology legitimated one another. Ideology was a source of strength for the Soviet state so long as there was no serious challenge to it. But the state's reliance on ideology also produced rigidity and dogmatism. The close control over communications stifled innovation and serious discussion of the trends affecting society. The rulers became blind to the real state of the system and wedded to an increasingly obsolete model of rule.

The party's demand for political loyalty meant that no alternative political ideologies could be propagated publicly. Soviet leaders acknowledged that the two great ideological alternatives in the world, socialism and capitalism, might be able to coexist, and even cooperate, at the level of diplomacy, trade, and cultural and scientific contacts, but that at the fundamental level of ideas, the two ideologies were ultimately incompatible and that in the end socialism would triumph over capitalism because of its intrinsic superiority. Soviet leaders, especially the more conservative of them, were always hostile to any notion that the struggle between the world system of capitalism and the world system of socialism could or should be ended in favor of a convergence of ideologies. They often quoted Lenin to the effect that any weakening of socialist ideology would inevitably lead to a strengthening of bourgeois ideology. The state's propaganda system thus had a twofold purpose: to persuade Soviet people of the correctness of party doctrine, and to prevent hostile ideologies from winning adherents.

The elaborate machinery for propagating and defending ideology included the following features:

1. Family. Efforts to persuade parents to make the family an instrument for raising children steeped in Communist morality, firm faith in the party and its leadership, a positive attitude toward labor, confidence in the socialist future, and intolerance toward hostile worldviews, such as religion. But, because the family was the least amenable to control by the party authorities, and because it tended to protect value systems at odds with the official ideology, the family was the most important agency of transmission of liberal democratic values, national awareness, and religious faith.

2. School. Schooling contributed to political socialization both through the curriculum, in which lessons in history, social studies, literature, and other subjects were used to reinforce political doctrines, and through a system of youth groups that organized schooltime and after-school activities.

3. Youth groups. The regime maintained a set of organized youth leagues for different age categories that combined political indoctrination with organized activities such as field trips, hobby clubs, service activities, summer camps, and study circles. The system of organized youth activities was divided into three age-specific groups: Octobrists, for 7- to 9-year-olds; Pioneers, for 9- to 14-year-olds; and Komsomol (the acronym for the Communist Youth League), for 14- to 28-year-olds. Each combined play, recreation, and basic socialization with political indoctrination appropriate to the age level. Many youths who remained active in Komsomol into their twenties were admitted directly to the Communist Party from Komsomol on the strength of their good records as Komsomol members.

4. The mass media. Officially the broadcast and print media were to serve as instruments of political socialization in addition to their roles as conduits of needed information, exhortation to work hard and well, criticism of problems, and some feedback from the public through letters. They were thus called on to mold the consciousness of the population while at the same time combating the system's inefficiencies. All mass media organizations were under the ideological authority of the party through its department of propaganda and similar departments charged with ideological oversight in every lower party committee.

5. Adult political education. The party oversaw a system of workplace talks and political study groups for various categories of the population—workers, managers, political executives, and so on. Party-run schools gave local party staff members up-to-date instruction on current party doctrine and policy and even gave graduate degrees in such topics as the theory of scientific communism.

Despite its immense scope, the Soviet political socialization machine never possessed, or even claimed, full control over all possible influences on citizens. Even in the darkest years of Stalinist tyranny, a sphere of private life survived, formed through powerful family and friendship links. So too did something of the legacy of Russian and Western humanism through the great classic works of prerevolutionary literature and art, which generations of Soviet schoolchildren were taught to know and respect. Throughout the Soviet Union, intellectuals, artists, and teachers preserved over a hundred different cultural legacies and national languages. The imperative of providing the Soviet regime with a powerful scientific and technological capability required the regime to accept a certain level of openness to outside influences: scientific and cultural exchanges of people and ideas, though closely monitored and directed, nonetheless kept open channels through which the diverse influences of the world society filtered in and out of the Soviet Union. As the regime's own ideological machinery grew increasingly ossified and ineffectual in the 1970s and 1980s, these internal and external cultural influences assumed an ever greater importance in shaping Soviet political culture and public opinion.

A second point to remember is that the discrepancy between the beliefs and values that the regime preached, and the actual behavior of officials and citizens, tended to weaken the credibility of regime propaganda. Nearly universal was the understanding that, in public, certain forms and observances needed to be respected: certain ritualistic words needed to be uttered and gestures made—one was to quote Lenin in a speech, article, or book. The vote taken at a meeting was to be unanimous; one would dutifully go to the polls to cast a ballot or attend a ceremony celebrating some official event. But these forms and observances had little bearing on one's ordinary, everyday life, both for officials and for citizens. They provided a certain stability and predictability in the forms of social interaction, which might have been comforting to people who had undergone the horrors of revolution, war, and terror in previous decades. These rituals and ceremonies also gave the authorities a convenient way to see whether anyone was bold enough to deviate from the accepted patterns. But few actually believed in the conventional doctrines and principles that were constantly echoed throughout the public domain. The actual rules governing behavior were quite different, and diverged strongly among different groups of the population. Younger generations might be attracted to Western popular culture, while the thinning ranks of the older generation still wept each year at the ceremonies commemorating the Soviet victory in the Second World War. In Central Asia, traditional clan ties came to determine the real distribution of power and status, whereas in the Baltic states, citizens of all strata cherished the dream that they would once again regain national independence. Behind the ritual obeisances to Marxist-Leninist dogmas, Soviet political culture was extremely diverse. This diversity has contributed to the very different trajectories that individual republics have followed since the breakup of the union. Thus the incompleteness and weakening of the political socialization effort, combined with the sharp divergence between what was preached and what was practiced, meant that actual Soviet political culture was being shaped by a variety of homegrown and international influences.

Thus while the state expended substantial effort in the 1960s and 1970s to inculcate its increasingly hollow Marxist-Leninist doctrine, intellectuals in the arts, the sciences, the professions, and even in policy institutes of the party and state were coming to abandon many tenets of Soviet ideology. Elements of social democratic and liberal democratic thought, ethnic nationalism, and a kind of pan-human internationalism gained strength. Some thinkers explicitly rejected Soviet doctrine and clandestinely shared with friends their writings or those of other authors whose writings had been suppressed.[28] Others tempered their dissent and stayed inside the system, while discussing their heterodox views in the intimate company of colleagues and friends.

By the time Gorbachev came to power, many intellectuals, including some in senior positions, were privately convinced that the old theory of an international "class struggle" between rival socialist and capitalist camps was leading the Soviet Union into a developmental dead end. The only way for the country to regain its economic and political strength was to adopt universal values of human rights and freedoms and to join in finding solutions to the challenges facing mankind as a whole. As Robert English has argued, this was a shift in the very conception of Russian national identity. Instead of seeing Russia as being defined by an ideological confrontation with the West, or even arguing that Russia must *cooperate* with the West, an influential body of intellectuals came to believe that Russia must become *part* of the liberal international community.[29] The philosophical ground was thus prepared for the leadership of Mikhail Gorbachev, who, remarkably, proved willing to embrace the radical new thinking that transformed Russia and the world.[30]

Why did the party persist in keeping its program of mass political indoctrination going despite the fact that its efforts were so unsuccessful? Various reasons have been proposed. One is inertia. The section of the party concerned with ideological propaganda and control justified its existence by ever greater quantitative displays of success, increasing the number of people reached and activists recruited. Another is fear. The leadership behaved as though it genuinely believed its claim that any weakening of socialist ideology must necessarily lead to a rise of hostile counterideologies. However ineffective the party's ideological effort may have been, it helped to combat the spread of ideas and values opposed to Marxism-Leninism. Ultimately, the reason ideological control over society was so important to the party was that it prevented the formation of opposition movements espousing alternative ideologies. In any event, no Soviet leader until Gorbachev was willing to relinquish the party's monopoly on ideology, and even Gorbachev, when he first came to office, used the traditional powers of the general secretary to reprogram and redirect party propaganda, rather than to dismantle the system itself.

At first, Gorbachev's attempt to reform the Soviet economy and to introduce an element of freer debate under the slogan of "glasnost" (openness) hardly affected either the forms or content of "Communist upbringing." But gradually, the glasnost campaign gained momentum.[31] Eventually it produced a significant feedback effect on the party's socialization program itself by revealing to people how widespread was the rejection of Marxism-Leninism. A poll of nearly 2,700 people throughout the Soviet Union in December 1989 found that 48 percent considered themselves religious believers, but only 6 percent thought that Marxism-Leninism had the answers to the country's problems.[32] Another countrywide survey in 1989 found that 61 percent of the respondents supported the principle of legalizing private property and only 11 percent opposed it.[33] Throughout 1989 and 1990 there were many other indications of the power and speed of popular rejection of Communist ideology. Close to two million members—one-tenth of the membership—quit the Communist Party before Yeltsin banned it in September 1991. A radical reform wing of the Communist Party itself threatened to break away from the party and form an alternative party.

At the same time, the policy positions taken by Gorbachev and the party leadership grew progressively more unorthodox, until by 1990 almost nothing of the old Marxist-Leninist doctrine remained. The theory of the international class struggle between capitalism and socialism was gone; the party's leading role had been abandoned in favor of support for multiparty competition and parliamentary politics; and Gorbachev called his domestic program a transition to a "social market economy." In a 1990 document adopted as a basis for economic policy, Gorbachev himself declared that "there is no alternative to switching to a market. All world experience has shown the viability and effectiveness of the market economy."[34] This was an admission that Marxism-Leninism had failed. The doctrine had been abandoned in all essential points by the Communist Party, and the party itself had lost its power to rule the country's ideological life. Both among the leadership and among the populace, only a small minority remained willing to defend Communist ideology. Both democratic and antidemocratic ideologies, however, arose to take its place.

SUPPORT FOR DEMOCRATIC VALUES

As soon as survey researchers were able to start conducting objective, scientifically structured opinion surveys in Russia, beginning in 1989–1990, they reported surprisingly high levels of support for democratic rights. For instance, in 1990, James Gibson and a team of American and Soviet researchers conducted a survey of 504 residents of the Moscow *oblast*—that is, the region around the city of Moscow—to determine support for important values associated with liberal democracy. They found strong support for liberal values. For instance, on such issues as whether freedom of speech should always be respected, they found that Soviet respondents held roughly the same views as citizens of West European countries (77 percent in agreement for the Moscow province population, 78 percent for the West Europeans). On a series of items, measured by the percentage agreeing that a particular right ought always to be respected, Soviet citizens were extraordinarily similar to West Europeans.

In addition, Gibson et al. found that education was positively associated with rights consciousness, much as age (and being female) were negatively correlated with it; these were the only significantly associated variables they established from analysis of demographic factors. The impact of education was particularly strong: on average, the higher a person's educational level, the more likely he or she was to endorse the principle of individual political rights. By the same token, the older a person was, all else being equal, the weaker the support for individual rights. And women were on the whole slightly less supportive of individual rights than were men, even after controlling for the effects of education and age.

Gibson's group extended the survey to the entire Western portion of the USSR in May 1990 and found remarkably similar responses—that is, extremely high levels of support for liberal values with the single exception of the freedom of association: fewer than half of the respondents agreed that the right must be respected always, and around 40 percent believed that it depends on circumstances.[35] Once again, age and education were significantly correlated with rights consciousness, education positively, age negatively.

On the other hand, Russians quickly lost faith in the new democratic institutions that were being constructed. Surveys over the past few years conducted have asked a battery of questions about how much Russians trusted various institutions to look after their interests. Consistently, Russians report much higher levels of confidence in nonelected institutions such as the Russian Orthodox Church and the army than in elective institutions. They also report high levels of faith in President Putin. Table 5.2 reports the results of a 2004 survey:[36]

Table 5.2 ■ Trust in Institutions, 2004

"To what degree, in your view, does each of the following merit confidence?"

	Percentage responding "fully merits confidence"
President of Russia	56
Church, religious organizations	43
Army	30
Press, radio, TV	26
Security organs	21
Regional (krai, oblast, republican) organs of power	19
Local (city, district) organs of power	19
Government of Russia	17
Courts	14
Procuracy	12
Federation Council	12
State Duma	11
Trade unions	11
Police	10
Political parties	5

Note: Survey conducted September 2004. N = 2,107. Margin of error 3%.

The results suggest that confidence in Putin's leadership far outstrips confidence in other institutions, even the army. The gap between Putin's rating and that of other elective institutions is striking.

Since he has come into power, Putin's approval ratings have consistently remained between 70 and 80 percent, higher by far than any other leader or institution.[37] As of late 2006, the number of Russians who approved of the activity of Putin was 81 percent (and only 18 percent disapproved), whereas the government's approval was only 40 percent (with 57 percent disapproving).[38] Putin is given credit mainly for reversing the deterioration of living standards (24 percent of the population cite this as his main achievement).[39] Half the population, polled after the presidential election in 2004, said their expectations for Putin had been justified.

These figures show how successful Putin has been at taking credit for positive developments in the country and allowing the government to catch the blame for continuing problems. Not surprisingly, Putin's popularity leads Russians to want to give him sweeping power over the political system. After the March 2004 presidential election, a nationwide survey found that 68 percent agreed with the statement that concentrating nearly all state power in Putin's hands "would be beneficial to Russia." 54% believed that the best system would be one in which the government "is fully subordinate to the president and his administration."[40]

Although most Russians welcome President Putin's success in strengthening the state, few believe that their own influence as individual citizens has grown stronger, as the results of a survey conducted in December 2003 show:[41]

Overall, Richard Rose and his collaborators conclude that Russia today reflects "resigned acceptance of an incomplete democracy," that is, their approval of the regime under Putin is relative. They tend to approve of the current political

Table 5.3 ■ Assessments of Changes in Political System since 1994 (in %)

Question: Ten years ago the first elections to the State Duma of "post-Soviet" Russia were held. In your opinion, in the last ten years has the political system of Russia:

Grown stronger	32
Grown weaker	26
Remained unchanged	28
Hard to say	14

In your opinion, in the last ten years, has the influence of ordinary citizens on the actions of the authorities:

Increased	13
Decreased	36
Remained unchanged	42
Hard to say	9

system, and majorities reject alternatives (such as restoring Communism, suspending parliament, installing a harsh dictatorship, or army rule). They see little chance of significant change in the regime, and they credit Putin with improving economic conditions in the country. Their support for the current regime is thus contingent on their judgment as to what has been achieved compared with what is possible. They are highly critical of the corruption and ineffectiveness in the state, but believe themselves to have little ability to make a difference—in part because of the widespread mistrust of parties and parliament as institutions affording ordinary people any real influence. Thus they may regard the current regime as less than ideal, but far better than many alternatives that are available.[42]

INFLUENCES ON RUSSIAN POLITICAL CULTURE IN THE SOVIET PERIOD

Both long-term and short-term forces act on Russian political culture. Modernization, including the rise in individual educational opportunities, geographical and career mobility, and economic productivity, has had a significant impact on political culture in Russia over time. Indeed, one major reason that the Soviet regime collapsed was its inability to meet the demands posed by a society that was far more educated and informed than had been the case when the Bolsheviks took power in 1917—thanks to the enormous efforts by the Soviet regime to educate and inform the populace. By the end of the 1980s, over 60 percent of the Soviet population over 15 years of age had attained at least a complete secondary education, and over 10 percent had higher educational degrees.[43] As many studies showed, education had the effect of reinforcing more critical and more demanding outlooks on the part of Soviet citizens.[44] Education, moreover, is closely linked to support for democratic principles: the more highly educated, the more likely an individual is to support values and principles associated with liberal democracy.[45] Consequently, over time, as Russian society comprised more and more people with secondary and higher educational degrees, levels of support for democratic principles grew.

The opening of career and geographic mobility (and particularly the industrialization drive) by the Soviet regime led rapidly to the urbanization of society. Even though old village mentalities and habits retreated only slowly, Russian society became predominantly urban in a relatively short span of time. By the late 1970s, more than two-thirds of the Russian population lived in cities; as of 2005, 73 percent of the population of Russia was classified as urban. But as recently as the late 1950s, the society was half urban, half rural. From 1950 to 1980 the urban population of the Soviet Union increased by nearly 100 million people—most of them immigrants from the countryside. Urbanization was in many respects driven by the imperatives of Soviet industrialization and many Soviet cities are little more than glorified dormitories serving major industrial enterprises. Yet urban life fostered new forms of interchange among people, new social identities, and, ultimately, new aspirations and expectations of government.

Generational Change

The effects of rising educational levels and of urbanization have been particularly important because each new generation of Soviet and Russian citizens has been more educated and urbanized than that of its parents. Political scientist Donna Bahry has compared surveys taken at different times to see how public opinion has evolved, and found that the single largest factor in the gradual change in political culture was the *turnover of political generations.*[46] The generation gap widened substantially by the time of the Brezhnev-era and Gorbachev-era studies. Those of the older generation might be critical of some features of the Soviet system, such as collectivized agriculture, but were more inclined to accept some of the political and economic values associated with state socialism. Not so the younger generations, which were significantly more critical of living conditions in the society and sympathetic to the loosening of political and economic controls. Thus, not age (and hence life-cycle effects), but generation, Bahry finds, affects the shift in public opinion: "Those born after World War II, and especially after 1950, had fundamentally different values from their elders."[47]

Generational change continues. Those who are in their twenties today were born in a period of intense turmoil as the old regime collapsed, opening unprecedented opportunities for individual freedom and prosperity, but at the same time producing widespread disillusionment, even cynicism, with the actual results of the regime transition. As expectations for rapid improvement in social conditions as a result of the regime change were disappointed, nationalism and xenophobia found a sympathetic following among many youth who embraced a simple division of the world into "us" and "them."[48] Many more simply reject all ideologies and focus instead on getting rich or getting by. Those who are in their twenties today have little memory of the Soviet period, but were strongly marked by the breakdown of Soviet ideological controls in the 1980s and the explosive growth in criminality, corruption, inequality, and materialism that followed.

The Putin administration has been extremely sensitive to the danger of an uncontrollable youth movement that might be politically mobilized against the authorities, as occurred in Serbia, Georgia, and Ukraine's "colored revolutions" (see Close-Up 7, Chapter 9, "The Orange Revolution") when mass movements— sparked by youth groups—brought down corrupt, authoritarian leaders who attempted to rig the results of elections. To prevent a "colored revolution" from breaking out in Russia, Putin's associates have formed their own youth movements (recruiting members, for example, from soccer fan clubs) devoted to patriotic and nationalist themes. These pro-Putin groups use belligerent anti-Western nationalist rhetoric but are fully loyal to the Kremlin. One, called "Ours" ("*Nashi*"), held a military-style two-week summer camp in 2005 for over 3,000 people featuring physical training, debate workshops, and lectures. The instructors warned that the West was trying to subvert Russia from without, while oligarchs, liberals, and other "fascist" elements were seeking to undermine it from within, so that patriotic youth must be ready to defend the country, by force if necessary, against both external and internal enemies.[49] All of Russia's major political parties also formed youth wings. Most youth, however, according to polls, are apathetic about politics, although they are also more opposed to authoritarianism than the older generations.

Political Socialization in Contemporary Russia

Whereas the Soviet regime devoted enormous effort to political indoctrination and propaganda, controlling the content of school curricula, mass media, popular culture, political education, and nearly every other channel by which values and attitudes were formed, today both the forms and content of political socialization have changed substantially. Gone is the comprehensive control over all forms of socialization by the ruling party. Citizens are exposed to a much broader array of values and beliefs. However, under Putin, the regime has tried to inculcate patriotic loyalty and national identification through the education system and to suppress the airing of opposition ideologies in the media. In place of the old Soviet doctrine of class struggle and the international solidarity of the working class, today's school textbooks stress love for the Russian national heritage. Historical figures who in the Communist era were honored as heroes of the struggle of ordinary people against feudal or capitalist masters are now held up as great representatives of Russia's national culture.[50] Patriotic education aims to build loyalty to Russia as a state as well as to Russia as a nation. This is logical, in view of Russia's effort to create a new sense of national community within the new post-Soviet state boundaries.

Contemporary political discourse also reflects a strong undercurrent of desire for some sort of restored union among at least some former Soviet republics. Russian television broadcasts pay a considerable amount of attention to activities in the "near abroad," as Russians term the other former Soviet republics. Russians continue to feel tied to the other republics by decades of shared social, economic, cultural, and political experience. Asked in a 2004 survey whether Russia's future lies with the countries of Western Europe or with the countries of the Commonwealth of Independent States (CIS), over half (57 percent) of Russians responded that it lay with the CIS. Only 28 percent were willing to say that it lay more with Western Europe.[51]

President Putin and other politicians actively play on this sentiment, calling for the reinforcement of ties between Russia and its neighbors in the CIS. Sergei Shoigu, the relatively popular minister for Emergency Situation, noted at a rally during the parliament election campaign in November 2003 that he hoped "to live to see the day when we have one big country within the borders of the [former] Soviet Union." A former KGB chairman went so far as to say that "if we do not reassemble the Soviet Union, we have no future at all."[52] Putin rarely goes so far as to call for rebuilding the Soviet Union, but he regularly declares that it is a strategic imperative for Russia to strengthen the CIS.[53] The neoimperial currents running through Russian political culture undercut the effort to create a new post-Soviet national community based on democratic values.

The authorities have also turned to the Orthodox Church as an instrument of political socialization. They regard the church as a valuable ally in building patriotic loyalty, national pride, and a framework of ethical behavior. The church in turn benefits from its ties to the state as a way of expanding its flock, protecting its traditional status as Russia's state church, and blocking other Christian denominations from proselytizing in Russia. As of the fall of 2006, a required course on "The Fundamentals of Orthodox Culture" had been introduced into the school curriculum in nearly 20 regions, and about 20,000 Orthodox priests were serving as chaplains in the armed forces.[54]

The Putin regime has also imposed far-reaching political controls over the mass media, although it has not used the media as part of a comprehensive political socialization program. Rather, its goals are defensive—the regime wants to deny political opposition access to the mass media. Nevertheless, the authorities under Putin have promoted a particular political message intended to build support for their foreign and domestic policies. Print and broadcast media consistently emphasize the principles of sovereignty and a strong state along with those of democracy, market economics, and the rule of law. Putin's team works to create the impression that they are finding a moderate middle ground between the extremes of the past—totalitarian Communism on the one hand, and unbridled oligarchic capitalism, on the other—and to restore continuity with the best traditions of Russia's political history.

At the same time, the Putin regime has consolidated its control over the media.[55] All the national television channels are controlled either through state ownership or indirectly, by ensuring that the business firms that own them maintain a pro-Kremlin editorial line. Most major newspapers are also careful to avoid offending the authorities. Journalists who defy the authorities with their investigative reports are subject to harassment and intimidation; some have been murdered. For example, the journalist Anna Politkovskaya, who wrote for one of the last remaining independent-minded national newspapers, was murdered at her apartment building in Moscow on October 7, 2006. She had received numerous death threats as a result for her reports of massive human rights abuses committed by federal and regional forces in Chechnia. She was the forty-second journalist murdered in Russia since the collapse of the Soviet Union.[56]

Therefore, even though there is no formal censorship agency as there was in Soviet times, most journalists are careful to avoid offending the authorities. Regional media are even more vulnerable to pressure from the regional political authorities.[57] The only communications medium that retains a certain amount of autonomy is the Internet, although periodically the authorities warn Internet service providers and Web site hosts that those who use the Internet improperly—for instance, to spread "extremist materials"—should be subject to prosecution.[58] However, only 9–12 percent of the population regularly uses the Internet for information (although in Moscow and St. Petersburg, over 20 percent of the population turn to the Internet).[59] Most Russians rely on central television channels for news, however: over three-quarters of Russians reported that they use central television as their news source.[60] The relative freedom enjoyed by Internet-based news organizations allows a relatively small part of the population to live in a freer news information while ensuring that the main conduits of news and opinion are under the control of the authorities.

Compared with the Soviet period, the channels of political socialization in Russia today are much more open and pluralistic. However, under Putin the authorities have reestablished some political controls over education, the media, and public discourse, less in order to propagate a comprehensive ideology than to control the boundaries of acceptable debate and opposition. As time passes, Russians' support for Putin's model of "sovereign democracy" will depend on the regime's performance in meeting its own goals.

CULTURAL DIVERSITY WITHIN RUSSIA

The opening of political activity in the late 1980s and early 1990s stimulated a surge of ethnic-national consciousness among ethnic minorities living in Russia's national republics and autonomous territories. Cultural centers, language revival movements, and political associations sprang up in many regions of Russia, including Tatarstan, Bashkortostan, Chechnia, Udmurtia, Tuva, and elsewhere.[61]

In the case of Tatarstan, for example, Tatars (who constitute Russia's largest ethnic minority, with 5.5 million or 3.7 percent of the population) nationalist groups voiced demands for sovereignty and even independence in the early 1990s. They traced their ancestry to Genghis Khan, who at one time had conquered much of Russia. They demanded an end to Russification and called for switching from the Cyrillic alphabet to Latin. In 1994, Tatarstan's president, Mintimir Shaimiev, signed a treaty with President Yeltsin that the Tatarstan authorities interpreted as an act of mutual recognition of sovereignty that acknowledged Tatarstan's "special relationship" with the federal government. The treaty was renewed in 1999 and again in 2005 despite Putin's hostility to such bilateral agreements with individual subjects of the federation. Putin also reappointed Shaimiev to another term as president in 2005. Thus even Putin, who has reversed the decentralizing trends of the 1990s in almost every area, deemed it wise to keep Shaimiev in power in view of his singular skill at balancing Moscow's demand for loyalty against local demands for the assertion of Tatar ethnic nationalism.

Tatarstan's ethnic revival has been reinforced by the resurgence of Islam in the republic. One of Shaimiev's major public acts was to rebuild the great mosque in the Kremlin of the capital city of Tatarstan, Kazan', which is the largest mosque in Russia. At its opening in 2005, Shaimiev observed that the fact that the mosque and the Orthodox cathedral stood side by side at the symbolic center of the city symbolized the multiethnic character of the republic. According to local officials, Shaimiev is careful to attend services at both the mosque and the cathedral. Shaimiev has tolerated (and no doubt encouraged) a certain level of ethnic-national political consciousness and Muslim religious activity, while keeping both well within safely defined boundaries. In turn, he has been able to use the existence of ethnic-national and Islamic religious movements in the republic as implicit threats to Moscow that too much centralization could trigger a nationalist or religious backlash movement that could spiral out of control.

Tatarstan is distinctive among Russia's ethnic republics in some ways. Tatarstan is populous (about 3.7 million), centrally located, well-endowed with oil, and heavily industrialized, and its Tatar population have a high level of ethnic self-awareness. President Shaimiev is an unusually skillful leader, adept at playing off Moscow against local political interests. At the same time, Tatarstan is characteristic of a number of the ethnic republics in Russia in that demands for cultural autonomy and a greater share of economic sovereignty have been granted by the federal government in return for the preservation of Russia as a multicultural federal state. Even under Putin, the center has shown a striking degree of flexibility, in fact, in handling the political implications of Russia's ethnic-cultural diversity. In all the republics except for Chechnia, both under Yeltsin and Putin, the central government has been able to find the necessary mix of concessions to demands for cultural and political autonomy and threats sufficient to satisfy all but the most irreconcilable separatists. But under Putin, there has been much less room for maneuver for ethnic nationalists than there was under Yeltsin.

Contemporary Russian political culture has been influenced by both slow-acting, long-term forces, including the impact of modernization, and by more immediate events such as the abrupt change in regime that occurred at the beginning of the 1990s. Through modernization, urbanization, and the turnover of generations, the Russian people gradually came to aspire to a freer and more prosperous standard of living than they had enjoyed under Communism. But the disappointments caused by the breakdown of the old Soviet social safety net, and the chaotic processes of marketization and privatization that led to extremes of wealth and poverty, led many to accept a heavier hand of state control as a necessary condition for order. Vladimir Putin's highly personalized and centralized regime, coupled with steady economic growth since 1999, has restored confidence in the regime after a decade of sharp disillusionment with the results of the regime change. Many Russians see Putin as a leader who can restore order and progress without sacrificing democratic principles—even as his actions belie this hope. Although most Russians would prefer not to have to choose between democracy and a strong state, most are also willing to endorse his use of authoritarian methods to achieve his goals. Putin has promoted the concept of "sovereign democracy" to legitimize his policies and he has used the United Russia as a vehicle to promote elite and mass acceptance of his program of authoritarian modernization. It is less clear whether Putin's associates can translate Putin's legacy into an ideology of "Putinism" that outlives his reign, as DeGaulle's associates in the French Fifth Republic were able to build a loose ideology of Gaullism as the foundation of a lasting political party.

Yet even in a period in which democratic institutions are increasingly hollowed out, democratic values remain alive. In Soviet times, a variety of democratic, religious, and cultural values diffused and competed behind the veil of apparent Marxist-Leninist solidarity. In view of the spread of liberal democratic values, Russian nationalism, and ethnic national consciousness that took form in interest group and political movements in the 1980s and 1990s, it is difficult to imagine how Russia's cultural diversity could ever be successfully confined to the iron logic of a single ideology again.

NOTES

1. There is a vast literature on the history of Russian national identity. Two valuable recent contributions are Ilya Prizel, *National Identity and Foreign Policy: Nationalism and Leadership in Poland, Russia and Ukraine* (Cambridge: Cambridge University Press, 1998) and Vera Tolz, *Russia* (New York: Oxford University Press, 2001).

2. Allen C. Lynch, *How Russia Is Not Ruled: Reflections on Russian Political Development* (Cambridge: Cambridge University Press, 2005).

3. An important recent book on this subject is Fiona Hill and Clifford Gaddy, *The Siberian Curse: How Communist Planners Left Russia Out in the Cold* (Washington, DC: Brookings Institution Press, 2003). They emphasize the factor of Russia's cold climate in particular, but note that the general problem of finding a suitable model of economic development in a country as large as Russia is a multidimensional challenge.

4. Lynch, *How Russia Is Not Ruled,* pp. 236–38.

5. For example, Nicolai N. Petro, *Crafting Democracy: How Novgorod Has Coped with Rapid Social Change* (Ithaca, NY: Cornell University Press, 2004); Nikolas K. Gvosdev, "'Managed Pluralism' and Civil Religion in Post-Soviet Russia," in Christopher Marsh and Nikolas K. Gvosdev, eds., *Civil Society and the Search for Justice in Russia* (Lanham, MD: Lexington Books, 2002), pp. 75–88.

6. James W. Warhola, "Revisiting the Russian 'Constrained Autocracy': 'Absolutism' and Natural Rights Theories in Russia and the West," in Marsh and Gvosdev, eds., *Civil Society and the Search for Justice in Russia,* pp. 19–40.

7. George Vernadsky, *A History of Russia* (New Haven, CT: Yale University Press, 1961), p. 244.

8. On the campaign against women's veiling in Central Asia, see Douglas Northrop, *Veiled Empire: Gender and Power in Stalinist Central Asia* (Ithaca, NY: Cornell University Press, 2003).

9. Gabriel A. Almond and Sidney Verba, *The Civic Culture: Political Attitudes and Democracy in Five Nations* (Boston: Little, Brown, 1965).

10. Gabriel A. Almond and Sidney Verba, eds., *The Civic Culture Revisited* (Boston: Little, Brown, 1980); Stephen White, *Political Culture and Soviet Politics* (London: Macmillan, 1979); Frederic J. Fleron, Jr., "Post-Soviet Political Culture in Russia: An Assessment of Recent Empirical Investigations," *Europe-Asia Studies* 48:2 (1996): 225–60; Harry Eckstein, Frederic J. Fleron, Erik P. Hoffmann, and William M. Reisinger, eds., *Can Democracy Take Root in Post-Soviet Russia? Explorations in State–Society Relations* (Lanham, MD: Rowman & Littlefield, 1998); and James Alexander, *Political Culture in Post-Communist Russia* (New York: Macmillan, 2000).

11. Ronald Inglehart, *Culture Shift in Advanced Industrial Society* (Princeton, NJ: Princeton University Press, 1990), p. 55.

12. James L. Gibson and Raymond M. Duch, "Emerging Democratic Values in Soviet Political Culture," in Arthur H. Miller, William M. Reisinger, and Vicki L. Hesli, eds., *Public Opinion and Regime Change* (Boulder, CO: Westview, 1993), pp. 69–94; William M. Reisinger, Arthur H. Miller, and Vicki L. Hesli, "Political Values in Russia, Ukraine and Lithuania: Sources and Implications for Democracy," *British Journal of Political Science* 24 (1994): 183–223; and Jeffrey W. Hahn, "Continuity and Change in Russian Political Culture," *British Journal of Political Science* 21:4 (1991): 393–421.

13. From a survey conducted by the Levada Center in June 2005 and posted to its Web site: http://www.levada.ru/press/2005070410.html.

The Levada Center is a widely respected independent public opinion survey firm.

14. From a survey in 2005 by the All-Russia Center for the Study of Public Opinion (VTsIOM) and reported by RFE/RL Newsline, March 7, 2005.

15. From a survey conducted by the Levada Center in January 2005 and posted to its Web site: http://www.levada.ru/press/2005031100.html.

16. Nationwide survey results conducted by the Public Opinion Foundation, reported by RFE/RL Newsline, December 10, 2001.

17. Colton and McFaul, *Popular Choice and Managed Democracy*, pp. 220–21.

18. Ibid., p. 222.

19. James L. Gibson, "The Resilience of Support for Democratic Institutions and Processes in the Nascent Russian and Ukrainian Democracies," in Vladimir Tismaneanu, ed., *Political Culture and Civil Society in Russia and the New States of Eurasia* (Armonk, NY: M. E. Sharpe, 1995), p. 57.

20. Cf. Richard Pipes, "Flight From Freedom: What Russians Think and Want," *Foreign Affairs* 83:3 (2004): 9–15.

21. James R. Millar and Sharon L. Wolchik, "Introduction: The Social Legacies and the Aftermath of Communism," in James R. Millar and Sharon L. Wolchik, eds., *The Social Legacy of Communism* (Washington, DC, and Cambridge: Woodrow Wilson Press and Cambridge University Press, 1994), p. 16.

22. Marcia A. Weigle, *Russia's Liberal Project: State–Society Relations in the Transition from Communism* (University Park: Pennsylvania State University Press, 2000), pp. 432–41.

23. Yuri Levada, "Svoboda ot vybora? Postelektoral'nye razmyshleniia," published on Web site Polit.ru, May 18, 2004.

24. William Zimmerman, "Markets, Democracy and Russian Foreign Policy," *Post-Soviet Affairs* 10 (1994): 103–26; William Zimmerman, "Synoptic Thinking and Political Culture in Post-Soviet Russia," *Slavic Review* 54 (1995): 630–41; Judith S. Kullberg and William Zimmerman, "Liberal Elites, Socialist Masses, and Problems of Russian Democracy," *World Politics* 51 (April 1999): 323–58.

25. See the speech Surkov gave to a group of United Russia party activists on February 22, 2006. The text (in Russian) may be found on the United Russia Web site at: http://www.edinros.ru/news.html?id=111148. Accessed 13 March, 2006.

For an overview of Surkov's political views, influence, and career, see Gregory L. White and Alan Cullison, "Putin's Pitchman: Inside Kremlin as It Tightens Its Grip: Ex-Aide to Tycoons; Domestic Adviser Surkov Hails Concentration of Power As 'Sovereign Democracy'; 'There'll Be No Uprisings Here,'" *Wall Street Journal,* December 19, 2006.

26. Timothy J. Colton, "Putin and the Attenuation of Russian Democracy," in Dale Herspring, ed., *Putin's Russia: Past Imperfect, Future Uncertain,* 3rd ed. (Lanham, MD: Rowman & Littlefield, 2007), p. 47.

27. On the impact of television in Soviet society, see Ellen Mickiewicz, *Split Signals: Television and Politics in the Soviet Union* (New York and Oxford: Oxford University Press, 1988); on propaganda and mass communications more generally, see Stephen White, *Political Culture and Soviet Politics* (London: Macmillan, 1979); and Thomas F. Remington, *The Truth of Authority: Ideology and Communication in the Soviet Union* (Pittsburgh, PA: University of Pittsburgh Press, 1988).

28. Comprehensive studies of Soviet dissent include Ludmilla Alexeeyeva, *Soviet Dissent: Contemporary Movements for National, Religious, and Human Rights* (Middletown, CT: Wesleyan University Press, 1987); and Frederick C. Barghoorn, *Detente and the Democratic Movement in the USSR* (New York: Free Press, 1976).

29. Robert D. English, *Russia and the Idea of the West: Gorbachev, Intellectuals, and the End of the Cold War* (New York: Columbia University Press, 2000), pp. 5–8.

30. Mikhail Gorbachev himself portrayed his reform program not merely as applying to Russia, but as a doctrine for the whole world, as the title of the book he published in 1987 indicates: *Perestroika: New Thinking for Our Country and the World* (New York: Harper & Row, 1987).

31. Thomas Remington, "A Socialist Pluralism of Opinions: Glasnost' and Policy-Making under Gorbachev," *Russian Review* 48 (1989): 271–304.

32. Yu Levada et al., "Homo Sovieticus: A Rough Sketch," *Moscow News*, no. 11 (1990): 11.

33. Tatiana Zaslavskaia, "Vesti dialog s liud'mi," *Narodnyi deputat*, no. 2 (1990): 25–27. Zaslavskaia is a distinguished sociologist who was one of the most important theorists of reform in the pre-Gorbachev and early Gorbachev periods. A member of the Academy of Sciences and a deputy to the Congress of People's Deputies, she founded a new institute to conduct public opinion surveys throughout the Soviet Union.

34. "Main Directions for the Stabilization of the National Economy and the Transition to a Market Economy," as published in the British Broadcasting System Summary of World Broadcasts (BBC SWB), SU/0900, 20 October 1990, p. C/1. This policy statement was adopted as the basis of national economic policy by the USSR Supreme Soviet on October 19, 1990. It is important mainly as a statement of goals and principles rather than as a working program of action.

35. Gibson and Duch, "Emerging Democratic Values," p. 79.

36. Levada-Tsentr, "Analiticheskii tsentr Yuriia Levady," http://www.levada.ru/press/2004092702.html, accessed September 30, 2004.

37. L. Sedov, "Obshchestvenno-politicheskaia situatsiia v Rossii v iune 2004," from Web site of Levada Center http://www.levada.ru/press/2004071402.print.html.

38. The Levada Center's approval ratings for President Putin can be found at: http://www.levada.ru/prezident.html. Those for the government are at: http://www.levada.ru/pravitelstvo.html.

39. Levada, "Svoboda ot vybora?"

40. Ibid.

41. Source: VTsIOM survey of sample of adult Russians, November 27–December 1, 2003. N = 1,600. Press release no. 38, "10 let Dumy," December 13, 2003. See http://www.levada.ru/press/2003121304.print.html. http://www.levada.ru/default_e.htm.

42. Richard Rose, William Mishler, and Neil Munro, *Russia Transformed: Developing Popular Support for a New Regime* (Cambridge: Cambridge University Press, 2006); Richard Rose and Neil Munro, *Elections without Order: Russia's Challenge to Vladimir Putin* (Cambridge: Cambridge University Press, 2002); and Richard Rose, Neil Munro, and William Mishler, "Resigned Acceptance of an Incomplete Democracy: Russia's Political Equilibrium," *Post-Soviet Affairs* 20:3 (2004): 195–218.

43. In the United States, according to the U.S. Census Bureau, as of 2005, 85 percent of Americans 25 years old and older had completed high school, and 28 percent had completed college. See http://www.census.gov/Press-Release/www.releases/archives/education/007660. html, accessed January 28, 2007.

44. Brian Silver, "Political Beliefs of the Soviet Citizen," in James R. Millar, ed., *Politics, Work, and Daily Life in the USSR* (Cambridge: Cambridge University Press, 1987), p. 127.

45. Gibson and Duch, "Emerging Democratic Values," p. 86; William M. Reisinger, Arthur H. Miller, Vicki L. Hesli, and Kristen Hill Maher, "Political Values in Russia, Ukraine and Lithuania: Sources and Implications for Democracy," *British Journal of Political Science* 24 (1994): 216–18; Jeffrey W. Hahn, "Continuity and Change in Russian Political Culture," in Frederic J. Fleron, Jr., and Erik P. Hoffmann, eds., *Post-Communist Studies and Political Science: Methodology and Empirical Theory in Sovietology* (Boulder, CO: Westview, 1993), pp. 319–22.

46. Donna Bahry, "Society Transformed? Rethinking the Social Roots of Perestroika, *Slavic Review* 52 (1993): 512–54." Bahry reanalyzes data from three surveys taken at different times: the Harvard Project of refugees to Europe after World War II, which reflects attitudes shaped in the 1920s, 1930s, and early 1940s; the SIP data from the emigre survey in the United States in the late 1970s; and a Times-Mirror survey conducted in 1991. This method allows her to compare public opinion on comparable issues for the *same* generations across different surveys taken at different times, and to track change and continuity in opinion *across* generations. She finds that both the earlier and later studies found an essential consistency in the values of

the prewar generations, even though members of those generations had grown much older by the 1970s and 1980s.

47. Bahry, p. 544.

48. *Washington Post* journalists Peter Baker and Susan Glasser present a vivid portrait of these groups in their book, *Kremlin Rising: Vladimir Putin's Russia and the End of Revolution* (New York: Scribner, 2005), ch. 3, "Time of the Patriots."

49. Claire Bigg, "Here Comes the Sun for Putin's Patriotic Youth," RFE/RL *Russian Political Weekly,* July 26, 2005.

50. Elena Lisovskaya and Vyacheslav Karpov, "New Ideologies in Postcommunist Russian Textbooks," *Comparative Education Review* 43:4 (1999): 522–32.

51. Rose, *Russian Responses to Transformation,* p. 7. The breakdown of responses was as follows: 20 percent said "definitely with the CIS," 37 percent said "more the CIS than Western Europe," 4 percent said "definitely with Western Europe," and 24 percent said "more with Western Europe than the CIS." Fifteen percent did not have an opinion.

52. RFE/RL Newsline, December 1, 2003.

53. For example, in July 2004 he warned that Russia must either work to strengthen the CIS or it will disappear. The fact that he made this statement at a meeting of the Security Council highlighted the strategic importance that he assigned to this task.

54. RFE/RL Newsline, February 15, 2006; August 31, 2006.

55. Sarah Oates, "Television, Voters, and the Development of the 'Broadcast Party,'" in *The 1999–2000 Elections in Russia: Their Impact and Legacy,* ed. Vicki L. Hesli and William M. Reisinger (Cambridge: Cambridge University Press, 2003), pp. 29–50; idem, "Framing Fear: Findings from a Study of Election News and Terrorist Threat in Russia," *Europe-Asia Studies* 58:2 (2006): 281–90; idem, "Media, Civil Society, and the Failure of the Fourth Estate in Russia," in Alfred B. Evans, Jr., Laura A. Henry, and Lisa McIntosh Sundstrom, eds., *Russian Civil Society: A Critical Assessment* (Armonk, NY: M.E. Sharpe, 2006), pp. 57–72.

56. RFE/RL Newsline, October 10, 2006.

57. Kelly M. McMann, *Economic Autonomy and Democracy: Hybrid Regimes in Russia and Kyrgyzstan* (Cambridge: Cambridge University Press, 2006). Kelly McMann has documented how authorities in some regions suppress independent newspapers and broadcast outlets, preventing opposition groups from enjoying any publicity, and keeping unwelcome investigative reports from appearing.

58. The Interior Minister and Prosecutor General called for new legislation giving them more effective means to treat the Internet as a communications medium and allowing them to prosecute service providers who allow the dissemination of extremist materials. RFE/RL Newsline, November 16, 2006.

59. RFE/RL Newsline, July 15, 2005, reporting on the results of a VTsIOM national survey.

60. Ibid.

61. A valuable study of ethnic nationalist mobilization in the Russian Federation is Dmitry P. Gorenburg, *Minority Ethnic Mobilization in the Russian Federation* (Cambridge: Cambridge University Press, 2003).

6

Interest Groups and Political Parties

INTEREST ARTICULATION: STATISM VS. PLURALISM

Regime change in Russia has had a powerful impact both on people's interests and on the way those interests are organized, that is, both the demand side and the supply side of interest groups. Decentralization, market reforms, privatization, ideological liberalization, and the weakening of the social safety net have reshaped people's needs and desires. Most people suffered losses in economic security and well-being in the 1990s.[1] At the same time, political liberalization has also allowed people to mobilize in defense of common interests, such as environmental protection and the rights of ethnic minorities, disadvantaged groups, business, and labor. Most people's lives are affected by the coexistence of surviving elements of the old socialist system with new quasi-capitalist, semidemocratic institutions established since 1991. The wider diversity of interests in society and the greater freedom for association have resulted in a far more differentiated spectrum of interest associations than existed under the old regime. But although there is much more organized interest articulation than there was in the past, the sharp increases in social inequality in the 1990s and the stricter state controls over interest articulation under Putin have limited the diversity of political expression.

In Chapter 4, we argued that the provision of honest and effective government is a public good; people face a collective action dilemma in trying to obtain good government. Public goods are goods that anyone may enjoy, whether they have expended any effort to obtain them or not, and the supply of which is not diminished as people use them. To explain where public goods such as honest and effective governance come from, we must look both at the supply side and the demand side. The problem of explaining the supply of good government arises because, as we know, public goods always tend to be undersupplied.[2] This occurs because few people are willing to assume the cost of organizing collective action for the common good of large groups of people if their own share of the benefit is worth less than the cost of the effort they make to achieve it. Those who do organize groups for collective benefit often are seeking some other private benefits for themselves by doing so. Some may have aspirations to become political leaders, for instance. By going to the trouble of mobilizing a group around a cause, they gain name recognition and followers.

It is easier to organize people for a collective endeavor if some organizational resources are already in place. If people belong to an organization, or share ties through previous acquaintance, it is easier to reach them and draw them into a collective endeavor. If organizational entrepreneurs have to start from scratch, and go around to people one by one to persuade them to sign a petition or contribute dues or turn out for a demonstration, large-scale collective action is much harder to produce. Consequently, when a regime changes, we would expect that interests that can be mobilized through existing organizational channels will have an easier time being heard than interests that are not already organized.

The same logic applies to the political calculations of leaders. Leaders who can take control of existing organizations, and make them vehicles for representing new groups of constituents, have an advantage winning influence over activists who have to start a movement or party from scratch. Therefore, even in a time of deep change in society, the way political and organizational resources were structured in the past will affect the way interests are articulated in the new regime. The legacy of the past therefore affects the *supply* of interest groups.

On the *demand* side, people's interests are strongly affected by a major change such as the shift from state socialism to market capitalism. In Russia, the demise of the old state-socialist economic system, in which the state was the universal employer, has affected everyone. In the first years of Russia's transition, a small minority of people became wealthy: most people grew poorer and more insecure. Inequality rose sharply, both across social strata and across regions. The collapse of Communist ideology has also spurred a number of groups to form around extremist ideologies, including xenophobic forms of Russian nationalism.

Interest articulation is thus affected both by the degree to which people are able to organize for collective action and by the shift in their own definitions of what they want and need from government. People's interests and identities create a potential for mobilization in the political arena, but whether that potential is realized depends a good deal on the distribution of organizational resources and the strategies of leaders who hope to build popular followings. In this chapter, we will examine how the regime change has affected people's material and social interests. We also will discuss the change in the organizational channels through which people convey their demands to the policymakers.

Socialism and Bureaucratic Politics

The Soviet regime did not tolerate the open pursuit of any interests except those authorized by the state. Soviet doctrine did recognize that there were diverse interests in society and encouraged the formation of a number of public organizations, such as labor unions organized by branch of the economy, professional unions for creative artists, and associations for particular groups of the population, such as youths, women, and veterans. But the regime required that organizations articulating interests support its goals. As we have seen, the regime treated such organizations as means of directing the participation of the population in public life. Stalin defined public organizations as "transmission belts" through which the state directed society.[3]

Although it did not take the form of open, competitive politics, interest articulation went on through intense behind-the-scenes maneuvering for power and advantage, especially within the state bureaucracy. Bureaucratic agencies, regional governments, and leadership factions vied quietly but vigorously for influence over policy and appointments. They were not allowed to appeal openly to the public for support, so the public had no means of holding leaders accountable, but they used methods familiar to bureaucratic infighters throughout the world: building tacit coalitions, manipulating the flow of information, favoring clients with patronage benefits. And, as we have seen, sometimes the expression of demands and ideas took the form of clandestinely circulated contraband literature that the regime treated as subversive.[4]

There was constant bureaucratic lobbying by state actors, including the myriad agencies of the state that ostensibly existed to carry out state policy but that, like bureaucratic organizations everywhere, developed a strong stake in their own organizational status and power. These included both the centralized branch agencies that managed the economy and society, as well as the leaders of the republics and regions of the union. Between the bureaucracy and the policymakers at the top there was a relationship of mutual dependence. The party leadership needed the branch and regional structures to achieve their policy goals. In turn the heads of ministries, state committees, republics, and regions needed the support of top party leaders for their institutional and career interests. As the center grew weaker, and depended more on the support of the state officialdom, the idea of any serious reform of the system became more and more threatening.[5]

Because the articulation of interests was regulated by the Communist Party, and there could be no open, active competition among political parties or interest groups for membership or support, the Communist Party was the major institution for weighing alternatives and deciding policy. In the Stalin era, party policies such as the collectivization of private farms were carried out using enormous coercion: collectivization resulted in the loss of millions of lives through the killing, deportation, and starvation of peasants.[6] But in the post-Stalin era, as the system grew bureaucratized, corrupted, and weak, entrenched interests became adept at ensuring that the system served them. Any policy initiative that threatened to upset the existing distribution of resources was watered down before it was adopted, and often was further blunted, distorted, or forgotten as it was implemented. Paradoxically, policymakers at the top of this seemingly centralized political system lacked the authority to break through the mass of bureaucratic inertia, and frequently lacked the information necessary for an accurate appraisal of the real state of affairs in many areas.

The statist model of interest articulation was upset by glasnost. Glasnost stimulated an explosion of political expression, which in turn prompted groups to form and to make political demands and participate in elections. It is hard today to appreciate how profound was the impact of glasnost on Soviet society: suddenly, it opened the floodgates to a gathering stream of startling facts, ideas, disclosures, reappraisals, scandals, and sensations. But if Gorbachev expected that glasnost would result in expression generally favoring his own strategy of perestroika, or restructuring, of Soviet socialism, he must have been surprised at the range and intensity of new demands, grievances, ideas, and pressures that erupted. In loosening the party's controls over communication sufficiently to encourage people to speak and write freely and openly, Gorbachev also relinquished the controls that would have enabled him to limit political expression when it went too far.

Ideology and organization in the Soviet regime were so tightly intertwined that by releasing controls over the ideological limits of speech, Gorbachev was giving up the party's traditional power to control public organizations. As people voiced their deep-felt demands and grievances, others recognized that they shared the same beliefs and values, and made common cause with them, sometimes forming new, unofficial organizations. Thus, as we have seen, a direct result of glasnost was a wave of participation in "informal" (i.e., unlicensed and uncontrolled) public associations. Daring publications in the media allowed people to see that they shared common interests with others, and prompted them to come together to form independent associations. When the authorities tried to limit or prohibit such groups, they generated still more frustration and protest. Associations of all sorts formed: groups dedicated to remembering the victims of Stalin's terror; ultranationalists who wanted to restore tsarism; nationalist movements in many republics. The devastating explosion of the nuclear reactor at Chernobyl' in 1986 had a tremendous impact in stimulating the formation of environmental protest, which also fed nationalist movements in Belarus and Ukraine.[7]

The mobilization of large-scale political activity led to the creation of new organizational outlets for nationalist movements, independent labor unions, and electoral coalitions. Some of these movements—which included new labor unions, women's groups, environmental protection groups, nationalist organizations, associations of cooperatives, farmers' groups, human rights and cultural groups—evolved into channels of interest articulation and aggregation in the post-Soviet era.[8]

Democrats, "Reds," and "Browns"

In Russia, as new organizations espousing political goals proliferated in the late 1980s, three distinct ideological tendencies arose and inspired collective action.

The first centered on principles of individualism, liberal democracy, market economy, and the rule of law—and a Western orientation for Russia. This group adopted the label "democrats" or "reformers." The second was the revival of a conservative, sometimes even Stalinist, version of Marxism-Leninism, whose advocates made up for their limited base of popular support with flights of extravagant rhetoric. They yearned for strong leadership, centralized state power, an assertive foreign policy, a collectivist, centrally planned economy, and preservation of an imperial Soviet Union—for them Stalin was a heroic figure in Russian history.

The third stream of ideology drew on conservative Russian and Slavophile nationalism. Like the ultra-Marxists, the nationalists wanted Russia to have a hierarchical and imperial state and rejected Western political and economic influences. They believed, however, that not Marxism but older Russian cultural values such as Orthodox religion should be the source for rebuilding society's exhausted moral fabric. At a deeper philosophic level, the conservative nationalists also rejected the rationalism and materialism associated with Marxism. But in more practical day-to-day politics, the conservative nationalists and the ultra-Marxists have often found common cause in their hatred for the West's impact on Russia (and in other forms of reactionary nativism, such as antisemitism). Thus the "red" Marxist-Leninists have often allied with the "brown" nationalists in opposition to the democratizing trends in Russia.[9] The "red-brown" strain of thought and feeling has continued to be powerfully felt in Russian politics to the present, and is represented by extremist groups such as Russian National Unity and, in slightly less virulent form, by the Communist Party of the Russian Federation. We shall say more about both of these groups below.

Toward Pluralism

The collapse of the Soviet regime brought a final end to the regime's ideological controls over political expression, which had already been weakened by Gorbachev's reforms. The transition created an opportunity for the rise of a variety of new groups that voiced a wide range of demands. But besides these fundamental political changes, the post-1991 period brought about another change of equal importance. The elimination of the state's monopoly on productive property resulted in the formation of new class interests, among them those of new entrepreneurs, commercial bankers, private farmers, and others interested in protecting rights of property and commerce. Another important category of interests was that of the managers of state-owned enterprises, who were facing a radically changed environment as state orders, credits, and sources of supply dried up, and as Yeltsin's privatization program took effect. Organized labor too found itself in a new position dealing with managers of privatized enterprises rather than, as in the past, with administrators of state property. Unions themselves were divided among competing labor federations. Also divided were the farmers: private farmers were represented by an association pressing for legal guarantees and state support for private farming; the collective farmers formed a powerful association and political party. Meanwhile, new associations representing banks, consumers, deceived investors, city governments, disabled persons, soldiers' mothers, defense industries, abused women, and a host of other interests began to form. No longer did the state demand that organized groups serve a single, state-defined political agenda, as was the case under the old regime. Now groups could form freely to represent a diversity of interests, compete for access to influence and resources, and define their own agenda. By 2001, there were over 300,000 nongovernmental, noncommercial organizations registered with the government, of which around 70,000 were active.[10] Over two million people work in these organizations as activists and employees, and as many as 15 or 20 million people receive assistance in some form from them.[11]

Political scientists have observed that interest groups generally pursue either "inside" or "outside" strategies for influencing policy. That is, either they tend to concentrate their resources on cultivating close, friendly relations with key policymakers, or they seek to build large public followings and membership bases that can apply pressure on policymakers through elections, demonstrations, letter-writing campaigns, and media attention.[12] The effectiveness of insider strategies depends on establishing relations of trust, which generally requires that the group's representatives and the policymakers keep each others' confidences. For this reason it can be difficult to judge from the outside how powerful an "insider" group is. In the case of Russian groups, we see various combinations of strategies. Some older organizations that survived into the new era cling to their organizational assets and legacies and take advantage of their "insider" access to the state. Some that have sprung up from scratch also work closely with legislative and executive authorities, but others play "outsider" roles, trying to influence government by mobilizing public attention and support. Still others try to use both.

The rapid changes in the structure of social relations have meant that both old and new organizations have had a difficult time keeping a firm base of support. Some organizations that appeared influential at first have turned out to be little more than an empty shell. Other interest groups have proved to be very strong politically even though they are not formally organized. Some formerly cohesive groups have split. The diversification of interests has generated a wide range of opportunities for organizers and activists.

At the same time, the political constraints on the ability of interest associations to form, seek supporters, and exercise influence have also evolved. The Soviet pattern of interest articulation was statist, that is, the Soviet state sponsored and controlled interest groups. In the 1990s, the prevailing pattern of interest articulation shifted to pluralism, in which multiple groups competed for members and influence. Under Putin, the model is shifting toward an authoritarian form of corporatism—one in which the state recognizes certain groups (and ignores or represses others) and controls the terms of the relationship between interest groups and policymakers. A good example is the formation of the Public Chamber, an organized forum through which certain societal groups are represented and consulted on public affairs. The regime chooses which associations are invited to participate in the Public Chamber and even controls the selection of those representatives. Groups that take an openly oppositional stance are subject to harassment and suppression. Interest groups thus need to choose whether to accept the boundaries of the role the regime has defined in order to exercise some influence, or to risk the consequences of open defiance of the regime. Most regional governments also have similar Public Chambers through which the regional administration consults with local interest groups.

It will be helpful to illustrate the patterns of interest articulation in contemporary Russian by examining four organizations in closer detail: the Russian Union of Industrialists and Entrepreneurs, the League of Committees of Soldiers' Mothers, the Federation of Independent Trade Unions of Russia, and the Russian Orthodox Church. These comprise both "old" and "new" types of interests and organization and will illustrate a range of strategies for collective action.

The Russian Union of Industrialists and Entrepreneurs

The case of the Russian Union of Industrialists and Entrepreneurs illustrates three points: some inherited Soviet-era organizations have proved resilient in the face of the considerable changes that have taken place in politics and society; the interests of the state industrial managers have slowly adapted to the new market conditions in the economy; and finally, although the voice of big business in Russia today is far stronger than that of any other organized interest, the state still has the upper hand in dealing with society.

Privatization has sharply changed the environment for industry. Most formerly state-owned industrial firms are now wholly or partly privately owned. Gradually their directors have come to respond to the incentives of a market economy, rather than those of a state socialist economy. Under the old regime, managers were told to fulfill the plan regardless of cost or quality, and profit was not a relevant consideration.[13] Now, managers are increasingly motivated to maximize profits and to increase the productive value of their firms. Some firms continue to demand subsidies and protection from the state. More and more, however, firms are demanding that the state provide a level playing field for all businesses, that is, an environment in which laws and contracts are enforced by the state, regulation is reasonable and honest, taxes are fair (and low), and barriers to foreign trade are minimized. As one consultant to a major firm explained, the CEO of the company at first did not understand why he should not simply "buy" a few government bureaucrats and members of parliament, and obtain the legislative and administrative decisions that he needed for his company through bribery. With time, however, he came to recognize that it was more efficient in the long run for him to work with other large companies in a business association to create a legal and regulatory environment that would favor growth and investment more generally. The association that is the vehicle for his lobbying efforts, and those of big business in Russia more generally, is the Russian Union of Industrialists and Entrepreneurs, or RUIE.

The RUIE is the single most powerful organized interest group in Russia. Its members are both the old state industrial firms (now mostly private or quasi private) and the newer financial-industrial conglomerates headed by the so-called oligarchs.[14] For its first 15 years, its president was Arkadii Vol'skii, who had been a senior CPSU official in charge of the Central Committee department overseeing industrial machine-building. During the Gorbachev period, Vol'skii headed an association of the heads of state enterprises called the "Scientific-Industrial Union."[15] The new organization sought to preserve economic ties among enterprises to offset the breakdown of the old system of central planning. In 1991, the organization reorganized as the Russian Union of Industrialists and Entrepreneurs. Although the RUIE professed to have no explicit political goals, it did seek to defend the interests of state industry—including their interest in obtaining credits and production orders—as well as to prevent the interruption of supply and trade ties in the face of economic upheavals.

In the 1990s, the RUIE twice sought to enter electoral politics through an alliance with the main trade union association that formed a party and ran candidates for the State Duma, with very poor results. But as an insider group voicing the interests of big business, the RUIE has been far more effective. It has been an influential behind-the-scenes force for compromise between management and labor, and a source of policy advice for government and parliament. The businesses belonging to it account for some 70 percent of Russian GDP and some 12 million employees. It has regional branches in most territorial units of the country and in all seven federal districts and a number of sector-specific subdivisions.[16]

The Putin regime took steps to bring all business interests together under a common umbrella and viewed the RUIE as the principal vehicle for its consultations with business. At the same time, it made sure that the RUIE's influence remained well within acceptable limits. In 2000, Putin let it be known that he wanted the oligarchs to join the RUIE rather to continue engaging in their free-wheeling and independent interest articulation.[17] (As then-president Vol'skii diplomatically put it, "the interests of the oligarchs are too diverse to create their own public association, and the RUIE can help them conduct civilized lobbying."[18]) In turn, the improvement in economic conditions beginning in 1999 made the RUIE's members themselves more interested in improving the business environment for Russia generally, rather than in capturing industry-specific privileges. The RUIE expanded its in-house capacity for working with the government and the parliament in drafting legislation. It maintains a number of specialized internal working groups that develop policy positions on a wide range of issues such as land reform; tax law; pension policy; bankruptcy legislation; reform of the natural gas, energy, and railroad monopolies; securities regulation; and the terms of Russia's entry to the WTO. By marshalling expertise, pooling the clout of its members, and maintaining friendly relations with the government, parliament, and presidential administration, the RUIE has become a quietly powerful force in shaping policy on a wide range of economic issues. To be sure, individual firms still lobby government for firm-specific benefits. But the RUIE is a recognized participant in high-level government and parliamentary policy making.

The Putin leadership been careful to avoid letting the RUIE gain too much influence. It has helped to create two rival business associations (OPORA, with a mandate to represent the interests of small and medium-size business firms, and "Business Russia," which is active in cooperating with the United Russia party) and to revive yet another business lobby, the Trade-Industrial Chamber. When Putin meets with business leaders, he often makes a point of including representatives of all these associations at the meeting, signalling that for all its prominence, RUIE is not the sole voice of business, and that the regime will set the terms for business's participation in policy making.

The limits of the RUIE's capacity to speak for business became dramatically evident when Putin launched his campaign against the Yukos oil firm (see Close-Up 6.1: The Yukos Affair). When the arrests of top leaders of Yukos began in July 2003, RUIE confined itself to mild expressions of concern. Its members, evidently fearful of crossing Putin, chose not to defend Yukos's head, Mikhail Khodorkovsky, or to protest the use of police methods to destroy one of Russia's largest oil companies. Instead, they promised to meet their tax obligations and to do more to help the country fight poverty. Putin pointedly avoided meeting with RUIE and other business association leaders from November 2003 to July 2004—and then agreed to meet with them only on the condition that the subject of Yukos not be discussed. Perhaps if big business had taken a firm and united stand, they could have had some influence. But the desire by each individual firm to maintain friendly relations with the government and the fear of government reprisals undercut business's capacity for collective action. The result was that the leadership of Yukos was jailed, the company was bankrupted, and its productive assets were taken over by firms friendly to the Putin regime.

Close-Up 6.1   The Yukos Affair

One of the most widely publicized episodes of the Putin era concerned the state's drive to break up the powerful oil company Yukos, whose head, Mikhial Khodorkovsky, was one of the most prominent of Russia's new post-Communist magnates. Khodorkovsky began as one of a group of young Komsomol activists working in the Moscow city government in the late 1980s who used their Komsomol resources and connections to start a bank called Menatep. Financing from the Menatep bank enabled them to acquire—at a bargain-basement price—80 percent of the shares of the Yukos oil company when the government privatized it under the "loans for shares" plan in 1995. At first, like some other newly wealthy business tycoons, Khodorkovsky sought to squeeze maximum profit from the firm. Soon, however, Khodorkovsky's business strategy changed, and he began to invest in the productive capacity of the firm. He made Yukos the most dynamic of Russia's oil companies. Khodorkovsky discovered that by emulating Western business practices, the company could increase its net worth and productive capacity. He made ownership and management of Yukos transparent in an effort to get his firm listed on Western stock exchanges. His was the first major company to make public information on its ownership structure. He reformed corporate governance practices and sought to have Yukos's shares listed on foreign stock exchanges. By improving the efficiency and transparency of the firm, Khodorkovsky found that share prices rose, and with them Khodorkovsky's own net worth. At its peak in 2002, the company's assets were estimated to be worth about $20 billion, of which Khodorkovsky owned nearly $8 billion. He was Russia's wealthiest citizen.

Meantime, concerned for the company's public reputation, Khodorkovsky created a foundation called Open Russia and launched several charitable initiatives in Russia, funding schools, hospitals, science, cultural exchange programs, and other causes. He recruited some distinguished international figures (among them Henry Kissinger) to his foundation's board and worked to polish his reputation in Europe and the United States. The company funded housing for its workers and youth programs for their families in regions where it operated. Khodorkovsky also was active in Russian politics, helping to fund the parties Yabloko and the Union of Rightist Forces, and sponsoring the election campaigns of several deputies to the State Duma. Critics accused him of wanting to control parliament and even of wanting to change the constitution to turn it into a parliamentary system. There was talk that he intended to seek the presidency.

Khodorkovsky himself refused to behave in a subservient manner toward the state authorities. Without consulting with the Kremlin, he began talks with foreign oil companies on selling a significant share of Yukos stock. In April 2003, Yukos and another oil company, Sibneft', announced an agreement to merge, which would have created Russia's largest oil company and the fourth-largest oil company in the world. In June 2003, he signed an agreement with China under which Yukos would build a major oil pipeline from Siberia to China that would supply a quarter of China's oil imports, a direct challenge to the state's preference for building a pipeline that would supply the Japanese market. At a meeting at the Kremlin in February 2003, Khodorkovsky even sparred with President Putin over a deal by which the state-owned oil company Rosneft' had acquired an oil company called Severnaia neft'. Khodorokovsky complained that the deal was corrupt, supposedly telling Putin that "Everyone feels that this deal had, so to speak, an additional level. The president of Rosneft is here, I don't know, will he confirm this? . . . Yes, corruption is spreading in the country. And you can say that it began with us. Well, it started, and sooner or later we'll have to stop

(Continued)

it!" Putin responded: ". . . Rosneft and its deal with Sevneft. . . . This is a state-owned company that needs to increase its reserves. Some companies, like Yukos, for example, have super reserves, and here's a question: How did it get them?"*

At some point in April or May 2003, the Putin administration evidently decided that Khodorkovsky and Yukos had grown too independent and must be destroyed. In a series of actions beginning in July 2003, several top figures in Yukos and companies associated with it were arrested and charged with fraud, embezzlement, tax evasion, and even murder. One case involved a privatization deal going back to 1993. The police raided the offices of the company and a number of its affiliates, seizing files and computer hard drives. They even raided the office of an orphanage sponsored by Open Russia.

In October, Khodorkovsky himself was arrested and charged with fraud and tax evasion. The courts consistently refused to release him on bail. At the end of December, the government opened another front against the company, charging it with failure to pay taxes in the years from 1998 to 2003. The tax ministry demanded that the company pay 100 billion rubles (about $3.4 billion) in unpaid taxes from 2000 and declared that more claims from 2001, 2002, and 2003 were pending. The government froze the company's bank accounts as collateral against the claims. In July 2004, the company defaulted on payments to foreign banks for loans and claimed that it could not meet the government's demands. It even threatened that it would have to begin laying off workers. The government stepped up the pressure, announcing that it would force Yukos to sell off its main production subsidiary, Yuganskneftegaz (responsible for about 60 percent of Yukos's total oil output), in order to meet its tax obligations. Ultimately, the government intended to drive the company into bankruptcy so that it could be broken up and pieces sold to other companies more loyal to the regime. The final breakup of Yukos began in December 2004, when the government auctioned off Yuganskneftegaz for a price that was a fraction of its actual worth to an unknown firm that sold it to a state-owned oil firm the next day. In May 2005, Khodorkovsky and an associate were each sentenced to nine years' imprisonment for tax fraud and embezzlement.

Many reasons have been suggested for the government's relentless campaign against Yukos, which has harmed Russia's economy, both in direct ways—Yukos had been Russia's fastest-growing and most forward-looking energy company, responsible for the rapid growth of Russian oil exports, and a model of the transformation of the "robber barons" of the 1990s into

---

* Reported in RFE/RL *Business Watch,* Vol. 3, no. 26, July 15, 2003.

entrepreneurial capitalists—and indirectly, through its chilling effect on Russian and foreign investment. Some have suggested political motives, arguing that Khodorkovsky, through his refusal to kowtow to the authorities and his liberal spending in the political arena, was challenging Putin. Some have taken the authorities' explanations at face value, accepting the argument that Yukos had indeed engaged in shady tax-avoidance schemes and that it was getting no more than its just deserts. The problem with this explanation is the selective and coordinated nature of the campaign against Yukos. All major Russian companies had behaved as Yukos had, seeking to take advantage of legal loopholes to minimize taxes and maximize profits, but only Yukos was singled out for attention; the dismantling of Yukos and prosecution of Khodorkovsky were very similar in this respect to the authorities' successful campaigns to break up the business empires of two other oligarchs in 2000, Boris Berezovsky and Vladimir Gusinsky, who had turned against Putin. In those cases as well, criminal and civil prosecutions were used as weapons to dismantle their companies and bring criminal charges against their owners.

Another, more plausible, explanation for the Yukos affair is that it is part of a struggle among intrabureaucratic factions ("clans," as some call them) over the distribution of control over profitable business assets. Knowledgeable insiders claim that a faction associated with senior officials in the security apparatus, who are linked with top officials in the presidential administration and with the government-owned Rosneft' oil company (the same company Khodorkovsky complained to Putin about in February), had its eyes on some of Yukos's choicest oilfields. According to this theory, elements tied to this faction persuaded Putin that moving against Yukos would be politically advantageous on the grounds that public opinion was hostile to the oligarchs, and would remove a threat to his own power. This theory gained credence when Rosneft' wound up the owner of Yukos's most valuable oil fields.

The Yukos affair shows that the authorities continue to manipulate the legal system for political purposes, that many of the most important political contests in Russia are fought out within the state bureaucracy rather than in the open arena of public politics, and that the fight for control over Russia's most lucrative natural resource assets continues to be a driving force in Russian politics.

The League of Committees of Soldiers' Mothers

The Soviet regime sponsored several official women's organizations, but these mainly served propaganda purposes. During the glasnost period, a number of unofficial women's organizations sprang up to voice the interests of groups who were otherwise unrepresented. One such group was the Committee of Soldiers' Mothers. It formed in the spring of 1989 when some 300 women in Moscow marched to protest the end of student deferments from military conscription. In response to their actions, Gorbachev agreed to restore the deferments. In 1990 and 1991, Gorbachev also acceded to other demands made by the Soldiers' Mothers, including creating a body to investigate noncombat-related deaths of servicemen, improving social benefits for the families of deceased servicemen, and granting a provisional amnesty to soldiers who deserted the army as a result of intolerable abuse.[19] Since the early 1990s the movement has grown. It has continued to focus on issues concerning military service. One of its enduring and most widely shared causes is its demand that the army end the common practice of subjecting new conscripts to brutal hazing, which results in numerous deaths and maimings of soldiers each year.[20] It also counsels families on how young men can avoid being drafted. Some 300 local committees sprang up in towns across the country and united into a nationwide League of Committees of Soldiers' Mothers that can call on a network of thousands of active volunteers for its work.

The onset of large-scale hostilities in Chechnia in 1994–1996 and 1999–2000 stimulated a new burst of activity by the Soldiers' Mothers. The organization has helped families locate soldiers who were missing in action or captured by the Chechen rebel forces; sent missions to Chechnia to negotiate for the release of prisoners and to provide proper burial for the dead; collected fuller information about the actual scale of the war and of its casualties than the Russian military; and continued to advise families on ways to avoid conscription and to lobby for decent treatment of recruits. It has even cooperated with Chechen women's groups in organizing antiwar protests. Through the 1990s, it became one of the most sizable and respected civic groups in Russia. Its St. Petersburg branch alone reports that some 300 people visit its office every week seeking consultations and legal advice, and that it has helped 57,000 young people escape the draft.[21] They visit wounded soldiers in hospitals and help military authorities in identifying casualties. One of the movement's greatest assets has been its moral authority as the voice of mothers defending the interests of their children; this stance has made it hard for their opponents to paint them as unpatriotic or power-hungry. The league has also avoided taking an explicitly antimilitary stance and has welcomed opportunities to cooperate with the military in such causes as ending hazing in the ranks.

The league has been active in lobbying parliament (for example, it worked for the adoption of legislation that would provide would-be conscientious objectors with a legal procedure for exercising their constitutional right to perform alternative civilian service instead of military duty[22]), but for the most part it has concentrated its efforts on helping soldiers and their families deal with their problems. Thus it performs multiple functions, combining political goals with services to clients. Unlike many Russian associational groups, the league has chosen to remain independent of government, not seeking any special privileges or recognition. As Elena Vilenskaia, one of the founders of the Committee of Soldiers' Mothers in St. Petersburg, put it, "we realized we had to form an organization of a completely different type. Not a committee which is manipulated by someone, but something fundamentally new, constructive. From the beginning we separated ourselves from all central structures."[23]

Like many nongovernmental organizations, the League of Committees of Soldiers' Mothers has cultivated ties with peace and women's groups in Europe and North America. It has won international recognition for its work and has presented reports to international organizations such as the UN Commission on Human Rights, the European Commission, and Amnesty International.[24] But, the league's high international profile and willingness to challenge the authorities over the sensitive issues of the Chechen War and the hazing of conscripts has made it vulnerable to the accusation that it is manipulated by foreign interests.[25] So far, however, its prestige at home and abroad has helped protect it from repressive actions by the regime.

The Federation of Independent Trade Unions of Russia

The cases of RUIE and the Committees of Soldiers' Mothers illustrate the point that the old regime was rich in state-sponsored organizations but poor in autonomous social groups that could provide organizational resources to new interests seeking to organize and voice their demands. Official Soviet public organizations were mouthpieces of state policy and "transmission belts" for controlling society. Yet in some cases they served to foster skills and social ties that became important resources for interest organizations in the post-Soviet environment. The RUIE suggests that an organization built on a Soviet-era association could adapt itself successfully to the new post-Communist environment and become an influential business association. The League of Committees of Soldiers' Mothers, in contrast, formed as an informal organization in the glasnost period, and has consciously chosen to keep its distance from the smothering embrace of the state. The RUIE made use of inherited networks of contacts and organizational resources from the old regime, whereas the Soldiers' Mothers group built itself up from scratch, taking advantage of the Internet to link branch organizations across the country as well as to win international recognition. Its prestige at home and abroad, its willingness to cooperate with the authorities when necessary and to avoid a directly political role for the most part, have helped preserve it.

The Federation of Independent Trade Unions of Russia (FITUR) is the successor of the official trade union federation under the Soviet regime.[26] It has adapted and survived, but is ineffective as a voice for organized labor despite inheriting substantial organizational resources from the old Soviet trade union movement. In the Soviet era, virtually every employed person belonged to a trade union. Branch trade unions represented all employed persons in a given industry, from shopworker to top management. In turn, all branch and regional trade union organizations were part of a single labor federation, called the All-Union Central Council of Trade Unions. With the breakdown of the old regime, some member unions became independent, whereas other unions sprang up as independent bodies representing the interests of particular groups of workers. Nonetheless, the shell of the old official trade union organization survived in the form of FITUR.

It remains by far the largest trade union federation in Russia; as of 2001, it claimed to represent about 60 percent of the labor force.[27] But this figure is doubtful. Surveys indicate that only about half of the employed labor force has trade unions at their place of work, and of these about 80 percent belong to a union. Thus only about 40 percent of the workforce are aware of belonging to a union.[28] Most of these belong to FITUR and smaller numbers belong to smaller independent trade unions. By comparison with big business, however, the labor movement is fragmented, weak, and unable to mobilize workers effectively for collective action.[29]

FITUR inherited valuable real estate assets from its Soviet-era predecessor organization, including thousands of office buildings, hotels, rest homes, hospitals, and children's camps. These generate a substantial stream of income for FITUR's leaders ($300 million per year, according to one 2001 estimate).[30] It also inherited the right to collect workers' contributions for the state social insurance fund. Although FITUR formally lost the right to collect and distribute social insurance funds, it still has substantial de facto control over these streams of income and their use. These assets and rights give leaders of the official unions considerable advantages in competing for members (for instance, they can deny members of rival unions from occupying apartments owned by FITUR). They also incline FITUR's officials to be more concerned about protecting their own organizational interests than in advancing those of the workers.[31]

Moreover, FITUR no longer has centralized control over its regional and branch members. In the 1993 and 1995 parliamentary elections, for instance, member unions formed their own political alliances with parties. Thus internal disunity is another major reason for the relative weakness of FITUR as an organization. Much of its effort is expended on fighting other independent unions to win a monopoly on representing workers in collective bargaining with employers rather than in joining with other unions to defend the interests of workers generally.[32]

The ineffectiveness of FITUR was illustrated by the tepid response of organized labor to the severe deterioration in labor and social conditions that occurred through the 1990s. Despite high unemployment, severe wage arrears, and a sharp drop in living standards, there was much less protest than might have been expected. Certainly there was some labor mobilization in the 1990s, mainly over wage arrears. Surveys found that in much of the 1990s, in any given year, three-quarters of all workers received their wages late at least once.[33] Teachers were particularly hard-hit by the problem of unpaid wages and organized numerous local strikes. Waves of strikes by teachers shut down thousands of schools in 1997, 1998, and 1999. Over 1999–2000 teachers' protests dropped off as wage arrears gradually were paid off thanks to the beginning of the economic recovery.[34] The Putin administration has paid attention to ensuring that wages and pensions are paid on time, and labor unrest subsided.

Still, when we consider how deep was the decline in living standards in the early and mid-1990s, it is reasonable to wonder why there was not more labor protest. One reason is workers' dependence on their workplaces for a variety of social benefits administered through the enterprise, such as pension contributions, cheap housing, and access to medical clinics and day care facilities.[35] A second is the organizational structure of FITUR, which replicates that of the Soviet trade unions. The fact that all members of each enterprise (blue collar, clerical, technical, and managerial) belong to the same union militates against mobilization around class interests. A final reason is the close, clientelistic relationship between the leadership of FITUR and government authorities. Any time that FITUR threatens any serious labor protest, the government threatens to take away its access to the distribution of social funds. Like RUIE, therefore, FITUR for the most part prefers to cultivate a docile relationship with the political authorities rather than to exert an independent role. In turn, the Putin regime has been content to keep the trade unions weak and dependent.

The Russian Orthodox Church

The great majority of the Russian people—as many as 89 percent, depending on how religious affiliation is measured—identify themselves with the Russian Orthodox Church. Another 9–10 percent identify with other faiths: 8–9 percent are Muslim, 0.5–0.6 percent are Buddhist, and 0.2–0.3 percent are Jewish.[36] The Russian Orthodox Church dates its origins to Prince Vladimir's baptism in 988 in the Kievan city-state, and considers itself to be the historic partner of the Russian state and people, providing spiritual guidance to society and sanctification of state authority in return for the state's protection. Its view of itself as a state church is at odds with the constitutional precept of the separation of church and state.[37]

Historically, the church was closely allied to the state authorities. For most of the two centuries before the Bolshevik Revolution, according to historian Firuz Kazemzadeh, "the Church acted as an arm of the State, teaching obedience to the governmeent, glorifying absolutism, and serving as a spiritual police."[38] After the Communists took power, the Russian Orthodox Church was not banned, but it was subject to persecution, at times violent, and to intense surveillance by the authorities. Young people were strongly discouraged from attending services; party members and political officials understood that their careers would be jeopardized if they openly practiced religion. Appointments of senior clergy had to be cleared by the state, and some clergy were in fact police agents. The church's public pronouncements had to be supportive of the state. For example, during the Cold War, church officials actively participated in the Soviet regime's propaganda campaign for "peace and justice" in the world, which was always directed against the "imperialist" world's policies, but never the Communist bloc's. The church never died out, as Soviet officials had once predicted it would, but its public role was severely restricted, and its clergy were infiltrated with police informers.

The collapse of Communism allowed the church to regain much of its status and freedom.[39] Under legislation passed in 1990, the church acquired the right of legal personhood, entitling it to own property and enter into contractual agreements. Many churches and monasteries that had been seized by the state were restored to the church, often in considerable disrepair. Religious education became legal, and was even introduced in some schools. The church also has benefited from the eagerness of the political elite to associate itself with the Church. Beginning with Gorbachev's celebration of the millenium of Russian Christianity in 1988 and continuing with Yeltsin's attendance at major church events and Moscow mayor Luzhkov's forceful drive to rebuild the Cathedral of Christ the Savior, torn down under Stalin, numerous Russian political leaders have found it expedient to embrace the church as a symbol of Russian national unity, continuity, and statehood. Although the 1993 constitution proclaimed the separation of church and state, state leaders have looked to the Orthodox Church to bless their actions. The church, for its part, has not been reluctant to take advantage of its newly privileged status. The Patriarch, for example, attended the inaugurations of Russian presidents Yeltsin and Putin.

The end of the Soviet regime also brought with it a religious awakening in Russia and other former Soviet republics. Many, including young people, sought to rediscover their religious heritage or to find a new religious identity. Thousands of foreign missionaries arrived to proselytize. Denominations and sects that had operated underground began to practice openly. New Protestant and Catholic churches were established. Muslim and Jewish organizations also gained strength. Various fringe sects won adherents. The Orthodox Church responded to the new activity by calling on the state to protect it against foreign competition. The church drew a sharp distinction between those religions that had a long history on Russian soil, and hence posed less of a threat, and those that were new and alien to it. Regarding proselytism from abroad as a hostile invasion,[40] the church pressured the president and parliament for protectionist legislation that would ban foreign missionary activity and would, in effect, require a state license for the exercise of the new religious freedom guaranteed under the Russian constitution.

The idea of such a law was very popular among lawmakers, particularly nationalists and Communists, who wanted to align themselves publicly with the moral authority of the church. In 1997 the Duma passed and, after an initial veto and some minor revisions, President Yeltsin signed a law that gave the church much of what it wanted. The law was euphemistically called "On Freedom of Conscience and Religious Associations." Declaring that there were four religious communities that were historically indigenous to Russia—Orthodox Christianity, Islam, Judaism, and Buddhism—the law required that any other religious organization that wanted to operate on Russian soil would have to reregister with the state by the end of 1998. If it wanted to use the word "All-Russian" (*Rossiiskii*) in its name, an organization would have to demonstrate that it had operated in Russia for at least 50 years and had local branches in at least half the regions of the country. Alternatively, it could register if it could prove that it had a central organization and at least three regional branches and had existed in Russia for at least 15 years. Moreover, the law listed a number of grounds on which registration could be denied. Foreign missionaries would only be allowed to operate in Russia if they were invited by registered religious organizations.[41]

Many Russian and international religious groups were alarmed by this law. As experts noted, it was directed not against Islam, Judaism, or Buddhism, but against rival Christian groups that the Orthodox Church considered to be "destructive totalitarian sects," as the Patriarch termed them.[42] Several groups challenged the constitutionality of the law. In November 1999 the Constitutional Court upheld the main tenets of the law but softened others. It ruled that the state could restrict the activity of foreign missionaries and could ban those groups that violated human rights and Russian law. But it also declared that the clause that religious organizations had to prove they had existed for 15 years did not apply to groups registered before the law was passed or to congregations that are part of centralized organizations. Therefore a local congregation of the Jehovah's Witnesses could be registered because the national organization had existed in Russia for more than 50 years.[43] A ruling several months later by the court went further and invalidated the other retroactive provisions.[44] Meantime, the deadline for registering religious organizations was extended, and several groups that were initially denied the right to register eventually succeeded.

The Orthodox Church holds that "the Russian people culturally, spiritually, and historically are the flock of the Russian Orthodox Church."[45] In contrast to the Western Christian doctrine of separation between the authority of the state and the authority of religion, Russian Orthodoxy regards church and state as interlocked elements of an organic national community.[46] It considers religious identification to be an attribute of a nationality, not simply a matter of individual taste, and it regards the Russian Orthodox Church as the patrimony of the Russians—whether they are believers or not. Therefore it is hostile to any efforts at conversion by outsiders, arguing that Western missionaries are trying to buy Russians' souls with promises of material prosperity. The Orthodox Church is amenable to coexisting with other religious communities in Russia, such as Muslims, Jews, and Buddhists, so long as the boundaries among the ethnic groups belonging to each religious community are respected. But it is deeply antagonistic to other Christian groups that believe that Russia should be religiously pluralistic. Because state leaders, both liberal and Communist, have been solicitous of the church for their own political interests, they have been unwilling to cross the church on matters of religious politics. The church's animosity toward the Catholic Church, for example, has made it impossible for the pope to visit Russia. The church has also sought to exert influence on matters of public education and culture. For instance, in January 2007, the head of the Orthodox Church, Patriarch Aleksii II, denounced the teaching of evolution in the schools.[47]

The church has formed a relationship of reciprocal dependence with state authorities, as in the prerevolutionary era: it looks to the state for protection and privileges, and in turn grants the state authorities moral sanction for their actions. Any change in this symbiotic relationship will probably come from within the church, as believers demand that it reduce its reliance on the state for its power and status and instead draw its strength from the commitment of the faithful.

New Sectors of Interest

We have seen that in a time when people's interests themselves are changing rapidly as a result of social change, both old and new organizations find it hard to stay united. As is true everywhere, smaller groups have an easier time acting collectively than do large, dispersed groups. We have also noted a pattern of behavior in which groups that gained new freedom in the post-Soviet era have used their influence to block competing organizations from recruiting support—as with FITUR's effort to use the new Labor Code to win exclusive collective bargaining rights on behalf of organized labor, and the Russian Orthodox Church's efforts to deny equality to competing religious denominations.

Overall, the trend has been an evolution in structure of interest articulation from statism to pluralism, and now, under Putin, to an authoritarian version of corporatism. The legacy of the Soviet system remains significant in the case of organizations such as the trade unions and RUIE, which are built on Soviet-era organizations. Elements of authoritarianism are evident in the Putin regime's efforts to limit the political rights of interest groups, and of corporatism in the effort to draw selected interest groups into the state's embrace.

Still, the system of interest articulation is far more pluralistic than it was in the Soviet period. Tens of thousands of new associations speak for interests that had never been organized in the past, such as the Committees of Soldiers' Mothers and tens of thousands of other organized associations. Among these are organizations that promote the interests of particular categories of officials, business, or social groups, such as associations for governors; associations of mayors of small towns and of mayors of closed cities; associations of small businesses and of entrepreneurs; associations for particular industries, such as the beer brewing industry; and associations for particular categories of the population, such as the Association of Indigenous Peoples of the North and the Far East. There are many new professional associations, which act to set guidelines for professional practice, seeking to fend off onerous government restrictions and to regulate entry into their fields. Television broadcast companies founded a National Association of Television Broadcasters on August 31, 1995, to seek the expansion of private ownership of television facilities and tax relief for broadcasters.[48] In May 2000, representatives of 150 auditing and consulting firms formed their own national federation to set professional standards with which to regulate their own activity.[49] In January 2001, heads of publishing and media firms from 20 different regions formed an Association of Independent Publishers and Editors. Public relations firms created the Russian Association of Public Relations, which celebrated its tenth anniversary in October 2001.[50] Reindeer breeders formed the Russian Union of Reindeer Breeders, which held a congress in Salekhard—located just south of the Arctic Circle, in the Yamalo-Nenets Autonomous Okrug—in March 2002, where they warned of the "tragic" consequences of the steep drop in the size of the reindeer herds.[51] A group called the Public Organization for the Defense of the Rights of Owners of Cars with Right-Hand Steering Wheels registered in Vladivostok. Press reports indicated that the aim of the group was to lobby against new customs duties on imported cars (many Japanese cars imported to the Far East have right-side steering wheels).[52]

Thousands of groups espousing charitable, social services, environmental, consumers' rights, and human rights causes have also formed. One of the most prominent is Memorial, which arose in the Gorbachev period to honor the memory of the victims of Stalin's repressions, and which has continued to work to protect human rights and democratic freedoms.[53] Most organizations are local. Examples are the Nizhnii Novgorod Society for Human Rights; the Center for the Support of Democratic Youth Initiatives in the city of Perm, which helps young men who want to do alternative service defend their legal rights; the Chukotka Ecology Society; the Magadan Center for the Environment; the Moscow Fellowship of Alcoholics Anonymous (AA started in Russia in 1987, and there are now some 300 AA groups around the country); and a group in Moscow called "the Circle" that offers special classes in music, dance, and theater to disabled children.[54] Many local groups join together in national associations to amplify their clout. Examples include the All-Russian Society of Invalids; the Association of Help Hotlines (which represents 200 crisis helplines in 68 cities); the Forum of Ecological Organizations; the Confederation of Consumers' Societies; and the Union of Charitable Organizations of Russia. Some groups act as facilitators of other nongovernmental organizations (an example is the Support Center for NGOs of Yaroslavl, which publishes directories with contact information for other organizations).[55]

Russian civic groups operate under very difficult circumstances, including unpredictable and sometimes hostile treatment by the authorities; scarcity of office space and other material resources; obstacles to communication with prospective members and with other groups; and habits of secretiveness and hoarding of information. Faced with economic and political pressure, many are dependent on foreign support, whereas others attempt to win official status and budget support from government. Some are simply fronts for commercial activity, and many are only sporadically active. Although only a very small number of citizens are members of such organizations, many more benefit from their activity. Taken together, they represent a substantial sector of independent civic activity.

In some regions, NGOs have cooperated with the local authorities on specific issues. For example, some NGOs are working with law enforcement agencies to improve policing and detention practices and to give training to police on handling domestic violence incidents.[56] One Siberian NGO offered free breast cancer screening exams, and a thousand women responded. Recognizing the pent-up demand for better women's health services, the local government offered funds to the NGO so that it could conduct similar screening sessions throughout the region. A center for Siberian NGOs (the Siberian Civic Initiatives Support Center) has been working with several local governments to develop better mechanisms for building citizen input into policy making. Several citizen-based advocacy groups have mounted campaigns for environmental protection (in one recent case, they persuaded the authorities to reroute a planned oil pipeline to reduce the chance that it could endanger the pure water of Lake Baikal).[57]

The Putin regime's policy toward NGOs has been driven by the twin goals of control and cooptation. Putin has repeatedly expressed his support for the concept that Russia needs a vigorous civil society, but he has also sought ways to structure and limit the political influence of Russian NGOs.[58] In 2006, following allegations that Western intelligence services were funding some Russian NGOs, Putin proposed new legislation tightening state control over NGOs, imposing stringent new registration requirements that give the authorities ample grounds to shut groups down, and expanding financial controls over their activity. All existing NGOs had to reregister. Compliance with the new rules was burdensome for many groups (for instance, they had to report the current home addresses and passport numbers of all the founding members of the organization) and a number of groups were denied reregistration on the grounds that their forms were improperly filled out.

At the same time, the regime has also sought to create formal mechanisms for consultation and collaboration with NGOs. In November 2001, the authorities convened a large assembly called the Civic Forum in the Kremlin's Palace of Congresses (where, in the past, the Communist Party used to hold its congresses every five years). Some 5,000 delegates representing civic groups from all over Russia assembled. President Putin and most of the senior officials of the presidential administration and government attended the meeting. Addressing the assembly, Putin had warm words for the principle of civil society, observing that "civil society cannot be formed at the initiative of government officials" and disavowing any desire to subordinate civil society to the state. Rather, he noted that civil society "grows up on its own, feeding on the spirit of freedom" and cited the Internet as an example of the way state and society can work together for mutual benefit.[59] The meeting broke into a number of thematic working sessions, which drew up resolutions that were signed by members of the civic associations and the government. Ultimately, however, little came of these documents, although one or two found their way into subsequent government policy planning on issues such as the problem of homeless children.

In September 2004, following the Beslan tragedy, Putin proposed the formation of a "Public Chamber." The Public Chamber was intended to give various social associations an outlet to bring their ideas and opinions to the attention of the authorities to improve the effectiveness and responsiveness of policy and to monitor the quality of public life. Similar consultative bodies already existed in a number of regions and several Western countries. Putin's proposed legislation creating a Public Chamber in Russia passed in 2005 and the body was formed soon thereafter. The chamber has 126 members, drawn from a wide array of organizations (including media; business; sports; environmental protection groups; the Orthodox Church; medical, legal, and academic professions; and youth groups). Putin named the first 42 members, who in turn chose another 42. These 84 then selected the final 42. No openly oppositional figures are represented in the chamber (nor did they wish to join) but the chamber does include a number of prominent intellectuals and social figures, such as the popular singer Alla Pugacheva, nuclear physicist Evgenii Velikhov, and the world chess champion Anatolii Karpov.

Although the Public Chamber has been careful to avoid taking directly political stands on controversial issues, it has weighed in on some topical questions. For instance, it called for softening some of the more repressive provisions of the 2006 law on NGOs. Perhaps of greater significance is the fact that regional governors have also been encouraged to create (or reorganize) public chambers in their own regions. Such chambers give governors opportunities to meet regularly with leaders of local civic groups, hearing their views and helping them in turn to shape public opinion.[60] Participation in such chambers gives some local NGOs greater legitimacy in voicing the interests of the groups they represent. In regions where such chambers did not already exist, Putin's creation of a Public Chamber at the federal level encouraged the governors to establish similar chambers in each region—and to invite local NGOs to join them. Thus a paradoxical consequence of Putin's authoritarian corporatism is that it has simultaneously limited freedom for some interest groups while expanding it for others—especially those that are willing to accept the terms of their relationship with the authorities and work within those constraints to advance the interests of their constituencies.

INTEREST AGGREGATION AND THE PARTY SYSTEM: RETURN TO A ONE-PARTY REGIME?

In democratic political systems, political parties are indispensable mechanisms for converting citizens' demands and groups' interests into policy options that give citizens choice and control over government. In the Soviet era, a monopoly party—the Communist Party of the Soviet Union—sought to guide all public organizations and serve as the sole means for aggregating the multiple interests of a vast and complex society. Since the end of the Communist era, a number of parties have arisen but a stable party system has yet to form. The dominance of United Russia under Putin, however, has led many observers to speculate that Russia is returning to some form of single-party rule.

Political scientists distinguish between the *articulation* of interests and their *aggregation*: interest articulation is the voicing of demands by organized groups seeking to advance particular causes and interests; interest aggregation refers to the combining of the demands of various groups of the population into programmatic options for government. Typically this is a by-product of the activity of political parties as they compete for voter support in elections and organize to assume responsibility for governing. Parties propose policy programs that they hope will attract wide support, generalizing the interests of the many in order to win a share of governing power. Although other political institutions also aggregate interests, among them the mass media, parliaments, and large interest groups, it is parties that are the quintessential agency performing this vital task of the political process. Indeed, most political scientists share the view that, as Seymour Martin Lipset put it, "modern democracy is unthinkable save in terms of parties."[61] This is because parties offer voters both choice and accountability: they give voters a choice over competing policy directions for government and make public officials responsible for their behavior in office. Without parties to organize the alternatives for public policy, and to compete for the power to put their plans into effect, the citizens lack power to participate in policy making.[62] The question of whether and how well parties in Russia are serving to aggregate interests, define choices for voters, and hold politicians accountable for their use of power is therefore central to assessing the level and quality of democracy in Russia.

In Russia, however, most parties have shallow roots; they appear suddenly and fade away quickly. Neither voters nor politicians develop lasting ties to them. Over time, hundreds of organizations have formed as parties and run candidates for elections, but very few have had staying power. The Putin regime has attempted to bring about greater stability to the party system but to place it under tight state control, allowing its preferred pro-Putin party, United Russia, to gain a commanding position of dominance among the parties.[63] The regime has taken a number of steps to accomplish these goals. New legislation passed in 2001 and 2004 raises the requirements for registration of parties: a party must have 50,000 members and branches in at least half the regions of the country to be legally registered. Moreover, only registered parties (and not other kinds of public organizations) are allowed to run candidates in elections. The new rules resulted in a massive winnowing out of the field. By January 2006, only 33 parties remained, and 27 had failed to clear the hurdle.[64] As of January 1, 2007, when the new legislation took force, 16 more parties were disqualified, leaving only 17 parties to have the legal right to compete in regional and national elections. The rest had dissolved or reorganized as social organizations.

In addition, legislation passed in 2005 eliminates single-member district seats from the Duma, so that all 450 seats will be filled by party lists. Parties have to collect large numbers of signatures or put down sizable deposits to qualify to run, and they will have to win at least 7 percent of the vote to win seats. All these provisions make it extremely difficult for small parties to compete. They also give federal and local authorities more legal grounds for denying parties access to the ballot. For instance, in the run-up to regional legislative elections held in 14 regions in March 2007, there were 17 instances when the authorities disqualified opposition parties; only completely loyal parties encountered no difficulty in registering their candidates to run.[65]

Table 6.1 lists the most prominent political parties as of early 2007 together with their levels of popular support.[66]

Today's parties have diverse origins. Some grew out of the "informal" groups and movements that mobilized during the glasnost period.[67] Others sprang up from the CPSU, as it fractured into hard-line and more liberal wings in 1989–1990. Still other parties are more recent creations formed by office-holding politicians who want to hold on to power by winning the next elections. One reason politicians join parties is simply that the law used for Duma elections requires that half the seats in the Duma (and all of them as of 2007) be filled from party lists. As a result, politicians who want to win or keep their seats find it useful to affiliate with a party. And once they are in the Duma, deputies affiliate themselves

Table 6.1 ■ Party Support, February 2007

If elections were to be held next Sunday for the State Duma, which party would you vote for?

United Russia	31
CPRF	7
LDPR	5
"Just Russia" (merger of Party of Life, Rodina, and Pensioners' Party)	4
Yabloko	1
Agrarian Party of Russia	1
SPS	1
Other	1
Wouldn't vote	22
Hard to say	27

Source: Fond, "Public Opinion," N = 1,500. Margin of error = 3.5 percent. Survey conducted February 3–4, 2007. From Web site: http://bd.fom.ru/report/map/d070601#Abs3.

with parliamentary parties. Parliamentary elections are strongly influenced by party competition—it is executive power that avoids partisanship and thus weakens electoral accountability.

Similarly, at the regional level, under legislation pushed by President Putin, at least half the seats of legislatures must be filled by proportional representation from party lists, again creating a legal incentive for politicians to affiliate with parties and run under party labels. Of course, this legislation has benefitted Putin's allies in the United Russia party most of all.

Russian parties tend to adopt one of two political strategies. Some espouse a particular ideological outlook, whereas others avoid taking a clear policy stance and instead identify themselves with broad, vague appeals to support the status quo. Of those with a definable ideological stance, three main strains are apparent: democratic, Communist, and nationalist. Although specific party names and organizational identities continue to evolve rapidly, the position of ideologically oriented parties can usually be identified in terms of support for a capitalist economy, liberal individualism, and a Western orientation (the democratic parties); a strong, centralized, state-dominated economic and political system (the Communist parties); and a pro-imperial or pro-ethnic nationalist, anti-Western orientation (the nationalist parties). The nonideological parties offer a bland mixture of appeals to noncontroversial values, such as "centrism," "unity," "pragmatism," and "a strong state." Often, such parties are simply political machines for officeholders, and are commonly termed "parties of power." United Russia is far and away the most successful "party of power" but there were earlier examples of the type as well.

Let us examine these categories more closely.

Party Families

Democratic parties

Democratic parties promote liberal democratic political values and market-oriented economic values; they want to dismantle the political and economic framework of state socialism and replace it with an open, pluralistic, free market system along Western lines. Some emphasize a more laissez-faire approach, others a more social-democratic approach. But they would all agree that Russia must guarantee political and economic freedoms for its citizens, protect private property rights, and strengthen the rule of law, and they fight against socialist and collectivist tendencies in the political and economic spheres.

Russia's democrats first mobilized in the glasnost era and formed, as we saw, a movement called Democratic Russia to compete for seats in the Russian parliament in 1990. Soon they split up into different groups, but in 1993 a number of democratic figures allied under the name "Russia's Choice" headed by Yeltsin's architect of economic reform, Egor Gaidar. After suffering setbacks in the 1993 and 1995 elections, some leaders of Russia's Choice and other groups pooled their resources and formed a new electoral alliance called the Union of Right Forces (SPS, for its Russian initials) to compete in 1999. They put a trio of younger leaders at the top of their party list, and their campaign emphasized that Prime Minister Putin had endorsed (if rather vaguely) their economic program. This time their strategy paid off, and they entered parliament. In 2003 they again fell below the 5 percent threshold in the Duma party list vote. They have won seats in several regional assemblies, however.

Yabloko is a party that presents itself as the "democratic opposition" to the government. It is headed by the prominent political leader Grigorii Yavlinsky. It espouses a general theme of a socially oriented economy and a pro-Western external policy. Yavlinsky himself ran for the presidency in 1996 and again in 2000, receiving around 7 percent of the vote in 1996 and 5.8 percent in 2000. Yabloko received a rather constant share of the vote in parliamentary elections in the 1990s, but failed to win 5 percent in 2003. SPS and Yabloko have repeatedly discussed uniting their efforts to avoid dividing the democratic vote between them and thereby keeping each other out of parliament. However, these efforts keep foundering on the ambitions of their leaders.

Communist Parties

The Communist Party of the Russian Federation (CPRF) is the major successor party to the old CPSU. Other splinter groups exist that are more militantly Stalinist; the CPRF has cautiously embraced certain elements of the market and has declared that it no longer believes in violence and revolution as means to achieve its policy goals but it vehemently opposed the market reforms and privatization programs of the Yeltsin era.[68] The CPRF also takes a nationalist stance, for instance, attacking Western influence in Russia. Its leader, Gennadii Ziuganov, has sought to align the party with the religious and spiritual traditions of Russian culture, glossing over Marx's and Lenin's militant enmity toward religion. Ziuganov frequently invokes the traditional mutual support between the Russian state and the Russian Orthodox Church.

The CPRF has a substantial organizational base, a well-defined electoral following, a large but declining membership (officially 184,000 as of early 2007), a large network of local party newspapers, and, probably most important, the tradition of Communist Party discipline that it inherited from the Communist Party of the Soviet Union. Divisions within the party are usually kept from exploding, although periodically the party expels dissidents. But the CPRF has clear weaknesses as well. Ziuganov lacks broad personal appeal, but no other Communist leader enjoys wide support in the party. CPRF voters tend to be older than average, and the party appeals to them by its association with the old regime. Moreover, it is ideologically straitjacketed: if it moves too much to the center of the political spectrum, it will lose its distinctiveness as a clear alternative to the government, but if it moves further to the left, it will marginalize itself. The result is that the CPRF's share of the electorate is declining but the party has been unable to mobilize new groups of voters. The ideology, reputation, and organization of the Communists give them a certain base level of electoral support, yet the same factors also set a ceiling on their success.

Until 1999, the Agrarian Party of Russia (APR) was closely allied with the CPRF, but its political activity was almost entirely focused on agricultural issues. The APR staunchly opposed the privatization of land in Russia and persistently lobbied for credits and subsidies, including price supports, to the country's collective and state farms. The APR is more a lobby for collective and state farm managers than a political party aggregating interests across sectors. Not only are the APR's interests focused specifically on the agricultural sector, but it also is willing to support the government's position on some issues on which the Communists are not. Splits between the hard-line and moderate wings of the party have weakened the agrarians' electoral strength, and they have failed to clear the 5 percent threshold since 1993.

Nationalist Parties

The most visible nationalist party, the Liberal Democratic Party of Russia (LDPR)—Zhirinovsky's party—differs from the Communists in certain important respects. Zhirinovsky's party stresses the national theme, even more than the Communists, appealing to feelings of injured ethnic and state pride. Zhirinovsky calls for aggressive foreign policies and harsh treatment of non-Russian ethnic minorities. However, his economic policy is much fuzzier. While demanding that the government relieve the distress of Russians who have suffered under market reforms, he also distances himself from the socialist economic system of the past and poses as a "third force," which is neither tied to the old Communist regime nor to the new order. Finally, he also sends a clear message that he is seeking the presidency, the powers of which he will use dictatorially to right wrongs and settle accounts with Russia's enemies.

Zhirinovsky cultivates a vivid, theatrical, even clownish, public persona, which works effectively on television. He appeals to many voters who are disaffected with both the government and the Communists. However, bombastic as Zhirinovsky's rhetoric is, the party's actual voting record is extremely supportive of the authorities. Zhirinovsky's party is also famous for putting figures identified with organized crime onto its candidate lists.[69] Rumors have circulated for years about the price for buying a good place on the list. Some consider the LDPR to be a business enterprise more than a political party.

Zhirinovsky's LDPR has been the most successful of the parties competing for the nationalist vote. A great many other parties have attempted to build successful followings around themes such as the need to restore the Soviet Union, or to make Russia a great world power again, or to cleanse Russia of the ethnic "outsiders" who contaminate it, or to bring back the tsar. But these parties have either failed in their bid for parliamentary votes and then splintered and faded, or have concentrated their efforts on forming a small but dedicated corps of militant (sometimes armed and militarily organized) followers. In the 2003 election, most parties tried to play the nationalist card by invoking patriotic rhetoric and putting forward candidates with reputations as strong nationalists. One, Rodina (Motherland), did well by running a list headed by a young economist with a protectionist program, Sergei Glaz'ev. A number of other prominent nationalists, including several extremists, were also added. This party was widely considered to enjoy the Kremlin's tacit sponsorship as a ploy to bleed votes away from the Communists and other nationalist forces.[70] But it split shortly after the election when its leaders fell out.

There are a number of small militant nationalist groups that have adopted fascist or protofascist ideologies and organizational models. Two examples are Russian National Union and Russian National Unity. The Russian National Union was planning to compete in the 1999 elections when it was charged with the crime of propagating fascist ideas, prompting a split in the organization. Russian National Unity, which uses a swastika-like symbol for an emblem and imitates Nazi styles in uniform and organization, has been banned in several regions. Still another group is the National Bolshevik Party, which has repeatedly been refused registration. Such groups have been able to attract media attention by staging marches and demonstrations, but they have little popular support.

Among the nationalist parties and splinter groups there are a variety of ideological tendencies: some want to see Russia form a great Eurasian union; others focus on purifying Russia of ethnically alien elements. This inability to define a common national program has been one factor inhibiting unity among the nationalist forces.

Parties of Power

Although many parties have called themselves centrist, that usually means that they lack any distinct policy positions that they could be held accountable for. In some cases, parties that are closely allied to the authorities call themselves centrist to reinforce their commitment to stability and continuity. Certainly the most successful "party of power" to have arisen—United Russia—considers itself to be centrist. For example, in its publicity, it describes itself as the "party of Russian political culture," "the party of sovereign democracy," "the party of stability, of self-reliant people."[71] In fact, it is centrist only in the sense that it avoids offering the voters any clear policy commitments at all, while voting loyally for any legislation proposed by the government or president. It often claims that it is the party of the middle class, but the middle class is far too small and undefined for that to be a successful electoral strategy. Its identification with Putin is total; it proudly declares that "the president is the moral leader of United Russia." A strategy of embracing the president will work only so long as the president is in office and popular. The question for United Russia is what will become of it once Putin leaves office.

The forerunner of United Russia as a party of power was "Our Home Is Russia." It originated in the run-up to the 1995 parliamentary elections, when President Yeltsin's political advisors decided to use the Kremlin's political resources to create a progovernment, centrist but moderately reformist, political movement. Yeltsin asked then-prime minister Chernomyrdin to head it. Benefitting from official government support and promoting a reassuring image of stability and pragmatism, Our Home won 10.3 percent of the list vote in the December election. However, Our Home never succeeded in defining a clear programmatic position, and was mostly a coalition of officeholders, particularly big-city mayors, regional governors, and presidents of ethnic republics. For this reason it soon became known as "the party of power." And once Chernomyrdin was dismissed from the government in 1998, Our Home imploded. In 1999 it only won 1.2 percent of the list vote. It dissolved soon thereafter.

The 1999 election was peculiar in that it offered voters at least three parties that had some claim to being a party of power. Besides Our Home Is Russia, two other blocs also competed that had strong links to the state authorities. The Fatherland-All Russia alliance united several powerful regional leaders and its list was headed by former prime minister Evgenii Primakov. But the real phenomenon of 1999 was the third party of power, Unity. Unity formed only three months before the election, by all accounts with the active assistance of Boris Berezovsky and President Yeltsin's entourage in the Kremlin. Its trump card was Vladimir Putin. Appointed prime minister on August 9, 1999, Putin actively aided in the formation of the new movement, commenting at one point that "as a citizen," he intended to vote for Unity. Thus state officials who wondered which was the "true" party of power (fearing to back the wrong party!) could safely conclude that Unity was the right choice, particularly as Putin's popularity soared. As the once-dominant Fatherland-All Russia bloc's ratings fell, Unity's support rose: Unity went from 4 percent on November 2, to 9 percent on November 22, to 18 percent on November 29; and it received 23.3 percent of the vote on election day.[72] The reason for its success was that governors and other elites quickly switched their allegiance to it once they saw that it was going to be the *real* party of power.

In parliament, Unity became the vehicle through which President Putin could enact his legislative program. Voting with remarkable discipline, Unity's members formed alliances with other parliamentary factions and passed nearly every bill proposed by Putin and the government.[73] Unity liked to describe itself as a "ruling party," but in fact it did not control either the government or the presidency: it was largely the parliamentary appendage of a very strong president. Putin spoke vaguely about the desirability of building a viable party system and even of moving to the point where parties would name the candidates for president. But, like Yeltsin before him, he himself found it expedient to remain above the battlefield of party politics. Still, the Kremlin lent its considerable resources to ensure the Unity would dominate the next parliament. In December 2001, "Fatherland" (Moscow mayor Yuri Luzhkov's party) merged with Unity to form "United Russia." The Kremlin signalled to federal and regional officeholders that it expected them to support United Russia. The result was a landslide electoral victory and an overwhelming majority in the Duma. United Russia succeeded in capitalizing both on President Putin's popularity and on the steady improvement in the economy.

In 2006, a quasi-opposition party of power formed to offer United Russia a challenge from the left side of the spectrum. Called "A Just Russia" (*Spravedlivaia Rossiia*), it is headed by Sergei Mironov, the chair of the Federation Council. Mironov had headed a minor party called the "Party of Life," which offered a vague, nonprogrammatic vision of improved living standards, but in October 2006, he engineered its merger with two other small parties to form "A Just Russia." The new party espouses a left-centrist, broadly social-democratic orientation, stressing the need for improved pay for workers, assistance to the poor, and higher pensions for the elderly. It attacks United Russia for tieing itself too closely to the government and big business, and promises to fight "wild capitalism," to nationalize natural resources, and to provide free, state-funded housing, education, and medical care to all citizens. Its member parties have already won seats in several regional legislatures, and the party itself was aiming to make a good showing in the wave of regional elections in March 2007. Campaigning in St. Petersburg in February 2007, Mironov confidently claimed that "Just Russia is the only real opposition currently. The others are just playthings."[74]

But whether in fact A Just Russia is a "real" opposition party is doubtful. Although it clearly reflects an effort by the Kremlin to organize a moderate leftist opposition to United Russia (a figure with the stature of Sergei Mironov would not be allowed to form a party without the explicit authorization of Putin), observers are unsure whether the Kremlin intends for it to have any real chance of winning a sizable share of the vote. The point of a party of power is that its status as the vehicle of officeholders is exclusive. Therefore any real competition beween United Russia and A Just Russia in the 2007 elections poses the risk of a divided elite, which in turn could spur an uncontrollable cascade of open popular mobilization.[75] Most likely, the Kremlin seeks to allow A Just Russia to win just enough votes to siphon off support from the Communists and nationalists, but not enough to pose a serious threat to United Russia's dominance.

The history of Russian parties of power illustrates the point that when parties are the creatures of official government sponsors, they lack the ability to formulate their own independent appeals to voters or to generate their own independent bases of organizational support. When their sponsors in the state lose power, they vanish. Parties of power are similar to patronage-based parties in some West European countries that exploit their entrenchment in government to provide material benefits to supporters and promises of elective office to ambitious politicians. The difference is that in Russia, the president, not the parliament, forms the government. As a result, Russian parties of power do not get an opportunity to take responsibility for government, and voters and politicians have little reason to make any long-term commitments to them.

Parties and Elections

The history of post-Communist Russia also shows that the greatest impetus to the development of political parties has been Duma elections. Each round of elections (1993, 1995, 1999, 2003, 2007) has stimulated a burst of organizational activity.[76] Presidential elections, on the other hand, held in 1991, 1996, 2000, and 2004, have not had a similar effect. Because Russia's presidential system encourages the president to avoid making commitments to parties, presidential elections have tended to concentrate attention on the candidates' personalities rather than their policy programs, and therefore have even undermined party development. The same has been true of gubernatorial elections. Other factors as well have stalled the development of the party system, including the trend for big business to sponsor candidates directly, the rise of governors' political machines, and the tendency for the Kremlin to intervene in the electoral system, both by sponsoring parties of power and by selective backing of individual gubernatorial and mayoral candidates. Political scientist Henry Hale terms these "party substitutes" and argues that they have impeded the development of the party system.[77]

Let us review the history of elections and party development more closely.

The 1989 and 1990 Elections

The development of parties began with the elections under Gorbachev to the reformed USSR and Russian Republic parliaments. Democratically oriented politicians coalesced to form legislative caucus in the USSR Congress of People's Deputies in 1989, and in turn helped a broad coalition of democratic candidates run for the Russian Congress in 1990. In parliament, democratic factions competed for influence with Communist, nationalist, agrarian, and other political groups. These parliamentary factions in turn became the nuclei of political parties in the parliamentary election of December 1993.

The 1993 and 1995 Elections

The 1993 election produced a shock—the pro-reform, pro-Yeltsin party, Russia's Choice, did unexpectedly poorly, whereas Vladimir Zhirinovsky's Liberal

Democratic Party of Russia (LDPR) did unexpectedly well. The Communists (Communist Party of the Russian Federation, or CPRF) took about 10 percent of the seats. Altogether the democratic factions received about 38 percent of the seats in the Duma, the left about 20 percent, and centrist factions about 20 percent. No political camp had a majority, but Zhirinovsky's oppositional stance meant the anti-Yeltsin forces had a narrow majority.

In the 1995 elections a wide array of political groups competed—far more than could possibly be accommodated given that the same 5 percent threshold rule was kept. Some 43 organizations succeeded in registering and winning a spot on the ballot. But in the end, only four parties crossed the 5 percent threshold: the Communists, Zhirinovsky's LDPR, the "Our Home Is Russia" bloc formed around Prime Minister Chernomyrdin, and the Yabloko party. Of these, the Communists were the most successful, winding up with nearly a third of the seats in the Duma. Altogether, half of the votes were cast for parties that failed to win any seats on the party list ballot.

The 1999 Elections

The 1999 election was dominated by the question of who would succeed Yeltsin as president. Many federal and regional officeholders wanted to rally around a new party of power in order to protect their positions. As we saw, a group of backroom Kremlin strategists formed the Unity bloc in late summer 1999 to serve as a political vehicle for Vladimir Putin. Conveniently for Putin, at just the same time as Unity's formation and Putin's appointment, Chechen rebels launched raids into the neighboring region of Dagestan, and bombings of apartment buildings attributed to Chechen terrorists occurred in Moscow and other cities. Putin's decisive handling of the military operations against the Chechen guerrillas gave him and Unity a tremendous boost in popularity during the fall campaign. Unity, which had not even existed until late August, ended up winning 23 percent of the party list vote.

The 2003 Election

Under Putin the ideological divide between Communists and democrats that had marked the transition era disappeared. The political arena was dominated by the president and his supporters. The loyal pro-Putin party, Unity, was renamed United Russia following its merger with its rival, Fatherland. United Russia came to hold almost a monopoly position in the party spectrum, squeezing other parties to the margins. The magnetic attraction of a successful party of power was demonstrated vividly in the 2003 parliamentary election, when United Russia won 38 percent of the party list vote and wound up with two-thirds of the seats in the Duma. The Communists suffered a severe blow, losing almost half their vote share, and the democrats did even worse; for the first time, none of the democratic parties won seats on the party list vote. The result underscored Putin's determination to eliminate any significant alternatives to his policies and power.

Table 6.2 indicates the results of the party list voting in the 1993, 1995, 1999, and 2003 Duma elections, and Table 6.3 shows the distribution of parliamentary parties' seats in the Duma following the 1999 and 2003 elections.

Unlike parliamentary elections, presidential elections have had very little positive effect on party development; it is more likely in fact that the "superpresidential"

Table 6.2 ■ Party List Vote in Duma Elections: 1993, 1995, 1999, and 2003

Party	1993	1995	1999	2003
Democratic Parties				
Russia's Choice	15.51	3.9	–	–
Union of Rightist Forces (SPS)	–	–	8.52	4.0
Yabloko	7.86	6.89	5.93	4.37
Party of Russian Unity and Concord (PRES)	6.76	–	–	–
Democratic Party of Russia (DPR)	5.52	–	–	0.2
Centrist Parties				
Women of Russia	8.13	4.6	2.04	–
Civic Union[1]	1.93	1.6	–	–
Parties of Power				
Our Home Is Russia	–	10.1	1.2	–
Fatherland-All Russia (OVR)	–	–	13.33	–
Unity/United Russia[2]	–	–	23.32	38.2
Nationalist Parties				
Liberal Democratic Party of Russia (LDPR)[3]	22.92	11.2	5.98	11.6
Congress of Russian Communities (KRO)[4]	–	4.3	0.62	–
Motherland (Rodina)	–	–	–	9.2
Leftist Parties				
Communist Party of the Russian Federation (CPRF)	12.4	22.3	24.29	12.8
Agrarian Party	7.99	3.8	–	3.69
Other parties failing to meet 5% threshold	10.98	26.81	12.55	11.1
Against all	4.36	2.8	3.34	4.8

[1] In 1995, the same alliance renamed itself the Bloc of Trade Unionists and Industrialists.

[2] In 2003, Unity ran under the name United Russia following a merger with the Fatherland party.

[3] In 1999, the LDPR party list was called the Zhirinovsky bloc.

[4] In 1999, this party was called "Congress of Russian Communities and Yuri Boldyrev Movement."

Source: Compiled by author from reports of Central Electoral Commission.

Table 6.3 ■ Seat Shares of Parliamentary Parties in State Duma, 2000 and 2004

	2000	2004
Unity/United Russia	16.9	67.0
Communist Party of the Russian Federation	18.6	11.6
Liberal Democratic Party of Russia	3.5	8.0
Motherland	–	8.7
Yabloko	4.4	–
Union of Rightist Forces	6.7	–
Fatherland-All Russia	9.4	–
People's Deputy*	12.1	–
Russia's Regions*	7.9	–
Agro-Industrial Group*	8.6	–
Unaffiliated	3.8	3.1

* These were groups made up of deputies elected in single-member districts who chose not to affiliate with any of the party-based factions, but were registered as official deputy groups on the basis of having at least 35 members. In the 2004 Duma, there were no such groups.

Source: Compiled by author from reports of State Duma.

NB: Figures taken as of January 2000 and May 2004. Percentages shift with time as members change factional affiliations. Note that United Russia was the result of a merger of the Fatherland party with Unity.

system in Russia has discouraged party development.[78] The two individuals who have run and won in Russia's presidential elections—Yeltsin and Putin—both conspicuously avoided running as partisans. (Technically, sitting presidents may not be party members—but this would hardly be a bar to a president who wanted to change the law.[79]) Rather, both Yeltsin and Putin evidently calculated that they would have broader appeal if they chose *not* to run as party candidates, but emphasized instead their personal qualities and their devotion to broad national goals. To be sure, some major challengers to Yeltsin and Putin have represented parties or political movements. It is possible, moreover, that Putin's successors may want to identify themselves with a "Putinist" party (whether United Russia or a different party of power) in order to claim the mantle of Putin's legacy—much as de Gaulle's associates in France chose to form a Gaullist party so as to link themselves with his popular image despite the fact that de Gaulle himself avoided a party label.

Let us review the history of presidential elections.

The 1996 Election

The 1995 parliamentary election was considered to be a test of strength for Russia's parties and leaders. The big unknown was how Yeltsin would perform in the 1996 presidential race. At the beginning of 1996 his approval rating was in the single digits.[80] But during the campaign, Yeltsin succeeded in persuading voters that the election was about a choice between him and a return to Communism. Yeltsin's displays of vigor during the campaign, his lavish promises to voters, and his domination of media publicity, all contributed to a remarkable surge in popularity and a victory over Gennadii Ziuganov, his Communist rival. The campaign took its toll on Yeltsin. Soon afterward he had major heart surgery and for much of his second term he was in poor health.

The 2000 Election

The presidential election of 2000 was held earlier than scheduled because of President Yeltsin's early resignation. Under the constitution, the prime minister automatically succeeds the president upon the premature departure of the president, but new elections for the presidency must be held within three months. Accordingly, the presidential election was scheduled for March 26, 2000. The early election gave the front-runner and incumbent, Vladimir Putin, an advantage because he was able to capitalize on his popularity and the country's desire for continuity. Putin ran the equivalent of a "rose garden" campaign, going about the normal daily business of a president rather than going out on the hustings and asking for people's votes. He counted on the support of officeholders at all levels, a media campaign that presented a "presidential" image to the voters, and the voters' fear that change would only make life worse. His rivals, moreover, were weak. Several prominent politicians prudently chose not to enter the race against him. In the event, Putin won an outright majority on the first round.

The 2004 Election

Putin's reelection as president in 2004 was a landslide: he won easily with 71.31 percent of the vote. European observers commented that the elections were "well administered" but hardly constituted "a genuine democratic contest" in view of the president's overwhelming control of media coverage of the race and the absence of genuine competition.[81] The Kremlin's use of administrative carrots and sticks (known in Russian as the "administrative resource"), its egregious manipulation of media coverage of the election, and Putin's genuine popularity all combined to make the outcome a foregone conclusion. Moreover, Putin's decisive victory underscored the point that United Russia needed Putin far more than Putin needed the party.

Table 6.4 lists the results of the presidential elections in 1996, 2000, and 2004, together with the party affiliations, if any, of the candidates.

As the history of party participation in elections demonstrates, there has been a great deal of turnover in the parties over time. Politicians are constantly starting new parties, only to abandon them after the election. Voters have relatively shallow attachments to parties and often associate them with particular politicians' personalities rather than with specific ideological stances. Each new election presents voters with a substantially new set of party choices, making it

Table 6.4 ■ Presidential Election Results, 1996–2004 (in percentage)

	Party Affiliation	First Round	Second Round
June–July 1996 (%)		**June 16**	**July 3**
Boris Yeltsin	none	35.28	53.82
Gennadii Ziuganov	CPRF	32.03	40.31
Aleksandr Lebed'	none	14.52	
Grigorii Yavlinskii	Yabloko	7.34	
Vladimir Zhirinovsky	LDPR	5.7	
Svyatoslav Fedorov	Party of Workers' Self-Management	0.92	
Mikhail Gorbachev	International Fund for Socioeconomic and Political Research	0.51	
Martin Shakkum	Party of Socioeconomic Reform	0.37	
Yurii Vlasov	National Patriotic Party	0.2	
Vladimir Bryntsalov	Russian Socialist Party	0.16	
Aman Tuleev	CPRF	0	
Against all candidates		1.54	4.83
March 26, 2000 (%)			
Vladimir Putin	none	52.94	
Gennadii Ziuganov	CPRF	29.21	
Grigorii Yavlinskii	Yabloko	5.8	
Aman Tuleev	none	2.95	
Vladimir Zhirinovsky	LDPR	2.7	
Konstantin Titov	none	1.47	
Ella Pamfilova	For Citizens' Dignity	1.01	
Stanislav Govorukhin	none	0.44	
Yuri Skuratov	none	0.43	
Alexei Podberezkin	Spiritual Heritage	0.13	
Umar Dzhabrailov	none	0.1	
Against all candidates		1.88	
March 14, 2004 (%)			
Vladimir Putin	none	71.31	
Nikolai Kharitonov	CPRF	13.74	
Sergei Glaz'ev	none	4.1	
Irina Khakamada	none	3.84	
Oleg Malyshkin	LDPR	2.02	
Sergei Mironov	Party of Life	0.75	
Against all candidates		3.45	

hard for voters to develop any lasting attachments to parties or to make sensible judgements about parties' past or future performance. As Richard Rose puts it, up until now, Russia has had "a floating party system."[82] The great question for the 2007–2008 electoral cycle is whether this pattern will end, and the party system will finally develop an anchor in the form of a lasting, stable, dominant party of power—United Russia.

Party Strategies and the Social Bases of Party Support

Survey researchers have found differences in party support among various categories of the population. Factors such as household income, age, urban or rural residence, and education levels are related to differences in party preferences.[83]

Table 6.5 indicates how the parties differed in the social bases of their support, based on a February 2007 survey conducted by the Moscow-based survey organization, the Foundation for Public Opinion. Note that the table should be read across. For example, it tells us that 47 percent of the respondents were male and that 28 percent of males support United Russia.

The table shows that age, gender, education, and economic situation all influence party choice. For example, the Communists depend much more on older voters than do other parties (note that 13 percent of those 55 years old and older support the Communists, whereas only 2 percent of 18–35 year-olds do so) and on voters with lower levels of education and lower income levels. In contrast, United Russia draws its support widely from across the political spectrum. The one way in which United Russia is distinctive is that it draws somewhat stronger support from women than from men, a fact consistent with the observation that female voters in Russia have tended to support parties promising stability and continuity in policy. Otherwise, however, United Russia's base of social support is strikingly even across social categories.

At the same time, surveys conducted by Timothy Colton on the determinants of party preferences in the December 2003 Duma election found that United Russia's support "is about much more than affection for Vladimir Putin."[84] A number of voters who had previously supported the Union of Right Forces or Yabloko evidently transferred their loyalty to United Russia in 2003 as the most viable alternative to the Communists. Certainly voters who viewed Putin favorably were much likelier to support United Russia, but voters also saw it as espousing a promarket economic ideology, and voted for it even so. United Russia's supporters were also influenced by the improvement in the country's economic conditions and by their own household's position (those who believed that economic conditions had improved for the country and for themselves were significantly more likely to vote for United Russia.) The Communists, in contrast,

Table 6.5 ■ Social Sources of Support for Political Parties

From question: "If elections to the Duma were to be held next Sunday, which party would you vote for?"

		Share of group in sample	United Russia	CPRF	LDPR	Just Russia	Yabloko	Agrarian Party	SPS	Other	Won't vote	Hard to say
All respondents		100	31	7	5	4	1	1	1	1	22	27
Sex	male	47	28	8	6	3	2	1	1	1	25	24
	female	53	33	6	3	4	1	1	1	1	20	30
Age	18–35	37	31	2	7	1	1	1	1	1	23	31
	36–54	37	31	7	4	3	2	1	1	1	25	25
	55+	26	28	13	3	7	1	1	1	1	18	26
Education	less than secondary	14	29	10	4	3	0	1	0	0	18	33
	secondary–general	33	30	6	6	3	1	1	1	1	23	29
	secondary–vocational	36	31	7	4	4	2	1	1	1	23	26
	higher	16	31	6	4	5	3	1	2	1	23	22
Income	<2000 rubles/mo.	24	34	8	4	3	1	2	1	1	18	29
	2001–4000 rubles/mo.	36	31	9	5	4	1	1	1	1	20	27
	4000+/mo.	27	28	5	6	4	2	1	2	2	28	23
Residence	Moscow	8	24	8	6	6	4	1	2	1	30	19
	megapolis	13	25	5	5	5	2	0	2	1	27	28
	large city	17	27	6	6	5	2	1	1	2	26	25
	small city	37	33	7	4	3	1	1	1	1	22	28
	village	25	35	7	5	3	1	2	0	0	16	31

Source: Fond, "Obshchestvennoe mnenie," http://bd.fom.ru/report/map/d070601#Abs2. Accessed February 15, 2007.

Survey based on N = 1,500, representative sample of adult population of Russia, conducted February 3–4, 2007. Margin of error 3.6%.

performed better among voters who believed that economic conditions had worsened. Both United Russia and Communist voters expressed a sense of attachment to their parties (as did, more strongly, the smaller numbers of voters who supported Zhirinovsky's LDPR and the Motherland party). Thus there is some evidence that voters are beginning to form attachments to political parties.[85] However, the progressive loss of open political contestation in Russia as the authorities manipulate the rules on ballot access and media coverage has made it difficult for opposition parties to win more than a small share of votes. Most politicians have recognized that career success today requires hitching their wagon to the principal party of power—United Russia.

The Future of the Party System

Party development in Russia has been hampered by institutional factors, such as the powerful presidency, the effectiveness of party politics, the fading of the ideological cleavages produced by the regime change, and the success of the party of power, United Russia. Strong presidentialism undermines the ability of parties to promise that electoral success will translate into policy influence, because the president can choose a government largely of his own liking. Moreover, both Yeltsin and Putin avoided party affiliations, preferring instead to remain above the partisan fray. Under these circumstances, politicians have little incentive to invest their efforts in building up party organizations. As a result, parties are weak at performing the functions of aggregating the interests of citizens and formulating practical policy options. In turn, voters have little basis on which to form definite opinions and attachments about parties.

The current situation is not likely to last indefinitely. The strongly presidential tilt to the constitution is not likely to change soon, but it is hard to predict what will happen once Putin is no longer the dominant institution in the political system. If Putin's authoritarian methods survive Putin, party competition will be nominal. President Putin and his allies have often called for a consolidation of the party system, and they have sponsored institutional changes to bring this about. However, their proposals appear to be intended to give United Russia, the current party of power, a near monopoly on power. Putin's political strategist, Vladislav Surkov, has indicated that he would like to see the political dominance of United Russia last 10 or 15 years or more, ensuring that Putin's long-term goals are achieved.[86]

To a large extent, politicians still treat parties as disposable objects, vehicles for winning and keeping office, and avoid having to be held to account for their actions. What little interest aggregation there is through political parties at present owes far more to the "top-down" and "supply-side" strategies of ambitious politicians than to the "bottom-up," "demand-side" processes of social mobilization. Whether Russia will succeed in producing a viable, competitive party system remains to be seen. There can be little doubt, however, that without it, democracy will remain a distant ideal.

NOTES

1. In October 2002, a national survey by VTsIOM found that 54 percent of the population consider that their lives had gotten "somewhat" or "significantly" worse in the last 15 years; only 29 percent said that their lives had improved.

Yuri Levada, "Ogliadyvaias' no proidennoe i neprodumannoe: 1987–2002," posted on Polit.ru Web site, December 27, 2002, www.polit.ru/printable/522413.html.

2. Mancur Olson, *The Logic of Collective Action: Public Goods and the Theory of Groups* (Cambridge, MA: Harvard University Press, 1965).

3. According to Gregory J. Kasza, such "administered mass organizations" as Stalin-era trade unions and youth groups have been a characteristic feature of a number of the mobilizing regimes of the twentieth century. Gregory J. Kasza, *The Conscription Society: Administered Mass Organizations* (New Haven, CT: Yale University Press, 1995).

4. Frederick C. Barghoorn, "Faction, Sectoral and Subversive Opposition in Soviet Politics," in Robert A. Dahl, ed., *Regimes and Oppositions* (New Haven, CT: Yale University Press, 1973), pp. 27–88.

5. Philip G. Roeder, *Red Sunset: The Failure of Soviet Politics* (Princeton, NJ: Princeton University Press, 1993).

6. Robert Conquest, *The Great Terror: A Reassessment* (New York: Oxford University Press, 1990). The terrible famine of 1932, which struck the Ukraine and certain other regions with particular force, was itself the product of deliberate policy as Stalin and his associates expressly prohibited sending relief to the affected areas, apparently in order to break any resistance to the collectivization campaign.

See also Robert Conquest, *The Harvest of Sorrow: Soviet Collectivization and the Terror-Famine* (New York: Oxford University Press, 1986).

7. Jane I. Dawson, *Eco-Nationalism: Anti-Nuclear Activism and National Identity in Russia, Lithuania, and Ukraine* (Durham, NC: Duke University Press, 1996).

8. On the emergence of informal social groups in the glasnost period, see Judith B. Sedaitis and Jim Butterfield, eds., *Perestroika from Below: Social Movements in the Soviet Union* (Boulder, CO: Westview, 1991) and Michael Urban, *The Rebirth of Politics in Russia* (Cambridge: Cambridge University Press, 1997). A valuable overview of the emergence of nationalist movements in the Gorbachev period is Ch. 4, "Nationalism and Nation-States: Gorbachev's Dilemmas," in Ronald Grigor Suny, *The Revenge of the Past: Nationalism, Revolution, and the Collapse of the Soviet Union* (Stanford, CA: Stanford University Press, 1993), pp. 127–60.

9. The labels "red" and "brown" are widely used to refer to these ideological tendencies in Russian discussions. "Red," of course, is the symbolic color of the Bolsheviks, of Communism and revolution; it was the dominant color of the Soviet flag. "Brown" represents extremist nationalism after the "brown shirts" who were early Nazi followers of Adolf Hitler in Germany in the 1920s. Thus they are regarded as quasi-fascist ultranationalists.

10. RFE/RL Newsline, June 13, 2001.

11. EastWest Institute, Russian Regional Report, Vol. 6, no. 42, November 28, 2001.

12. Jack L. Walker, Jr., *Mobilizing Interest Groups in America: Patrons, Professions, and Social Movements* (Ann Arbor: University of Michigan Press, 1991), p. 9.

13. In a system in which all prices were set by the state, there was no meaningful measure of profit in any case. Indeed, relative prices were profoundly distorted by the cumulative effect of decades of central planning. The absence of accurate measures of economic costs is a major reason that Russia's economy continues to be so slow to restructure.

14. Chapter 7 will discuss the oligarchs in more detail.

15. Information on Civic Union may be found in Stephen White, Graeme Gill, and Darrell Slider, *The Politics of Transition: Shaping a Post-Soviet Future* (Cambridge: Cambridge University Press, 1993), pp. 166–69. A more detailed study is Peter Rutland, "Business Elites and Russian Economic Policy" (London: Royal Institute of International Affairs, 1992). See also Michael McFaul, "Russian Centrism and Revolutionary

Transitions," *Post-Soviet Affairs* 9:3 (July/September 1993): 196–222. Wendy Slater, "The Diminishing Center of Russian Parliamentary Politics," *RFE/RL Research Report* 3:17 (April 29, 1994), discusses the fate of Civic Union through the 1993 elections.

16. Information drawn from the RUIE's Web site, http://www.rspp.ru/Default.aspx? CatalogId=1282, accessed February 11, 2007.

17. Peter Rutland, "Business and Civil Society in Russia," in Alfred B. Evans, Jr., Laura A. Henry, and Lisa McIntosh Sundstrom, eds., *Russian Civil Society: A Critical Assessment* (Armonk, NY: M. E. Sharpe, 2006), p. 85.

18. *Segodnia,* October 7, 2000.

19. Lisa McIntosh Sundstrom, "Soldiers' Rights Groups in Russia: Civil Society through Russian and Western Eyes," in Evans, Henry, and McIntosh Sundstrom, eds., *Russian Civil Society,* p. 180.

20. Figures on the number of soldiers who die each year as a result of hazing (*dedovshchina*) are hard to come by. According to the Ministry of Defense, only 16 soldiers died as a result of improper treatment in 2005. However, another 276 committed suicide, and 1,064 died as a result of "crimes and incidents." Polit.ru, January 27, 2006. The Prosecutor General reported in August 2006 that so far that year, 17 servicemen had died as a result of hazing and over 100 had been injured, and that there had been some 3,500 reported cases of hazing. RFE/RL Newsline, August 4, 2006.

Occasionally a particularly shocking case comes to light, resulting in a public outcry and provoking the military to arrest and try those guilty. But despite the public and official condemnation of the practice, it clearly continues.

21. http://www.soldiersmothers.spb.org/. On the Soldiers' Mothers, see Valerie Sperling, *Organizing Women in Contemporary Russia: Engendering Transition* (Cambridge: Cambridge University Press, 1999), pp. 206–07; *Christian Science Monitor,* February 24, 2000.

22. Article 59 of the 1993 Constitution provides that young men of conscription age who are conscientious objectors to war may do alternative service rather than being called up to army service, but legislation specifying how this right is to be exercised only passed in 2002 as a result of the strong opposition by the military. Thus would-be conscientious objectors and courts were in a legal limbo for nearly ten years.

23. Quoted in Annemarie Gielen, "Soldiers' Mothers Challenge Soviet Legacy," on Web site of Initiative for Social Action and Renewal in Eurasia, www.isar.org/isar/archive/GT/GT8Gielen.html. July 5, 2002.

24. Sundstrom, "Soldiers' Rights Groups," p. 182.

25. James Richter, "Evaluating Western Assistance to Russian Women's Organizations," in Sarah E. Mendelson and John K. Glenn, eds., *The Power and Limits of NGOs: A Critical Look at Building Democracy in Eastern Europe and Eurasia* (New York: Columbia University Press, 2002), p. 80.

26. On the transformation of the trade unions as a result of the regime transition, see Sue Davis, *Trade Unions in Russia and Ukraine, 1985–95* (New York: Palgrave, 2001) and Linda J. Cook, *Labor and Liberalization: Trade Unions in the New Russia* (New York: Twentieth Century Fund Press, 1997).

27. Sue Davis, "Russian Trade Unions: Where Are They in the Former Workers' State?" in Evans, Henry, and Sundstrom, *Russian Civil Society,* p. 203.

28. Richard Rose and Neil Munro, *Elections without Order: Russia's Challenge to Vladimir Putin* (Cambridge: Cambridge University Press, 2002), p. 225.

29. See Paul J. Kubicek, *Organized Labor in Postcommunist States: From Solidarity to Infirmity* (Pittsburgh, PA: University of Pittsburgh Press, 2004), for a comparative study of the changes in trade union organization in post-Communist countries since the end of the Communist regime.

30. Davis, "Trade Unions," p. 202.

31. Ibid., p. 203.

32. FITUR reached a Faustian bargain with the government over the terms of a new Labor Relations Code, which was adopted in 2001. Under the new legislation, employers no longer have to obtain the consent of the unions to lay off workers. But collective bargaining will be between the largest union at

each enterprise and the management unless the workers have agreed on which union will represent them. Thus the new labor code favors FITUR at the expense of the smaller independent unions.

33. Richard Rose, *New Russia Barometer VI: After the Presidential Election* (Glasgow: Centre for the Study of Public Policy, University of Strathclyde, Studies in Public Policy, no. 272), p. 6; Richard Rose, *Getting Things Done,* p. 15. In 1996, the question was: at any point during the past 12 months, have you received your wages or pension late? In 1996, 78 percent responded yes, 21 percent no. In 1998, the question was: at any point during the past 12 months, have you received your wages late? 75 percent responded yes, 25 percent no.

34. RFE/RL Newsline, January 13, 1997; January 17, 1997; February 18, 1997; November 25, 1998; January 14, 1999; January 27, 1999; September 15, 1999; and June 26, 2000.

35. Linda J. Cook, *Labor and Liberalization: Trade Unions in the New Russia* (New York: Twentieth Century Fund Press, 1997), pp. 76–77.

36. RFE/RL Newsline, October 3, 2000, citing estimates published in *Nezavisimaia gazeta—religii.* Another survey placed the number of Russians considering themselves to be Russian Orthodox at 55 percent; 9 percent were adherents of other religions, while the number calling themselves atheists was 31 percent. See RFE/RL Newsline, May 10, 1999, citing a survey by the Russian firm Public Opinion.

Religious identity is closely tied to ethnicity. A few ethnic groups of Russia, including the Buryats, are Lamaist Buddhist by tradition. Many groups, among them the Tatars, Bashkirs, and most of the Northern Caucasus nationalities, are historically Muslim. The Jews are considered an ethnic group of their own. A number of other nationalities have preserved and even revived traditional animist rites and practices, including shamanism.

37. An accessible and sympathetic introduction to Orthodox history and doctrine is Timothy Ware, *The Orthodox Church* (New York: Penguin Books, 1984).

38. Firuz Kazemzadeh, "Reflections on Church and State in Russian History," in John Witte, Jr., and Michael Bourdeaux, eds., *Proselytism and Orthodoxy in Russia: The New War for Souls* (Maryknoll, NY: Orbis Books, 1999), p. 237.

39. John Dunlop, "The Russian Orthodox Church as an 'Empire-Saving' Institution," in Michael Bourdeaux, ed., *The Politics of Religion in Russia and the New States of Eurasia* (Armonk, NY: M. E. Sharpe, 1995), pp. 15–40; and Dimitry V. Pospielovsky, "The Russian Orthodox Church in the Postcommunist CIS," in ibid., pp. 41–74.

40. Metropolitan Kirill of Smolensk and Kaliningrad, "Gospel and Culture," in Witte and Bourdeaux, *Proselytism and Orthodoxy in Russia,* p. 74.

41. *Segodnia,* June 19, 1997.

42. RFE/RL Newsline, September 22, 1997.

43. RFE/RL Newsline, November 24, 1999; *Segodnia,* November 24, 1999.

44. This came in a case involving the Jesuits, whose right to registration was upheld by the Constitutional Court in April 2000 although the Society had only existed in Russia since 1992.

45. RFE/RL Newsline, February 14, 2002.

46. John Witte, Jr., "Introduction—Soul Wars: The Problem and Promise of Proselytism in Russia," *Emory International Law Review* 12:1 (Winter 1998): 38.

47. RFE/RL Newsline, January 30, 2007.

48. RFE/RL Daily Report, September 1, 1995.

49. EastWest Institute, Russian Regional Report, May 5, 2000 (Internet edition).

50. RFE/RL Newsline, October 22, 2001.

51. RFE/RL Newsline, March 12, 2002.

52. Polit.ru, November 28, 2002.

53. Nanci Adler, *Victims of Soviet Terror: The Story of the Memorial Movement* (Westport, CT: Praeger, 1993).

54. Sophie Lambroschini, "Russia's Growing Network of Private Associations," RFE/RL Newsline, Part I, December 2, 1999.

55. EastWest Institute, Russian Regional Report, Vol. 5, no. 33, September 13, 2000.

56. Brian D. Taylor, "Law Enforcement and Civil Society in Russia," *Europe-Asia Studies* 58:2 (2006): 193–213.

57. I am indebted for information about the Siberian Civic Initiatives Support Center to Sarah Lindemann-Komarova. Its Web site is: www.cip.nsk.su.

58. Harley Balzer, "Managed Pluralism: Vladimir Putin's Emerging Regime," *Post-Soviet Affairs* 19:3 (2003): 189–227.

59. Polit.ru, November 21, 2001; RFE/RL Newsline, November 26, 2001.

60. Novgorod's governor, for example, has had such a consultative body in place for many years. See Natalia Dinello, "What's So Great About Novgorod-the-Great: Trisectoral Cooperation and Symbolic Management," *NCEEER Working Paper* (Washington, DC: 2001).

61. Quoted in Richard Rose, Neil Munro, and Stephen White, *The 1999 Duma Vote: A Floating Party System* (Glasgow: Centre for the Study of Public Policy, University of Strathclyde, 2000), p. 3.

62. E. E. Schattschneider, *The Semi-Sovereign People* (New York: Holt, Rinehart and Winston, 1960), pp. 140–41; Robert A. Dahl, *Polyarchy: Participation and Opposition* (New Haven, CT: Yale University Press, 1971).

63. Regina Smyth, "Building State Capacity from the Inside Out: Parties of Power and the Success of the President's Reform Agenda in Russia," *Politics and Society* 30:4 (2002): 555–78; Vladimir Gel'man, "From Feckless Pluralism' to Dominant Power Politics'? The Transformation of Russia's Party System," *Democratization* 13:4 (2006): 545–61.

64. A list of the parties currently registered may be found at the Justice Ministry's Web site: http://www.rosregistr.ru/index.php?menu=3010000000.

65. Steven Lee Myers, "Russians to Vote, but Some Parties Lose in Advance," *New York Times,* February 15, 2007, http://www.nytimes.com/2007/02/15/world/europe/15russia.html?_r=1&oref=slogin&pagewanted=print. The most common grounds for denying registration was disqualification of a proportion of the signatures on the petition documents. Typically, the election officials disqualified the signatures so close to the registration deadline that the parties had no opportunity to contest the decision in court or to obtain fresh signatures.

66. The figures are taken from the Levada Center (formerly VTsIOM) and reflect percentages supporting the given party of those intending to vote.

67. M. Stephen Fish, *Democracy from Scratch: Opposition and Regime in the New Russian Revolution* (Princeton, NJ: Princeton University Press, 1995); Michael Urban, with Vyacheslav Igrunov and Sergei Mitrokhin, *The Rebirth of Politics in Russia* (Cambridge: Cambridge University Press, 1997).

68. On the CPRF, see Joan Barth Urban and Valerii D. Solovei, *Russia's Communists at the Crossroads* (Boulder, CO: Westview, 1997) and Richard Sakwa, "Left or Right? The CPRF and the Problem of Democratic Consolidation in Russia," *Journal of Communist Studies and Transition Politics* 14:1 & 2 (March/June 1998): 128–58.

69. For example, a founding member of the notorious Tambov organized crime gang was elected to the Duma in 1995 on the LDPR list. See Vadim Volkov, *Violent Entrepreneurs: The Use of Force in the Making of Russian Capitalism* (Ithaca, NY: Cornell University Press, 2002), pp. 112–13.

70. Alexei Titkov, *"Party Number Four": Rodina: Whence and Why?* (Moscow: Panorama Center, 2006).

71. Slogans taken from the party's Web site, http://www.edinros.ru/news.html, accessed February 13, 2007.

72. Olga Shvetsova, "Resolving the Problem of Pre-Election Coordination: The Parliamentary Election as an Elite Presidential 'Primary,'" in Vicki Hesli and William Reisinger, *Elections, Parties and the Future of Russia: The 1999–2000 Elections* (Cambridge: Cambridge University Press, 2002).

73. Thomas F. Remington, "Presidential Support in the Russian State Duma," *Legislative Studies Quarterly* 31:1 (2006): 5–32.

74. Myers, "Russians to Vote, but Some Parties Lose in Advance," *New York Times,* February 15, 2007.

75. Such a scenario occurred in the cases of the "colored revolutions" in Serbia, Georgia, and Ukraine in 2000, 2003, and 2004, respectively. See Michael McFaul, "Conclusion: The Orange Revolution in a Comparative Perspective," in Anders Aslund and Michael McFaul, eds., *Revolution in Orange: The*

Origins of Ukraine's Democratic Breakthrough (Washington, DC: Carnegie Endowment for International Peace, 2006), pp. 165–95. On the Orange Revolution and its predecessors, see Close-Up 9.1 in Chapter 9.

76. On the political campaigns surrounding the 1989 and 1990 elections include Brendan Kiernan, *The End of Soviet Politics: Elections, Legislatures, and the Demise of the Communist Party* (Boulder, CO: Westview, 1993); and Michael McFaul and Sergei Markov, *The Troubled Birth of Russian Democracy: Parties, Personalities, and Programs* (Stanford, CA: Hoover Institution Press, 1993). For accounts of the elections of 1993, 1995, and 1999, see Stephen White, Richard Rose, and Ian McAllister, *How Russia Votes* (Chatham, NJ: Chatham House, 1997) and Richard Rose and Neil Munro, *Elections without Order: Russia's Challenge to Vladimir Putin* (Cambridge: Cambridge University Press, 2002). On the 2003 election and its impact on party development, see Henry Hale, *Why Not Parties in Russia? Democracy, Federalism, and the State* (Cambridge: Cambridge University Press, 2006).

77. Hale, *Why Not Parties in Russia?*

78. M. Steven Fish, *Democracy Derailed in Russia: The Failure of Open Politics* (Cambridge: Cambridge University Press, 2005), pp. 226–29.

79. Hale, *Why Not Parties in Russia?*, p. 206.

80. Stephen White, Richard Rose, and Ian McAllister, *How Russia Votes* (Chatham, NJ: Chatham House, 1997), p. 254.

81. Quoted from a press release of the election observer mission of the Organization for Security and Cooperation in Europe posted to its Web site immediately following the election, as reported by RFE/RL Newsline, March 15, 2004.

82. Rose and Munro, *Elections without Order,* pp. 118–19.

83. Survey researchers have found that younger and better-educated voters are likelier to respond "yes" to the question, "Is there a party which represents your interests?" See Arthur H. Miller, Gwyn Erb, William M. Reisinger, and Vicki L. Hesli, "Emerging Party Systems in Post-Soviet Societies: Fact or Fiction," *Journal of Politics* 62:2 (May 2000): 464–66.

84. Timothy J. Colton and Henry E. Hale, "Context and Party System Development: Voting Behavior in Russian Parliamentary Elections in Comparative Perspective," Paper presented at Annual Meeting of the American Political Science Association, Chicago, September 3, 2004, p. 19.

85. Ibid.

86. Surkov made these comments at a United Russia party school session on February 7, 2006. They are taken from the United Russia Web site: http://www.edinros.ru/news.html?id=111148, accessed March 13, 2006. He noted that Japan's Liberal-Democratic Party and Sweden's Social-Democrats had each held power for 40 years or more, and that there was nothing strange or undemocratic about such party dominance.

Chapter 7

State and Market in Russia's Economic Transition

THE DUAL TRANSITION

Russia's transition from Communism required a complete overhaul of both its political *and* economic systems. This is because the two were tightly intertwined. The Communist political system rested on state ownership of all productive wealth, thus eliminating class divisions based on property ownership, and allowing the Communist Party to manage the economy on behalf of the state. Observing the sharp difference between Russia's and China's economic performance in the 1990s and 2000s, many observers argue that Russia's strategy of loosening political controls and engaging in radical economic reform opened the door to a surge of corruption, oligarchic predation, and extremes of wealth and poverty. In contrast, China, where the Communist Party has maintained tight political controls and moved more slowly to dismantle state economic controls, has been far more successful in achieving sustained economic growth. Certainly China's thriving economy is all the more impressive when compared to the spectacle of breakdown and decline seen in Russia over the last decade, as Figure 7.1 and Tables 7.1 and 7.2 show. Note that Figure 7.1 shows per capita income levels in Russia and China as expressed in terms of "purchasing power parity," which provides a more accurate estimate of the actual incomes based on the purchasing power of incomes in the country. The figure underscores the sharp drop in incomes in Russia before their sustained growth since 1999, in contrast to the much steadier trend in China for average incomes to rise.

Considering the dismal economic performance of the Soviet model and the dynamic rates of growth in most market-oriented economies, few doubt that

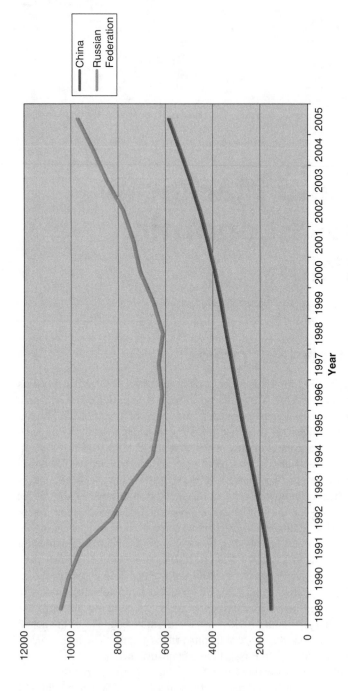

Figure 7.1 ■ **Per Capita Income Growth, Russia and China, 1989–2005 (GDP per capita [PPP], in constant 2000 $US).**

Table 7.1 ■ Russian Annual GDP Growth and Price Inflation Rates, 1991–2006 (in %)

	1991	1992	1993	1994	1995	1996	1997	1998	1999	2000	2001	2002	2003	2004	2005	2006
GDP	−5	−14.5	−8.7	−12.6	−4.3	−6.0	0.4	−11.6	3.2	7.6	5.0	4.0	7.3	7.1	6.4	6.9
Inflation	138	2323.0	844.0	202.0	131.0	21.8	11.0	84.4	36.5	20.2	18.6	15.1	12.0	11.7	10.9	9.0

NB: GDP is measured in constant market prices.

Inflation is measured as the percentage change in the consumer price index from December of one year to December of the next.

Source: Press reports of Russian State Statistical Service (www.gks.ru).

Table 7.2 ■ Russian and Chinese Development Compared

	GDP (2001) (billions of $US)	GDP/ capita (2001)	PPP gross national income (2001) $ blns	PPP gross national income/cap $ (2001)	GDP growth (average annual % growth, 1990–2001)	Inflation (average annual %, 1990–2001)	External debt (% of gross national income, 2000)	% living below poverty line	Gini index (1998)	Life expectancy at birth (2000)	Adult illiteracy[1]
Russia	253.4	1,750	1,255	8,660	−3.7	139.6	60	25.0[2]	48.7	65	0
China	1,131.0	890	5,415	4,260	10.0	6.2	13	4.6[3]	40.3	70	16

[1] % of people aged 15 and above, 2000.

[2] Russian State Statistical Agency figure for 2002 (refers to percentage of population living below subsistence level).

[3] 1998.

Source: World Bank, *World Development Report 2003: Sustainable Development in a Dynamic World: Transforming Institutions, Growth, and Quality of Life* (Washington, DC: World Bank, 2003), pp. 234–39.

a market economy leads both to higher economic growth and greater dynamism over the long term than does state socialism. But the transition from a state-controlled economy to a market system in Russia resulted in economic depression, the collapse of social welfare structures, and the concentration of wealth and power in the hands of a small circle of tycoons. Based on Russia's experience, many argue that liberalization of the economy should wait until the institutional infrastructure of capitalism is in place.[1]

By comparison with other post-Communist countries, Russia's growth performance is lower than that of the successful Central European countries but higher than most of the post-Soviet countries. Figure 7.2 provides the figures on economic growth in several post-Communist countries, taking the economy as of 1990 as a baseline for tracking annual growth or decline of GDP through 2005. Those countries that remade their economies along capitalist lines were most successful, whereas those that reformed only partially experienced the deepest declines before beginning to recover. The great debate, therefore, is between those who think Russia's reforms in the early 1990s were too radical, too "Bolshevik," to succeed, and those who believe that Russia's reforms did not go far enough to eliminate the distortions blocking the breakthrough to a dynamic of self-sustaining growth.[2] The fact that Putin's accession to power coincided with economic recovery in Russia makes it hard to resolve this debate conclusively.

Certainly the economy Putin inherited had few of the institutions needed for a successful market economy: impartial regulatory bodies to referee market competition; law enforcement and judicial bodies to enforce contracts and property rights; financial markets to allocate capital efficiently; transparent corporate governance and protection for shareholder rights; wide access to information about economic activity; insurance markets to spread the risk of business activity. Nor were the representative political institutions, such as parties and parliament, able to channel popular demands for fair play in the economy into public policy. Many Russians became convinced that the privatization of state assets in the 1990s had allowed a handful of unscrupulous oligarchs to loot the state's wealth. Under these circumstances, Putin's strategy of renationalizing the industries most critical to his domestic and foreign policy goals, while encouraging market capitalism in the rest of the economy, has enjoyed a broad base of public support.

Stabilization

To understand the mixture of state control and market capitalism that characterizes Russia's economy today, we have to go back to the beginning of the 1990s and examine the radical reforms enacted under Yeltsin. Russia pursued two major sets of reforms in the 1990s, macroeconomic stabilization and privatization. The stabilization program was nicknamed "shock therapy," which underscores its drastic and painful nature. Stabilization imposes an austerity regime on an economy in order to restore a balance between what society spends and what it earns. It is usually adopted as a response to a crisis in government finances, comparable to an emergency-room

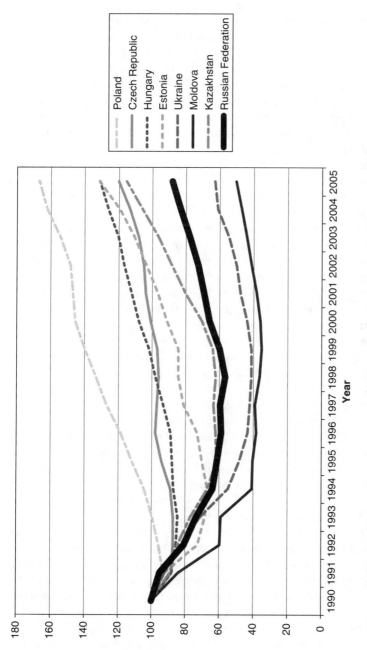

Figure 7.2 ■ Selected Postcommunist Countries, GDP Growth (1990 = 100).

operation on a patient bleeding to death. In the case of economies, the trauma is uncontrollable inflation—skyrocketing prices, plummeting currency.

The goal is to stabilize the national currency, which requires eliminating chronic sources of inflation. This means making drastic cuts in state spending, raising taxes, ending price controls, and eliminating restrictions on foreign trade so that foreign products can compete with domestic ones. Structural reform of this kind always lowers the standard of living for some or most groups of the population, at least in the short run. Therefore, until living standards begin to rise again, such reform creates powerful political opponents. These include the groups that formerly had enjoyed the benefits of state-controlled wages and prices, high state spending to subsidize priority sectors of the economy, protection from competition from foreign industries, and welfare entitlement programs. In many countries undergoing stabilization programs, these groups are well-organized, voicing their opposition to reform through strong trade unions, associations of directors of state-owned firms, and political parties whose primary constituencies are those most vulnerable to reform.

Those who are made worse off by stabilization are not the only enemies of reform, however. Joel Hellman has argued persuasively that in a number of the post-communist countries, it was precisely the reform's "early winners" who stepped in to block subsequent measures to open the economy to free competition. These included managers who acquired ownership rights to monopoly enterprises and then worked to shut out potential competitors from their markets. Others were state officials who benefited from collecting "fees" to issue licenses to importers and exporters or permits for doing business. Still others were bankers who took out cheap state-subsidized loans from the central bank and then lent out money to entrepreneurs at exorbitant rates. Many enterprise directors set up profitable sideline businesses, using the state enterprise as a cheap source of production equipment, raw materials, and labor; the state enterprise then recorded losses while the private sideline business made the director and his friends a tidy profit. All these newly advantaged groups cultivated ties with policymakers who protected them from both a rollback of the reforms and their advancement to the next stage. Hellman argues that these groups were a powerful brake on reform in post-Communist countries such as Russia.[3] The result was that after the initial reforms, the economy did not become more open to competition: those who took advantage of the initial steps prevented the deepening of reform.

The Russian stabilization program took shape in the fall of 1991. The August 1991 coup had fueled support for radical reform. The response to the coup was a surge of support for Yeltsin and his radical reform program both in the Russian Congress of People's Deputies and in society more generally. Addressing the Congress on October 28, 1991, Yeltsin demanded special powers to enact radical reform by decree, and on November 1, received them by a decisive margin. He named himself prime minister and head of government, and formed a cabinet of young, radically minded intellectuals drawn from academic institutes. Egor Gaidar, then 35 years old, became deputy prime minister and overall architect of the reform program. Yeltsin proceeded to issue a set of decrees liberalizing foreign trade and the circulation of hard currency.[4] On January 2, 1992, under Yeltsin's political protection, the new government undertook a major initiative to push Russia toward a market system by abolishing most controls on wholesale and retail prices and cutting government spending sharply.

Almost immediately, opposition to the new program began to form. Within two weeks of its introduction, Ruslan Khasbulatov, chairman of the Russian Supreme Soviet, spoke out strongly against the program and called on the government to resign. Because Yeltsin formally was head of government, this was a direct attack on him. Yeltsin's vice president, Alexander Rutskoi, sided with Khasbulatov and the opposition in parliament. Economists and politicians chose sides. Dispassionate analysis of, and even basic information about, the effects of the stabilization program became virtually impossible to get. The shock therapy program was an easy target for criticism, even though there was no consensus among critics about what should be done instead. Opponents demanded that the pace of reform be slowed so that Russians would have more time to adjust to the new conditions; they complained that the Gaidar team might be capable theorists but had no idea how to run a government. They demanded creation of a safety net to cushion the blow of the transition for the indigent, the elderly, and the displaced. It became commonplace to say that the program was all shock and no therapy.

Evaluating Stabilization

Why did Yeltsin and his government adopt so radical a program of reform? The fact is that they had very little choice. They were faced with an array of undesirable alternatives, and they chose the least bad among them.[5] The breakdown of state planning and administrative controls over the economy had progressed too far for an easy or painless solution. Ministries and regional governments were no longer responding to the old hierarchical command system, but a system of market-based price signals was not in place that could guide producers and consumers. In their power struggle, leaders such as Gorbachev, Yeltsin, and Khasbulatov had freely issued decrees giving away valuable assets or rights that left the state with ever fewer means to control the economy.[6] Hyperinflation was about to erupt, and the policymakers needed to bring demand and supply in the economy back into some rough equilibrium.[7] Like policymakers in other countries facing a financial collapse, they adopted a draconian combination of tax hikes, spending cuts, and monetary stringency.[8] It led immediately to a severe and protracted economic recession.

One line of criticism directed against the Yeltsin/Gaidar government, its Western advisers, and the international financial organizations that were supplying loans, was that they were seeking to "de-industrialize" Russia—that is, trying to destroy the great industrial plant that had been built up at such cost over many years. Some critics went further and said that the West was deliberately trying to sabotage Russia by forcing it to follow the shock therapy prescription. Communists and nationalists got a rise out of audiences by depicting Gaidar and the other radical members of the 1992 government as the traitorous hirelings of a malevolent, imperialist West.

A more widespread viewpoint, however, is that the principles underlying the reform program were fundamentally flawed.[9] These ideas are sometimes referred to as the "Washington consensus" because they represented the conventional wisdom promoted by the United States and many economists in the 1980s and 1990s. The Washington consensus emphasized macroeconomic stabilization, privatization, deregulation, and trade liberalization as ways of squeezing out inflationary pressures and injecting painful but necessary doses of competitive pressure into the economy. The idea was to reduce the amount of state intervention into the economy as much as possible and as quickly as possible. You can't jump across an abyss in gradual steps, they pointed out; if you prolong the pain of reform, the opposition will only grow stronger.

Gaidar and his team embraced this philosophy, both for economic and political reasons. Economically, they believed that Russia would never progress if it remained wedded to a Stalin-era industrial system in which heavy and defense industry received the lion's share of investment, while consumer goods and services sectors were perennially starved of resources. Politically, they wanted to act as quickly and decisively as possible in order to make movement toward the market economy irreversible. The team of reformers who enacted stabilization in Russia in 1992 acted on the assumption that they had only a very short window of opportunity in which to act, or otherwise the forces opposed to market capitalism—Communists and their supporters, powerful state officials and enterprise managers, workers and peasants dependent on state-owned factories and farms—would rise up and restore the old system. Therefore the reformers had to be pragmatic. They calculated that they would have to make concessions to potential allies, such as industrial managers and regional governors, by giving them a stake in the success of reform, and they used the privatization program to do so.[10] The problem was that because insiders ("early winners") ended up with so many advantages, they acted to block further reform and thus protracted the pain of transition.

Both critics and defenders of the program assume that the government's policies actually had the effects they intended. In fact, the program was never carried out comprehensively. Moreover, many officials simply circumvented the policies. Directors of important industries wheedled credits out of the Central Bank (which was not under the government's control) or persuaded ministries to place orders for products simply to keep production going.[11] Rather than respond to the new financial austerity, many directors simply continued to turn out and ship their products without being paid, allowing interenterprise arrears to mount. The Gaidar government lacked full control over the state bureaucracy, so it could not completely shape the structure of incentives to which enterprise managers responded. The credibility of its policies was never secure. Since the effectiveness of a stabilization program depends on producers' calculation of the government's commitment to staying the course, the government's imperfect control over the money supply distorted the effects of the policy. The government did not carry price liberalization out fully in any case, keeping heavy controls on energy and electric power, which may have protected consumers and producers but at the cost of allowing severe price distortions to accumulate throughout the economy.

Certainly the Gaidar team had a very limited choice of policy instruments to use, and it inherited an economy on the verge of breakdown. Through 1991, as traditional lines of control via the Communist Party and state bureaucracy weakened, regional and local governments began erecting barriers to interregional trade. Some set tariffs; others erected roadblocks preventing the "export" of goods from their territories. Moscow and other big cities introduced identity cards to prevent out-of-towners from coming in and purchasing goods from the relatively better-stocked stores in cities. The network of internal wholesale and retail trade was breaking down. Administrative measures probably would have failed to restore them, short of martial law. But the drastic price liberalization of January 2, 1992, which allowed producers and retailers to set any price that the market could bear for most goods and services, immediately eliminated the internal trade wars and restored the circulation of goods, albeit at high and often ruinous prices.

Privatization

Stabilization was followed shortly afterward by another, equally important program—the privatization of state assets. In contrast to the shock therapy program, privatization at first enjoyed considerable public support, which helped offset the unpopularity of stabilization. Privatization is the transfer of ownership of state enterprises to private owners. Market theory holds that under the right conditions, private ownership of productive assets is more efficient for society as a whole than is monopoly or state ownership because, in a competitive environment, owners are motivated by an incentive to maximize their property's ability to produce a return. Whereas a monopolist does not care whether the firm he or she owns is inefficient, in a market system, the owner wants to increase the productivity and therefore the market value of his or her firm. For this reason, most economists consider it essential to transfer ownership of state assets from the state to private owners as part of the transition from socialism to a market economy in order to stimulate growth and productivity in the economy as a whole. In short, a system of clearly established property rights benefits not only the individual owners, but also benefits the whole society.

The theory is generally valid. But, as is often true of good theories, much can interfere with its application to the real world.

We must distinguish between the privatization of state-owned firms in Russia and the creation of new, private start-up businesses. Although private entrepreneurs and foreign interests have created a large number of new, independent businesses, these are usually small in scale. The fate of Russia's state enterprises has profound political importance because the overwhelming majority of the population is tied to them for their livelihoods as well as the wide circle of social benefits that, as we have noted, are supplied through jobs at state enterprises. Privatization's form also has major political repercussions. One method is simply to give away state assets to the public as a democratic gesture that quickly turns the entire population into property holders and gives them a stake in the reform process. An alternative is to require auctions in which groups and individuals submit competitive bids to purchase assets, thereby creating real value that can be used as investment capital, but allowing rich or corrupt elements of the population to capture control of state enterprises. Russia combined these two methods, first distributing free vouchers to all citizens, who were then able to use the vouchers to bid for shares of privatized firms at special auctions, and then holding auctions of shares for cash.

Giving people the right to start private businesses was much less controversial than was the design of the privatization program. As early as 1986, Soviet law was changed so as to permit individuals and family members to start their own businesses, as well as to allow groups of people to start private commercial businesses organized as cooperatives.[12] Small-scale firms have sprouted up, although as a sector, small business is much smaller than in Western economies and has not grown in the last decade (the number of small businesses has stayed at fewer than one million for the last decade). In the United States, firms employing fewer than 500 people employ just over half of all workers. In Russia, small businesses—defined as those employing 100 or fewer workers—account for only about 11 percent of all employees.[13]

Firms that are wholly or partly state-owned are often large, whereas start-up private firms tend to be small (about two-thirds of private firms are small in scale). The privatization of larger state firms affects the livelihoods of large numbers of employees. Because many towns were built around giant enterprises, privatization of a state firm can affect a whole region. And of course, privatization of important industrial or natural resource assets has substantial implications for the distribution of wealth.

For these reasons, privatization programs are profoundly political acts. Someone must decide how to set value on state enterprises in the absence of capital markets; whether to privatize enterprises for cash or for government-provided coupons; how much to favor the workers and managers of the enterprise in gaining control over their own workplace; whether to allow foreigners to buy privatized enterprises; and which levels of government can privatize which assets. Disputes over these issues have often stalled privatization programs in countries undergoing the transition from Communism. The decisions that Russia made in the 1990s about privatization are still the subject of passionate debate and bitter recrimination.

Voucher Privatization

The Russian parliament gave Yeltsin and his government the authority to enact privatization by decree but disagreements within the government produced fits and starts in the policy. Some in the government wanted to use auctions as much as possible to sell off state enterprises, especially retail and service establishments where it was reasonable to think that purchasers might have sufficient resources to buy them. Others believed it was more just to distribute some sort of coupon to every citizen, which they could use to bid on and buy shares of enterprises. Although the government generally agreed that for the sake both of fairness and social stability, workers should have priority in acquiring title to the enterprises in which they worked, there were two objections to taking this idea too far. One was that not every citizen worked in an enterprise that could be privatized. Retired people, military servicemen, ballerinas, scientists, teachers, and government employees, for instance, would not be able to share in privatization. Another was that if workers were able to gain control over their enterprises, the managers would be able to use their power over the workers to gain both ownership and control of the firm.

In the forms of privatization used in 1991 and the first half of 1992, buyers used cash rather than state-issued vouchers. Auctions and the sale of shares were supposed to stimulate economic productivity by creating a material interest on the part of an investor in the value of the newly acquired assets. It was hoped that investors, be they the workers of the firm themselves or outside buyers, would be interested in maximizing the return on their investment by seeing that the firms were run profitably and efficiently. But when efficiency became the principal objective of cash privatization schemes, fairness was jeopardized. Cash privatization had the effect of making the rich richer and giving ownership of enterprises to the officials who had run them before. Ordinary citizens often were excluded from benefiting from the most profitable opportunities as insiders acquired the stock of the most promising firms. And the poor, of course, had no chance at all to buy shares. In the interests of dispersing ownership rights as widely as possible, parliament's law envisioned that all citizens would be given special bank accounts to buy shares of privatized enterprises.

In April 1992, as opposition to the stabilization program was gaining force, Yeltsin issued a decree launching a program of voucher privatization beginning in the fourth quarter of 1992. Under the program, every citizen of Russia would be issued a voucher with a face value of 10,000 rubles (the equivalent of about $30). People would be free to buy and sell vouchers, but they could only be used to acquire shares of stock in privatized enterprises through auctions at which voucher owners could bid vouchers for shares of enterprises. People were also allowed to use their vouchers to acquire shares of mutual funds investing in privatized enterprises, or they could sell them to other people. The program was intended to ensure that everyone became a property owner instantly. Politically the aim was to build support for the economic reforms by making citizens into stock owners and thus giving them a stake in the outcome of the market transition. The designers of the program hoped that even though the voucher privatization program did not itself represent new investment capital, it would eventually spur increases in productivity by creating meaningful property rights.[14]

Beginning in October 1992, 148 million privatization vouchers were distributed to citizens. The program established three ways in which state enterprises could be privatized by means of voucher auctions. These methods differed according to how much stock could be acquired by employees of privatized enterprises and on what terms. Each method balanced the demands of managers and workers of state enterprises for control over their own enterprises against the demand of outsiders for the right to bid freely for shares, and each combined the objective of letting citizens acquire stock for free with that of creating a real capital market where stock had tradable value. The State Privatization Committee and its regional and local offices oversaw the entire privatization process, organizing auctions and approving privatization plans drafted by enterprises. This powerful agency, and its chairman, Anatolii Chubais, became targets for vehement criticism from all sides—from those accusing the committee of selling off assets too cheaply and not protecting enterprises, to those distressed at the way in which state managers usually wound up with the controlling share of stock. With Yeltsin's protection, however, Chubais carried out the program over the objections of all critics.

Chubais's team was reluctant simply to give away Russia's vast capital stock to the powerful state enterprise directors. Instead, it wanted to diffuse ownership rights as broadly as possible. The political realities, however, dictated that the government allow enterprise directors certain advantages. In the short run, at least, the directors' consent to the program was essential to maintaining economic and social stability in the country. The managers could ensure that workers did not erupt in a massive wave of strikes. The managers also represented one of the most powerful collective interests in the country. The government, therefore, allowed a good deal of "insider privatization," in which senior enterprise officials acquired the largest proportion of shares in privatized firms. On average, only 22.5 percent of shares of enterprises were sold at voucher auctions, where the public could bid for them. In most enterprises, both ownership and control wound up in the hands of the managers.[15]

Around 18,000 medium- and large-scale firms were privatized by 1996. Privatization for most of them did not immediately bring about major changes in the way they were run. One reason is that privatization did not bring an infusion of new investment capital to modernize their plants and equipment, in part because managers strenuously resisted allowing their firms to be taken over by outside investors. Asked in one major survey of enterprise directors whether they would be willing to sell a majority of their enterprise's shares to an outside investor who would bring the capital needed to invest in modernizing the firm, two-thirds said no. In other words, they preferred to remain majority owners of an unprofitable enterprise than the minority owners of a much more profitable one.[16] Very few firms experienced much management turnover and even fewer engaged in extensive restructuring of their operations to make them more productive or efficient.

All vouchers were to have been used by December 31, 1993. President Yeltsin extended the expiration date until June 30, 1994. By that time 140 million vouchers had been exchanged for stock out of 148 million originally distributed, according to Anatolii Chubais.[17] Some 40 million citizens had become property owners. About 70 percent of large- and medium-size firms and 80 percent of all small businesses had been privatized. The voucher privatization phase had ended. The next phase was to bring about the privatization of most remaining state enterprises, but by means of auctions of shares for cash. This also included the infamous "loans for shares" scheme, which we will discuss below. By 1996, about 90 percent of industrial output was being produced by privatized firms and about two-thirds of all large- and medium-size enterprises had been privatized.[18] As of 2006, nearly 80 percent of all Russian firms, accounting for just over half the workforce and about 70 percent of GDP, were in the private sector.[19]

Once the voucher privatization campaign was completed, the government turned to other methods to sell off shares in state enterprises. One method used in 1995–1996 came to be called "loans for shares." Although ownership rights and wealth had been concentrated before this, the program enabled a handful of ambitious entrepreneurs to acquire title to some of Russia's most desirable assets at low prices. The episode resulted in the emergence of the so-called oligarchs, a handful of wealthy magnates who took advantage of the government's weakness in the mid-1990s to acquire ownership and control over some of Russia's most lucrative natural resource, industrial, and media assets. (See Close-Up 7.1: The Rise and Fall of the Oligarchs.)

Close-Up 7.1   The Rise and Fall of the Oligarchs

The term *oligarchs* has come to refer to a small group of wealthy and powerful individuals who succeeded in taking advantage of the opening of the Russian economy to acquire ownership of Russia's most lucrative industrial and natural resource assets.[1] Political contacts helped them win crucial licenses and monopolies early in the post-Communist period; by building up great economic empires they also became immensely powerful in the political realm.

The rise of the oligarchs was helped by Yeltsin's privatization policies, but in fact they got their start well before the Soviet regime fell. As the system of centralized administrative control over economic resources collapsed in the late 1980s, well-placed officials in the party, the KGB, and the Komsomol (Soviet Youth League) began cashing in on their power and privileges. Some quietly liquidated the assets of their organizations and secreted the proceeds in overseas accounts and investments.[2] Others created banks and businesses in Russia, taking advantage of their insider positions to win exclusive government contracts and licenses and to acquire financial credits and supplies at

---

[1] Similar oligarchs have also arisen in Ukraine and several other post-Communist countries, where the state opened the economy just enough to allow entrepreneurs to profiteer from partial reform but not enough to force them to compete with other entrepreneurs on a level playing field.
[2] Steven L. Solnick, *Stealing the State: Control and Collapse in Soviet Institutions* (Cambridge, MA: Harvard University Press, 1998).

(Continued)

artificially low, state-subsidized prices in order to transact business at high, market-value prices. Great fortunes were made almost overnight. Access to capital and contacts from the old regime helped these new *"biznesmeny"* considerably. Some called this wave of quasi-market activity *"nomenklatura* capitalism." By the time that the Soviet regime fell and the Yeltsin government began to try to establish a working market economy, some of the *nomenklatura* capitalists had already entrenched themselves as powerful players.

The concentration of immense financial and industrial power extended to the mass media. One of the most prominent of the financial barons, Boris Berezovsky, who controlled major stakes in several banks and companies (including Aeroflot), acquired an 8 percent stake in the main state television company, ORT, when 49 percent of its shares were auctioned off; one of Berezovsky's banks was part of a banking consortium that owned 38 percent of ORT. Berezovsky himself became deputy director of the company and was considered to exert extensive influence over its programming. Berezovsky and the other ultrawealthy and well-connected tycoons who controlled these great empires of finance, industry, energy, telecommunications, and media became known as the oligarchs. Through the "loans for shares" program, Yeltsin and his entourage had given them a royal opportunity to scoop up some of Russia's most desirable assets in return for help in his reelection effort. In the spring of 1996, with Yeltsin's popularity at a low ebb, the oligarchs agreed to cooperate in securing Yeltsin's reelection. How much money they poured into Yeltsin's reelection campaign is still a matter of dispute—some say the quantity was relatively insignificant—but there is no question about the fact that the media properties that they controlled were all turned to the service of ensuring Yeltsin's reelection. The media painted a picture of a fateful choice for Russia, between Yeltsin and a return to totalitarianism, directly serving Yeltsin's campaign strategy and unquestionably helping him win.

Some saw the oligarchs as a cabal controlling Yeltsin's administration and, through it, Russia. Boris Berezovsky was probably being more boastful than candid when he told the *Financial Times* a few weeks after Yeltsin appointed him deputy secretary of the Security Council (October 1996), that there was now a group of seven individuals, with substantial influence over government, who controlled banks and businesses that together controlled half of the economy. Berezovsky went on to justify this situation: "I think two types of power are possible. Either a power of ideology or a power of capital. Ideology is now dead, and today we have a period of transition from the power of ideology to the power of capital." Echoing the famous comment (by General Motors' chairman) that "what's good for General Motors is good for the USA," Berezovsky observed: "I think that if something is advantageous to capital, it goes without saying that it's advantageous to the nation. It's capital that is in a condition, to the greatest extent, to express the interests of the nation."[3] Berezovsky was surely exaggerating both the public-mindedness of the oligarchs, and the degree to which they formed a coherent, coordinated group.

For a moment in 1996, when Yeltsin's reelection hung in the balance, the oligarchs came close to forming a kind of board of directors for Russia; however, once Yeltsin was reelected they fell out and began feuding with one another. The 1998 financial crash hurt all of them and nearly wiped several out. Their influence as a group depended on the unique environment of Yeltsin's presidency, when a weakened Yeltsin, faced with substantial political opposition and uncontrollable government deficits, gave them enormous assets at bargain basement prices.

Putin's presidency sharply altered the relationship between the state and big business. In July 2000, Putin held a widely publicized meeting with several of the most influential oligarchs. There he told them what the terms of their relations with the state would be under his rule. He promised that the oligarchs' property would be secure, no matter how dubious the manner in which it had been acquired, so long as they kept their noses out of high politics and as long as they began investing in Russia rather than sending their money abroad.[4] Since then, most of the oligarchs have been content to abide by the new rules of the game. They have competed to build political machines at the level of regional government, but generally refrain from seeking broader political influence. However, a few oligarchs continued their involvement in high politics, even daring to oppose Putin and his policies. They paid a high price for their defiance. Through a series of criminal and civil prosecutions in 2000–2001, Putin forced Boris Berezovsky and another prominent oligarch, Vladimir Gusinsky, to relinquish their substantial media holdings. Both men are now under indictment and living abroad. Beginning in 2003, the Putin administration began another series of moves intended to strip Mikhail Khodorkovsky, who had played an increasingly prominent role in politics, of his control of the Yukos oil firm and to break it up so that it could be sold cheaply to other firms more subservient to Putin's political interests. (See Close-Up 6.1: The Yukos Affair.) The lessons of these actions were clear: So long as heads of big businesses do not challenge the president, they are welcome to amass wealth. But as soon as they cross Putin, they are crushed.

---

[3] Quoted in Rose Brady, *Kapitalizm: Russia's Struggle to Free Its Economy* (New Haven, CT: Yale University Press, 1999), p. 207.

[4] Peter Rutland, "Putin and the Oligarchs," in *Putin's Russia: Past Imperfect, Future Uncertain*, ed. Dale R. Herspring (Lanham, MD: Rowman & Littlefield, 2003), p. 1141.

How "loans for shares" worked can be illustrated by the case of Norilsk Nickel, a giant metallurgical firm in Russia's North that produces over 20 percent of the world's supply of nickel. An inefficient, debt-ridden behemoth of a company, Norilsk Nickel was also potentially one of Russia's most valuable assets. In 1995, with elections approaching and the government desperate for cash, a prominent entrepreneur named Vladimir Potanin proposed a deal to the government. His bank would bid on the right to manage a bloc of 51 percent of the shares of Norilsk Nickel in return for granting a loan to the government. If after a year's time the government failed to repay the loan, the bank would have the right to purchase the shares outright. He proposed conducting similar auctions for several other companies of strategic importance as well. Yeltsin and the government approved the plan despite the fact that it was clearly designed to turn over ownership of some of Russia's crown jewels to a small coterie of tycoons. Potanin's bank organized the auctions and banks he controlled were the sole bidders for Norilsk Nickel. Not surprisingly, his bid won. A year later, when the government failed to repay the loan, Potanin proceeded to acquire majority ownership in Norilsk Nickel. This was an astonishing bargain: for $170 million, Potanin bought a company whose output accounts for 1.9 percent of Russia's GDP.[20]

The case of Norilsk Nickel was only one example of the infamous "loans for shares" scheme. Controlling interests in several of Russia's largest oil companies were auctioned off to other oligarchs, also at dirt cheap prices. The entire "loans for shares" program stands as one of the most flagrant examples of the cozy, collusive relationship between Russia's oligarchs and the Yeltsin regime. Along with the other forms of privatization, "loans for shares" resulted in extremely high levels of ownership concentration in Russia. As of 2003, the top ten families in Russia owned approximately 60 percent of the value of the stock market. This is high by European standards (typically in the larger European countries, the top ten families own less than 30 percent of the value of the stock market) but it is characteristic of other middle-income developing countries, such as Indonesia (58 percent) or the Philippines (52 percent), and it is lower than in the United States and Europe a century ago. Moreover, close analysis suggests that firms owned by oligarchs in Russia have been more productive than state-owned firms.[21]

Consequences of Privatization

Initially, privatization contributed little to the urgent task of modernizing and retooling the economy. Vouchers, the instrument used in the first phase for mass privatization, were not inflationary because they could not be used as legal tender for other transactions.[22] But neither were they forms of productive capital, as stocks and bonds are in countries with established financial markets. So the vouchers did not expand the pool of resources enterprises could use to increase productivity and efficiency. They were intended as an impetus to a process that would end in the consolidation of a market economy. The policymakers believed that mass privatization would establish an interest on the part of new property owners in increasing the value of their assets, which they would achieve by investing in the modernization and retooling of the firms. In turn, the need for capital would induce a healthy capital market into being. However, the lack of an institutional infrastructure for market exchange and a lack of confidence in the future deterred entrepreneurs from investing capital. Capital investment rates in Russia are rising, but they were extremely low in the 1990s (and capital flight very high), and they remain below the levels of other transitional and mature economies.[23]

There is a famous theorem in economics that holds that if the costs of economic transactions are sufficiently low, then regardless of how property rights over some set of economic assets are initially allocated, bargaining among owners will eventually achieve a socially efficient distribution of ownership and control rights over those assets as owners buy and sell property and enter into mutually advantageous contractual relations.[24] That is, each asset ultimately winds up with its highest and best use. But note the *if.* The theorem stipulates that the distribution of property rights reaches the social optimum *if* the costs of bargaining and reaching agreements among owners are low and *if* the state enforces property and contract rights. In fact, in any real society, the costs of transactions—the absence of trust, incomplete information about the qualities of what is being sold, the problem of enforcing an agreement after it has been reached—can be formidable.[25] In Russia, the uncertainty surrounding the change in economic and political conditions made transaction costs extremely high. As a result, owners of many firms preferred to capitalize on their political leverage and take advantage of inefficiency rather than to maximize the value of their assets. For example, many owners initially stripped newly privatized firms of assets and sent the proceeds to offshore bank accounts. Many owners avoided restructuring their firms and depended on state life-support systems such as cheap loans and subsidies.[26] Many newly wealthy owners preferred to spend their money on lavish personal consumption rather than to reinvest it in their firms. Only in the late 1990s, when the political system became more predictable, did private owners begin to behave as though they cared more about the long-term value of the assets they owned than about maximizing short-term returns.

Weak Capital Markets and the August 1998 Crash

Privatization was carried out in the absence of effective, impartial institutions regulating capital markets, and the newly minted big business owners have not been eager to see such institutions created. The channels by which market economies convert private savings into investment in companies, such as financial institutions, pension and insurance funds, and stock and bond markets, are extremely weak in Russia. For so large a country, with so great an industrial potential, stock and bond markets are tiny.[27] Enterprises, starved for working capital, failed to pay their wages and taxes on time, and traded with one another using barter. By 1998, at least half of enterprise output was being "sold" through barter trade.[28] Barter creates a world of unreal values, a "virtual economy," as economists Clifford Gaddy and Barry Ickes termed it, where it is impossible to calculate the cost of goods and where investors cannot make intelligent judgments about where capital investment will have the greatest return. A virtual economy is profoundly inefficient.[29]

By the mid-1990s, the government's own long- and short-term goals were in conflict. In the long run the government hoped privatization would create property rights and capital markets. But in the short term, the government needed to raise cash to compensate for shortfalls in its tax revenues. Privatization of enterprises for cash allowed the government to generate one-time infusions of revenue into the budget by auctioning off state-owned shares of stock in industrial firms. Unfortunately, the government found that demand for shares was often weak, and sold off the assets at embarrassingly, even scandalously, low prices. Moreover, at the same time the government was trying to auction off shares in enterprises, it was also trying to raise revenues by issuing bonds (GKOs), at extremely high rates of return.[30] The market for the lucrative GKOs crowded out the capital market for investment in industry. One government policy goal—that of financing budget expenditures by issuing bonds—was in direct competition with another—that of accelerating private ownership of state-owned enterprises.

Making matters worse was a collapse in oil prices on the world market. The price of a barrel of oil on the world market fell by half from January 1997 to December 1998, cutting deeply into Russia's export earnings. International markets were shaken as well by a financial crisis that rippled across Asia, and nervous investors pulled out of many emerging markets. This double blow of external pressure and an unsustainable fiscal situation at home pushed Russia's government into a debt trap. The government needed to borrow to meet current obligations. To pay off the interest on the loans it had taken out, it needed to raise still more cash, which it did through still more borrowing, including credits from the IMF, high interest-bearing domestic bonds, and privatization. As lenders grew worried that the government could not make good on its obligations, they demanded ever higher interest rates, deepening the trap.

Finally, in August 1998 the bubble burst. The state could not honor its obligations. The government declared a moratorium on its debts, and let the ruble sink against the dollar. Overnight, the ruble lost two-thirds of its value and credit dried up.[31] Government bonds held by investors became almost worthless. Importers went out of business. The effects of the crash rippled through the economy. The sharp devaluation of the ruble made exports more competitive and gave an impetus to domestic producers, but also significantly lowered people's living standards. Although recovery resumed surprisingly fast, the 1998 crash was the culmination of nearly a decade of economic decline.

How severe was the economic depression? No doubt official figures overstate its depth. Consumption fell less than production. Observers skeptical of official output statistics pointed out that in the past, managers had every reason to *overstate* their actual output, as they were under pressure to fulfill the production plan, whereas now they were more likely to *understate* their output in order to avoid taxes. Moreover, the very structure of national income shifted. Much more of Russia's economic activity is occurring in the sphere of services, which is poorly captured in output statistics. The share of services in the economy dropped much less than that of industry or agriculture. There is certainly a great deal of off-book economic activity taking place, some of it legal but untaxed, and some of it illegal.

Still, Russia's economic decline in the 1990s was deeper and more protracted than was the Great Depression experienced by the United States or Western Europe following 1929. It was about half as severe as the catastrophic drop caused by the effects of World War I, the Bolshevik Revolution, and the Civil War.[32] The depression in the 1990s was the aggregate result of many individual survival strategies. Starved of cash, some enterprises formed alliances with regional governors to pay lower taxes to the regions, while pressuring the regional branches of the federal tax collectors to let them defer their tax obligations to the central government.[33] Recognizing that major oil, gas, and electric power firms were suffering from huge unpaid bills from their customers, the federal government effectively allowed them to avoid paying much of their federal taxes in return for keeping key customers, such as military bases and major industrial enterprises, supplied with energy and power. Each link in the chain coped with the shortage of cash and credit in the economy, but the net outcome was a deep structural crisis. The government was perennially short of money with which to meet its obligations, including pensions and pay for teachers and other state employees. People coped by working outside the official economy, earning unrecorded incomes and hoarding money. No one knows exactly how much cash is sitting under people's mattresses, both in rubles and in dollars, but the state statistical agency estimated in 2000 that people had some $17 billion stashed away at home.[34] This sum, and another $12 billion or so held in ruble and dollar savings accounts in banks, could be an enormously important source of investment capital, if only banks and other institutions were working more effectively to translate savings into financial assets.

Since 1999, however, the economy has grown steadily, fueled by three factors. First, many domestic firms that had not been competitive when the value of the ruble was relatively high against the dollar suddenly became competitive on domestic and foreign markets. Second, President Putin's early policy moves reassured many economic actors that he was intent on restoring order in the state and establishing a business-friendly economy. Third, and perhaps most important, the prices of oil and gas began rising again on the world market. By 2006, the world price of oil was about five times what it had been in 1999.

As a result of these factors, the economy commenced a period of steady growth. Output has grown at an average rate of over 6 percent from 2000 through 2006. Liquidity returned. Barter transactions largely ended; enterprises started paying taxes and wages on time. Real incomes have risen to well above their 1998 levels, as wages and pensions have increased (and now are usually paid on time). Unemployment has fallen from over 13 percent in 1998 to around 7.5 percent in 2005.[35] The share of people living in poverty has fallen to 17.8 percent in 2004.[36] Higher tax collections have allowed the government to realize significant budget surpluses, which it has used to accelerate the repayment of foreign debt and to create a reserve fund (called the "stabilization fund") that had accumulated nearly

$100 billion by early 2007.[37] By the end of 2006, according to official estimates, Russia's total GDP had finally caught up with its 1990 level.[38]

Because so much of Russia's growth has been driven by the rising prices of oil and gas on the world market, Russia may be subject to the so-called resource curse.[39] A former economic advisor of Putin has warned of the "Venezuelanization" of Russia, meaning that Russia may be falling into the trap of allowing high resource-based revenues to drive populist fiscal policies, increased state control over the economy, and authoritarian political tendencies—to the detriment of both long-term economic performance and democratic politics. William Tompson, an economist with the Organization for Economic Cooperation and Development (OECD) argues that although Russia is far from becoming a classic petro-state, the windfall from high energy prices has indeed allowed Putin to roll back the democratic trends of the 1990s and to avoid enacting structural reforms of the economy.[40]

As of 2005, oil and gas exports account for 62 percent of the total value of Russian exports (as opposed to 52 percent in 2000), suggesting how dependent Russia's economy is on natural resource exports.[41] To be sure, other sectors of the economy have been growing as well. Investment has been increasing in agriculture and other sectors. However, fuel and metals make up nearly two-thirds of the value-added in industry. As Putin and his aides themselves have often pointed out, Russia's continued economic progress cannot be dependent solely on high world energy prices. Russia must raise the productivity of other sectors of the economy, and of human capital, if its recovery is to continue. But Putin and his associates also rely on access to resource-based revenues to build political support. This means they find it convenient to extend state control over much of the economy rather than promoting competition and investment.

Social Conditions

The economic changes in the country have had an enormous impact on living standards. For most of the 1990s, unemployment, inflation, and nonpayment of wages and pensions led to distress and insecurity for a majority of households. Richard Rose's 2005 survey of Russians asked how people rated their family's economic situation. Eighty percent rated it as unsatisfactory or very unsatisfactory.[42] Fifty-eight percent reported that their household living standards had fallen by comparison with 1991. Yet most households have some major consumer goods: 28 percent of households have a car, 47 percent have a VCR, 14 percent use the Internet, and 90 percent have a color TV set.[43]

Poverty rose as a result of the transition for several reasons, including unemployment and the persistent lag of wages behind prices. Large-scale unemployment was particularly painful for a country whose citizens were used to nearly full employment in the Communist era and where the state-funded social safety net works poorly. Because the vast majority of single-parent households are headed by women, rising unemployment pushed more women and children into poverty.[44] Also vulnerable to the economic disruptions of the 1990s were groups whose incomes were paid directly out of the state budget, such as those living on pensions and disability payments, as well as teachers, scientists, and health care workers. Although they received periodic increases in their earnings levels, these were insufficient to keep up with rising prices. People often went for months without receiving their wages or pensions.

Other changes offset the decline in living standards to some extent. First, many people receive in-kind and unreported forms of income (such as enterprises paying workers in the goods they produced, or people's consumption of products they grew themselves on garden plots). Many earn incomes from off-book employment, often second and third jobs (for example, a worker might use income from the primary place of work as the basis for declaring his or her taxable income, and then refrain from declaring the income from side jobs). Second, whereas in the prereform period, goods were scarce at the official state prices, people spent long hours standing in line at stores, and prices on the black market were high, after the 1992 radical reform, consumer goods became available in all major cities and lines disappeared. Because the cheap prices on basic subsistence goods set by the Soviet authorities had often been purely hypothetical—what use is a cheap price if the good is unavailable?—many people's living standards have improved. One estimate is that by early 2002, living standards had recovered to their 1993 levels if the quality and availability of goods are taken into account.[45]

Along with poverty, inequality has grown sharply since the end of the Soviet era. While most people suffered falling living standards, a few became wealthy. One commonly used measure of inequality is the Gini index, which is an aggregate measure of the total deviation from perfect equality in the distribution of wealth or income in a country. In a highly egalitarian country such as Finland, Sweden, or Norway, the Gini index for income distribution stands at about 25. Countries with moderately high levels of income inequality, such as Great Britain, France, and Italy, fall in the range between 27 and 37. High-inequality countries such as the United States have a Gini index of around 40. In Russia, the equivalent index reached 48 in 1993, double the level of 1988, and higher than any other post-Communist country except Kyrgyzstan.[46] Then as incomes grew again starting in 1999, the gap closed somewhat. Today Russia's Gini index is about 40, equivalent to the level of the United States.

Another way to look at inequality is to divide the population into five equal groups, or quintiles, and compare the share of national income that each receives. Figure 7.3 displays the results for Russia and five other countries. In Russia, as in the United States, the richest 20 percent of the population receives over 45 percent of total income; in China, the richest fifth receives half the income; in Mexico, the richest fifth receive almost 60 percent. The richest fifth of the population receive eight times as much income as does the poorest fifth in Russia, and the ratio is similar in the United States. (The ratio is nearly 20 in Mexico, and only 4.3 in Germany.) But although Russia's level and structure of inequality resemble the United States, the huge rise in inequality represents an enormous shock to a society brought up on the socialist doctrine of class equality.

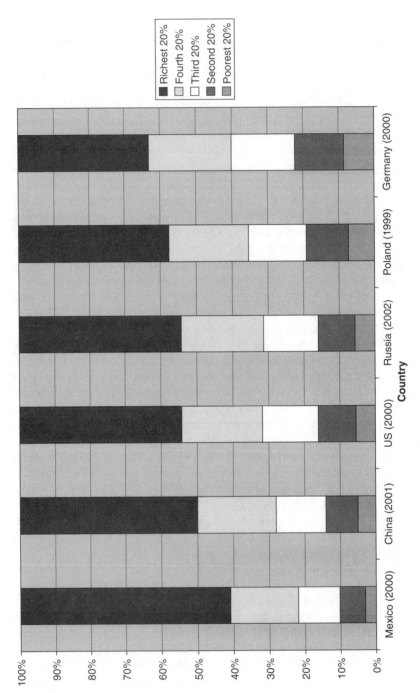

Figure 7.3 ■ Structure of Income by Quintile.

An especially disturbing dimension of the social effects of transition has been the erosion of public health. Although public health had deteriorated in the late Communist period, the decline worsened after the regime changed. Mortality rates have risen sharply, especially among males. Life expectancy for males in Russia is at a level comparable with poor countries. Russia's State Statistics Committee estimated that life expectancy at birth in 2004 for males was 58.9 and for females 72.3. Despite the economic recovery since 1999, these figures have been almost unchanged since 2000, and are lower than in 1990. The disparity between male and female mortality—enormous by world standards—probably owes to the much higher rates of abuse of alcohol and tobacco among men. Demographers warn that at the present rate of mortality, 40 percent of Russia's 16-year-old boys will not reach their sixtieth birthday.[47] Other demographic indicators are equally grim. Every year Russia's population declines by over half a million people or more due to the excess of deaths over births. The rate of deaths per year is 70 percent higher than the rate of births.[48] Rates of incidence of HIV and other infectious disease, murders, suicides, drug addiction, and alcoholism are rising. Russia's leaders consider the demographic crisis to be one of the gravest threats to the country's national security both because of the growing shortage of labor in some regions and the army's inability to recruit enough healthy young men.[49]

As a result of the declining population, Russia is becoming increasingly reliant on immigrant labor. For example, the Volgograd region contracts with China to bring in around 600 temporary laborers each year. Russian policymakers have proposed offering young men from Central Asia and other CIS republics Russian citizenship if they will serve in the army. There are 8–12 million illegal immigrants in Russia, according to the Federal Migration Service[50] (equivalent to the number estimated to be in the United States). A large number are from Muslim republics to the south. The growing dependence of the economy on them has led to social tensions and urgent debates over appropriate policy responses, including the desirability of a blanket amnesty, a guestworker program, or other means of managing the influx.

Putin's Dual Agenda

Vladimir Putin has repeatedly stated that he intends to set the economy firmly on the path of growth by creating an economic climate conducive to investment and entrepreneurship. Some reformers who were part of the Gaidar team of the early 1990s—including Gaidar himself—were involved in drafting legislation on tax reform, administrative reform, privatization, and other policies in Putin's first term. Putin's initial legislative agenda sought to lower marginal tax rates, protect property rights, reduce burdensome government regulation of business, liberalize the labor market, shift the pension system more toward pension insurance and private savings, eliminate the tariff and bureaucratic obstacles that prevent Russia's entry into the World Trade Organization (WTO), and create a market for buying and selling land. Legislation on most of these reforms was enacted.

But by 2003, the president's commitment to economic reform flagged. Some of the most ambitious plans were quietly shelved, such as the aim of breaking up the large natural monopolies and overhauling the state bureaucracy. Instead of trying to break up the giant natural gas monopoly, Gazprom, into several competing companies, Putin decided to use Gazprom as a means to expand state control over the entire oil and gas industry. The government's interest in reforming the housing and utilities sectors and the electric power monopoly abated. Plans to restructure the dangerously shaky banking industry were forgotten. Instead, the government began taking back control of major oil, gas, electric power, automotive, machine-building, aviation, nuclear power, and other enterprises; the most visible of these was the drive to break up Yukos and absorb its most lucrative assets into the state-owned oil company, Rosneft.[51] The government also began squeezing foreign investors out of their majority stakes in major oil and gas ventures, forcing them to accept minority shares as a condition of doing business in Russia. In short, Putin's growth agenda was overtaken by a new emphasis on placing big business under tight state control, and renationalizing some firms of strategic importance.

Putin now appears to be pursuing two policy agendas at the same time. On the one hand, he wants an orderly, efficient, business-friendly economy that will attract domestic and foreign investment and yield high, self-sustaining economic growth. On the other, he wants to recentralize political power, curb the power of big business, and take direct control of important sectors of the economy in order to strengthen the state's power at home and abroad. Ultimately, these agendas are incompatible. Steady, self-sustaining economic growth requires creating an environment in which economic actors have an incentive to invest in Russia's future. The more that Putin reverts to the traditional Russian model of patrimonial rule, the greater the likelihood that Russia's economy will once again stagnate.

NOTES

1. The former chief economist of the World Bank, Joseph E. Stiglitz, is a vehement critic of the "Washington Consensus" and the radical liberalization policies it pursued in the 1980s and 1990s. He is especially critical of IMF policy in Russia. See Joseph E. Stiglitz, *Globalization and Its Discontents* (New York: W. W. Norton, 2002); Joseph E. Stiglitz, *Making Globalization Work* (New York: W. W. Norton, 2006).

2. Among those critical of the radical reforms of the early 1990s are Stephen F. Cohen, *Failed Crusade: America and the Tragedy of Post-Communist Russia* (New York: W. W. Norton, 2001); Peter Reddaway and Dmitri Glinski, *Tragedy of Russia's*

Reforms: Market Bolshevism against Democracy (Washington, DC: US. Institute of Peace, 2001); Jerry F. Hough, *The Logic of Economic Reform in Russia* (Washington, DC: Brookings Institution Press, 2001). Among those arguing that the reforms did not go far enough in removing obstacles to an open, competitive market system are Anders Aslund, *Building Capitalism: The Transformation of the Former Soviet Bloc* (Cambridge: Cambridge University Press, 2002); Andrei Shleifer and Daniel Treisman, *Without a Map: Political Tactics and Economic Reform in Russia* (Cambridge, MA: MIT Press, 2000). Shleifer and Treisman argue that the compromises made by the reformers were conscious concessions to important stakeholders in order to weaken resistance to the larger goals of the reforms.

3. Joel S. Hellman, "Winners Take All: The Politics of Partial Reform in Postcommunist Transitions," *World Politics* 50:1 (1998): 203–34.

4. Hard currency is the term used for the U.S. dollar, German mark, Japanese yen, and other national currencies that are freely traded on world markets and used as currency reserves by governments. Soft currencies are those for which governments set a value and then protect that value against foreign currency markets. Thus they do not have an established international market value.

5. Shleifer and Treisman, *Without a Map*; William Tompson, "Was Gaidar Really Necessary? Russian 'Shock Therapy' Reconsidered," *Problems of Post-Communism* 49:4 (July/August 2002): 12–21.

6. For example, the oil company Lukoil—Russia's largest oil company—was created by a directive issued by the Russian Council of Ministers in November 1991, shortly before the final dissolution of the Soviet Union. Needless to say, creation of this company enabled a small group of owner-managers to become hugely wealthy overnight.

See Peter Maass, "The Triumph of the Quiet Tycoon," *New York Times Magazine,* August 1, 2004.

7. Economists generally say that once prices start rising by 50 percent a month and more, the economy is in a state of hyperinflation.

8. For a discussion of stabilization in Poland, see Jeffrey Sachs, *Poland's Jump to the Market Economy* (Cambridge, MA: MIT Press, 1993).

9. Cf. Joseph Stiglitz, *Globalization and Its Discontents* (New York: Norton, 2002), esp. ch. 5, "Who Lost Russia?" and Stiglitz, *Making Globalization Work.*

10. A good account of the political choices faced by the reformers is Shleifer and Treisman, *Without a Map.* For memoirs by two of the key policymakers from the period, see Anatolii B. Chubais, ed., *Privatizatsiia po-rossiiski* (Moscow: Vagrius, 1999); and Yegor Gaidar, *Days of Defeat and Victory* (Seattle: University of Washington Press, 1999).

11. Joseph R. Blasi, Maya Kroumova, and Douglas Kruse, *Kremlin Capitalism: Privatizing the Russian Economy* (Ithaca, NY: Cornell University Press, 1997), 171; Shleifer and Treisman, *Without a Map,* p. 42. A good account of the Central Bank's high-handedness in this period is Juliet Johnson, *A Fistful of Rubles: The Rise and Fall of the Russian Banking System* (Ithaca, NY: Cornell University Press, 2000), Ch. 3, "The Central Bank of Russia," pp. 64–97.

12. In a cooperative, all the employees are co-owners of the business and share in its profits.

13. Goskomstat Rossiia, *Rossiiskii statisticheskii ezhegodnik 2005* (Moscow: Goskomstat, 2006), p. 356.

14. The goals of the privatization program are laid out in a volume of essays by its chief Russian designers and their Western advisers. See, in particular, Anatoly B. Chubais and Maria Vishnevskaya, "Main Issues of Privatisation in Russia," and Maxim Boycko and Andrei Shleifer, "The Voucher Programme for Russia," both in Anders Åslund and Richard Layard, eds., *Changing the Economic System in Russia* (New York: St. Martin's Press, 1993), pp. 89–99 and 100–11. Another book by three individuals closely involved in the privatization program gives both lucid theoretical rationalization and frank insider insight into the program. See Maxim Boycko, Andrei Shleifer, and Robert Vishny, *Privatizing Russia* (Cambridge, MA: MIT Press, 1995).

15. Pekka Sutela, "Insider Privatization in Russia: Speculations on Systemic Changes," *Europe-Asia Studies* 46:3 (1994): 420–21.

16. Blasi, et al., *Kremlin Capitalism,* pp. 179–80. The authors conducted a major national annual survey of the managers of privatized enterprises in Russia.

17. Radio Free Europe/Radio Liberty Daily Report, July 1, 1994.

18. Blasi, et al., *Kremlin Capitalism,* p. 50.

19. *Rossiiskii statisticheskii ezhegodnik 2005* (Moscow: Goskomstat Rossii, 2006), pp. 148, 349; Rudiger Ahrend and William Tompson, "Fifteen Years of Economic Reform in Russia: What Has Been Achieved? What Remains to Be Done?" OECD Working Paper No. 430, ECO/WKP(2005)17 (Paris: OECD, 13 May 2005), p. 23.

20. http://www.nornik.ru/page.jsp?page Id=about.

21. Sergei Guriev and Andrei Rachinsky, "The Role of Oligarchs in Russian Capitalism," *Journal of Economic Perspectives* 19:1 (2005): 131–50.

22. They were backed by the federal government's share of the proceeds of the sale of stock from state enterprises. Each enterprise had to offer at least 35 percent of its stock for vouchers. This corresponded to the share of ownership that the federal government claimed for itself. The federal government's share in the sale of privatizing enterprises was thus distributed to the citizens in the form of vouchers.

23. The OECD estimates that Russia's rate of gross fixed capital investment as a share of GDP is about 18 percent, compared with around 40 percent for China. Organization of Economic Cooperation and Development, *OECD Economic Surveys: Russian Federation* (Paris: OECD, November 2006), pp. 26–27.

24. This is known as Coase's Theorem, after the economist Ronald H. Coase. It is very often misrepresented: Coase was calling attention to the sensitivity of markets to the costliness of transactions. Where contracts and property rights are not consistently enforced and information is scarce, the theorem predicts that the high cost of reaching and enforcing agreements will be an obstacle to efficiency-improving economic exchange.

25. This perspective underlies the field of institutional economics. Cf. Douglass C. North, *Institutions, Institutional Change and Economic Performance* (Cambridge: Cambridge University Press, 1990).

26. Blasi, et al., *Kremlin Capitalism*; Michael McFaul, "State Power, Institutional Change, and the Politics of Privatization in Russia," *World Politics* 47 (1995): 210–43.

27. For example, the total capitalization of Russia's 300 largest companies reached around $250 billion in fall 2004, which is less than the capitalization of General Electric. *Kommersant-Dengi*, September 14, 2004.

28. European Bank for Reconstruction and Development (EBRD), *Transition Report 1998: Financial Sector in Transition* (EBRD: London, 1998), p. 186.

29. On the virtual economy, see Clifford G. Gaddy and Barry W. Ickes, "Russia's Virtual Economy," *Foreign Affairs* 77 (September–October 1998): 53–67; and David Woodruff, *Money Unmade: Barter and the Fate of Russian Capitalism* (Ithaca, NY, and London: Cornell University Press, 1999); Stephen S. Moody, "Decapitalizing Russian Capitalism," *Orbis* 40:1 (Winter 1996): 123–43.

30. In spring 1996, when the presidential election campaign was at its height, Russian state treasury obligations were selling at ruinously high interest rates—over 200 percent effective annual yields on six-month bonds. Little wonder that investors were uninterested in the stock market. Because of the instability of the political climate and the fear of default, the great bulk of this paper was short-term.

31. Thane Gustafson, *Capitalism Russian-Style* (Cambridge, England: Cambridge University Press, 1999), pp. 2–3, 94–95.

32. The Russian Civil War (1918–1921) was fought between the Bolshevik ("Red") forces and the anticommunists ("Whites") following the Communist revolution. The Whites comprised a diverse set of enemies of the new regime—among them both monarchists and socialists—whose inability to unite against the Bolsheviks ensured their ultimate defeat at the hands of the Red Army.

33. Shleifer and Treisman, *Without a Map*, pp. 113–36.

34. RFE/RL Newsline, March 30, 2000.

35. *OECD Economic Survey, Russian Federation 2006*, p. 18.

36. Goskomstat, *Rossiiski ekonomicheskii ezhegodnik 2005*, p. 205.

37. A stabilization fund is used by countries that realize large windfalls when the world prices of their commodity exports rise sharply. The purpose is twofold: to prevent the revenues from high prices of exported goods from artificially inflating domestic prices; and to hold reserves for a rainy day, so that if export revenues drop suddenly, the government can dip into the reserve fund to meet its current spending needs.

38. Polit.ru, February 26, 2007.

39. The "resource curse" refers to the observation that countries that rely on natural resources for a high proportion of national income tend not to invest in other sources of productivity (such as human capital) and fail to develop effective institutions of accountability

and governance. For this reason they tend to have weaker long-term economic performance and to undergo transitions away from democracy. See David L. Epstein, Robert Bates, Jack Goldstone, et al., "Democratic Transitions," *American Journal of Political Science* 50:3 (2006): 551–69; Michael L. Ross, "The Political Economy of the Resource Curse," *World Politics* 51:2 (1999): 297–322.

40. William Tompson, "A Frozen Venezuela? The 'Resource Curse' and Russian Politics," in Michael Ellman, ed., *Russia's Oil and Natural Gas: Bonanza or Curse?* (London: Anthem Books, 2006), pp. 189–212; also see William Tompson, "The Political Implications of Russia's Resource-Based Economy," *Post-Soviet Affairs* 21:4 (2005): 335–59; and M. Steven Fish, *Democracy Derailed in Russia: The Failure of Open Politics* (Cambridge: Cambridge University Press, 2005), pp. 114–38.

41. *OECD Economic Survey, Russian Federation 2006,* p. 50.

42. Richard Rose, William Mishler, and Neil Munro, *Russia Transformed: Developing Popular Support for a New Regime* (Cambridge: Cambridge University Press, 2006), p. 160.

43. Ibid., p. 159.

44. Gail Kligman, "The Social Legacy of Communism: Women, Children, and the Feminization of Poverty," in James R. Millar and Sharon L. Wolchik, eds., *The Social Legacy of Communism* (Washington, DC: Woodrow Wilson Center Press and Cambridge University Press, 1994), p. 261; Mary Buckley, "The Politics of Social Issues," in Stephen White, Alex Pravda, and Zvi Gitelman, eds., *Developments in Russian and Post-Soviet Politics,* 3rd ed. (London: Macmillan, 1994), pp. 192–94.

45. Vesa Korhonen, "Looking at the Russian Economy in 2001–02," Bank of Finland, Institute for Economies in Transition; "Russian Economy: The Month in Review," February 11, 2002, on Web site www.bof.fi/bofit.

46. Branko Milanovic, *Income, Inequality, and Poverty during the Transition from Planned to Market Economy* (Washington, DC: The World Bank, 1998), p. 41; see the World Bank figures for most countries in the world in its annual World Development Indicators.

47. REF/RL Newsline, March 8, 1999.

48. RFE/RL Newsline, March 23, 2000; March 20, 2002.

49. Russian military commanders reported that one-third of the men they had called up in the fall of 2004 were unfit to serve as a result of health problems. Polit.ru, December 9, 2004.

50. Polit.ru, December 4, 2006.

51. *OECD Economic Survey, Russian Federation 2006,* p. 38.

Chapter 8

Politics and Law

DEMOCRATIZATION AND THE RULE OF LAW

In Russia, the law has often been an instrument in the hands of the strong. Consequently, one of the most important goals of democratic reformers has been to establish the rule of law, that is, to make the enforcement of law independent of the will of the authorities. In this effort, there has been some progress but also many setbacks. The legal system continues to be subject to corruption and political abuse. Under Putin, the authorities have tried to weaken the ability of wealthy private interests, such as oligarchs and organized crime, to manipulate the legal system but they have done so by reasserting the state's political control over it. President Putin has often emphasized the importance of the rule of law, yet his regime frequently bends judicial institutions to its will when major political interests are at stake.

The constitutional scholar Stephen Holmes has distinguished between the "rule of law" and "rule by law." In rule *by* law, a powerful elite concentrating political power uses law to protect its prerogatives. In rule *of* law, power is sufficiently dispersed among groups and organizations in society to prevent any one group from monopolizing access to the law. Many citizens and groups can turn to the law to defend their rights and interests, and their diversity and competition help to preserve the law's independence.[1] This means that reforming legal codes and structures alone is not sufficient to make the legal system impartial: as Holmes argues, "Russia's legal reforms will succeed only to the extent that the country as a whole develops in a liberal, pluralistic, and democratic direction."[2]

In the Soviet regime, the authorities regarded the law as an extension of state power, to be used for the state's purposes.[3] However, the mass terror of the Stalin period persuaded Stalin's successors that the regime would benefit from limiting the arbitrary power of the secret police—if only so that state officials could perform their duties with less fear. After Stalin's death in 1953, legal reformers attempted fitfully and with mixed results to reform both the codes of law and procedure so as to build more guarantees of rights into the legal system. One of the most important institutional changes made in the late 1950s was to place the secret police under stricter legal control. Extrajudicial trials, judgments, and sentences, which were a common practice in the time of Stalin's terror, were prohibited, and criminal defendants were granted important rights. New codes of criminal law and criminal procedure were adopted in the union republics, and official policy promoted a concept of "socialist legality." Like many slogans of the post-Stalin period, this was a formula meant to paper over contradictory policy goals. The idea was that the legal system, while still upholding socialist principles and practices, should be less subject to political caprice than under Stalin.

In fact, in the post-Stalin era, the party and police continued to use legal procedures as a way of legitimating actions taken in the service of the regime's power and security. The criminal codes themselves contained articles providing legal penalties for "anti-Soviet agitation and propaganda" and for "circulation of fabrications known to be false which defame the Soviet state or social system."[4] In the post-Stalin period these were frequently used against individuals whom the regime considered to be political dissidents. Alternatively the authorities sometimes resorted to the practice of declaring a dissident mentally incompetent and forcibly incarcerating him in a mental hospital, where he could be further punished by being administered mind-altering drugs.[5] The continuation of these practices as means of political repression into the late 1980s attests to the inability of the law to protect the rights of individuals whom the party or KGB for any reason considered a threat.

When Mikhail Gorbachev came to power in 1985, one of his major goals was to strengthen the legitimacy and authority of legal institutions. He declared the establishment of a "law-governed state" (*pravovoe gosudarstvo*) to be a cardinal objective of his reform program.[6] By a "law-governed state," Gorbachev meant that both rulers and ruled would obey the law. Its opposite would be a condition in which the rulers exercised power arbitrarily; the rulers could freely violate the state's own constitutional and statutory rules, as had often happened under the Soviet regime when Communist Party, KGB, and other officials often ignored constitutional and legal norms in exercising their power, but they expected their subjects to obey the law. Since 1991, the ideal of the law-governed state has continued to attract lip service from Russian leaders even when they took actions violating the constitution. Putin, for instance, declared that Russia must be governed by a "dictatorship of law," which certainly has ambiguous implications (does it mean that the law must be supreme over the state, or a dictatorship by means of law?). Since the end of the Communist regime, reforms of the constitutional and judicial systems have strengthened legal institutions by making them less subject to political abuse. The judicial system has grown somewhat more independent and effective. The legal principles essential to a democratic and pluralistic society have begun to be established. One significant change is the creation of a Constitutional Court empowered to adjudicate disputes arising between the branches of government and between the federal level of government and the constituent territories. An important statutory change is the adoption of a body of law recognizing private property rights.

Still, movement toward a genuinely independent judicial branch has been stymied by several problems. At the federal level, the enormous power of the president limits the courts' ability to apply the law impartially. For instance, the Constitutional Court has been very cautious about crossing the president on matters concerning presidential prerogatives; under Yeltsin, the court was willing to defy the president occasionally, but since Putin took power, the court has never tried to check the president. Many lower court rulings go unenforced because of the ability of powerful interests to flout judicial decisions, and some decisions clearly reflect high-level political intervention. At the regional and local levels, courts remain susceptible to political influence. On a range of contentious issues—electoral disputes, federalism issues, property rights conflicts, national security cases—the courts routinely bow to the will of those in power. Although this can mean that the courts can sometimes uphold federal law against runaway local officials when the federal authorities want to curb regional autonomy, it also means that the courts almost never issue a ruling that defies the president.

A second problem is corruption. Russian surveys have found that the courts and police are among the most highly corrupted of Russian institutions.[7] To some extent, this stems from the rapidity of the change in the political and economic system. The meltdown of the Soviet system created opportunities for criminals to amass wealth and use it to corrupt law enforcement officials. Legitimate business owners often find themselves forced to turn to illegal protection rackets because the police and courts fail to protect their basic interests.[8] Many citizens report that they cannot afford to turn to the law for the redress of their grievances, because they cannot afford to pay the bribes that they believe are expected. Trust in the courts and procuracy is low, as Table 5.2 illustrated.[9]

Yet despite the low trust, people turn to the courts in rising numbers. The chairman of the Russian Supreme Court, Viacheslav Lebedev, estimated in 2000 that the number of cases heard in Russian courts had tripled since 1994.[10] Judges are overwhelmed by the caseload, are often paid far less than the attorneys who appear in court, and face primitive or substandard working conditions (for example, it was reported in 2000 that only 40 percent of judges had computers).[11] There are only a quarter as many bailiffs as are needed to enforce judicial rulings.

Legal reformers emphasize two basic principles: individual rights should take precedence over the power of the state, and judicial power should be separated from legislative and executive power. Observance of these two principles would represent a large step toward greater respect for law and away from the many abuses of law that the Soviet state committed in the past. For instance, the Bolsheviks held that, because "revolutionary justice" was higher than any written law, the rights and obligations of rulers and citizens must be subordinate to the political interests of the regime. But this instrumental view of the law was not held only by the Bolsheviks. Many in and outside of President Yeltsin's administration expressed a similar view that the goal of eliminating the foundations of Communist rule took precedence over observance of the letter of the law: the populace must obey the law—but the authorities (*"vlast"*) could choose when to observe it and when not to, according to their judgments of expediency.

President Putin has repeatedly proclaimed his adherence to the principle of an independent judicial branch and procuracy, but he and his staff routinely instruct the procurators and courts how to handle important cases. Under Putin, the political authorities use the machinery of the law to repress real and imagined political opponents, much as the Soviet authorities did in the 1960s and 1970s. There is a difference, however. Today, there are no provisions in the criminal code outlawing "anti-state agitation and propaganda." Instead, the authorities use seemingly nonpolitical criminal and civil laws as political instruments. For example, criminal prosecutions on charges of tax law violations, embezzlement, and other crimes, as well as civil suits for recovery of debts, figured in the Putin administration's campaigns against several top figures of major financial and industrial groups. A good example is the use of selective prosecution to dismantle the Yukos oil firm so that it could be taken over by the state. (See Close-Up 6.1: The Yukos Affair, in Chapter 6.)

Judicial reform affects many interests, including the bureaucratic self-interest of the agencies directly responsible for law enforcement. Law enforcement in Russia has traditionally given considerable responsibility to the *procuracy*—the agency charged with supervising the justice system, investigating crimes, preparing and prosecuting cases, and ensuring that the rights of *both* state *and* individuals were upheld. Judicial reformers long have urged that judges be given greater authority with which to supervise pretrial investigations and court proceedings, and that individuals accused of criminal acts have more effective means to defend themselves. But the procuracy has proved itself to be a powerful bureaucratic interest group, and has blocked many reforms that might improve the justice system.

Judicial Reform

Full establishment of the rule of law would mean that no arm of the state would be able to influence or violate the law for political ends. In turn, this would require that the judiciary be independent of the executive. Through much of the Soviet period, however, judges were readily influenced by political pressures, some direct, some indirect. One of the most notorious forms of political influence was called "telephone justice." This referred to the practice whereby a party official or some other powerful individual would privately communicate instructions to a judge on a particular case.[12] "Telephone justice" was symptomatic of a prevalent pattern in which the law was held in relatively low repute and legal institutions possessed little autonomy of the policy-implementing organs of government. The party might direct judges to be especially harsh in passing sentences on a particular class of criminals if it was attempting to conduct a propaganda campaign against a social problem, such as alcoholism, hooliganism, or economic crimes. A party official might direct prosecutors to crack down on some previously tolerated activity, or to gather incriminating evidence on someone it wished to punish. In the past, pressures such as these often pushed adjudication over the line from full and vigorous enforcement of the law into abandonment of the law in pursuit of political ends.[13] By the same token, an unwritten but firmly observed norm made it impossible to prosecute a high-ranking member of the political elite without the party's consent. Even when improper political influence was not involved, many judges routinely accepted the prosecutor's case for a defendant's guilt, a reflection of the procuracy's advantage over the defense in criminal proceedings.

The judicial reforms under Gorbachev set in motion significant policy changes but did not bring them to fruition. Still, the record of judicial reforms undertaken during the Gorbachev period was significant. It also showed that both right and left can agree on the principle of a fair and impartial judicial system because it serves ultimately to protect all citizens, regardless of their political persuasions, from the arbitrary exercise of political power. The obstacles to achieving judicial independence have less to do with the struggle between reformers and conservatives than with the powerful desire by state authorities to retain their power over the legal system. Often a consensus between legal experts of very different ideological camps emerges on the principles of judicial reform, but is opposed by the bureaucratic groups whose power would be threatened by reform.

Since 1989, reforms of Russia's legal system have taken some steps to improve the effectiveness and independence of judicial institutions and to strengthen individual legal rights vis-à-vis the state. These institutional and statutory changes have not always pitted democrats against Communists, but have often met the resistance of powerful agencies of the state, such as the procuracy, that are threatened by losing power to judges, defense attornies, and juries. In the 1990s parliament passed and the president signed a number of significant institutional changes, including a reorganization of the court system and statutory changes affecting the criminal code, code of criminal procedure, and criminal corrections code. At the same time, progress in the other factors that would enable Russia to move toward the rule of law has been slower. Those in power still sometimes intervene in judicial decision making, and the poor working conditions under which the police and courts operate invite corruption.

Let us now consider in more detail the degree of change and continuity since the Communist era in three domains of the legal system: the procuracy and other agencies of law enforcement; the judiciary and in particular the Constitutional Court; and the codes of law and legal procedure.

Law Enforcement

Russia's legal system traditionally vested a great deal of power in the procuracy, which was considered to be the most prestigious branch of the law. The procuracy is somewhat comparable to the system of federal prosecutors in the United States, but has wider powers and duties. The procuracy is given sweeping responsibilities for fighting crime, corruption, and abuses of power in the bureaucracy, and for both instigating investigations of criminal wrongdoing by private citizens and responding to complaints about official malfeasance. The procuracy has the primary responsibility for bringing criminal cases to court. It supervises the investigation of a case, prepares the case for prosecution, and argues the case in court. In addition, the procuracy has traditionally been seen as the principal check on illegal activity and abuses of power by officials: One of its assigned tasks is to supervise all state officials and public organizations to ensure that they observe the law.

Another critical role of the procuracy is to enforce federal law throughout Russia. When regional political establishments grew powerful and independent in the 1990s, the center's ability to compel compliance with federal law in the regions declined, placing more pressure on the procuracy to enforce federal law. Formally, the regional branches of the procuracy are subordinate to the Procurator General in Moscow, but in practice some local procurators formed alliances with strong governors. President Putin has demanded that the procuracy once again be centralized so that it can enforce common legal standards throughout the country. When Putin created the seven new federal "superdistricts" in May 2000, the procuracy announced that it was creating new branches of the procuracy in each new superregion. These were charged with riding herd on the branches of the procuracy in each of the 89 subjects of the federation, and thus helping to recentralize control within the procuracy. These new branch offices were instructed to comb through regional statutes to find instances of laws contradicting federal law and to correct these problems. They found hundreds of such cases in each federal district, and pressed regional legislative and executive bodies to rewrite the offending legislation. Putin hailed this effort for "its important role in implementing the important task of creating a unified legal space in the country."[14]

The procuracy has substantial political influence, which it exercises to protect its institutional prerogatives. Complaining that its resources leave it grossly underequipped to meet even the most elementary demands placed on it, such as investigating the most serious violent crimes and bringing the offenders to justice, the procuracy's representatives plead for more resources rather than fewer responsibilities. The procuracy has even lobbied vigorously in defense of its institutional prerogatives when it believed that a proposed reform would weaken its power. For example, it has staunchly opposed giving arrested persons the right to consult with an attorney at any time during the pretrial investigation; it stubbornly opposed the adoption of the jury trial system; it fought reforms giving the courts the right to review procurators' decisions on the pretrial detention of criminal suspects; and it has battled successfully to retain the responsibility to supervise criminal investigations. The procuracy has won some of its fights, and in others it has succeeded in watering down reforms intended to strengthen other legal institutions. Both Russian statist tradition (including the experience of legal institutions in the Soviet and prerevolutionary eras) and Russia's use of a continental, or inquisitorial, system of legal procedure,[15] reinforce the procuracy's central role in the judicial system.

However, the reformed Criminal Procedure Code that came into effect on July 1, 2002, significantly reduced the legal powers of the procuracy by providing that warrants for arrests, wiretaps, searches, seizures, and a number of other pretrial procedures could no longer be issued by the procuracy, but only by the courts.[16]

Because of the centrality of the procuracy in the Russian legal system, the position of Procurator General—who directs the procuracy throughout the country—is of enormous political sensitivity. Under the 1993 constitution, the president nominates a candidate for Procurator General to the Federation Council, which has the power to approve or reject the nomination. Likewise, the president must obtain Federation Council approval to remove the Procurator General. Only rarely in post-Communist Russia has the Procurator General taken a position directly opposing the president, but in one important precedent-setting instance at least, the procuracy did demonstrate its political independence. In February 1994, the State Duma approved an amnesty for several categories of persons, including those who were in jail awaiting trial for their participation in the attempted coups d'état of August 1991 and October 1993. The Duma was exercising the power of amnesty that the newly adopted constitution had granted (although no law had yet been adopted specifying how this power was to be exercised). However, President Yeltsin expressed outrage at the decision and his advisors presented a variety of legal opinions purporting to demonstrate that the Duma's action was unlawful. Nonetheless, the Procurator General at the time, although believing that the Duma had exceeded its constitutional powers, complied with the Duma's decision, and ordered the release of the prisoners. When Yeltsin pressured him to halt the release, the procurator refused to comply and resigned instead. The release was duly carried out. Then, for several months afterward, the Federation Council refused to confirm Yeltsin's nominee for a new Procurator General.[17]

Under Yeltsin, the procuracy exercised greater independence of the executive branch; since Putin came to power, the procuracy has been a loyal instrument of the Kremlin's political will. It has carried out a large effort to identify laws adopted by regional legislatures that violate federal law and taken them to court to have them overturned. It has opened criminal cases against regional government officials accused of committing crimes. The procuracy has taken advantage of the tightening of political controls under Putin to claim greater responsibility in investigating corruption among government officials. As Procurator General Vladimir Ustinov put it in a speech in May 2004, because civil society in Russia is so underdeveloped, the procuracy has assumed the functions of civil society in curbing abuses by the state bureaucracy.[18] It is clear, however, that the procuracy's actions are closely coordinated with the Kremlin. Ustinov has said that he meets at least once a week with Putin in order to "report" to the president, although he insists that the procuracy is entirely independent of the authorities in its enforcement of the law.[19] This is a dubious claim, however. The record suggests that the procuracy is often used as an instrument against figures whom the Kremlin wants to remove from the political arena.

The procuracy has overall responsibility for investigating suspected violations of the law by ordinary citizens and public officials, but the power to investigate crimes and arrest suspects is vested in a series of police agencies. Some of them are administered by the Ministry for Internal Affairs (MVD), and others are specialized successor bodies of the old Soviet-era KGB (Committee for State Security).

The Ministry for Internal Affairs manages both regular uniformed police (known as the *militsiia*) and militarized security forces that carry out riot control and other functions. They also operate specialized police forces, such as the branch of the police that monitors road safety. As with other branches of law and law enforcement in Russia, the MVD is a hierarchically organized federal structure, but in practice, the federal-level authorities have a hard time subordinating regional branches of the police to the center because regional governments have a great deal of day-to-day influence over the material and career interests of police in their regions. One important trend under Putin has been to appoint new regional heads of the MVD, procuracy, and security police to reinforce central control over law enforcement in those regions. According to Nikolai Petrov of the Moscow Carnegie Center, Putin in his first term replaced 85 percent of the federal procurators in the regions, 70 percent of the regional police chiefs, 60 percent of the heads of the regional security services, and half of the chief federal inspectors in the regions.[20] Politically, this turnover has had the effect of weakening the governors' control over the regional branches of the federal power structures while simultaneously expanding Putin's own network of loyal political clients.

The KGB, or Committee for State Security, exercised very wide powers in the Soviet regime, including responsibility for both domestic and foreign intelligence. It also conducted extensive surveillance over society to prevent political dissent or opposition, and in its exercise of power, it often operated outside the law. In October 1991, following the August 1991 coup (when the KGB chairman was one of the principal organizers of the seizure of power), Yeltsin dissolved the Russian republican branch of the KGB and divided it into several new agencies: the Ministry of Security, which was to guard the state's security in domestic matters; the Foreign Intelligence Service, which took over the KGB's overseas espionage and intelligence functions; the Federal Agency for Governmental Communications and Information (FAPSI), which maintained security in the country's telecommunications system, the Federal Border Guard Service (FSP), and the Federal Tax Police (FSNP). The reorganization altered the structure and mission of the successor bodies, but they were never subjected to a thorough purge of personnel. Like Gorbachev, Yeltsin and Putin have preferred to cultivate a close political relationship with the security agencies rather than to antagonize them. Although many of the archives containing documents on the past activities of the secret police[21] have been opened to inspection, thus exposing many aspects of the Soviet regime's use of terror, no member or collaborator of the security service has ever been prosecuted legally for these actions. None of the KGB's informers have been exposed to public judgement. Indeed, the security police claim that they were themselves a victim of arbitrary rule and terror under Stalin, and therefore that today they strongly uphold the rule of law. Whether this position is credible is another matter.

Throughout the 1990s, the successor bodies were further reorganized. In 1993 the Ministry of Security was reorganized as the Federal Counter-Intelligence Service, and in 1995 President Yeltsin reorganized it yet again into the Federal Security Service (FSB), assigning it comprehensive duties and powers. Some idea of how wide-ranging its powers are is suggested by the description of the new body's mandate given by a senior Russian government official to the press. The new FSB, he stated, would "be able to infiltrate foreign organizations and criminal groups, institute inquiries, carry out preliminary investigations, maintain its own prisons, demand information from private companies, and set up special units and front enterprises." Its duties would include foreign intelligence activities to boost Russia's "economic, scientific, technical, and defense potential" and "to ensure the security of all government bodies."[22]

The KGB's successor agencies have been skillful at adapting to the new post-Soviet political environment, and have found new security tasks that enable them to retain power and resources. An example is the Federal Agency for Governmental Communications and Information (FAPSI), which is responsible for ensuring the security of state telecommunications. FAPSI is believed to provide telecommunications services to a number of governmental, financial, and commercial organizations, giving it unusually privileged intelligence-gathering opportunities. FAPSI's role in monitoring all forms of mass communications and telecommunications systems has been greatly enhanced by the approval of a sweeping new doctrine on "information security," which the Security Council drafted and which Putin signed on September 12, 2000. Defining virtually all areas of information processing, communication, and use as vital to Russia's national security, the doctrine enumerates a series of threats to Russia's information security. Among them are Russia's inability to compete effectively in world markets for news and information, the leakage of state secrets, the ability of unauthorized persons to gain illegal access to Russian databases and electronic servers, vulnerability to "information weapons" directed against Russia, and efforts by "western countries" to "further destroy the scientific-technological integrity" of the former Soviet Union by trying to bring it under Western influence. The document establishes doctrinal grounds for a considerable expansion of the powers (and budget allocations) of FAPSI and other security agencies in order to control the flow of information in and out of Russia.[23]

Although they have been eager to aggrandize power, the security agencies that were created out of the KGB have had a reputation for competence and honesty. Many former security officers have gone to work for private organizations because they are considered to be honest and professional. And a number of leading politicians have backgrounds in the security organs, including, most famously, President Putin. Putin has drawn on the security agencies for many of his senior personnel appointments. Certainly a number of figures who were associates of Putin from his days working in St. Petersburg have wound up with senior positions in the presidential administration and as heads of major government-run business corporations—sometimes simultaneously.[24]

Since the end of the Soviet era, despite taking on new tasks such as fighting international narcotics trafficking and terrorism, Russia's security police have continued to demonstrate a Soviet-style preoccupation with controlling the flow of information about the country. In 2002, embarrassed by the defections to the West of two senior officers, they obtained convictions in absentia of both defectors on charges of treason. Under Putin the authorities have arrested several Russian journalists and scientists for espionage, and in 2001 the security police sent a directive to the Academy of Sciences demanding that scholars report all contacts with foreigners. A deputy director of the FSB denied that his agency was fanning a "spy-mania" but claimed that the activities of foreign intelligence services in Russia had become "more aggressive, conspiratorial, and sophisticated."[25] In January 2006, the FSB announced that it had caught four British Embassy employees engaged in spying and claimed that they were financing Russian human rights NGOs. The case (given extensive coverage in the media) thus implied both that the West was trying to subvert the Russian state and that Russian NGOs were a fifth column inside the country.

The fact that the police were reviving Soviet-era practices under a president who made his career in the KGB has raised serious concerns about Putin's commitment to the rule of law. Some Russian political figures have expressed serious concern that under Putin, the security police have become more powerful and assertive and have cast a long shadow over society.

A further step in the strengthening of the state security police under Putin was the decision in March 2003, enacted in a series of presidential decrees, to dissolve FAPSI and the Federal Border Guard Service (FSP) and merge them into the Federal Security Service. As both of these services had operated as divisions of the KGB in the Soviet era, observers commented that the FSB was returning to the old model of "superagency." Some idea of the breadth of the FSB's power is suggested by the agency's claims about its successes. In December 2006, at the security police's annual holiday celebration, FSB director Nikolai Patrushev declared that the FSB had fought terrorism, subversion, extremism, corruption, and foreign espionage operations. He claimed that the FSB had saved Russia 45 billion rubles that year, investigated 70 criminal cases, and brought 35 local and 17 regional state officials to justice.[26] Their broad mandate and the secrecy surrounding their operations make the FSB and other successor agencies to the KGB extremely difficult to monitor. Effectively, the only institution to which the secret services are accountable is the president. Putin, meantime, has continued to expand their mandate and budget. Like many previous Russian rulers, Putin has found the security police an indispensable source of political support.

The Judiciary

In contrast to the clout that the procuracy has traditionally wielded in Russia, the bench has been relatively weak and passive. Traditionally judges have been the least-experienced and lowest-paid members of the legal profession, and the most vulnerable to external political and administrative pressure.[27] This situation is changing; the professionalism and prestige of the bench have been rising.[28] But in order for judges to exercise their powers impartially and without fear of retribution, the political environment in which they operate must value the principle of judicial independence. However, the regime changes in Russia have had contradictory effects on the development of an effective, autonomous judicial branch. In the 1990s, the rise of powerful business interests, coupled with the reach of organized crime, subverted judicial autonomy. In a few instances, judges were murdered when they attempted to thwart organized crime. In the 2000s, judges have been reluctant to cross the executive branch.

In addition, many judges have left the bench to take higher paying jobs in other branches of the legal profession. As the volume of court cases that come before the courts increase, judges find themselves hard-pressed to keep up. There are around 30,000 judges in courts of general jurisdiction, and many are holdovers from the Soviet era. They hear almost six million cases each year.[29] The workload of the courts continues to rise as market relations spread and more and more disputes spill over into the courts. Despite the introduction of a new institution of "bailiff-enforcers" in 1997 to assist in compelling parties to legal judgments to comply with court decisions, courts still often find it difficult to implement their decisions in the face of determined resistance.[30] Judges continue to complain that there are too few bailiffs to enforce judgments and secure their courtrooms.

Policymakers recognize the importance of an independent judiciary but disagree on the conditions needed to achieve it. In the past, judges were formally elected by the local soviet of the jurisdiction in which they served; in actuality they were part of the Communist Party–controlled *nomenklatura* system and thus were appointed to their positions by the party staff. Reforms beginning in the late 1980s attempted to increase judges' independence by lengthening their term of office and placing their election into the hands of the soviet at the next-higher level to that of the jurisdiction in which they served. But this still allowed powerful regional executives to sway judicial decision making. Therefore reformers pushed a law through the Federal Assembly that put the power of appointment of all federal judges into the president's hands, although the president must choose from among candidates screened and proposed by judicial qualifications commissions. The president was also obliged to take into account the suggestions of the legislatures of the regions where federal judges would serve. Judges now have lifetime terms, but under legislation passed in 2001, they must retire at age 65 (age 70 for the highest courts).

The judicial reform law passed at the end of 1996 took a significant step in the direction of establishing a single legal order throughout the Russian Federation.[31] Over the objection of some heads of the national republics and other regions, both chambers of parliament and the president agreed that all courts of general jurisdiction would be federal courts and would be guided by federal law, the federal constitution, and the instructions of the federal Supreme Court.

The law establishes an institution of local justices of the peace (*mirovye sud' i*), which had existed in Russia in the prerevolutionary era, but they may only consider minor cases. These courts have spread rapidly and now hear a large proportion of all civil and criminal cases. It is important to note, however, that in contrast to the United States' multitiered federal system of courts, Russia's law establishes a common federal judiciary throughout the country.[32]

Until recently, all judicial decisions in Russian courts in criminal cases were rendered by a judge and two "lay assessors." Lay assessors are ordinary citizens who are given paid leave from their place of work for a period of time in order to serve as co-judges in presiding over criminal trials; their participation is a form of community service for citizens designed to bring the justice system closer to the values and interests of the public. The judge and lay assessors have equal votes in deciding on the verdict and sentence, but, in practice, lay assessors tend to defer to the superior legal knowledge and experience of judges. More recently, a serious practical problem has arisen with the system of lay assessors. Fewer and fewer citizens are willing to leave their jobs to serve as lay assessors, and many trials must be conducted without them.

Putin has lent his support to efforts by legal reformers to replace the old system of judges and lay assessors with a jury trial system in serious criminal cases. Gradually, the jury trial system has been introduced into courtrooms throughout the country. The jury system remains controversial. Supporters believe that it helps make citizens consider themselves to be part of the legal system, and, by extension, the political system, rather than passive and helpless objects of its will. Jury service, at least in theory, allows people to experience directly the responsibilities associated with democratic self-government. Reformers assert that jury trials also make the legal system more honest and effective, since it is more difficult for police, investigators, prosecutors, and judges to get away with abuses and misconduct. Finally, they argue that the jury trial redresses the bias of criminal procedure by countering the strong advantages traditionally possessed by the procuracy and establishing a more level playing field between accuser and accused. As the distinguished Russian legal scholar, Alexander M. Yakovlev, wrote:

> The introduction of jury trials into the Russian system of justice marked an important step from the inquisitorial principle to the accusatorial one. The jury represented the real third party, the umpire before whom the defendant and the prosecutor became equal. This meant a great deal in a country where the prosecutor personified the omnipotence of the state and the defendant was considered just a despised transgressor of the laws prescribed by the state, where the presumption was not of innocence but of guilt, and where to be accused meant mostly to be sentenced and punished.[33]

Trial by jury certainly is not a *necessary* condition for democracy: other judicial fact-finding procedures are also perfectly consistent with democratic principles. But in Russia, where there are long traditions of local self-government and strong if latent norms of egalitarianism and communalism, the jury trial may indeed have indirect effects that reinforce democratic values. Moreover, it is an institution with substantial roots in Russian society. It was introduced and widely used in Russia as part of the great reforms of the 1860s, and juries became an important instrument of civic participation.[34] Following the October 1917 revolution, however, the Bolsheviks eliminated the jury trial.

As in the Anglo-American world, juries are somewhat more sympathetic to defendants than judges would be; acquittal rates are significantly higher than in regular courts.[35] Some acquittals have prompted second thoughts about the jury system. For example, in 2006 a jury in St. Petersburg acquitted a group of youths who had been accused of killing a Vietnamese student out of ethnic hatred. Eight of the 17 accused were let off entirely, and the rest were convicted of other charges. In another 2006 trial involving a gang of Russian youths armed with chains and knives who had beaten a 9-year-old Tajik girl to death, a jury concluded that the charges of murder had not been proved and therefore, that the accused were not guilty of her murder. The youths were found guilty of hooliganism instead, and given light sentences. In a third case, involving the hate killing of a student from the Congo, four accused youths were acquitted. These cases attest either to the sloppy work of the investigators and prosecutors, or to the sympathies of jury members with the young men accused of the charges.[36] Public opinion about the jury trial system is divided, but it is probably too soon to assess the impact of the system on the quality of justice.[37]

The courts of general jurisdiction form a pyramid of local and regional courts. At its pinnacle is the Russian Supreme Court, which hears cases referred from lower courts and also issues instructions to lower courts on judicial matters. Its reasoning in rendering decisions is published and may be taken as guidance by lower courts in reaching decisions (bringing the Russian system closer to the recognition of legal precedents as binding). The Supreme Court does not have the power to challenge the constitutionality of laws and other normative acts adopted by legislative and executive bodies. That power is assigned by the constitution to the Constitutional Court. Under the constitution, judges of the Supreme Court are nominated by the president and confirmed by the Council of the Federation. Likewise, the chairman of the Supreme Court is appointed by the president and confirmed by the upper house.

There is another system of courts designed to adjudicate cases arising from civil disputes between firms, including bankruptcy proceedings, and between firms and the government. These are called "arbitration" or "commercial" courts (*arbitrazhnye sudy*).[38] There is one arbitration court in each subject of the federation, and there are another ten interregional courts to hear appeals. At the apex of this system stands the Supreme Commercial Court. Like the Supreme Court, the Supreme Commercial Court is both the highest appellate court for its system of courts, as well as the source of instruction and direction to lower commercial courts. Also, as with the Supreme Court, the chairman of the Supreme Commercial Court is nominated by the president and confirmed by the Council of the Federation. As the volume of commercial transactions in Russia has grown, so has the workload of the arbitration courts; in 2000 they handled over 600,000 cases, and the caseload is growing.[39] These courts also handle an increasing number of cases arising from tax disputes (including a rapidly growing number of cases, often successful, when private firms take the government's tax authorities to court). The new commercial courts have issued a number of crucial rulings that have helped establish the legal foundation for a market economy. The courts have often had a hard time enforcing their rulings, but the new institution of judicial bailiffs has helped somewhat. Moreover, enterprises sometimes find it useful to obtain a ruling in a dispute against another enterprise, even if they are unsure whether it will be enforced, in order to have a precedent that they can use in future litigation.[40] The chairman of the Supreme Commercial Court, Veniamin Yakovlev, commented that even though the arbitration courts are a part of the state and paid by it, the judges consider themselves an independent branch of state power, and have been reasonably successful at defending their independence even in litigation where the state has been a party.[41]

In 2001 the Putin administration drafted a comprehensive set of legislative proposals to reform the judicial system. One aim of the reforms was to increase the accountability of judges for their actions, but increasing accountability and independence at the same time proved problematic. After extensive deliberation by legal experts, judges, presidential staff people, and parliamentarians, the reforms were enacted. They consisted of a substantial increase in judges' salaries and improvement in their working conditions; organizational changes in the way judges were appointed and removed; and the changes to the criminal procedure code that were noted earlier that expanded the rights of judges to supervise pretrial criminal procedures.[42] Putin also reformed the system of judicial qualifications commissions, which regulate the selection and disciplining of judges, by bringing a larger number of laypeople onto them.[43] Reports indicate that Putin has used this reform to place a number of executive branch representatives—including former security police officials—onto the regional commissions.[44] The Putin reforms were ostensibly designed to increase the status and political independence of the judiciary and to expand the judicial protection of civil liberties. Undoubtedly the president wants to increase the autonomy of the judiciary vis-à-vis regional and business interests, consistent with his aim of centralizing power. On the other hand, Putin's efforts to increase judicial accountability also appear intended to subject judges to tighter political control from above.

The Constitutional Court

The creation of the Constitutional Court is one of the more important achievements of the democratization movement of the late 1980s and early 1990s. Because the Soviet regime had no legal institution to ensure that legislative and administrative acts of the state conformed with the Soviet constitution, legal reformers in the Gorbachev period called for creating a constitutional court, equivalent to such bodies as the Constitutional Council in the French Fifth Republic or the Constitutional Court in Germany, which would rule on the constitutionality of laws and would adjudicate disputes between the union and the republics. As a cautious initial experiment with such a body, a constitutional amendment creating a "committee on constitutional supervision" (*komitet konstitutsionnogo nadzora*) was passed in December 1988. This body came into being on January 1, 1990. One of its early decisions was that there would be no Communist Party organization within it—a small symbolic indication that the committee's members considered the law superior to the dictates of the party. The committee's first official decision, in September 1990, found that Gorbachev had acted unconstitutionally when he had decreed earlier in the year that, as president, he had the power to forbid or allow demonstrations within Moscow. Gorbachev did not challenge the committee's ruling. But the committee found itself powerless to overcome the paralyzing effects of the "war of laws" between union, republican, and local government authorities. Moreover, as it was not a court, the committee could not adjudicate cases. Nevertheless, the committee's creation, and the care it exercised to avoid making decisions that would be flagrantly ignored, indicated that an important precedent had been established.

The committee dissolved along with the rest of the union government in December 1991. Russia, however, had established a constitutional court by a constitutional amendment in July 1991. The 15 members of the Constitutional Court were elected by the Congress of People's Deputies for life terms. The Congress elected a relatively young legal scholar, Valerii Zor'kin, as chairman.

The Russian Constitutional Court made several significant decisions in its first year of existence. Among them was a finding in December 1991 that an action of President Yeltsin merging two state ministries into a single body was unconstitutional; the president complied with the decision, establishing the precedent of effective judicial review. Another important decision concerned Yeltsin's decrees in the fall of 1991 outlawing the Communist Party and nationalizing its property. Reviewing the constitutionality of his actions, the court held in November 1992 that Yeltsin acted within his rights when he banned the Communist Party's executive organs but that he had no right to prohibit members of the party from forming primary organizations (PPOs or cells). Moreover, the court said that the state had the right to confiscate the party's property, but that in cases in which the title of an asset was unclear or disputed, only the Supreme Commercial Court could rule on the state's rights. This decision was widely regarded as juridically sound and politically shrewd, in that it allowed both the Communists and the president's side to claim victory. The court also, perhaps wisely, avoided taking sides on the president's assertion that the CPSU was itself unconstitutional. The court thus positioned itself as a politically neutral institution. This was no mean achievement in the tense, polarized environment of the time.

A final success for the court in the 1991–1993 period was the intervention by its chairman into the severe confrontation that arose between President Yeltsin and the Congress of People's Deputies in December 1992 over the rightful powers of the president and the legislature. Chairman Zor'kin proposed a resolution of the crisis, which both sides accepted: that a national referendum be held to decide on the basic constitutional principles to govern Russia. Here the chairman of the court came close to entering the political fray directly, but, unfortunately for the court, he did not stop there. Zor'kin soon came to agree with the chairman of the Supreme Soviet, Ruslan Khasbulatov, that the referendum should not be held after all, and supported the Congress's decision in early March 1993 to cancel it. When Yeltsin immediately thereafter appeared on television to declare his intention to suspend the Congress and impose special presidential rule, Chairman Zor'kin quickly issued a condemnation of Yeltsin's statement: but he did so without having reviewed the text of Yeltsin's proposed decree and on his own authority, rather than as a decision of the court's full membership. When Yeltsin's decree was finally published a few days later, it had dropped the legally offensive provisions about declaring a special form of presidential rule and suspending the activity of the Congress. Perhaps Zor'kin's condemnation had helped to deter Yeltsin from taking such authoritarian steps. But it was clear that Zor'kin had acted precipitously, revealing a zeal more political than juridical.

Soon Zor'kin began supporting Khasbulatov's political positions routinely and thus forfeiting the court's claim to be politically neutral. In October 1993, following Yeltsin's decrees dissolving parliament and calling for new elections and a constitutional referendum, Yeltsin also suspended the operation of the Constitutional Court until the new constitution was ratified, new judges elected to fill vacancies, and a new law governing its activity was enacted by parliament. Under the new law on the Constitutional Court passed by parliament in summer 1994, there were to be 19 members and the members themselves would elect their own chairman. Their terms were limited to 12 years. Thirteen of the original members of the court remained members (including Zor'kin, whom Yeltsin removed as chairman of the court but who continued as a full member and eventually was reelected chairman in 2003). The president then nominated six new justices to fill the vacancies on the court and presented them to the Council of the Federation for confirmation. The council refused to confirm three and the stage was set for a new round of political bargaining between the president and parliament to find mutually acceptable candidates. Over the next 8 months, the president proposed 14 different candidates altogether, and the Federation Council rejected 8, until finally the full complement of 19 judges was confirmed.

When the newly configured court resumed work in March 1995 it quickly established its right to interpret the constitution in a variety of areas. It ruled on several ambiguous questions relating to parliamentary procedure. It overturned some laws passed by ethnic republics within Russia, and struck down a provision of the Russian Criminal Code that limited individual rights. Generally, in cases involving disputes between individuals and state authorities, the court has favored individual rights. For example, the court issued an important ruling in March 2002 demanding that the new legislative rule that the arrest of a person for more than 48 hours required a court order must take effect as of July 1, 2002.[45]

Of all the spheres in which the Constitutional Court has made politically significant rulings, its decisions in the area of *federalism* are probably the most important. Repeatedly the court has been called on to delimit the powers of territorial subjects of the federation in relation to the federal constitution. Generally, it has defended the legal unity of the federation in the face of the regions' demands for autonomy.[46] However, it has also tried to be careful not to issue rulings that will be ignored and thus undermine the court's legitimacy. A particularly contentious example of the type of dispute it has decided arose from the ethnic republic of Udmurtia. The legislature of the Udmurt Republic (an industrial territory located in the western part of the Urals area), passed a law in 1996 that dissolved the elected governments of the cities and districts throughout the republic, and required that the executive branch instead be headed by officials appointed by the republic government. The mayor of the capital city, joined by President Yeltsin and the Russian State Duma, took the matter to court and sought a ruling from the Constitutional Court. In January 1997 the court ruled that although the Udmurt legislature was within its constitutional rights to pass a law on local government for the republic, it did not have the right to nullify the authority of previously elected government officials without taking into account the will of its citizens. An interesting outcome of the decision was that both sides claimed that they had won. For several weeks the regional legislature ignored the court's requirement that it reinstate the officials it had removed from office. Twice Yeltsin went so far as to issue an edict demanding the region's compliance with the court's decision. After temporizing briefly, the region finally backed down.[47] Observers hailed this as an important precedent in establishing the court's legitimacy in adjudicating disputes arising from ambiguities in the rules of Russian federalism.

Throughout the 1990s, the court rendered a series of decisions upholding federal law against the efforts by regional executives and legislatures to assert their autonomy. However, the court was always mindful of the political climate and therefore recognized that the federal government had only limited capacity to enforce its decisions in the regions. The election of President Putin changed the political balance sharply. Putin made it clear that he intended to reclaim for the federal government some of the power and prerogatives that had been claimed, de facto, by regional governments. Two major decisions by the Constitutional Court in the spring of 2000 reinforced Putin's position. First was a ruling in April 2000 that procurator (in fact, *any* citizen) could challenge the legality of a law or regulation passed by a regional or local authority. An ordinary court (court of general jurisdiction) was entitled to suspend such a law or regulation if it found that it did indeed violate federal law. Only the Constitutional Court had the power to strike down such a law as completely invalid. But a local court, guided by previous decisions of the Constitutional Court and its own reading of the federal law, could declare that the law or regulation was "not in force."[48] The effect of this ruling was to allow procurators and courts throughout the country to enforce the primacy of federal law over arbitrary acts by local authorities.

The other major decision by the court came in response to an appeal by the president of the ethnic republic of Gorno-Altai, who sought clarification about the constitutionality of several provisions of its constitution. Among other things, he asked the court to rule whether its constitution had the right to declare the republic "sovereign" and to declare the natural resources located on its territory the "property" of the republic. The court ruled that not only did the provisions on sovereignty and the ownership of natural resources violate the federal constitution (on the grounds that only the Russian Federation is sovereign), but declared explicitly that the analogous provisions in all the other republic constitutions that contained such points were also unconstitutional. To drive the point home, the court met with the heads of the constitutional courts of all six republics whose constitutions possessed such provisions. It explained that these provisions were all automatically rendered invalid and should be removed. Clearly the court was taking advantage of Putin's vigorous drive to centralize power to assert its own legal doctrine of the primacy of federal law and constitution over regional claims to sovereignty.

Because the court has been politically prudent, reluctant to issue a decision that will be flagrantly ignored, it has tiptoed cautiously around the huge domain of presidential authority. In the Yeltsin period, however, the court did limit the president's power. One instance was its ruling in the "trophy art" case, when it decided that President Yeltsin was required to sign a law after both chambers of parliament overrode his veto.[49] Another was its decision that the use of the proportional representation system in the electoral law to elect half of the deputies of the Duma was entirely compatible with the constitution (observers generally thought that the case, which was brought by one of the regional legislatures, had the tacit support or even sponsorship of the Kremlin). And the court ruled that Yeltsin was not entitled to run for a third term as president.[50] In other and more significant cases, however, the court has tended to side with the president. One of the court's first and most important decisions concerned a challenge brought by a group of Communist parliamentarians to the president's edicts launching the war in Chechnia. The court ruled that the president had the authority to wage the war through the use of his constitutional power to issue edicts with the force of law.

The Constitutional Court proceeds by deciding whether to accept a case or inquiry. (It receives some 15 thousand petitions each year.) Usually, if it does so, it has determined that a challenge to an existing law, decree, or official action has legal merit. It then holds hearings at which parties and experts representing both sides of the issue make statements to the court. Each side listens to the arguments presented by its opponents, and seeks to counter them with superior arguments. The court then takes the information presented under advisement and renders its judgment. Dissenting opinions are published separately, but in recent years there have been very few of these; the court much prefers to speak with a single voice.

The court tends to act slowly. Most cases require 2–4 weeks to decide, with most of that time being spent on the painstaking task of drafting their decision. The court issues only about 20 full rulings per year. The court issues, however, several hundred "findings" (determinations, or *opredeleniia*) per year. These fall short of being full rulings on a case but find that the issues it raises were decided in a previous case. It therefore has begun to introduce a form of law by precedent. This form of decision making eases the strain on the court's growing workload.

The court has had a very difficult time in the Putin period. It has sought to steer a course between being regarded as a tool of the president, and crossing the president on a significant issue only to have its ruling flagrantly ignored. In an interview with the newspaper *Izvestiia* in October 2004, the court's chairman demonstrated his awareness of the Constitutional Court's need to stay attuned to the president's policy priorities, noting that the court "of course interprets the spirit of the constitution in the context of the times." The court, he said, "cannot be guided purely by the letter of the constitution, but must find its spirit."[51] Undoubtedly the court's interpretation of the "spirit" of the constitution requires acute sensitivity to the current political climate.[52]

Putin meantime has made clear his view that the court will not be allowed to obstruct his drive to recentralize state power by pushing a law through parliament that will move the seat of the court to St. Petersburg in March 2008 (over the objections of the judges of the court). This change of venue is widely regarded by observers as an effort to reduce the court's political prestige by distancing it from the network of central state bodies headquartered in Moscow.

Reforms in the Law Codes

In addition to these changes in judicial institutions, Russia has made far-reaching modifications to the codes of criminal, civil, and administrative law and procedure since the end of the Soviet era. The changes extend protections for individual legal and civil rights, at least on paper, and replace many Communist-era provisions with norms compatible with a capitalist economy. More generally, they create legal conditions for civil society through laws recognizing the rights of social and public organizations such as religious communities, political parties, charitable associations, labor unions, and business firms. To a surprising degree, this legislation has been achieved by the laborious process of bargaining and consensus-building among interested groups, including judges, legal experts, and politicians of the left and right, rather than by decree or dictate. As has been emphasized, both reformers and conservatives can support the principles of judicial independence, impartiality, and fairness.

One milestone of statutory reform of legal procedures is the new Civil Code, which regulates civil relations among individuals, organizations, and the state, and provides legal guarantees for property rights.[53] Another important achievement was the new Criminal Code, finally signed into law by President Yeltsin in June 1996 following a year and a half of negotiations and deliberations among specialists, concerned state bodies, the presidential administration, and members of parliament. The new code brought the criminal law into closer conformity with the demands of the post-Soviet environment. It reduced the number of crimes subject to capital punishment, differentiated closely among crimes according to their seriousness, emphasized the need to protect individual legal rights as opposed to the state's interests, decriminalized some activities that had been illegal in the Soviet era, and at the same time introduced definitions of new types of crimes that had been previously unheard of, such as money-laundering and unfair competition. "On the whole," Peter Solomon remarked, "the new code represented a moderate consensus document that promised to de-Sovietize and modernize Russian criminal law."[54] The set of laws reforming the judiciary adopted in December 2001 was a significant step toward improving the working conditions of courts and expanding the legal powers possessed by courts.[55] In 2002, a new Code of Criminal Procedure was passed that increased individual legal rights.[56] For these statutory changes to bring about major progress toward real judicial independence, however, the necessary political conditions must also be met and political interference in the operation of the justice system be ended.

OBSTACLES TO THE RULE OF LAW

By comparison with the Soviet system, the structural and statutory changes that have been made in Russia's legal system, and the far higher level of political pluralism, have expanded civil rights substantially. Individuals and organizations have greater opportunity to defend their rights through the legal system than they did in the Soviet era. Still, the reforms have not managed to eliminate the arbitrary use of state power by executive authorities, and there is much evidence to suggest that the problem of manipulating the legal system for political purposes by those in power is growing under Putin. The continuing threat of terrorism has also given Putin the opportunity to enact severe restrictions on the civil rights of individuals and groups, which the authorities can invoke when they deem it necessary to do so on national security grounds. Putin's repeated claim that shadowy "foreign interests" are trying to break up Russia's integrity as a state has been his justification for enacting a series of legislative and administrative measures that limit the freedom of individuals, political groups, and the mass media.

Other obstacles to the rule of law are long-standing, persistent problems. Bureaucratic autonomy and nontransparency continue to be a barrier to the rule of law, by allowing state officials to defy the will of both executive and legislative policymakers and apply law arbitrarily. Together with the widespread corruption in the legal system, the pattern of the abuse of law by the authorities undermines respect for the law. Let us consider these issues in greater detail.

Bureaucratic Rule Making

The immense inertia of a heavily bureaucratized state remains a challenge for central policymakers no less than for democratic accountability. In Russia today, as in Russia in centuries past, the power of the state's rulers is frequently thwarted by the tendency of administrative agencies to issue rules—decrees, regulations, instructions, orders, directives, circular letters, and many other kinds of official and binding rules, many of them secret—applying not only to subordinates in the same agency but, often, to other governmental agencies and to Russian citizens generally. In the Soviet period, the practice of bureaucratic rule making through what are called "sublegal normative acts" was extremely widespread. Some indication of the magnitude of this practice is suggested by the fact that over the first 70 years of Soviet power, the USSR legislature adopted fewer than 800 laws and decrees, whereas over the same period, the union-level government issued hundreds of thousands of decrees and other normative acts. In 1985, according to one estimate, there were 27,000 legal norms enacted by the USSR Council of Ministers that were still valid.[57] Tens of thousands more binding rules issued by particular government ministries and state committees also remained on the books. The profusion of rules and regulations—complementing, interpreting, and often contradicting one another—creates ample opportunities for evasion, as well as incentives for intervention by powerful individuals seeking to cut through the jungle of red tape. Although the rules and regulations that the departments issue are supposed to be consistent with both the language and spirit of the law, in practice they frequently gut it, so that reforms adopted by the legislature may be eviscerated and weightless by the time they reach the level where they are supposed to be acted upon.

The 1993 constitution does not give parliament an explicit right to oversee (*kontrolirovat'*) the executive branch, a power considered essential to the checks and balances between the American legislative and executive branches. However, as parliament has gained experience in using the powers it does have—particularly the budget process, investigations, hearings, and the Auditing Chamber[58]—it has gradually acquired greater de facto power to oversee the bureaucracy's compliance with legislative requirements. On the other hand, it is frequently difficult to know what the legislature's will is. A persistent problem with legislation passed by the Federal Assembly and signed into law is that as laws pass through the legislative mill, their more controversial points are removed or replaced with bland statements that give bureaucrats wide latitude to issue rules "interpreting" the law. The ambiguity of formal rules invites a reliance on "informal institutions" by state officials and ordinary citizens alike.[59] Officials have wide latitude to use state institutions for their own personal benefit and to minimize openness and transparency in their work.

Personalization of power, secretiveness, and excessive discretion in the hands of administrative officials are obstacles not only to the primacy of law, but also to the ability of a central leader to ensure the implementation of his policies. For this reason, President Putin has repeatedly denounced the bureaucracy's propensity to sidetrack laws with rules and regulations that distort or block federal laws and decrees. For example, in his April 2001 message to parliament he called on the bureaucracy to eliminate excessive rules and regulations and on parliament to pass better quality laws[*]:

> Bureaucratic rule-making [*vedomstvennoe normotvorchestvo*] is one of the chief brakes on the development of entrepreneurship. A bureaucrat is used to acting according to an instruction which, after one or another law has

---

[*] Translated from the presidential Web site, http://president.kremlin.ru/events.

come into force, often is inconsistent with the law itself, but yet for years is never rescinded. . . . The government, ministries and departments should, finally, take radical measures with respect to bureaucratic regulation—even going so far as to eliminate the whole body of departmental regulations in cases where there are already federal laws of direct force in place.

Putin has demanded a major reform of the entire system of state service in order to raise the quality and professionalism of civil servants. In 2002 he issued two decrees laying out general principles to guide the state bureaucracy, but these are extremely broad. A state employee, Putin decreed in August, must show "tolerance and respect toward the customs and traditions of the peoples of Russia, facilitate interethnic and interconfessional concord, observe political neutrality, and respectfully relate to the activity of representatives of the mass media." "Observing and defending human rights and freedoms," the decree stated, "constitute the meaning and content of the activity of organs of state power." Legislation was passed in 2003 and 2004 codifying the organizational principles of the state service that regulated recruitment, pay, evaluation, and promotion, but how effectively it will be implemented remains to be seen.[60]

In 2003, Putin issued another decree demanding a comprehensive reform of the structure and operation of the state bureaucracy.[61] This resulted in a reorganization of the federal executive in March 2004 that was widely regarded as a failure (for one thing, the restructuring was not accompanied by procedures laying out how job responsibilities were to be allocated among the new organizations). In late 2005 the government issued a new document intended to improve the efficiency, responsiveness, and transparency of state administration. The success of this initiative will depend not only on pressure from President Putin and his successors but also on the ability of other political and social institutions—including parliament, interest groups, courts, and media—to subject the bureaucracy to continuous scrutiny.[62]

Terrorism and National Security

Terrorism and the measures taken to combat it pose twin threats to the rule of law, in Russia as in other contemporary states. The large-scale violent attacks against civilians carried out by radical Islamic groups in the United States, Europe, Africa, and Asia have prompted even democratic states to adopt policies giving the authorities far-reaching powers to restrict civil liberties in the interest of fighting terrorists.[63] These powers are readily subject to abuse by rulers wishing to suppress their political opposition. In several Central Asian states, for instance, the authorities have suppressed a number of religious and political groups by charging their leaders with complicity in terrorist acts (acts which in some cases may have been staged by the authorities themselves as a pretext to eliminate their rivals). In Russia, the terrorist threat has been used by President Putin to expand the range of powers at his disposal to restrict civil and political liberties.

Russians in recent years have been the victims of a series of shocking terrorist incidents, most of them arising from the war in Chechnia. Some of these have involved attacks against military, police, and civilian targets, and others have taken the form of seizing large numbers of civilians as hostages. The series of terrorist attacks in 2004 had a particularly high political impact, because they revealed how serious were the problems of corruption, indiscipline, and incompetence among the agencies charged with protecting the country's security. In June a small group of terrorists was able to take over the main headquarters building housing the police, procuracy, and other law enforcement bodies in Nazran', capital of Ingushetia, meeting little or no resistance, and killing almost 100 law enforcement officers inside. Female suicide bombers were able to bribe their way on board airliners leaving from a busy Moscow airport in August 2004 and set off bombs that downed both planes. A lack of coordination among the military and special forces units who surrounded the school in Beslan allowed the hostages to kill hundreds of hostages amid the confusion at the end. (See Close-Up 3.1: Chechnia and the Terrorist Threat.)

Putin has responded to the terrorist incidents with a series of laws intended both to centralize political power and to expand the powers of the security police. As we saw in Chapter 3, Putin responded to the Beslan incident with legislation abolishing the direct election of regional governors, creating the Public Chamber, and eliminating all single-member district elections to the Duma. More directly related to the antiterrorist campaign was legislation passed in 2006 that assigned the FSB primary responsibility for fighting terrorism in the country and giving it increased powers to command the armed forces in case of an act of terrorism, to wiretap individuals suspected of terrorist activity, and even to shoot down hijacked airplanes. The law outlaws organizations "whose purposes and actions include the propaganda, justification, and support of terrorism."[64] A second law passed in 2006 following the capture and killing of several Russian diplomats in Iraq authorizes the president to use both armed forces and special forces against terrorists outside the borders of Russia.[65] Several observers have commented that this law, in effect, legalizes assassinations overseas of individuals designated as terrorists.[66]

This legislation and the other measures that the Putin administration has taken to tighten political, administrative, and police controls in response to the terrorist attacks of the past few years give the authorities new legal powers that can easily be abused. The authorities can prevent unflattering media coverage of their activity and suppress opposition groups on the suspicion that they are abetting terrorism. In view of the history of the abuse of law for political repression in the Soviet era and again under Putin, the antiterrorist legislation has ominous implications for the rule of law.

Organized Crime and Corruption

Organized Crime

A threat of another kind to the principle of the rule of law is the widespread corruption of state officials, particularly in law enforcement and the judiciary.

The worsening of corruption after the end of the Communist regime owes a great deal to the rapid growth in the organized crime's power in the 1990s. But although organized crime has been discussed extensively in the Western and Russian press, reliable indicators of its scale are elusive.[67] By all accounts, however, organized crime is deeply entrenched and broad in scope. A 1994 article in the newspaper *Izvestiia* observed:

> 'Godfathers' of the mafia exist in many countries, but there for the most part they control illegal business, such as narcotics, gambling, thieves' hangouts. Here they have established total control over ordinary commerce. As a result we pay for our daily bread, for our basket of consumer goods, around 20–30 percent more. In the farmers' markets exotic fruits cost less than tomatoes and cucumbers—because of the tribute to the mafia that is paid. Thus the population is supporting two states with its money—the legitimate government and the criminal one—that exist in parallel. Or rather, the legal state more and more depends on the power of the criminal one.[68]

Certainly the police often appear to be incapable of solving major crimes committed by organized crime groups. Hundreds of prominent individuals—politicians, businesspeople, bankers, journalists, and others—have been assassinated in contract murders, but few cases have resulted in an arrest, let alone a conviction. A number of Duma deputies have been murdered. In October 2006, Anna Politkovskaya, a journalist who had written scathing exposes of the tactics used by federal forces in Chechnia and by the Moscow-backed government in Chechnia was murdered. The following month, a former KGB officer, Alexander Litvinenko, was killed by radiation poisoning in London. Two prominent banking officials were murdered in the fall as well. All were believed to have been victims of contract killings, which criminal gangs often use to settle accounts. In 2004, an official of the Security Council estimated that organized crime groups had carried out some 5,000 contract murders in 2003.[69]

Analysts agree that two conditions contribute to the entrenchment of organized crime groups: first, the state bureaucracy is highly susceptible to corruption and has allowed organized crime to penetrate it deeply; and second, regular businesses frequently find it impossible to operate except by turning to organized crime for "security services," which include paying protection rackets, forcing partners to make good on agreements, and obtaining scarce supplies. The persistence of crime and corruption is the product of a vicious circle formed by the interlocking relationship among three sets of actors: government, legitimate business, and criminal organizations. Many businesses, both small-scale entrepreneurs and the owners of large companies, purchase protection from protection rackets (of course, racketeers often commit acts of violence against businesses to force them to purchase their protection services). Government, particularly the police, is weak, and weakened further by corruption. Organized crime groups penetrate both business and government, providing business with services such as protection as well as short-term loans and the enforcement of business contracts, and paying off law-enforcement officials to let them operate with impunity.[70]

Each side in this triangle depends on the others. Businesses frequently find that they must pay bribes to corrupt government officials simply to be able to operate or to be allowed to get around the law. Moreover, unable to count on the courts to protect their property rights and enforce their business agreements, they often turn to organized crime rackets for protection. Taking advantage of the state's inability to enforce the law (and, through penetration of the state, keeping it weak), organized crime preys on business and corrupts government. And government officials often find it easier, safer, and more lucrative to accept bribes than to fight crime and corruption or to provide legitimate public goods such as fair enforcement of the laws. The fact that Russia is a federal state probably exacerbates the problem, as the existence of governments at different levels multiplies the number of officials who demand bribes as a condition for doing business.[71]

Corruption

Corruption is fed both by the interests of businesses in evading laws and regulations and by organized crime rackets that want to keep government weak and subservient. Although corruption is notoriously difficult to measure with any precision, all observers agree that it has increased substantially since the end of the Soviet period and that it is has increased further under President Putin. It is widespread both in everyday life and in dealings with the state. A recent large-scale survey by Indem, a respected Moscow research firm, gives some indication of the nature and scale of corruption. At least half the population of Russia is involved in corruption in daily life.[72] For instance, the survey found that the probability that an individual would pay a bribe to get an automobile inspection permit was about 60 percent. The likelihood of paying a bribe to get one's child into a good school or college, or to get good grades, was about 50 percent. There was about a one-third probability that one would bribe a repairman to fix a problem in one's apartment. There was a 26 percent chance of paying a bribe to get a favorable ruling in a court case. Altogether, the study estimated that the country spends the equivalent of about $2.8 billion every year in bribes for everyday services of this type. The areas where the largest sums are spent are health care, education, courts, and automobile inspections; these alone make up over 60 percent of the market for corruption in everyday life.[73] A senior official in the procuracy recently estimated that corruption costs the country some $240 billion per year, a sum comparable to the total revenues of the federal budget.[74]

Despite the efforts by the Putin regime to tighten accountability in the state bureaucracy, corruption has been growing. Sixty percent of respondents in a public opinion survey in 2006 report that corruption is rising (only 4 percent think it is falling). The international consulting firm Transparency International, which publishes an annual "Corruption Perceptions Index," finds that Russia's rating has been worsening since the early 2000s and that Russia is now 126th of 159 countries in the magnitude of corruption.[75] One reason for the apparent rise in corruption is that officials are increasingly replacing private racketeers in providing "protection" to businesses. A survey of small businesses in 2006 found that total payments to criminal protection rackets ("roofs") were declining whereas payments to government officials were increasing.[76] This is consistent with findings by the World Bank and European Bank for Reconstruction and Development find that "unofficial payments" to officials (tax inspectors, fire safety officials, construction regulators, etc.) are on the rise.[77]

Corruption in Russia has deep roots and many Russians assume that it is an ineradicable feature of Russian society. Comparative studies of corruption demonstrate, however, that the culture of corruption can be changed by changing the expectations of the public and the government. For example, some countries have created powerful independent agencies to fight corruption. When their commitment to their mission is credible, people begin resisting corruption and refusing to engage in it, and government officials begin providing services without expecting to receive bribes.[78] The key is for the political leadership to make a serious commitment to fighting corruption, and to back this commitment up with institutional reform and sustained attention to the problem.

Senior officials in Russia have repeatedly called corruption a grave threat to state security. The head of the FSB declared in December 2006 that there is "a growth of corruption among officials, first and foremost at the regional and municipal level. . . . Criminal elements are making active attempts to penetrate government structures, take enterprises and banks under their control, [and] get hold of the levers of influence in certain territories."[79] A number of high-profile cases have been prosecuted, among them that of a former deputy finance minister who is accused of embezzling $231 million through a sale of fighter jets to India in 1997.[80] The regime's commitment to eradicating corruption is called into question, however, by the fact that prosecutions usually focus on officials who have already fallen out of favor with the authorities. The question is not whether the leadership recognize the problem, but whether they have the political will to address it.

Conclusion

Despite some steps toward realizing the ideal of the rule of law since the end of the Communist regime, Russia remains closer to a system of rule by law than to the rule of law. The precedence of law over political and administrative power in the state would reduce the ability of officials in the bureaucracy, the security police, and the president to exercise power arbitrarily. Respect for the law on the part of officials and citizens would help establish habits of civic initiative and responsibility, which are essential to democracy. These are among the reasons that legal reformers in Russia have propagated the ideal of the "law-governed state." As with many other institutional reforms, however, success in the realm of law will ultimately require a commitment on the part of the highest officials in the country. Policymakers must be willing to take a long-term view of the rule of law's importance for economic progress, and to refrain from abusing legal institutions for their short-term political gains. It will also require the development of political pluralism where resources for political influence are widely distributed, allowing groups to monitor the behavior of state officials and preventing any one group from monopolizing access to the law.

The radical implications of a shift to a law-governed state have generated opposition from a number of entrenched interests both inside and outside the state. In some cases, the opposition is due to bureaucratic unwillingness to relinquish administrative power; in other cases, it stems from the lucrative opportunities that lax and corrupt practices create for self-enrichment by officials. The fact that many who wield power and even the general population continue to hold a traditionally skeptical attitude toward the law—that it is no more than an instrument of the policy goals of those in power—may also impede movement in this direction. However, there is ample evidence that a substantial base of support exists for the concept of law as a set of impartial rules to which both state officials and ordinary citizens would be subordinate.

But there are still many obstacles to the realization of the rule of law. The inefficiency and corruption of law enforcement bodies, the penetration of the state by organized crime, and the old habit on the part of Russian rulers and Russian citizens of treating the law instrumentally continue to impede progress toward the primacy of law. Under President Putin, the state has taken a number of steps that compromise the independence of the judiciary. Although Putin has also sponsored reforms that strengthen efficiency and accountability in the legal system, it appears that he is more intent on making law independent of regional and business interests that might interfere with his own power than he is with advancing the rule of law. His use of the procuracy, Tax Police, and courts to prosecute selected targets on political grounds, and the wave of new legislation strengthening the powers of the security police in the face of possible terrorist threats, indicate that the Kremlin will not soon relinquish its political influence over the legal system.

NOTES

1. Stephen Holmes, "Introduction," *East European Constitutional Review* 11:1/2 (Winter/Spring 2002): 91.

2. Holmes, "Introduction," 92.

3. A seminal study of the influences on the development of law in the Soviet Union is Harold J. Berman, *Justice in the U.S.S.R.,* rev. ed. (Cambridge, MA: Harvard University Press, 1963).

4. Full texts of these articles of the RSFSR Criminal Code together with commentary will be found in Harold J. Berman, ed., *Soviet Criminal Law and Procedure: The*

RSFSR Codes, 2nd ed. (Cambridge, MA: Harvard University Press, 1972). Analogous articles were contained in the criminal codes of other republics as well.

5. Sidney Bloch and Peter Reddaway, *Psychiatric Terror: How Soviet Psychiatry Is Used to Suppress Dissent* (New York: Basic Books, 1977).

6. On the legal reforms of the Gorbachev period, see Donald D. Barry, ed., *Toward the "Rule of Law" in Russia? Political and Legal Reform in the Transition Period* (Armonk, NY: M. E. Sharpe, 1992); and Alexandre Yakovlev

with Dale Gibson, *The Bear that Wouldn't Dance: Failed Attempts to Reform the Constitution of the Former Soviet Union* (University of Manitoba, Canada: Legal Research Institute, 1992).

7. See the discussion of corruption, below.

8. Federico Varese, *The Russian Mafia: Private Protection in a New Market Economy* (New York: Oxford University Press, 2001); Vadim Volkov, *Violent Entrepreneurs: The Use of Force in the Making of Russian Capitalism* (Ithaca, NY: Cornell University Press, 2002).

9. See pp. 134.

10. Robert Orttung, "A Long Way to Go in Establishing Effective Courts," Russian Regional Report, EastWest Institute, 5:46 (December 13, 2000).

11. Orttung, "A Long Way to Go."

12. One early product of glasnost was the exposure of "telephone justice" as a prevalent practice. See, for example, Arkadii Vaksberg, "Pravde v glaza," *Literaturnaia gazeta* (December 17, 1986): 13.

13. Robert Sharlet, "The Communist Party and the Administration of Justice in the USSR," in Donald D. Barry et al., eds., *Soviet Law After Stalin, Part III: Soviet Institutions and the Administration of Law* (Alpen aan den Rijn, The Netherlands, and Germantown, MD: Sijthofff and Noordhoff, 1979), pp. 321–92. In another article, Sharlet details several ways in which the regime acted to repress individuals for political acts, including administrative penalties such as job dismissal, officially sponsored acts of hooliganism, psychiatric internment, forced emigration, and criminal trials. See Robert Sharlet, "Party and Public Ideals in Conflict: Constitutionalism and Civil Rights in the USSR," *Cornell International Law Journal* 23:2 (1990): 341–62.

14. Quoted in Brian D. Taylor, "Russia's Regions and Law Enforcement," in Peter Reddaway and Robert W. Orttung, eds., *The Dynamics of Russian Politics: Putin's Reform of Federal–Regional Relations,* vol. II (Lanham, MD: Rowman & Littlefield, 2005), p. 74.

15. Inquisitorial procedure is contrasted with the adversarial model used in Anglo-American judicial proceedings. In the inquisitorial system, the presiding officer (judge, magistrate) actively seeks to determine the full truth of the case at hand rather than serving as an impartial referee in a contest between an accuser and a defendant. In Soviet and Russian tradition, the powerful procurator is the central figure in the proceeding; the judge may actively participate in questioning witnesses and ruling on matters of law, but the procurator is expected to serve the higher cause of justice and not simply to present the state's best case against the accused. From the standpoint of the Anglo-American tradition, this puts the procurator in a potentially contradictory position: the procurator is required to ensure the legality of the entire proceeding (including, as appropriate, the obligation to defend the accused's rights), and yet he or she must also seek to prosecute and win the case. Given that the procurator has already overseen the pretrial investigation and concluded that there is sufficient evidence to proceed with the trial, it is extremely rare for a procurator to decide that the case lacks merit and should be dropped. From the standpoint of the Anglo-American criminal process, it is as though the procurator were wearing the hats of prosecutor, defender, judge, and jury all at the same time. In any case, in Soviet times, judges tended to be highly deferential to the procurators. As a result of the procuracy's power and prestige, very few criminal cases in the Soviet period resulted in acquittal, although in some cases, a higher court set aside a questionable conviction or remanded it for further investigation, effectively reversing a lower court's verdict.

For a discussion of the Soviet procuracy that places it in the context of both Western continental models and earlier, Russian historical precedents, see Berman, *Justice in the USSR,* pp. 238–47.

16. Peter H. Solomon, Jr., "Putin's Judicial Reform: Making Judges Accountable as Well as Independent," *East European Constitutional Review* 11:1/2 (Winter/Spring 2002): 121.

17. Donald D. Barry, "Amnesty under the Russian Constitution: Evolution of the Provision and Its Use in February 1994," *Parker School Journal of East European Law* 1:4 (1994): 437–61.

18. RFE/RL Newsline, May 17, 2004.

19. From an interview with *Komsomol'skaya Pravda,* July 19, 2002, cited in RFE/ RL Newsline, July 19, 2002.

20. Nikolai Petrov, "Federal'naia reforma i kadry," *Brifing moskovskogo tsentra Karnegi,* 4–5:6 (April–May 2004): 1.

21. The KGB was the institutional successor to the powerful instruments of coercion that the Soviet regime used since the revolution to eliminate its political enemies, including the Cheka (created within six weeks of the October Revolution), the GPU, and the NKVD. In the post-Stalin era, according to its press representatives, the KGB had nothing in common with these predecessor organizations, and was dedicated to upholding the law while carrying out its mission of defending the security of the state and its citizens. Often KGB press representatives discussed the modern efforts of the organization in combating drug trafficking and terrorism. Evidently keen to be portrayed in a positive light in the media, the KGB promoted itself in the 1980s as a heroic organization, a body performing its difficult duties with scrupulous respect for the law as well as ingenuity and courage.

22. OMRI Daily Digest, April 7, 1995.

23. The doctrine was posted to the Internet on several sites, among them www.regions.ru.

24. Among these are Sergei Ivanov, recently promoted to first deputy prime minister and previously the defense minister; Nikolai Patrushev, Federal Security Service director; Sergei Lebedev, Foreign Intelligence Service director; Georgii Poltavchenko, presidential envoy to the Central federal district; Yevgenii Murov, Federal Bodyguard Service head; and Viktor Zolotov, head of the presidential security service. Several other associates of Putin's from his work in St. Petersburg combine positions in his administration with board chairmanships of major companies. Among these are Igor Sechin, deputy chief of the presidential administration, who is chairman of the board of the state-owned oil company, Rosneft'; Dmitrii Medvedev, another first deputy prime minister, who is chairman of the board of the natural gas monopoly, Gazprom; and Viktor Ivanov, an advisor to Putin who is chairman of the board of the company Almaz-Antei. The latter is a major defense contractor manufacturing (and selling abroad) some of Russia's most advanced air-defense systems. These connections not only ensure close control of major firms by the state, but they give Putin personal control over the strategic direction of the companies.

25. RFE/RL Newsline, May 7, 2002.

26. Ivan Sas, "FSB okhvatila vse sfery," *Nezavisimaia gazeta,* December 20, 2006.

27. Eugene Huskey, "The Administration of Justice: Courts, Procuracy, and Ministry of Justice," in Eugene Huskey, ed., *Executive Power and Soviet Politics: The Rise and Decline of the Soviet State* (Armonk, NY: M. E. Sharpe, 1992), pp. 224–31.

28. Kathryn Hendley, "Putin and the Law," in Dale R. Herspring, ed., *Putin's Russia*, 3rd ed. (Lanham, MD: Rowman & Littlefield, 2007), p. 108.

29. Hendley, "Putin and the Law," p. 110. Of these, 1.2 million are criminal cases. *Vedomosti,* October 20, 2006.

30. On the new system of bailiffs, see Solomon and Foglesong, *Courts and Transition in Russia*, pp. 165–71; also Peter L. Kahn, "The Russian Bailiffs Service and the Enforcement of Civil Judgments," *Post-Soviet Affairs* 18:2 (April–June 2002): 148–81.

Press reports indicate that the introduction of the new system of "bailiff-enforcers" has helped reduce noncompliance somewhat, but there are still numerous cases in which court decisions are ignored. For example, in one incident, a group of 18 bailiffs appeared at a factory on the outskirts of Moscow at 6:30 one morning. They were enforcing a court order upholding the decision of a shareholders' meeting of the company to replace the old director with a new one. The bailiffs were there to ensure that the new director gained access to the director's office, and to prevent the old director from entering the premises. A group of workers and guards attacked the bailiffs with rocks and stones, water from a fire hose, and tear gas. Four bailiffs were wounded and all 18 suffered injuries from the tear gas. As the news report put it, "further attempts to enter the firm have been called off for the time being." See Polit.ru, April 10, 2002.

31. Eugene Huskey, "Russian Judicial Reform after Communism," in Peter Solomon, ed., *Reforming Justice in Russia, 1864–1994* (Armonk, NY: M. E. Sharpe, 1997).

32. All courts of general jurisdiction must apply federal criminal and civil law and procedural codes. The only nonfederal courts

operating at the regional level are the constitutional courts of ethnic republics and the "charter courts" in regular administrative territorial units. These courts adjudicate disputes involving a republican constitution or the charter of a subject of the federation, but they too must adhere to federal statutory and constitutional law.

33. Yakovlev, *Striving,* p. 208.

34. In one of the most famous trial verdicts in Russian history, Vera Zasulich, a young Russian revolutionary who had attempted to assassinate the chief of police of St. Petersburg in 1878, was acquitted by a jury following a fiery speech by her lawyer that scathingly denounced the injustices of the Russian government.

35. In jury trials, the acquittal rate was 8.5 percent in 2002 but less than 1 percent in ordinary trials.

Hendley, "Putin and the Law," 113. Note that a majority of 7 votes out of the 12 jurors suffices to decide on a conviction, but only 6 votes are needed to acquit. Solomon, "Limits," 103.

36. *Vedomosti,* October 20, 2006.

37. Hendley, "Putin and the Law," 114.

38. It is misleading to call these "arbitration" courts, as they use judicial procedure, not arbitration, to adjudicate disputes. They were created out of the "arbitration boards" used in Soviet times to resolve disputes among economic entities such as enterprises and ministries, but now form a separate branch of the federal judiciary.

39. *Segodnia,* February 20, 2001.

40. See Kathryn Hendley, Barry W. Ickes, Peter Murrell, and Randi Ryterman, "Observations on the Use of Law by Russian Enterprises," *Post-Soviet Affairs* 13:1 (January–March 1997): 19–41.

41. *Segodnia,* November 30, 1999.

42. Peter H. Solomon, Jr., "Putin's Judicial Reform: Making Judges Accountable as Well as Independent," *East European Constitutional Review* 11:1/2 (Winter/Spring 2002): 117–23.

43. Hendley, "Putin and the Law," 106–07.

44. RFE/RL Newsline, August 26, 2005.

45. The new Criminal Procedure Code that was passed by parliament in December 2001 and came into force on July 1, 2002, included this provision, which had been opposed by the procuracy. The Duma agreed to delay its implementation, however, on the grounds that the courts needed time to prepare for it (judicial administrators claimed that they would need another 3,000 judges and 700 million rubles to handle the increased caseload that would result from implementation of the reform). The Constitutional Court ruled that the provision must be implemented immediately on July 1, along with the rest of the new Code.

46. Robert Sharlet, "The Russian Constitutional Court's Long Struggle for Viable Federalism," paper presented at annual meeting of the American Association for the Advancement of Slavic Studies, Boston, MA (December 2–5, 2004).

47. *Segodnia,* January 30, 1997; OMRI Daily Digest, March 10 and March 11, 1997.

48. *Segodnia,* April 12, 2000.

49. This case arose when President Yeltsin refused to sign a law that parliament had passed that he considered unconstitutional. The law nationalized cultural artifacts and artworks that the Soviet Army had seized in Nazi-occupied Europe during World War II. Parliament overrode his veto but Yeltsin still refused to sign. Parliament sent a protest to the Constitutional Court, which found that Yeltsin had no right to withhold his signature when parliament overrode a veto; it did find some provisions of the law unconstitutional but warned that a president had no right to declare a duly passed law unconstitutional— only the court had that power.

50. *Segodnia,* February 21, 2000.

51. Both comments cited in RFE/RL Newsline, October 25, 2004. Interestingly, the chairman was Valerii Zor'kin, who had incurred Yeltsin's wrath as chairman of the Constitutional Court at the time of Yeltsin's confrontation with parliament in 1992 and 1993. Zor'kin was elected chairman of the court once again in February 2003. Zor'kin has been much more circumspect in his politics the second time around.

52. A thorough examination of the recent history and legal status of the court is the article by Herbert Hausmaninger, "Towards a 'New' Russian Constitutional Court," *Cornell International Law Journal* 28 (1995): 349–86. Also see Robert Sharlet, "Transitional Constitutionalism: Politics and Law in the Second

Russian Republic," *Wisconsin International Law Journal* 14:3 (1996): 495–521. Other information on the court is drawn from interviews with judges on the court.

53. Parts 1 and 2, recognizing private property and regulating commercial transactions, passed in 1994 and 1995; Part 3, regulating inheritance rights, passed in 2001. An important amendment to the Civil Code passed in early 2001 when the Duma lifted a suspension on the right to buy and sell land.

54. Solomon, "Limits," 93–94.

55. For a review of these laws, see Solomon, "Putin's Judicial Reform," 117–23.

56. Hendley, "Putin and the Law," 104.

57. Eugene Huskey, "Government Rulemaking as a Brake on Perestroika," *Law and Social Inquiry,* 15:3 (Summer 1990): 421–22.

58. The Auditing Chamber (*Schetnaia palata*) is an auditing agency created by the parliament, comparable to the General Accounting Office in the United States. Like the GAO, it serves the legislative branch by conducting audits of the books of executive agencies and presenting reports of its findings.

59. Vladimir Gel'man, "The Unrule of Law in the Making: The Politics of Informal Institution Building in Russia," *Europe-Asia Studies* 56:7 (November 2004): 1021–40.

60. OECD Economic Survey, pp. 128–29.

61. Polit.ru August 13, August 14, and November 21, 2002; OECD Economic Survey Russian Federation 2006, p. 125.

62. OECD Economic Survey, pp. 129–40.

63. In the United States, the Patriot Act, passed a month after the September 11 attacks, significantly expands government power to conduct surveillance of U.S. citizens suspected of involvement in terrorist activity, allows indefinite detention of noncitizens, and creates a new category of crime called "domestic terrorism."

64. Polit.ru, February 27, 2006; RFE/RL Newsline, March 7, 2006.

65. Polit.ru, July 5, 2006.

66. The secret police conducted one such operation even before the law was passed. In 2004 two Russian agents were arrested, tried, and convicted in Qatar for the assassination of a former Chechen rebel leader and his son and bodyguard. The Qatar authorities released them after five months in prison. Upon their return to Russia, they were awarded with decorations.

67. A useful but somewhat lurid account of the subject is the book by Stephen Handelman, *Comrade Criminal: Russia's New Mafiya* (New Haven, CT: Yale University Press, 1995); two recent studies of the operation of protection rackets are Federico Varese, *The Russian Mafia: Private Protection in a New Market Economy* (New York: Oxford University Press, 2001) and Vadim Volkov, *Violent Entrepreneurs: The Use of Force in the Making of Russian Capitalism* (Ithaca, NY: Cornell University Press, 2002). Also see Vadim Volkov, "Who Is Strong When the State Is Weak? Violent Entrepreneurship in Russia's Emerging Markets," in Mark R. Beissinger and Crawford Young, *Beyond State Crisis? Postcolonial Africa and Post-Soviet Eurasia in Comparative Perspective* (Washington, DC: Woodrow Wilson Center, 2002), pp. 81–104.

68. "Neizvestnaia voina korruptsiiei," *Izvestiia,* October 22, 1994.

69. Jeffrey Donovan, "Contract Killings Once Again on Rise in Russia," RFE/RL Newsline, October 12, 2006.

70. Varese, *The Russian Mafia;* Volkov, "Who Is Strong?."

71. Political scientist Daniel Treisman has conducted a comparative analysis of corruption in Russia and other countries. He found that most corruption in countries could be explained by four factors: relatively low per capita income, low experience with democracy, low level of foreign trade, and its federal structure. Once these factors were accounted for, Russia was not particularly more corrupt than other countries. See Daniel Treisman, "The Causes of Corruption: A Cross-National Study," *Journal of Public Economics* 76:3 (2000): 399–457.

72. G. A. Satarov, *Diagnostika rossiiskoi korruptsii: Sotsiologicheskii analiz* (Moscow: Fond INDEM, 2002).

73. Satarov, *Diagnostika,* pp. 16–17.

74. RFE/RL Newsline, November 8, 2006.

75. OECD Economic Survey 2006, p. 123. The Corruption Perceptions Index is based on reports by officials, journalists, businesspeople, and others who have extensive dealings in the countries surveyed.

76. Kommersant, October 12, 2006.

77. OECD Economic Survey 2006, p. 123.

78. Susan Rose-Ackerman, *Corruption and Government: Causes, Consequences, and Reform* (Cambridge: Cambridge University Press, 1999), pp. 159–62.

79. RFE/RL Newsline, December 15, 2006.

80. RFE/RL Newsline, February 26, 2007.

Chapter 9

Russia as Regional Superpower

Russia's thousand-year history of expansion, war, and state domination of society has left behind a legacy of autocratic rule and a preoccupation with defending national borders. In the twentieth century, Russian society underwent several traumas that deeply affected its relations with the outside world. Twice the regime collapsed—in 1917 and again in 1991—and twice world wars took tens of millions of lives. During the Soviet era, civil war and Stalin's terror killed tens of millions more. Little wonder that Russians should regard the preservation of statehood in an anarchic world as the foremost priority for their country. Likewise this history of catastrophe, much of it self-induced, helps explain why President Putin calls for continuity with the past rather than another rupture, and why Russians remain so averse to any more social transformations. It explains the strongly pragmatic streak in Russian foreign policy: Russian leaders tend to be acutely sensitive to the international balance of power and their country's place in it. However bitterly they may regard the loss of their country's status as a superpower, Russians have little desire to provoke a conflict with the United States or other international powers.

Russians harbor a high sense of insecurity for their country. Not only do most Russians worry that the country will fall apart (a survey in April 2005 found that 62 percent of the respondents think that there is a strong chance that the country will break up), 60 percent of respondents believe that there are outside forces working "purposefully and persistently" to bring about Russia's disintegration. The countries that were named most often as being interested in seeing that disintegration occur were the United States, Japan, China, Israel, Ukraine, Georgia, and the Baltic states, in that order.[1] A 2007 survey sponsored by the European Union found that almost half of Russians regard the European Union as a threat to Russia, and specifically to its financial and industrial independence. Only a third consider Europe as a neighbor and partner with which Russia should develop long-term relations.[2] And Russians' anxiety has increased in recent years. About half of Russians answered affirmatively when asked whether they thought that there is a military threat to Russia today from other countries, a figure that has gone up substantially since the late 1990s.[3]

Some of this insecurity stems from the fear that outside powers will take advantage of the state's vulnerability at a time of regime change.[4] Russians historically have learned to associate periods of domestic turmoil with attempts by foreign powers to exploit Russia's weakness. Interludes of regime collapse and civil disorder, such as the Time of Troubles in the early seventeenth century or the fall of the Romanov dynasty in 1917 during World War I, which led to the February and October Revolutions, tempted external powers to intervene in Russia and to seize Russian-ruled territories. Many Russians today regard the period of the late 1980s and early 1990s in a similar light, believing that Gorbachev's concessions to the West, his willingness to allow the union to dissolve, and his abandonment of Communist Party rule left Russia weakened and humiliated and subject to the dictates of the West. A major source of Russian suspicion of outside powers is the widespread view that the West, especially the United States, is trying to squeeze Russia out of its traditional sphere of influence. This includes the belt of countries in Eastern Europe, but most especially the states of the former Soviet Union.

There is a strong sense of loss among Russians over the breakup of the union. Around two-thirds of Russians express regret over the collapse of the Soviet Union (around a quarter do not).[5] And there is strong support for rebuilding some sort of union from among the former Soviet republics. A survey in spring 2005 found that about two-thirds of Russians would like to see the CIS countries unite and form a single state. But 53 percent believed that this was unlikely to happen and only 25 percent thought it likely.[6]

President Putin's foreign policy has addressed the widespread sense of insecurity and loss following the collapse of the Soviet state. The worldwide increase in the price of oil has strengthened Putin's hand enormously in this effort. Certainly Putin's policy is far from seeking to isolate Russia from the international capitalist economy, as the Soviet regime did. Nor is it intending to compete with the United States as a global superpower. However, it does seek to become, in the words of one Russian analyst, a "regional superpower." In this effort Putin has had considerable success. But Russia also faces substantial obstacles to maintaining its dominant position in the region.

A LIBERAL EMPIRE?

The most important factor in Russia's effort to rebuild its status as regional superpower is its energy resources. It has used its economic power to consolidate its control over the economies and infrastructures of the region. As former defense minister (and current first deputy prime minister) Sergei Ivanov commented in October 2003, "The CIS [Commonwealth of Independent States] is a very crucial sphere for our security. Ten million of our compatriots live there, and we are supplying energy to them at prices below international levels. We are not going to renounce the right to use military power there in situations where all other means have been exhausted." On the same day, speaking in another Russian city, Putin declared that Russia would never give up control of the pipeline system in the former Soviet states. The pipelines were built by the Soviet regime, he observed, and only Russia can keep the system operating, "even those parts of the system that are beyond Russia's borders."[7]

Russia's policies have been consistent with the stated goal of preserving Russian influence in the countries of the region by controlling the energy infrastructure. This is in part a reflection of a fundamental dilemma that Russia faces: Russia has to export energy to sustain its economy. As we saw in Chapter 7, exports of oil and gas account for over 60 percent of Russia's export earnings. The energy sector makes up about a quarter of Russia's GDP and roughly 40 percent of budget revenue."[8] Therefore, Russia's economic growth, and status as a great power, depends in the short run on maintaining its exports of oil and gas. This in turns means that Russia relies on ensuring a reliable way to get its oil and gas to world markets. Likewise, Europe depends on imported Russian energy, especially Russian gas, which accounted for 40 percent of total imports and 28 percent of total gas demand in 2004 in Western Europe.[9]

Both sides thus depend on secure transit routes through Russia's neighbors. For instance, three-quarters of Russian gas exports to Europe go through Ukraine and most of the rest transits through Belarus. Consequently, Russia is deeply concerned about the possibility that Ukraine or Belarus could divert gas or block Russian exports (as they have done). One reason for Putin's strategy of using energy to consolidate control over the pipeline infrastructure in the region, therefore, is to guarantee uninterrupted access to its European markets.

Even before he became president, Putin regarded Russian energy resources as the major source of its international power. Putin's 1997 dissertation concerned natural resources and their contribution to development strategy; he wrote an article in 1999 about the importance of creating a set of vertically integrated oil and gas companies that would work as the state's partners in exercising strategic influence to restore Russia's status as a great power.[10]

As president, Putin has put his theory into practice. He has made the state-owned gas monopoly Gazprom, and other state-owned and state-controlled energy firms, into instruments of his strategy to become a regional superpower. Gazprom is a behemoth. It has over 400,000 employees, annual revenues of $76 billion, and reported profits of $20 billion. Its market value is estimated at $230 billion.[11] Although it has taken several steps toward improving the transparency of its corporate governance, it is still widely criticized by foreign observers (and even by some Russian officials) for its resistance to reform and the slowness with which it has moved to modernize the gas industry.[12] Gazprom has a near-total monopoly over the extraction, processing, and distribution of natural gas in Russia, and through a series of acquisitions, is now one of the largest oil firms as well. It owns and controls the entire gas pipeline system in Russia, and much of the pipeline system in neighboring countries. In recent years Gazprom has raised prices substantially on the gas it sells Russia's neighbors, bringing them much closer to world market prices. Although Russian leaders and Gazprom managers insist that they are basing these decisions on market forces rather than maintaining Soviet-era price subsidies, the price increases have allowed Gazprom to acquire greater control over the pipeline networks within the neighboring transit countries as part of the price agreements.

For example, Gazprom had been selling gas to Ukraine for about $50 per one thousand cubic meters; then as negotiations for a new contract beginning in 2006 began, Gazprom raised the price to about $220 (close to the price paid by West European customers). Gazprom offered to take partial control in Ukrainian pipelines or shares in Ukrainian companies as payment, but Ukraine refused. By January 1, 2006, no new contract had been signed. Russia cut the gas supply to Ukraine and Ukraine in turn cut the supply of Russian gas to Europe. Eventually an agreement was reached. Russia agreed to supply gas to Ukraine at a discounted price through a shadowy supply company that was partly owned by Gazprom and partly by a firm whose principals have been investigated by the authorities in Ukraine and United States for their ties to organized crime.[13] Similarly, Gazprom raised prices to Moldova, the Baltic states, Georgia, Armenia, and Belarus. In several cases, it negotiated deals under which it acquired stakes in the pipeline companies of the partner country. Currently, Gazprom owns a majority stake in the gas pipeline transiting Belarus that delivers gas to Europe, and it owns all the gas pipelines transiting Armenia. The key is the Ukrainian gas pipeline network, and Gazprom is attempting to use its negotiating leverage to trade price concessions on gas for greater control over Ukraine's pipeline system.[14]

Russia has also consolidated its control over the electric power networks of neighboring countries. The Russian national electric power company, Unified Energy Systems, whose chairman is the durable Anatolii Chubais, now owns Armenia's electric power generation and distribution system through an offshore subsidiary.[15] The EES company has also acquired substantial stakes in the electric power companies of other neighbors, including Georgia and Moldova, and aims to expand its holdings in Latvia, Lithuania, Belarus, Ukraine, Tajikistan, and Kyrgyzstan, as well as several other countries such as Bulgaria, Romania, and Turkey.[16] Chubais himself has proposed that Russia take the lead in creating what he calls "a liberal empire," in which Russia would exercise its influence through consolidated control over electric power and energy supplies in neighboring countries to promote Russian interests as well as to support the values of freedom and human rights and create a favorable view of Russia. In Chubais's view, this means that Russia should emphasize common economic and political interests rather than forcing its neighbors to accept Russian dominance. The Putin team undoubtedly regards Chubais's efforts at consolidating the electric power grids of the former Soviet states as useful for their goal of making Russia a regional superpower, whatever their views of the concept that the Russian imperial project should be "liberal."[17]

Other versions of the imperial idea are also popular. For example, it is increasingly acceptable for Russian politicians to express their desire to see the former Soviet Union reconstructed under Russian domination. A former KGB chairman was quoted in late 2003 to the effect that "if we do not reassemble the Soviet Union, we have no future at all." The popular minister for emergency situations, Sergei Shoigu, campaigning for the United Russia party, said he hoped "to live to see the day when we have one big country within the borders of the [former] Soviet Union."[18] A political strategist with close Kremlin ties declared that the only way Russia could thrive in the twenty first century was to dominate "the post-Soviet space," which was its natural "historical-geographical area." Another strategist commented that Putin needed to offer Russians an inspiring new national project, which could only be a "Great Russia": "history has left us no other choice," he argued. "Russia can only be great."[19] Putin himself said that the countries of the CIS were "now working to restore what was lost with the fall of the Soviet Union but are doing it on a new, modern basis," in a speech at Lev Gumilev University in Kazakhstan in June 2004.[20]

THE CIS AND ITS DESCENDANTS

Although Putin and others still pay lip service to the idea that the CIS can serve as the organizational framework for the reintegration of the union, Russia has invested little in realizing that goal. As we saw in the first chapter, the CIS was formally created simultaneously with the dissolution of the Soviet Union by agreement of the leaders of Russia, Ukraine, and Belarus in December 1991. Yeltsin and his colleagues regarded the CIS as a vehicle for maintaining the economic, military, infrastructural, and political ties linking the states of the former Soviet Union until a new set of relations among them was worked out. Many in the Russian leadership assumed that the breakup of the union would be temporary, and that following a period of time in which the former Soviet states would discover that they could not survive as independent states, the union would be restored in some new form. Neither Russia nor other successor states were willing to devote much effort to building a strong CIS: the other states feared Russian dominance in it, whereas Russia preferred to concentrate on carrying out its own far-reaching political and economic reforms. In any event, the CIS never became more than a loose framework for periodic consultations among its members.

Certainly one major obstacle to the growth of integration and hence of coordinating power for the CIS is the enormous difference between Russia's power and size and the power and size of the other members. As Table 9.1 indicates, Russia's population is almost three times larger than that of the next most populous member, Ukraine. Russia was never willing to turn over sovereign power to any organization not under its immediate control, and the other member states of the CIS were unwilling to turn over much power to a governing body controlled by Russia. This issue simply underscores the point that the Soviet Union itself functioned as a sovereign state only by submerging Russia's own status as a political

Table 9.1 ■ Population and Income of Former Soviet States, 2005 (excluding Baltic states)

	Population (millions)	GDP per capita (constant 2000 $US)
Russian Federation	143.15	2,443.94
Western neighbors:		
Ukraine	47.11	959.17
Moldova	4.2	428.83
Belarus	9.77	1,867.98
Transcaucasus:		
Armenia	3.02	1,127.61
Azerbaijan	8.39	1,181.53
Georgia	4.47	971.18
Central Asia:		
Kazakhstan	15.15	1,972.45
Kyrgyz Republic	5.16	318.53
Tajikistan	6.51	237.25
Turkmenistan*	4.83	752.5
Uzbekistan	26.59	673.33

* Turkmenistan GDP per capita figure reported for 2001.

Source: World Bank, World Development Indicators.

actor within the larger Soviet state, and investing power instead in the Communist Party–dominated structures of the union. For this reason, Russia probably had no chance of becoming a democratic state until it jettisoned the union. But without Russia, of course, there could be no union.

Moreover, several states that were formerly republics of the Soviet Union regard Russia as their major source of external insecurity, and seek to protect themselves through membership in Western-oriented security and economic alliances. Former Soviet republics Estonia, Latvia, and Lithuania are members of NATO (legally, the United States never recognized them as union republics of the USSR), and Ukraine and Georgia are in a status of "intensified dialogue" with NATO as a step toward possible future membership. The United States sent a small team of military trainers to Georgia, specifically to assist Georgia in apprehending Chechen terrorists who had fled across the border into Georgia to escape Russian attacks, but more broadly to demonstrate American support for Georgia's aspirations to be democratic and free of Russian pressure. Moreover, following the September 11, 2001, attacks on the United States by Al Qaeda–backed terrorists, the United States sought and received basing privileges at air force facilities in two former Soviet republics in Central Asia, Kyrgyzstan and Kazakstan. The immediate justification for American use of these bases was to assist American air strikes against the Taliban regime in Afghanistan. Russia accepted this American military presence on the condition that it be for a limited time and restricted in scope, no doubt recognizing that the removal of the Taliban regime also served Russian security interests. Thus there is some basis for Russians' anxiety over the American presence in the former Soviet region.

Russian leaders are also convinced that the hand of the United States and other hostile Western powers are behind the wave of "colored revolutions" that swept across the former Soviet states and intend to prevent any more such threats to regional stability or to their own ability to hold power. We will examine these upheavals in more detail below.

The region of the former Soviet Union remains a major focus of Russian foreign policy, but the CIS never became a new state structure filling the vacuum left by the collapse of the old union. A decade after the formation of the CIS, more and more Russian figures have publicly called the CIS a dead letter. Although Putin himself has not gone so far, the fact that senior figures in and around the Putin administration have taken this position indicates that it is an official view of the Russian leadership. As Putin commented in March 2005, the formation of the CIS was intended to make possible "a civilized divorce" among the former members of the union. One official, deputy director of the CIS Institute in Moscow, extended the metaphor by saying that it was time for Russia to stop paying "alimony" in the form of cheap energy to CIS members.[21] As early as August 2000, Russia ended the right of citizens of CIS countries to travel to Russia without visas.

Instead of trying to make the CIS a viable instrument of collective action among the former Soviet states, therefore, Putin's administration has chosen to work through subsets of the CIS for specific sets of tasks. Four in particular are important: the troubled "union state" between Russia and Belarus; the Eurasian Economic Community; the Collective Security Treaty Organization; and the Shanghai Cooperation Organization.

The Russia–Belarus Union

The leaders of Russia and its smaller Western neighbor, Belarus (formerly known as Belorussia), have made sporadic attempts to form a union since the mid-1990s. Belarus is led by its dictatorial president, Alyaksandr Lukashenka, who has pinned his hopes for a political future on a union of Belarus and Russia. This would elevate his own political status to that of a coequal with Russia's president and tie his country's failing economy to Russia. Six times between 1996 and 1999, Presidents Yeltsin and Lukashenka held showy ceremonies at which they signed agreements promising to unite their two countries.[22] New institutions (such as a joint parliament) were created on paper, but neither side was willing to cede any real power to the union structures.

In 2002, President Putin poured cold water on the idea of a union by pointing out the obvious—that Russian could never allow a union with Belarus to proceed at the expense of Russia's economic or political interests. At the end of 2006, the relationship then took a further sharp downturn when Russia more than doubled the price Belarus would have to pay for natural gas and imposed a substantial new export tax on oil shipped to Belarus. Belarus initially refused to pay the higher rates and imposed a transit fee for oil shipped across Belarus territory. Russia in turn accused Belarus of siphoning off oil from its pipelines sending oil to Europe via Belarus and cut off the supply of oil to Belarus for three days. Belarus then shut off the supply of oil through its pipelines to Europe, sending shockwaves throughout Europe. The incident dramatized both the illusory nature of the Russian-Belarus "union" and the willingness of Russia to use coercive tactics to force its neighbors to accept its terms for energy purchases. Clearly Russia was unwilling to continue subsidizing Belarus with cheap energy for the sake of a special political relationship. Putin has made it clear that if Belarus is to merge with Russia, it will be as one or more of the constituent federal subjects of Russia, rather than as a coequal state.

The Eurasian Economic Community

Under the CIS's auspices, a customs union made up of Russia, Belarus, Kazakstan, Kyrgyzstan, and Tajikistan formed. The objective was to facilitate trade among the members by eliminating customs barriers. In 2000, the members formally created the Eurasian Economic Community (EEC), along the lines of the European Community. Under the weighted voting scheme it uses for decision making, Russia has the preponderance of decision-making power. In addition to lowering trade barriers among the member states, the group has also discussed energy cooperation. However, Russia is probably more interested in joining the WTO than in developing the EEC as an alternative to integration into the international economic system.

The Collective Security Treaty Organization

If the EEC resembles a post-Soviet European Community, the Collective Security Treaty Organization (CSTO) resembles a post-Soviet NATO. The CSTO was formed by a treaty in April 2003 out of a predecessor agreement, the Tashkent Treaty, established originally in 1992. It is devoted to collective defense and promotes the goal of collective response to security threats. Its members, Russia, Armenia, Belarus, Kazakhstan, Kyrgyzstan, and Tajikistan, maintain elements of the old Soviet unified air defense grid. They also have agreed to form their own rapid deployment force. However, Uzbekistan dropped out of the Tashkent Treaty in 1999 and Russia has been keen to see it join the CSTO, as Uzbekistan is by far the most populous country of Central Asia.[23] The CSTO's role has been limited. As the Tashkent Treaty, it provided a framework for Russia's intervention in the civil war in Tajikistan in the early 1990s, and it facilitates consultations among members on responses to terrorist threats.[24] It has been overshadowed as an instrument for collective action, however, by the Shanghai Cooperation Organization, which does include Uzbekistan.

The Shanghai Cooperation Organization

The Shanghai Cooperation Organization (SCO) comprises Russia, China, Kazakhstan, Kyrgyzstan, Uzbekistan, and Tajikistan. It is a vehicle through which Russia, Central Asian states, and China coordinate security policies in matters concerning cross-border flows of drugs, weapons, and terrorists. It formed in 2001 and has evolved rapidly. An indication of its significance is the fact that when the heads of government of its members met in the fall of 2005, the foreign minister of India, prime minister of Pakistan, and vice president of Iran attended as observers.[25] The SCO has planned joint military training exercises (to address a hypothetical terrorist threat) and adopted joint declarations about regional security policy. Under its auspices, a regional antiterrorist center was created in Kyrgyzstan under Russian military command. In July 2005 the SCO formally requested that the United States set a deadline for the removal of its military forces from the airbases in Kyrgyzstan and Uzbekistan, and shortly afterward, Uzbekistan formally requested the United States to withdraw from the base it was leasing there. This followed a bloody incident in May when Uzbek security forces killed several hundred protesters, provoking strong U.S. criticism of the regime's actions and a cooling of U.S.–Uzbek relations. The American withdrawal from Uzbekistan was viewed by Russian analysts as a loss for American influence in the region and a gain for Russia.[26] Russia regards the SCO as an organization with substantial potential for influence, but whether it becomes an effective instrument of collective security will depend above all on China's interest in cooperating with Russia and its Central Asian neighbors on issues of common interest.[27]

OBSTACLES TO REGIONAL HEGEMONY

Although Russia's economic and military influence in the former Soviet region has increased as a result of these organizational initiatives and its immense energy resources, it faces serious challenges to its effort to become a regional superpower. First is the fact that several of its neighbors are weak states with repressive regimes and uncertain stability. In recent years, there have been several large-scale popular protest movements against autocratic and unpopular governments in the region. Two of them (Georgia's "Rose Revolution" in fall 2003 and Ukraine's "Orange Revolution" in fall 2004) represented democratic movements aimed against efforts by old-guard leaders to falsify the results of elections in order to hold on to power.[28] In another case, that of Kyrgyzstan in May 2005, a popular opposition group succeeded in driving the president from office but not in establishing democratic rule. In all three cases, the popular movements organized around the fact of election fraud, and swelled until they ultimately forced the presidents to resign. (See Close-Up 9.1: The Orange Revolution.) But whereas these revolutions were generally regarded as democratic breakthroughs by Western observers, they were deeply unsettling to the Russian authorities because they threatened the seeming stability of the region. The Orange Revolution in Ukraine was particularly embarrassing to Russia because Russia had intervened so openly in the election campaign in favor of its preferred candidate, who ultimately had to relinquish power in the face of massive popular protest and a unified Western stance against his efforts to manipulate the outcome. Russia's inability to prevent a humiliating political defeat reinforced the fears of many officials in the Kremlin that they could not be sure how deep popular discontent runs in Russia and neighboring states, and their conviction that Western agents were stirring up trouble against them. As though to reinforce these fears, in Kyrgyzstan, a new wave of popular protests erupted in November 2006, indicating that the new regime's stability was also tenuous.

Close-Up 9.1   The Orange Revolution

Ukraine's presidential election of 2004 resulted in a fiasco for Russian policy. Of the two leading candidates—Prime Minister Viktor Yanukovych and former prime minister Viktor Yushchenko—Russia strongly favored Yanukovych with visible and heavy-handed support. Yanukovych took a line favoring closer ties between Russia and Ukraine. He promised, for example, that if elected he would make Russian (along with Ukrainian) a state language of Ukraine, and would introduce dual citizenship so that Ukrainian citizens could be citizens of Russia as well. Putin made no pretense of neutrality. Yanukovych was given prominent play in the Russian media. For example, he was shown together with Ukraine's president, Leonid Kuchma, meeting with Putin to celebrate Putin's birthday in October and addressing a national congress of Ukrainians in Russia at the Kremlin. Billboards supporting Yanukovych were visible throughout Moscow; his opponent, Yushchenko, hardly figured at all in the Russian media. President Putin went so far as to pay a three-day visit to Ukraine on the eve of the first round of the election, where he made clear Russia's backing for Yanukovych. Pro-Kremlin Russian political consultants and strategists were sent to Ukraine to ensure Yanukovych's victory.

Yanukovych was closely tied to the political establishment in Ukraine and to some of Ukraine's leading oligarchs. Much of his support came from the Russian-speaking industrial regions of eastern Ukraine. Yushchenko, in contrast, had a reputation as a competent, honest reformer. He had served as prime minister in 1999–2001 and before that as chairman of Ukraine's Central Bank. Much of his support came from the western regions of the country, where Ukrainian national feeling and antagonism toward Russia are strong. The cultural and political divide between the nationalist West and the pro-Russian East in Ukraine was expressed with unusual intensity during the campaign. Many participants and observers claimed—with the

(Continued)

hyperbole that elections often fan—that the contest between Yanukovych and Yushchenko represented a choice between Russia and Europe in Ukraine's basic political orientation.

The election campaign was marked by an unusually high level of acrimony and dirty tricks. In the course of the campaign, Viktor Yushchenko was poisoned. In early September he became violently ill and had to be rushed for treatment in Vienna. He recovered sufficiently to resume campaigning later in September, but his face had been badly disfigured. Later, pathologists in Vienna reported that he had been poisoned with a high dose of dioxin, the active ingredient in the powerful defoliant Agent Orange. The fact that the night before he fell ill he had had dinner with the head of Ukraine's secret service only fueled suspicions about who had poisoned him.

The first round of voting, held on October 31, resulted in a dead heat between the two top finishers, Yushchenko and Yanukovych. Yushchenko received 39.87 percent of the vote, Yanukovych 39.32 percent. The runoff took place on November 21. Putin paid another visit to Ukraine to aid Yanukovych. Exit polls on the day of the voting suggested that Yushchenko had a comfortable lead. However, the country's Central Electoral Commission declared Yanukovych the winner, by 49.46 percent to 46.61 percent. Observers from Europe and the United States reported, however, that there had been widespread falsification. The OSCE's election observation mission stated that the vote fell below democratic election standards. U.S. Senator Richard Lugar, observing the election as President Bush's representative declared in Kiev that "It is now apparent that a concerted and forceful program of election-day fraud and abuse was enacted with either the leadership or cooperation of government authorities." Two days later, the European Union announced that "we don't accept these results and we think they are fraudulent." U.S. Secretary of State Colin Powell warned of "consequences" for U.S.–Ukrainian relations if the Ukrainian authories failed to investigate "the numerous and credible reports of fraud and abuse." Observers reported that the fraud was most prevalent in the eastern regions of the country where Yanukovych's support was strongest.

However, President Putin rejected any suggestion of fraud. He telephoned Yanukovych to congratulate him on his victory, commenting that "the battle has been hard-fought, but open and honest." Putin and other Russian policymakers furiously criticized the West for refusing to accept the election results. Putin called the OSCE's characterization of the election as fraudulent "inadmissible." Russia's ambassador to the European Union declared that "it's impossible not to see the direct involvement of the American Congress, individual congressmen who are spending their days and nights in Kyiv— foundations, nongovernmental organizations, consultants, experts. It's clear and obvious to everyone."[1] An editorial comment in the Russian daily, *Izvestiia,* claimed that the events clearly demonstrated that the West was trying to weaken Russia by stripping away territories from its sphere of influence, but pointed out that Russia had made matters worse by intervening so ineptly.[2]

As soon as the Ukrainian election commission announced its official report, Yushchenko supporters streamed into the central squares of Kiev and other cities to protest the official results. The demonstrations were large in scale and well organized. The opposition adopted the color orange as their symbol, and wore orange ribbons and scarves. Denouncing the official results as fraudulent, they demanded new and fair elections. Led by a youth movement called "Pora" ("It's Time"), they erected tents, set up field kitchens and first aid stations, and handed out ribbons, scarves, and literature. A 19-year-old leader of Pora noted that they had been ready for action: "We heard that Yanukovich would try to organize this fraud, and we were prepared for this kind of situation," she said. "We decided we also had to do something, to raise the people's will."[3] Hundreds of thousands of people participated; the central square in Kiev was filled with protesters 24 hours a day, day after day for nearly two weeks. Yushchenko's supporters appealed to the Ukrainian Supreme Court to nullify the results of the November 21 runoff on the grounds that they had been falsified, and to require holding new elections. As the days passed and the opposition movement gained in strength, pressure on the Ukrainian authorities to find a peaceful resolution mounted.

Putin faced a serious dilemma. Russia's support for Yanukovych and its refusal to acknowledge the election fraud in the Ukraine was already discrediting Russia in the West and threatening to spoil his plans for closer ties with Europe. A summit meeting between the European Union and Russia on November 25, overshadowed by the Ukrainian crisis, failed to produce a planned agreement on a "strategic partnership." But Putin also feared the consequences of allowing Yushchenko to win, which would complicate relations between Russia and Ukraine and represent another humiliating defeat for Russia. The Russian Duma passed a resolution on December 3 accusing the European Parliament, the European Union, and the Organization for Security and Cooperation in Europe (OSCE) of "destructive foreign interference in the development of the situation in Ukraine." Ukrainian president Kuchma flew to Moscow to consult with Putin to find a way out of the impasse. Representatives of the Yanukovych and Yushchenko camps

---

[1] RFE/RL Newsline, November 29, 2004.
[2] www.izvestia.ru/comment/article763957, November 29, 2004.
[3] Quoted in C. J. Chivers, "Youth Movement Underlies the Opposition in Ukraine," *New York Times,* November 28, 2004.

(*Continued*)

met to discuss possible political solutions. Yanukovych proposed a power-sharing agreement under which the powers of the president would be reduced, the powers of the prime minister strengthened, and the two would divide the offices between them. Yushchenko, sensing that his political support in Ukraine and abroad was growing, rejected the deal and held out for a new runoff election. Yanukovych then agreed to participate in a new runoff if Yushchenko would agree to constitutional changes weakening the powers of the presidency and strengthening those of the prime minister. The two camps edged toward a deal.

On December 3, the Ukrainian Supreme Court ruled that the November 21 election was invalid as a result of large-scale fraud, and called for holding a new election. Five days later, the Ukrainian parliament passed a package of laws that included reforms of the election system intended to reduce opportunities for election abuses, and a set of constitutional amendments that would reduce the powers of the president and strengthen those of the prime minister. In effect, the legislation bundled together reforms that both camps had demanded: a cleaner election process, as Yushchenko's supporters sought, in return for a less presidentially dominant system, as Yanukovych's supporters, fearing that Yushchenko would win the December 26 election, had wanted. On December 9, at a meeting of the Russia-NATO Council in Brussels, the Russian foreign minister and the other NATO foreign ministers issued a statement declaring that all sides agreed to respect the outcome of the new elections. On December 26, the new runoff election was held. Yushchenko won with 52 percent of the vote.

Although the immediate crisis was over, the episode revealed how far apart were the interests and perceptions of Russia and the West. For many Russian policymakers, Ukraine is an integral part of Russia's sphere of influence; indeed, many Russians find it hard to conceive Ukraine as a separate country. For them, therefore, Western support for Yushchenko amounted to an effort to separate Ukraine from Russia and turn it against Russia. Many Russians were convinced that it was the CIA and other Western secret services that had underwritten the "Orange Revolution." They pointed out that events in Ukraine unfolded very similarly to those a year before in Georgia. At that time a mass movement that became known as the "Rose Revolution" protested the large-scale falsification of presidential elections, with the West's support, and forced President Shevardnadze to leave office, bringing the young leader of the opposition, Mikhail Saakashvili, to power. (Saakashvili's supporters, which included an organized youth movement called "Kmara," or "Enough," marched on parliament carrying roses, as a symbol of their nonviolent protest.) Russians also recalled the similar sequence of events in September–October 2000 in Serbia. There, President Milosevic attempted to falsify the outcome of an election he had lost, provoking mass protests, strikes, and a march on parliament; ten days after the election, he was forced from office. For some Russians, the similarity of these events was hardly coincidental; it simply confirmed that they were all part of a concerted Western strategy to exploit the denunciation of election fraud as a means to deny Russia its traditional allies and expand Western power in Russia's natural sphere of influence.

From the standpoint of the West, such charges reflected a fundamental lack of acceptance of the force of popular demands for democratic elections. To be sure, efforts by Western foundations, NGOs, and government democracy-building programs contributed to these popular uprisings. In each case the popular movements supported the opposition because the opposition had won elections but were being denied the right to claim victory. Western assistance has gone to efforts to promote civil society, free elections, and competitive parties and therefore benefited opposition movements at moments when the authorities attempted to steal elections. International monitoring of elections is intended to ensure that the election results are credible and the winners hold power by right, rather than by force. To regard Western insistence on fair elections in zero-sum terms, as an attempt to invade Russia's natural sphere of influence, is to reject the principle that Russia is part of a community united by democratic principles. As Michael McFaul put it, "democracy is not an American plot."[4] But although Putin ultimately found it prudent to accept the outcome of the decision in Ukraine to hold new elections, the failure of his own clumsy efforts to intervene in the election proved to be a humiliating setback and one likely to reinforce Russian grievances about the country's ambiguous place in the international system.

The Orange Revolution also illustrates the point that peaceful protest movements are better at overthrowing a repressive regime than ensuring the stability of a new democratic region. A year after the Orange Revolution, Ukrainians expressed widespread disillusionment with its results. After a falling out between President Yushchenko and his prime minister, Yulia Timoshenko, parliament brought down the prime minister and Yushchenko had to bring the discredited former president Yanukovich back into government. New parliamentary elections in March 2006 led to a stalemate and protracted negotiations over the formation of a new government. Ultimately, President Yushchenko had to call on the former president Yanukovich to head the government—under the new constitutional rules making the prime minister more powerful than before. The aftermath of the Orange Revolution indicates that a popular revolution may be able to force a regime to call a new election, but be unable to guarantee that the new government will govern honestly or effectively.

---

[4] Michael McFaul, "'Meddling in Ukraine': Demoracy Is Not an American Plot," *Washington Post,* December 21, 2004.

There have also been indications of popular unrest elsewhere in Central Asia. In eastern Uzbekistan, a protest against the government in the town of Andijan in May 2005 was suppressed by violence when Uzbek security forces opened fire on several thousand demonstrators, reportedly killing hundreds of them. The government claimed that the organizers were linked to a radical Islamist movement. When the eccentric dictator of Turkmenistan died in December 2006, some feared that the succession could be contested, leading to a colored revolution in that country. However, the election was managed peacefully. Nevertheless, the fear that popular unrest could spill out into a large-scale organized protest movement and force current leaders from power strongly influences the calculations of Russian and other regional leaders, and is used to justify repression against potential opposition groups.

Related to the concern over the stability of the states on its periphery is the continued threat of Islamic fundamentalist movements in Central Asia and the Transcaucasus, linked to the Taliban and other international Islamist groups. It is hard to gauge the influence of radical Islamist groups in Central Asia and the Caucasus because the authorities tend to label any manifestation of Islamic piety as politically inspired. Nevertheless, there are radical Islamic terrorist organizations operating in Central Asia, notably the Islamic Movement of Uzbekistan (IMU), which has been linked to several terrorist acts in Central Asia. The IMU's access to the region is eased by the fact that its militants are able to slip back and forth between Tajikistan and Afghanistan. The Tajik border with Afghanistan is very weakly controlled (the Uzbek-Afghan border is better guarded). The resurgence of the Taliban and the opium trade in Afghanistan has given the IMU an opportunity to exploit the drug trade for its own benefit. Experts estimate that the IMU controls most of the drugs trafficked across Afghanistan's borders into Tajikistan and Kyrgyzstan.[29]

Russian leaders have also consistently accused Chechen rebels of being supported by international Islamist terror groups. A prominent Chechen rebel leader killed in 2005, named Khattab, was a Jordanian who helped to infuse the Chechen independence movement with Islamic political ideology. The serious concern over the spread of international Islamist ideology was a strong motivation for Putin's decision to offer help to the United States following the September 2001 attacks in New York and Washington and the cooperation with the American campaign to eradicate the Taliban regime in Afghanistan.

Finally, Russia's leverage in the region from its oil and gas wealth is precarious; already, Russia needs to mix Central Asian natural gas with its own reserves to meet its current commitments to the European market. Gazprom's ability to expand production of gas in Russia in the short term is limited; production at its major fields is declining rapidly and substantial investment is needed to increase production significantly in the coming years.[30] Therefore, in order to meet its growing export commitments, Gazprom needs to acquire cheap gas from Turkmenistan. (Russia was able to agree to a discounted price for gas supplied to Ukraine, an important regional ally, because of a long-term agreement with Turkmenistan for a below-market price on its gas.) Russia's dependence on Central Asia for its gas supply therefore requires a close political relationship between Russia and the Central Asian states, together with political stability in the region. Russia's leverage over Turkmenistan, Kazakstan, and other Caspian Sea gas-producing states was substantial until the late 1990s, because all their gas had to be exported through Russian-controlled pipelines to export markets. Now, however, Turkmenistan can export gas to Iran, bypassing Russia, and if the long-discussed Trans-Caspian gas pipeline is ever built, Turkmenistan will have still greater leverage over the terms of its gas sales to Russia.[31]

Russia's control over the oil export pipelines from Central Asia faces a similar challenge. Until recently, all Central Asian and Caucasus oil was exported through Russian pipelines. Since 2005, however, when a major new pipeline from Azerbaijan through Georgia to a Turkish port on the Mediterranean Sea (the "Baku-Tbilisi-Ceyhan pipeline"), Russia's monopoly on the transit of Caspian Sea oil to export markets was broken. The pipeline project, which took ten years, was strongly backed by the United States over Russian objections; the U.S. Secretary of Energy spoke at the opening ceremonies of the pipeline. The American interest in diversifying supply routes for Caspian oil reinforces Russian fears that the United States seeks to push Russia out of its natural sphere of influence in the region.

RUSSIA AND THE INTERNATIONAL COMMUNITY

The drive to make Russia a regional superpower is not the same as creating an empire or restoring the Soviet Union. It is important to bear in mind that Russia today is far more open than it was under Soviet rule and its leaders recognize that it cannot retreat into isolation and autarky. President Putin clearly recognizes that Russia's economic interests require closer trade and investment ties with the outside world and that its security requires the avoidance of provoking confrontations with any powerful potential enemies. The post–Cold War environment has been more favorable to Russia's strategic interests than most observers expected, however. While having to accept the United States' preeminent military power and the limits this imposes on Russia's own security strategy (for instance, requiring it to accept NATO's expansion and the end of the ABM treaty regime), it has also given Russia new opportunities to develop its own international role by playing on the world's concerns about international terrorism. The new vulnerabilities and divisions created in the post–Cold War world and Russia's immense energy resources have given Russia an opening to develop influence not dependent solely on its legacy as the heir to the Soviet Union's nuclear arsenal. This opening encourages Russia to seek a place in the international community commensurate both with its means and its long-term interests.

Russia's vast size, weak government capacity, and cultural legacy of state domination make it likely that the primary objective of its leaders for the foreseeable future will be to strengthen the state, both in its internal and international dimensions. The end of the Communist regime and the dissolution of the Soviet Union brought about a severe weakening of the state's capacity to enforce its laws, protect its citizens, and provide basic social services. Russian history has seen periods when the breakdown of an old regime and the rise of a new one led to internal weakness and external vulnerability. Putin has responded to the threat that an internal breakdown of order could weaken its external security by rebuilding Russia's state capacity and asserting its power internationally. He has especially emphasized the goal of consolidating political and economic influence in the post-Soviet region by relying on energy resources to gain control over the energy and power infrastructure of the region. Much of the success of this strategy, however, depends on high world market prices for its energy exports; lower oil and gas prices would deprive it of its competitive advantage in the international power struggle. Putin's successors therefore will need to overcome the temptation to collect short-term rewards from Russia's natural resources and instead to carry out deep reforms of its political and economic structures that make it worthwhile for individuals to invest in endeavors, such as education and innovation, whose return will only be realized over the long term.

Russia's rulers are seeking to reconcile the imperative of strengthening a weakened state with the need for economic growth. But setting Russia on a path of self-sustaining economic development will require the rule of law; the traditional patrimonial model of rule is incompatible with market capitalism. While President Putin may give priority to the rebuilding of a coherent administrative structure for implementing state policy, the viability of Russia's post-Communist state will ultimately depend on how responsive and adaptive its institutions are to the demands of Russia's citizens in a globalized and interdependent world.

NOTES

1. RFE/RL Newsline, April 25, 2005, reporting on the results of a survey conducted by the Fund for Public Opinion.

2. From the Web site of the Levada Center: Levada Center, February 15, 2007 release: reception of European values by Russians, http://www.levada.ru/press/2007021501.html.

3. From a Levada Center survey conducted in February 2007. Between 1998 and 2007, the number of people who responded "definitely yes" or "probably yes" to the question, "Do you think there is a military threat to Russia today from other countries?" went up from 33 percent to 49 percent, and the number answering "probably not" or "definitely not" declined from 59 percent to 43 percent. Levada Center, February 22, 2007, http://www.levada.ru/press/2007022201.html.

4. A valuable overview of the deep continuities in the evolution of Russia's relations with the outside world through the twentieth century is Robert Legvold, "The Three Russias: Decline, Revolution, and Reconstruction," in Robert A. Pastor, ed., *A Century's Journey: How the Great Powers Shape the World* (New York: Basic Books, 1999), pp. 139–90.

5. RFE/RL Newsline, January 6, 2005, reporting on a survey by the Levada Center in December 2004.

6. From a survey by the Fund for Public Opinion, reported by Polit.ru, April 8, 2005.

7. RFE/RL Newsline, October 10, 2003.

8. Country Analysis Briefs: Russia (September 2003), http://www.eia.doe.gov/emeu/cabs/russia.html.

9. Jonathan Stern, "The Russian-Ukrainian Gas Crisis of January 2006," Oxford Institute for Energy Studies, January 16, 2006.

10. Putin's ideas were hardly original. Indeed, an American scholar, Clifford Gaddy,

discovered that much of the dissertation had been plagiarized from an earlier American book. RFE/RL Russian Political Weekly, March 29, 2006.

11. Shawn McCarthy, "Putin's Power Play," *Globe and Mail,* March 5, 2007.

12. Jonathan Stern, "The Future of Russian Gas and Gazprom," Oxford Energy Forum, November 2005, p. 14.

13. Tom Warner, "RosUkrEnergo Hits at Critics by Naming Owners," *Financial Times,* April 27, 2006.

14. Economist Intelligence Unit, "Belarus's Gas Deal with Russia Marks the End of an Era," January 3, 2007, http://economist.com/agenda/displaystory.cfm?story_id=E1_RQRVPNV.

15. RFE/RL Newsline, September 27, 2006.

16. RFE/RL Business Watch, September 23, 2003.

17. On Chubais's conception of a "liberal empire," see his speech "Russia's Mission," delivered at the St. Petersburg State Engineering-Economic University on September 25, 2003, as reprinted in Polit.ru, September 26, 2003, http://www.polit.ru/docs/625760.html; his interview in *Izvestiia,* November 26, 2003; and the report of his interview with the editor of the nationalist newspaper *Zavtra,* Polit.ru, September 20, 2006.

18. RFE/RL Newsline, December 1, 2003.

19. RFE/RL Newsline, January 5, 2004.

20. Lev Gumilev, who was the son of the famous Russian poet Anna Akhmatova, was a historian and philosopher who popularized the idea of "Eurasianism." Eurasianism is a perspective emphasizing Russia's ethnic and cultural links with the peoples of Central Asia and Mongolia, as opposed to Russia's European heritage and identity.

21. RFE/RL Newsline, August 26, 2005.

22. Agreements or treaties of union were signed by the two presidents on April 2, 1996; April 2, 1997; May 23, 1997; December 28, 1998; and December 8, 1999.

23. Uzbekistan's population is over 26 million; the next largest in population is Kazakhstan, with 15 million.

24. See Fiona Hill, "The Eurasian Security Environment," Testimony before the U.S.

House of Representatives Armed Services Committee Threat Panel, September 22, 2005, p. 7.

25. Fred Weir, "Russia, China Looking to Form 'NATO of the East'?" *Christian Science Monitor,* October 26, 2005, http://www.csmonitor.com/2005/1026/p04s01-woeu.html.

26. The United States did renegotiate its treaty with Kyrgyzstan and continues to lease an airbase there.

27. Hill, "Eurasian Security Environment," p. 7.

28. On the commonalities among these democratic revolutions, see Michael McFaul, "Conclusion: The Orange Revolution in Comparative Perspective," in Anders Aslund and Michael McFaul, eds., *Revolution in Orange: The Origins of Ukraine's Democratic Breakthrough* (Washington, DC: Carnegie Endowment for International Peace, 2006), pp. 165–95.

29. Fiona Hill, "Eurasian Security Environment," p. 5.

30. Claire Bigg, "Putin Receives Turkmen President for Gas Talks," RFE/RL Russian Political Weekly, vol. 6, no. 2, January 26, 2006. Although experts believe that Western technology and capital will be needed to develop the new fields where future gas production will be concentrated, Gazprom has recently forced international energy companies to reduce their stakes in joint ventures from majority to minority positions.

31. Jonathan Stern, "The Future of Russian Gas and Gazprom," Oxford Energy Forum, November 2005; Theresa Sabonis-Helf, "The Rise of the Post-Soviet Petro-States: Energy Exports and Domestic Governance in Turkmenistan and Kazakhstan," in Daniel L. Burghart and Theresa Sabonis-Helf, *In the Tracks of Tamerlane: Central Asia's Path to the 21st Century* (Washington, DC: National Defense University, 2004), pp. 167–68; Robert M. Cutler, "New Chance for Trans-Caspian Pipeline," *Asia Times,* February 27, 2007; U.S. Department of Energy, Energy Information Administration, "Caspian Sea Region: Natural Gas Export Options," July 2002, http://www.eia.doe.gov/emeu/cabs/caspgase.html.

Index

267